First World War
and Army of Occupation
War Diary
France, Belgium and Germany

24 DIVISION
Divisional Troops
41 Sanitary Section
2 September 1915 - 31 March 1917

WO95/2203/2

The Naval & Military Press Ltd
www.nmarchive.com
Published in association with The National Archives

Published by

The Naval & Military Press Ltd

Unit 10 Ridgewood Industrial Park,

Uckfield, East Sussex,

TN22 5QE England

Tel: +44 (0) 1825 749494

www.naval-military-press.com

www.nmarchive.com

This diary has been reprinted in facsimile from the original. Any imperfections are inevitably reproduced and the quality may fall short of modern type and cartographic standards.

© Crown Copyright
Images reproduced by permission of The National Archives, London, England, 2015.

Contents

Document type	Place/Title	Date From	Date To
Heading	WO95/2203/2		
Heading	41st Sanitary Section Sep 1915-1917 Mar		
Heading	24th Division 41st Sanitary Section Vol I Sep 15		
War Diary	Havre	02/09/1915	03/09/1915
War Diary	Beaurainville	04/09/1915	24/09/1915
War Diary	Bethune	25/09/1915	25/09/1915
War Diary	Bouvry	26/09/1915	28/09/1915
War Diary	Fouquerquil	29/09/1915	30/09/1915
Diagram etc	Ablution Bench		
Diagram etc			
Heading	War Diary of 41st Sanitary Section from 1st Oct/15 to 31st Oct/15 Volume 2		
War Diary	S' Hilaire	01/10/1915	02/10/1915
War Diary	Steenvorde	03/10/1915	06/10/1915
War Diary	Reninghelst	06/10/1915	31/10/1915
Miscellaneous	Unit M. O.		
Heading	24th Division Nov 15		
Heading	War Diary of 41st Sanitary Section from 1st Nov 15 to 30th Nov 15 Volume 3		
Miscellaneous	No 41 Sanitary Section Nov. 1915		
War Diary	Reninghelst	01/11/1915	24/11/1915
War Diary	Tilques	25/11/1915	30/11/1915
Heading	24th Div San. Sect. 41 Dec 1915		
Miscellaneous	41st. Sanitary Section. Dec. 1915		
Heading	War Diary of 41st Sanitary Section from 1st Dec./15 To 31st Dec/15 Volume		
War Diary	Tilques	01/12/1915	31/12/1915
Heading	24th Division 41st Sany. Section		
Heading	San. Sect. 41 Vol. 5		
Heading	War Diary of 41st Sanitary Section. From 1st Jan to 31st Jan 1916 Volume 5		
War Diary	Tilques	01/01/1916	08/01/1916
War Diary	Map 28. G.15.a5.9	09/01/1916	17/01/1916
War Diary	G.15.c.5.9	17/01/1916	31/01/1916
Diagram etc	Manure Destructor		
Diagram etc			
Heading	41st Sanitary Section Volume 6 from 1st February 1916 to 29th February Private of		
War Diary	Map 28 G. 15.c.5.9	01/02/1916	14/02/1916
War Diary	6 15.c.5.9	15/02/1916	21/02/1916
War Diary	Map 28 G 15.c.5.9	21/02/1916	29/02/1916
Diagram etc	Treatment Soapy Waste		
Heading	War Diary of the 41st Sanitary Section Volume 7		
War Diary	Map 28 6.15.c.5.9	01/03/1916	22/03/1916
War Diary	Fletre	23/03/1916	29/03/1916
War Diary	St Jans Capelle	30/03/1916	31/03/1916
Heading	41st Sanitary Section War Diary Volume 8		
War Diary	St Jans Cappel	01/04/1916	18/04/1916
War Diary	Bailleul	18/04/1916	30/04/1916
Diagram etc	Dranoutre Baths		

Diagram etc	Dranoutre Baths.		
Diagram etc			
Diagram etc	Dranoutre Baths		
Diagram etc			
Miscellaneous	Material required for Destructor		
Diagram etc	Brick Destructor		
Heading	41st Sanitary Section War Diary Volume 9		
War Diary	Bailleul	01/05/1916	31/05/1916
Heading	41st Sanitary Section War Diary Volume 10 from 1st June to 30th June 1916		
War Diary	Bailleul	01/06/1916	30/06/1916
Miscellaneous	Appendix		
Diagram etc	Dranoutre Baths		
Diagram etc			
Diagram etc	Dranoutre Baths.		
Diagram etc			
Diagram etc	Dranoutre Baths.		
Diagram etc	Manure Destructor		
Diagram etc	Grease Trap		
Heading	41st Sanitary Section Volume XI From 1st July 1916 to 31st July 1916		
War Diary	Bailleul	01/07/1916	03/07/1916
War Diary	Sheet 28 M. 29.a.8.8	04/07/1916	08/07/1916
War Diary	S. 14.a.07	09/07/1916	10/07/1916
War Diary	Sheet 28 S.14a.0.7	11/07/1916	13/07/1916
War Diary	6.14a.0.7	14/07/1916	20/07/1916
War Diary	27 R 36b 4.1	21/07/1916	25/07/1916
War Diary	Cavillon	26/07/1916	31/07/1916
Heading	41st Sanitary Section War Diary Volume 12 From 1st Aug. to 31st August 1916		
War Diary	Corbie	01/08/1916	02/08/1916
War Diary	F 25.b. 6.1	03/08/1916	05/08/1916
War Diary	F. 26.c.5.3	06/08/1916	12/08/1916
War Diary	Citadel	13/08/1916	19/08/1916
War Diary	Sheet 62D Citadel	20/08/1916	22/08/1916
War Diary	F 26.c.6.3	23/08/1916	25/08/1916
War Diary	D 28.d.8.5	26/08/1916	26/08/1916
War Diary	Sheet 62 D D.28.d.8.5	27/08/1916	31/08/1916
Heading	41st Sanitary Section War Diary Volume 13 from 1st Sept. to 30th Sept. 1916		
War Diary	Sheet 62 D E.11.c.	01/09/1916	06/09/1916
War Diary	Ailly	07/09/1916	19/09/1916
War Diary	Bruay	20/09/1916	25/09/1916
War Diary	Camblain L'Abbe	26/09/1916	30/09/1916
Diagram etc			
Diagram etc	Ailly-Le-Haut-Clocher		
Map	Map Of Rest Area		
Diagram etc			
Miscellaneous	24th Division No. A. 4891/2		
Heading	41st Sanitary Section War Diary Volume 14 From 1st Oct to 31st Oct. 1916		
Diagram etc	Estree Cauchie		
Miscellaneous	Estree Cauchie		
Diagram etc			
Miscellaneous	Gouy Servins		
Diagram etc	Camblain L'Abbe		

Miscellaneous	Comblain L'Abbe		
Miscellaneous	Personnel Latrine for type		
Miscellaneous	Comblain L'Abbe		
War Diary	Comblain L'Abbe	01/10/1916	27/10/1916
War Diary	Les Brebis	28/10/1916	30/10/1916
War Diary	Braquemont	30/10/1916	31/10/1916
Diagram etc			
Diagram etc	Petit Servins		
Diagram etc	Gauchin Legal		
Diagram etc	Grand Servins		
Miscellaneous	Comblain L'Abbe		
Heading	24th Div 41st Sanitary Section		
Heading	41st Sanitary Section War Diary Volume 15 From Nov 1st to Nov. 30th 1916		
War Diary	Braquemont	01/11/1916	30/11/1916
Heading	24th Div 41st Sanitary Section		
Heading	G.C 41st Sanitary Section		
War Diary	Braquemont	01/12/1916	31/12/1916
Heading	41st Sanitary Section War Diary Volume 17 from 1st Jan to Jan 31st 1917		
War Diary	Braquemont	01/01/1917	31/01/1917
Miscellaneous	Drawings Of Sanitary Appliances For The Field		
Diagram etc	Latrines & Urinals		
Diagram etc	Ablution Bench And Disposal Of Soapy Waste Water		
Diagram etc	Inanerators & Manure Burnings		
Diagram etc	Food Safe & Grease Trap.		
Heading	24th Div. 41st Sanitary Section		
Heading	41st Sanitary Section War Diary Volume 18 from February 1st to February 28 1917		
War Diary	Braquemont	01/02/1917	13/02/1917
War Diary	Labeuvriere	14/02/1917	28/02/1917
Diagram etc	Labeuvriere Plan Of Village		
Map	Hazebrouck Sheet 5a		
Diagram etc	Lapugnoy		
Diagram etc	Hesdigneul		
Diagram etc	Annezin		
Diagram etc	Cantrainne		
Diagram etc	Busnettes		
Diagram etc	Le Hamel		
Diagram etc	Bas Rieux		
Diagram etc	Fouquieres		
Diagram etc	Ecquedecques		
Map	Allouagne		
Miscellaneous	Allouagne		
Heading	War Diary of 41st Sanitary Section from March 1st to March 31st 1917 Volume No. 19		
War Diary	Labeuvriere	01/03/1917	05/03/1917
War Diary	Boyeffles	06/03/1917	31/03/1917
Diagram etc	Boyeffles		
Diagram etc	Bully Grenay		
Diagram etc	Sains En Gohelle		
Diagram etc	Bois De Noulette		
Diagram etc	Fosse No. 10		
Diagram etc	Aix Noulette		
Diagram etc	Bouvigny		
Diagram etc	Fosse Calonne		

Diagram etc	Key Plan Of Area
Diagram etc	Barlin Key Plan [Not to Scale
Diagram etc	Barlin
Diagram etc	Petit Sains
Diagram etc	Braquemont
Diagram etc	Les Brebis

W095/22032

24TH DIVISION
MEDICAL

41ST SANITARY SECTION
SEP 1915 - DEC 1916
1917 MAR

(TO 1 ARMY)

S

24th Division

Summarised but not copied

121/6991

Sep '15

41st Sanitary Section

Vol: I

Sept. 15 – Dec '16

Sept.

41st Sanitary Section

Army Form C. 2118.

H.S. Smithers Lieut R.A.M.C. O.C.

WAR DIARY
or
INTELLIGENCE SUMMARY.
(Erase heading not required.)

Instructions regarding War Diaries and Intelligence Summaries are contained in F.S. Regs., Part II. and the Staff Manual respectively. Title pages will be prepared in manuscript.

Place	Date	Hour	Summary of Events and Information	Remarks and references to Appendices
HAVRE	2/9/15	7 a.m.	Arrived from SOUTHAMPTON at 2 a.m. Disembarked at 7 a.m. Whole section given fatigue work unloading transport. Left Docks at noon for REST CAMP No. 5. Supplied guard for Motor Lorry & Orderly Room from 1.30 p.m. to midnight.	H.S.S.
	3/9/15	12.30 a.m.	Left CAMP at 12.30 a.m. for railway station. Left by train at 4.30 a.m. Arrived at MARESQUET at 5 p.m. Left by road at 9.30 p.m. Arrived BEAURAINVILLE 10 p.m. Secured billets for men in Mayor's barn, for self in house.	
BEAURAINVILLE	4/9/15		Arranged P.O. re letters. Approached Private LAW Bn. Orderly Room re stamping letters. Arranged with Colonel in Divisional Orderly Room re new billets – secured satisfactory one for self in Café bleu. – all billets for men not satisfactory – they will remain in Mayor's premises.	H.S.S.
		5 p.m.	Received ① from Lieut. Colonel STEWART, Gen. Staff "Scheme of Training and of Organisation for units of the 1st Division, during the period they are in reserve. ② from Brigadier General FORD, Hqrs. "Instructions regarding Casualties + Strength Returns" No A/2/1. Date 4/9. ③ from Brigadier General re communication "Control over Issues of Supplies in the Field" - tally of supplies to be sent to S.O. every Saturday.	

Page 2.

Army Form C. 2118.

WAR DIARY
or
INTELLIGENCE SUMMARY.

(Erase heading not required.)

Place	Date	Hour	Summary of Events and Information	Remarks and references to Appendices
BEAURAINVILLE	Sep 1st cont.	8 P.M.	Received 24th Div. Routine Orders, 1st Sep. 1915. The sections referred to in par 3 which apply to us will be copied into Order Book and explained to the men. So "Extracts from General Routine Orders" is not to hand par 2 has not yet been included in orders.	
			Received 24th Div. Routine Orders, 2nd Sep. 1915. Noted instructions re Sick & Correspondence.	
			Received 24th Div. Routine Orders 3rd Sep. 1915, Par 3. Divine Service:- All men other than cook assistant, orderly & clerk given permission to attend the local church at 8 & 11 a.m. Par 4. Interpreters:- A man in this section speaks French will act as our Interpreter. Par. 6 Latrines. Men informed of the contents of paragraph.	
	Sep 3		Received 24 Division Part I Orders by Major General Sir John G RAMSAY K.C.B. 3/9/15. Men will be practised in making bivouac shelter.	
			Received Extract from Gen. Routine Orders re Requisitions Billeting. The first certificate will be used from Sep 3rd to 12th inclusive.	
			Received Orders by Col. CLARKE A.D.M.S. O.C. R.A.M.C. Men training as laid down in par 2 will be continued. There are no outstanding vaccinations & reinoculations.	

WAR DIARY
or
INTELLIGENCE SUMMARY

Place	Date	Hour	Summary of Events and Information	Remarks and references to Appendices
BEAURAINVILLE	5/9/15		Received 24th Div Routine Orders 4th Sep 1915. Par 11 Trees copied into Order Book and explained to men. Par 13 Stationary duty complied with Part 17 Discipline. Men warned re wearing "Cap Comforter" during the time they are on duty. Par 18 Supplies Change in time noted & N.C.O. responsible informed. Received 24th Div Routine Orders 5th Sep 1915. Par 21 re Coal noted. Groom informed of Sou. 20 Care of Horses.	
		A.M.	Duties performed. Visited HdQrs. Saw Major WESTON, D&R&M to whom I reported our arrival. Col. CLARKE, A.D.M.S having gone to Étaples	
		P.M.	Cap. MARETT - Sanitary Officer, Adv. Base called re Station Policing at BEAURAINVILLE. At present he has a Corporal in charge of fatigue parties supplied by R.T.O. Went with him to H.Q. where Major Weston arranged for my Section to undertake this duty. In the Orders a Sergeant & 2 men were detailed for to-morrow. During the day the men have dug latrines for themselves & Officers billeting here in the field near	NSL

Page 4

Army Form C. 2118

WAR DIARY
or
INTELLIGENCE SUMMARY.
(Erase heading not required.)

Instructions regarding War Diaries and Intelligence Summaries are contained in F.S. Regs., Part II. and the Staff Manual respectively. Title pages will be prepared in manuscript.

Place	Date	Hour	Summary of Events and Information	Remarks and references to Appendices
BEAURAINVILLE	6/9/15		Received Orders by Col. CLARKE, A.D.M.S. 6/9/15. Par.4 Gas – copied in Order Book. Par. 5 Nominal Roll Ref. letter 1320/234 d/3x 4/9/15 from O/C R.A.M.C. received. Reply will be forwarded by morrow's post. Received General Routine Orders 3/9/15. Par. 1132. Censoring of Parcels & Par. 1135 Spies – Staked up. Nails will appear in to-morrow's Orders. Received Group Orders "A" at Div 5/9/15. Note Par 2 - Post - Part Gas - "Instruction in Protection against" Lecture at the Divisional Train at 2 p.m. on the 8 inst. Received Part I Orders 6/9/15. Par. 6. Training Programme. The men of my Section are now engaged on their regular sanitary duties as I have not thought it necessary to submit a Training Programme. Their work will depend largely on the requirements of Officers commanding other Units. Received 2nd Div Routine Orders 6/9/15. Par 23 Draughtsmen – No men in this Unit are qualified draughtsmen. Par. 65 Rations – I have full supply. Report to this effect made out.	

T2134. Wt. W708-776. 500000. 4/15. Sir J. C. & S.

WAR DIARY
or
INTELLIGENCE SUMMARY.

Army Form C. 2118

Page 5.

Place	Date	Hour	Summary of Events and Information	Remarks and references to Appendices
BEAURAINVILLE	6/9/15		Duties performed :- Detailed 1 Sergeant & 2 men for duty at Station	
			6 men for Water Duty for factory	
			1 man " " at 194th Coy A.S.C.	
			Special " " at 194th Coy A.S.C.	
			Remainder - Latrine building + C	
			Visited H.Q.Rs + Ordnance Dept re making up Establishment as laid down in latest Schedule dated Aug. 1915. Withdrew Station duty men at noon as the previous squad was still at work Here. Extracts from Divisional Orders read & explained to whole section as required by A.D.M.S.	WSL
	7/9/15		Despatched Answers to Gen. Routine Orders No 1129 re A.S.C. men's allotment; Nominal Roll with details req.d in Order Ref. 1329/234 4 Sep. 1915. 1st Div. Routine Orders No. 25 Ration dated 6/9/15. Duties performed Detailed 1 Sergeant + 6 men for duty at Ry Station	
			1 " " + 2 " " Supply Column	
			to instruct fatigue squad in construction of latrines, grease traps, urine pits & incinerators.	
			1 man performed special Water Duty at 194 Coy A.S.C. Remainder at Billet. Received from Field Cashier 165 francs whole of money paid out to men. Acquittance Rolls forwarded to A.9	WSL

Page 6

Army Form C. 2118

WAR DIARY
or
INTELLIGENCE SUMMARY.

(Erase heading not required.)

Instructions regarding War Diaries and Intelligence Summaries are contained in F. S. Regs., Part II. and the Staff Manual respectively. Title pages will be prepared in manuscript.

Place	Date	Hour	Summary of Events and Information	Remarks and references to Appendices
BEAURAINVILLE	8/9/15		Received 24th Div. Routine Orders 1/9/15. Note alterations re Sick par 31. Note Par. 37 re Instructions – Quartermasters. Re Par 34 G.R.O. Nos 1132 & 1135. These were read over to the Section last evening. Received "Summary of Information" – Operations of 3/4/5 Sep 1915. The men will be interested in the contents. Duties performed. Detailed 1 Sergeant & 1 Men for duty at Meringuet. 1 NCO + 3 Men "Water" – 194 Co Ade. 1 NCO + 2 Men "Disinfecting" – 106 Hd Qu. 1 NCO & 3 Men "duty at Rail Head" 2 NCO's & 4 Men – " – Supply Column. Remainder of Men on duty at the Billet.	
		AM	Visited all the above sections. Met Col CLARKE at Rail Head – informed of Scarlet Fever patient at Rimboyal. RIMBOYAL	
		PM	Together with Staff Serg't & 2 men I went to Rimboyal found that patient (Private A.G. Gibbs, Royal Sussex) stood "unity" had been removed. Disinfected room by spraying unbroken burnt straw bedding. M.O. Lt WHITTON immediately isolated & other men who occupied the same room	

WAR DIARY
or
INTELLIGENCE SUMMARY.
(Erase heading not required.)

Army Form C. 2118

Page 1.

Place	Date	Hour	Summary of Events and Information	Remarks and references to Appendices
BEAURAINVILLE	8/9/15	P.M.	Received reports from NCOs on work done during the day. At 16b. Hd.Qrs R.F.A. the clothing of 14 men suffering from body lice, & of 1 man suffering from scabies was disinfected. Received "Orders by Col. CLARKE, O.D" nd 7/9/15. Par 8 – Saluting. This order has been included in the Orders for the day read to the men. Received "Group Orders by Brig.Gen.Sir G.T. THOMAS.K.C.B., D.S.O. 7/9/15". Note Par 6 – Gas Instruction in rotation against Col. WATSON will now give instructions to Officers of Group "A" at BEAURAINVILLE at 12 noon on the 10th inst. Received D.R.O. 5/9/15. Note Par 4 & 2 Chaplains – Senior Chaplain 24th Divn. as % 6th Bedford Regiments. Par 45 – G.R.O. Nos 1125, 1128, & 1130 have been noted. Received Part I Orders by Maj. Gen. Sir John G. RAMSAY, K.C.B. Bar.y Gas – Protection against. Information herein contained in Group Orders above. Received "Summary of Information 5 to Sept 1915". Took steps to see that each man takes a bath regularly.	

WAR DIARY or INTELLIGENCE SUMMARY

Place	Date	Hour	Summary of Events and Information	Remarks and references to Appendices
BEAURAINVILLE	8/9/15	P.M.	"Instructions for use of Respirators Smoke Helmets" distributed to NCOs & men	MS2
	9/9/15	A.M.	Detailed Duty lections for the day as follow:-	
			Supply Column — 3 NCO's & 6 men.	
			Rail Head — 1 NCO & 4 men	
			H.Q. — 1 NCO & men for Supplies, Water Duty, Preparation of new latrines, urine pits, grease trap & soakage pit	
			Summary of work done by above sections	
			Supply Column Section under Serg¹ GOODING at back of Offices:- Cleaned garden-filled in latrines - constructed new one - made new urine pit - filled in Officers' latrine & constructed another on rail system - built incinerator & pit for refuse from same. Following plan for drainage of yard & field kitchen made & partly carried out:- An ablution bench with lime compartments to be made - water falling through grease trap into channel leading into garden where it passes through a series of three soakage pits. The sinking drainage system the yard is not to be used & sullage water from kitchen is to pass through same channels. A proper field kitchen fireplace to be erected work partly carried out.	1 2

Page 9

Army Form C. 2118

WAR DIARY
or
INTELLIGENCE SUMMARY.
(Erase heading not required.)

Instructions regarding War Diaries and Intelligence Summaries are contained in F. S. Regs., Part II. and the Staff Manual respectively. Title pages will be prepared in manuscript.

Place	Date	Hour	Summary of Events and Information	Remarks and references to Appendices
BEAURAINVILLE	9/9/15		Supply Column cont. Section under Sergt DINNIS. Construction of incinerators attached to field kitchens. Made grease trap soakage pit for each. Constructed one large urinal. Latrines filled in new ones constructed. Rail Head. Filled in latrines - new ones constructed. New urine pit made. Cleared yard & burnt burned all refuse in turf incinerator made two days ago. Headquarters - Water from pump sloped declivinated for use of section. Latrines filled in - new ones constructed. Large soakage pit for ablution water from bath made.	
		4pm	Received from Sub Qre. Instructions as to local purchasing of supplies re 8/2/3/6/9/15	
			" " " "Reinforcements - Division. Arrangement for meeting 9/9/15	
			" " " Summary of various circulars on subject of supplying canteens	
			" " " List of Returns to be rendered to Div. H.Qrs. with specimen sheets. Note AB 231 ~ A.F.B. 213 specially	
			" " " Tg A 11 11 Expeditionary Force Canteens	
			" " " Extract from G.R.O. dated 8/8/15 re 1059 Revised A.F.B. 213 - instructions as to compilation	

Army Form C. 2118

WAR DIARY
or
INTELLIGENCE SUMMARY.
(Erase heading not required.)

Instructions regarding War Diaries and Intelligence Summaries are contained in F.S. Regs., Part II. and the Staff Manual respectively. Title pages will be prepared in manuscript.

Page 10.

Place	Date	Hour	Summary of Events and Information	Remarks and references to Appendices
BEAURAINVILLE	9/9/15	4 p.m.	Received from A.A.Qr. G. 1431. 24 HQ. No. A. 13/3 "Billeting in France & Belgium"	52
			- " - " " Summary of Information - Operations of 6/7 September	
			" " 2nd DRO 8/9/15. Note especially par. #9(4) & (1). Both copied in Order	
	10/9/15	9 a.m.	Book for to-day; par. 50 "Billets - the time has been advised to revise our arrangements"; par. 51 "Baths - no expense will be incurred during existing arrangements"; par. 52 "Care & preservation of shoes" Received Part I Order 9/9/15 "Musketry" Received Confidential letter S+T re suspected civilians in car. Received from StQrs No. A 24. 9/9/15 "Method of reporting casualties"	
		10 a.m.	Despatched by post to Colonel KENNY A.A. + Q.M.G. copy of letter forwarded by Signal Messenger at 6.15 p.m. yester 1915 re him letters in answer to telegram (demanding return) of yesterday's date.	
			Duty sections for to-day are:-	
			Supply Column : 3 NCO's + 5 men	
			Rail Head : 1 " + 5 men	
			Water Duty & Hd. Qrs. : 1 NCO + 5 men	
			Stables : 3 men	
		11 a.m.	Rec'd from A.D. R.A.M.C. section Copy of Nominal Roll. Certified same to be a correct copy. Returned same	

WAR DIARY
or
INTELLIGENCE SUMMARY

Army Form C. 2118

Page 11.

Place	Date	Hour	Summary of Events and Information	Remarks and references to Appendices
BEAURAINVILLE	10/9/15	7.55pm	Received Corps Routine Orders IM Ops 1/9/15 A.G. Branch No. 1. "Tying of Horses to Trees" etc. noted. A/Ops No. 2. "Road Discipline" – will be carefully observed. Received 24th D.R.O Sep 10th 1915. No. 53, 54 & 56 duly noted. Re 56 "Divine Service" – the men will be given facilities for attending the Parish Church as last Sunday. Re par 59 CRO No 1 Certificate forwarded to Admin Staff Officer that my horse is tied up in accordance with instructions. (by post 11/9/15) Re par 60 "Vehicles" – instruction given to S/Sgt. for necessary obliterations to be made. Re par 61 "Protection from Poisonous Gas" – Necessary indent for 28 new Smoke Helmets or Respirators signed & will be despatched (by post 11/9/15) ① The dating will be carried out first same was 1/9/15 Par 63 Traffic has been communicated to the drivers of the Motor Lorry & will be followed. Received from XI Corps Staff Ops 9/9/15 Summary of Information No 5. Forwarded to Div HQrs & to O.C. at the Base copy of Field Return for 11/9/15	
		3.45pm	Personally visited the Qr. at ROYON & left Field State for 11/9/15	

Page 12.

WAR DIARY
or
INTELLIGENCE SUMMARY.
(Erase heading not required.)

Army Form C. 2118

Place	Date	Hour	Summary of Events and Information	Remarks and references to Appendices
BEAURAINVILLE	10/9/15.		Work done. Supply Column Section under Sgt GOODING - back of Shops.	
			(a) In garden. Picked up channel, laid pipes to conduct water from grease trap at end of ablution bench to soakage pits. Soakage pits covered with wooden covering earth. Men's latrines filled in - 5 closets constructed on pail system surfed in. Emptied filled in existing urine pit - dug pit for latrine refuse.	
			(b) In yard - Cleaned same - mud carted away & buried - gullies cleaned out - ablution bench fitted with water tight compartments with hole plugs for waste, also with lower trough for carrying same to channel.	NSL
			Rail Head - ordinary routine work continued.	
	11/9/15.		Duty Sections for to-day are:-	
			Supply Column - 3 NCOs & 5 men	
			Rail Head - 1 NCO & 5 men	
			Water Duty & Stores - 1 NCO & 5 men	
			Mess Orderlies - 2 men	
			Headquarters - 3 men	

Page 13

Army Form C. 2118

WAR DIARY
or
INTELLIGENCE SUMMARY.
(Erase heading not required.)

Place	Date	Hour	Summary of Events and Information	Remarks and references to Appendices
BEAURAINVILLE	11/9/15	10 a.m.	Indent for 28 Smoke Helmets or Respirators forwarded to H.Qrs. ROYON by host. Duty Sections for to-day continued previous day's work. Work at Supply Column conducted Details Section under Sergt. GOODING. – Constructed fitted two grease traps, one at each end of ablution bench for village water from kitchen, this going first into larger one made from half a barrel passing into second at other end of ablution bench, the second one also receiving waste water from washing benches. Water spouts from adjoining outhouses connected to main drainage to soakage pits. Babies hut under pump to prevent flushing of yard with waste water after using pump. Two unused WCs belonging house thoroughly cleaned & disinfected at request of O.C. Supply Column. All necessary notices on closets, urine pits, incinerators, refuse pits, soakage pits &C. Soakage pits were railed off from rest of garden. Recommendations made by O.C. & Sergt. GOODING & Corporal i/c San Squad @ Member of San. Squad to visit latrines at frequent intervals & see if exereta is properly covered.	

Page 14.

Army Form C. 2118

WAR DIARY
or
INTELLIGENCE SUMMARY.
(Erase heading not required.)

Place	Date	Hour	Summary of Events and Information	Remarks and references to Appendices
BEAURAINVILLE	11/9/15		(a) Renew notices when required. (b) See that soil, scraps, papers are provided daily in all latrines (c) See that filtering material in all grease traps is exchanged once daily, soiled material burnt at once (d) See that all refuse except latrine refuse is burnt or else deposited in the pits covered with soil. (f) See that all latrine pails are emptied into pit provided - cover with soil - wash pails with sol: of chloride of lime or creol (g) Keep fires in incinerator burning (h) See that no water is emptied down the gutters in the yard. (i) See that the permanent grease trap in the water channel in garden is removed periodically, cleaned, & replaced (j) Repair & renew all sanitary conveniences & appliances immediately they require same. Duties performed by O.C.	
		A.M	Visited & inspected work done by detailed sections in BEAURAINVILLE.	
		11.30	Received request by telegram from M.O. Norfolks at MONTCAVREL to disinfect vermenous	
		P.M.	clothing of 4 men. Took 2 men, disinfector, 2 N.C.O's & 2 men there early in afternoon. Owing to delay in receiving wire M.O Norfolks had dealt with the men's underclothing which had been soaked in creol solution. Visited Suffolks at ALETTE same afternoon for same purpose. Discovered that message sent by telegraph was sent by M.O. Norfolks & misinterpreted. Reported this to Signalling Officer.	

Page 15.

Army Form C. 2118

WAR DIARY
or
INTELLIGENCE SUMMARY.
(Erase heading not required.)

Place	Date	Hour	Summary of Events and Information	Remarks and references to Appendices
BEAURAINVILLE	11/9/15	5.30pm	Received instructions from D.A.D.M.S. to disinfect billet used by Private MIDDLETON belonging to Supply Headquarters who is suffering from measles. The M.O. of Remount, Lieut. Col. FLYNN having taken the case to ÉTAPLES I saw Officer i/c & arranged to isolate the one contact of this man until return of M.O. These two men had slept together alone in a motor lorry since arrival here. Lorry is used for Supply purposes & is emptied daily. It has now been removed to another district so disinfection could not be undertaken.	
	12/9/15	A.M.	Received Group Orders "A" HdQrs 11/9/15. No 4 "Link" - details noted.	NSL
			" 2nd D.R.O. HdQrs 11/9/15. Par 65 "Returns-Officers" return in triplicate left by me at HdQrs. Par. 66 "Returns (Religion)" - Jewish Faith - return (I man) left by me at HdQrs. Par. 64 Stationery - noted	
			Received Memorandum No. A 13/4 IInd Corps No. Q/35/2. Q/3793 "Occupation of Officers' Messes"	
			Received 3rd D.R.O. HdQrs 12/9/15 Par. 70 re A.F. B. 213 to be rendered through Div HdQu. Note Par. 72 re A.F.B. 213 to be rendered through Div HdQu. Note Par. 71 Field Cashier at BEAURAINVILLE Sat. 2pm	
			Received Confidential Letters re suspects & perfected motor cars.	

WAR DIARY
or
INTELLIGENCE SUMMARY.

(Erase heading not required.)

Army Form C. 2118

Page 16.

Place	Date	Hour	Summary of Events and Information	Remarks and references to Appendices
BEAURAINVILLE	10/9/15		Received Summary of Information No. 7 Hqrs XI Corps 11/9/15 Memo. No. G 85 HQ 2d Div: re Maps of BELGIUM - this Unit has none of these	WSL
	11/9/15	5.50 am	Telegram from Ottawa 9th Bn: re Smoke Helmets & Rockets.	WSL
	12/9/15	9.30	Went to ROYEN to draw 35 new Smoke Helmets & Rockets - also to return 40 damaged ones. The damaged ones are to be returned to C.O.O. ABBEVILLE via R.T.O. Saw Major WESTON on various matters connected with the work of the Section.	
		10 am	Received telegram from M.O. Norfolks requesting me to arrange for the disinfection of Clothing belonging to 3 men infested with lice, who had been attending Machine Gunnery Instruction Course at MASQUES.	
		1.30 pm	Took Dry disinfector S/Sgt & 2 men to do this work. All their clothing was disinfected by steam. Men bathed themselves with soft soap mineral oil after disinfection. They washed their spare underclothing in a similar solution.	
		8 pm	Report of action taken sent to D.A.D.M.S. by foot with suggestion that directions be given to M.O.'s of other units who have sent men to the same instruction Place to examine these men on their return. Course considered advisable for two reasons: - (1) Men frequently hide this complaint. (2) blankets at MASQUES are used in common by men attending classes & by men from the trenches.	

Page 14

Army Form C. 2118

WAR DIARY
or
INTELLIGENCE SUMMARY.

(Erase heading not required.)

Place	Date	Hour	Summary of Events and Information	Remarks and references to Appendices
BEAURAINVILLE	13/9/15		Duty Sections detailed as follows:—	
			Supply Column — 1 NCO + 5 Men ⎫ In each case the work is a	
			Rail head — 1 NCO + 4 Men ⎬ continuation of last week's work	
			Water Duty & Stores — 1 NCO + 4 Men ⎭ Sections have been so arranged	
			Mess Orderlies — 2 Men ⎫ that every man has the opportunity	
			Headquarters — 2 NCOs + 4 Men ⎬ of seeing everything that has been done	
		6.30pm	Received Circular 24th Divn No. A 1/4 re Minor Claims for Damage.	
			" Q.29 "Smoke Helmet". Each man in this Unit now possesses	
			Two. The dating of both (par. 6) will be done after "Orders" to-morrow evening	
			Received Circular Memorandum 3. Q.59 "Prevention of Waste" — contents duly	
			noted. At present the stores are easily controlled & there is no waste.	
			The men in my Unit thoroughly understand the need of economising	
			& reducing preventible waste to the lowest possible minimum.	
			Received "Summary of Information" No 8.	
			Received 24th D R.O. 93/9/15. Par. 46 "Returns". This Unit possesses One	
			30cwt. Motor Lorry — letter to this effect will be left at HdQrs. by me	
			to-morrow morning before 9 a.m	

Page 16.

WAR DIARY
or
INTELLIGENCE SUMMARY.
(Erase heading not required.)

Army Form C. 2118

Place	Date	Hour	Summary of Events and Information	Remarks and references to Appendices
BEAURAINVILLE	13/9/15			WSL
	14/9/15	6.30am	Received Memo. 24th Div. No. G.523 13/9/15 re No. of Smoke Helmets in my possession	
		8.40am	Visited Hd Qrs at ROYEN. Left billeting certificate (duplicate), letter re no. of Motor Lorries, letter re Smoke Helmets (2 per man)	
		9.30am	Forwarded by foot to C.O.O. Meat Transport. A.S.C. ABBEVILLE indent for 2 brushes. Spoke for use on Motor Lorry Duty Sections for to-day are — Work done
			Railhead — 2 NCO's & 4 Men — Supply/dump — Inspected sanitary arrangements made
			Supply Column — 2 NCO's & 5 Men — Dry section. Started incinerator which had been
			Water Duty Stores — 1 NCO & 4 Men — choked with wet refuse. Completed Ablution bench
			Special Duty — 1 Man — Railhead — Dug new latrines. Cleaned yard. Burned
			H.Qrs. — 3 Men — refuse.
			Headquarters — 2 Men	
		6 pm	Inspected all Smoke Helmets — all serviceable — new pockets all sewn in	
			All helmets dated 11/9/15 or 12/9/15 — after Orders for the day	
		4.30pm	Received Summary of Information No. 9; Rect. Part I Orders 24th Div. H.Q. 14/9/15; Note both dated 18 & 9 "Interpreters", "Maps". Received March Data 24th Division. G.O. 14/9/15. Recd W.O. letter 9/Infd/9984 (F2) with 3 enclosures.	

WAR DIARY or INTELLIGENCE SUMMARY

Army Form C. 2118

Place	Date	Hour	Summary of Events and Information	Remarks and references to Appendices
BEAURAINVILLE	14/9/15		Received 24th D.R.O. 14th Sept. 1915. Note Par. 85 "Billets" – ① included in Orders for to-morrow further emphasising previous instruction. ② carefully observed by us. ③ have asked Staff Qrs. for copy of G.R.O. No. 654 dated 28/7/15. Par. 86 "Blankets" – Return will be left by me at H.Qrs. to-morrow. Par. 87 "Smoke Helmets" – note unserviceable ones to be forwarded to C.O., O.S.H. Depôt, ABBEVILLE. Par. 90 "Returns" – Med. Transport to Divl H.Qrs. at 11 p.m. every Saturday.	NSL
	15/9/15	8 A.M.	Duty Sections for to-day similar to yesterday. Work at all stations continued except that at the Supply Column the work was chiefly that of Sanitary Police. Smoke Helmets forwarded by post to ABBEVILLE (see above)	
		10 A.M.	Visited H.Qrs. at ROYON. Saw Col. CLARKE, A.D.M.S. & Major WESTON D.A.D.M.S. Instructed by Col. CLARKE to visit all troops in Div. 24 for the purpose of inspecting all sanitary arrangements; advising & instructing the various Sanitary Squads either personally or by deputy. I purpose visiting LOISON & OFFIN with 3 N.C.O's + 3 Men to-morrow.	
		2 P.M.	Visited the various Sections at work. Saw O.C. Supply Column re Sanitary Police. Made arrangements for reliefs in afternoon.	
		12 noon		

Army Form C. 2118

WAR DIARY
or
INTELLIGENCE SUMMARY.
(Erase heading not required.)

Instructions regarding War Diaries and Intelligence Summaries are contained in F. S. Regs., Part II. and the Staff Manual respectively. Title pages will be prepared in manuscript.

Place	Date	Hour	Summary of Events and Information	Remarks and references to Appendices
BEAURAINVILLE	15/9/15	7 P.M.	Received from Div'l HdQrs. Army Orders, War Office, Aug 27th 1915 "Permanent Commissions in the Regular Army." Rec'd Circular A.B/23. 24th Div re Return of all Officers to be rendered on the 1st of each month commencing with Oct. 1st. Received 24th DRO 15/9/15. Par. 94 "Photography will be included in Orders for to-morrow 16th inst. Mentioned in G.R.O. "1/9/15 No. 1137 received to-day. No. 1148 "Registration of letters or packets containing coin or articles of value" will be included in Orders for 16th inst. Last Summary of Information. No. 10.	hSL
		10.30 p.m.	Received Telegram from H.Q. 24 D.A. asking for Route Return. Same has been forwarded.	
	16/9/15		Duty Sections for to-morrow are:— OFF I N — Staff-sergeant, 1 S/Cpl + 1 Man } O.C. accompanying. LO I S DN — S/gt. GOODING + 2 Men Railhead — 1 N.C.O. + 4 Men Supply Column — 1 N.C.O. + 4 Men Water Duty + Stores — 1 N.C.O. + 3 Men H. Qrs. — 5 Men	

Page 21

WAR DIARY
or
INTELLIGENCE SUMMARY.
(Erase heading not required.)

Army Form C. 2118

Place	Date	Hour	Summary of Events and Information	Remarks and references to Appendices
BEAURAINVILLE	10/9/15	A.M.	Visited OFFIN. Inspected billets with Lieut WALLACE, M.O. & R.E. All billets were satisfactory. A Sanitary Squad has been detailed by C.O. but duties are only carried out when men are not required for purely regimental duties. Inspected Field Kitchen & Sanitary Area. Saw Water Carts & examined men working on them in their duties. These were properly performed except that amount of alum used in clarifier was not known owing to Unit not being supplied with Horrock's case & amount of bleaching powder used was merely guessed. Detailed Sergeant & 2 Men to instruct this Sanitary Squad in construction of new type of urinal & grease trap. Took M.O. to Supply Column, BEAURAINVILLE to see ablution bench erected by men of my section, with the drainage arrangements made. Visited LOISON. An unfinished elementary school is used as billet. Went round with Lieut WALLACE. The Company of R.E. using billet was away on duty for the day so did not see the Sanitary Squad. Submitted various suggestion to M.O. through A.D.M.S especially as regards Sanitary Area & Ablution Place	
		P.M.	Visited Glasgow Yeomanry at HESMOND with Lieut WALLACE. Two R.A.M.C. men have been detailed for duty from their training centre with the Unit. Went through Chateau & horse lines & billets with the C.O. At present there is no Water Cart. Water provided from pumps is boiled before use. One	

Army Form C. 2118

Page 22.

WAR DIARY
or
INTELLIGENCE SUMMARY.
(Erase heading not required.)

Instructions regarding War Diaries and Intelligence Summaries are contained in F. S. Regs., Part II. and the Staff Manual respectively. Title pages will be prepared in manuscript.

Place	Date	Hour	Summary of Events and Information	Remarks and references to Appendices
BEAURAINVILLE.	10/9/15	P.M.	One is expected shortly. Made arrangements to install these men in its use when it arrives. Bulletin 46. C.O. at my suggestion will arrange with local farmers to remove manure daily from horse lines. All other refuse is to pass through an incinerator. Latrines were on short trench system but epidiascope was unsevered. C.O. will take necessary action.	
		7.15	Received 24 D.R.O. Suppt 11th Sept. 1915. Note Par. 95 "War Diaries". Have no copy of G.R.O. No 546. Note Par. 96 "Billeting". Cut offs in future to be forwarded to G.H.Q. not Div. H.Q. Par. 98 "Smoke Helmets" has already been complied with.	M.S.C.
	14/9/15	A.M.	Visited Div. H.Qrs at ROYON. Disinfected with steam verminous clothing of one man at request of D.A.D.O.S. Man was instructed to wash his underclothing afterwards in Isonnigale supply to seamen of time. Detailed Sgt. & 2 men to continue the instruction to Sanitary Squad of R.E. stoves.	
		P.M.	Visited Sherwood Foresters at St DENŒUX. Inspected with Lieut. MIDDLETON billets & sanitary arrangements. A Sergeant & 8 Men form the Sanitary Squad & they perform no other duties. Billets were outhouses of farms & in no case was ventilation good. In many there was no windows. Three billets were very insanitary — one was over a cowshed with a dangerous floor — another adjoins a cowshed with a thin partition split in many parts — this contained a stove used for making high food which was stored in billet during night. All the latrines were of the long pattern & the many were fouled — no urine pits are provided, the trenches being used.	

T2134. Wt. W708—776. 500000. 4/15. Sir J. C. & S.

WAR DIARY
or
INTELLIGENCE SUMMARY.

(Erase heading not required.)

Army Form C. 2118

Page 23

Place	Date	Hour	Summary of Events and Information	Remarks and references to Appendices
BEAURAINVILLE	17/9/15		Excellent arrangements were made for bathing purposes, water being heated in a copper boiler placed over fire which was supported surrounded by turf. Men bathed in tubs in an adjoining room. The Sanitary Squad was well instructed but as the Unit was expected to move at any moment many of their duties had been neglected. Water is properly chlorinated. No work is now being used, and is stored in water carts.	
		7 P.M.	Received "Summary of Information" No 12. Recd. Memo "Return of deficiencies of Equipment". Note that this Return must reach D.H.Q. by 6 p.m. each Thursday. Recd. Corps R.O. 159/15. Note Sec. 5 "Horses" — not to be tied to vehicles except in cases of emergency. Recd. G.R.O. 1150, 1, 2. Ref. 2nd DTW HQ 17/9/15. Note 102 "Pcls" & 103 "Purchase of clothing." Aus. Name in "Div" Ø 5/23. 11th Corps. No Q/20/4. O.S.G. 7350/396 with regard to "Smoke Helmet Respirators."	NOS?
	18/9/5	8 A.M.	Took Cpl. LOTT & 45th Field Ambulance at LEBIEZ for advanced knee. Left dept & 2 Men to instruct San Squad at OFFIN. Left Field Shab. & Field Return at DHQ at ROYON where I received instructions from A.D.M.S. to visit to HUMBERT to disinfect billet occupied by case of meningitis.	
		P.M.	Visited HUMBERT & found billet occupied by 26 contacts so disinfection was impossible. Visited billets with Lieut POTTER, M.O. Majority are badly ventilated — all are anything but sanitary. Squad consists of Sergt & 16 Men who have no other duties to perform in forms sanitary squad enough of Sergt & 16 Men who have no other duties to perform. They are well instructed	

T2134. Wt. W708—776. 500000. (4/15. Sir J. C. & S.

Page 24

Army Form C. 2118

WAR DIARY
or
INTELLIGENCE SUMMARY.
(Erase heading not required.)

Instructions regarding War Diaries and Intelligence Summaries are contained in F. S. Regs., Part II. and the Staff Manual respectively. Title pages will be prepared in manuscript.

Place	Date	Hour	Summary of Events and Information	Remarks and references to Appendices
BEAURAINVILLE	18/9/15	7 P.M.	Water is drawn from pump in the middle of a manure heap. To prevent such a case in providia. Coirifer cloth only two in number – the pump unsanitary drain. the Unit possesses two Water Carts. Field kitchens – ten in number – no clean other duty. Latrines: three pits are made for each company but they are too far away from huts. The latrines are not properly used. Urine pits were of V shape but were too large. These were also not provided or well made; they are however too large a step for away so as not as a step for away so they ought to the. No shoved provision made for bath. Received "Summary of Information" No 15. Recd Memo XI Corps G 195 – Map 36C amended according to instructions. Recd m BRO HQ 189/15. Par 112 "Location of Units" specially noted to day. men have been on duty at the Railhead. Supply Column Staffs as on preceding days. Work has followed ordinary lines. Pay Parade – had out Frs 165 Recd 24th BRO 54G 19/9/15. Note Par 117 "Casualties." Recd Memo. 11th Corps Q 77 m 49w of Road Discipline. Acknowledged receipt of same Rear Summary C. 148 m Road Discipline. Acknowledged receipt of same Rear Summary of Information No.14.	NOSL
	19/9/15	7 P.M.	Duty Section provided for at Supply Column Railhead, etHq Qu until 1.30 p.m. – similar work done as on previous days. Returned Two rifles (ale Drew) to R.T.O. BEAURAINVILLE for transmittance to HAVRE.	NOSL

Page 25

Army Form C. 2118.

WAR DIARY
or
INTELLIGENCE SUMMARY.
(Erase heading not required.)

Place	Date	Hour	Summary of Events and Information	Remarks and references to Appendices
BEAURAINVILLE	20/9/15	6.30pm	Received 24th BD R O dated 20/9/15. Note Par. 121 "Weekly Field State". A.3.B. 231 to be made up to noon Friday. Recd 24th Div "A "4/40" Confidential Memorandum re "Honours & Rewards". Recd Summary of Information No. 15. Duty Section worked as follows:- Château, BEAURAINVILLE — 2 Men to instruct Sans Squad in cleaning of usual sanitary conveniences &c. Supply Column, Railhead, Water Duty, Staff — work continued.	NASL
	21/9/15	5 A.M	NEUVILLE — Went with 2 Sergeants & 4 Men to instruct Bedfords in water & sanitary duties. Found everything in excellent order. Went to MONTCAVREL to inspect billets.	NASL
		11.30	Returned & found no news re moving of my Unit so went to Staff at MARESQUEL. Learnt here that we were expected at LEBIEZ at noon to join the 43rd Field Ambulance. Left billets at 3pm arriving LEBIEZ at 4.5pm.	
		5.30	Left with Ambulance Column — marched all night — billeted at HEZELQUE	
	22/9/15		Halted all day. Left HEZELQUE at 6p.m. — arrived MANQUEVILLE 4 A.M.	NASL
	23/9/15		Changed billets — men rested all day	NASL
	24/9/15		Left MANQUEVILLE at 5.30pm for BETHUNE. Billeted with 43rd F. Ambulance in unfinished church	NASL

WAR DIARY
or
INTELLIGENCE SUMMARY.

Army Form C. 2118

Page 26

Place	Date	Hour	Summary of Events and Information	Remarks and references to Appendices
BETHUNE	25/9/15		Left BETHUNE at 3pm with 2nd Field Ambulance Workshop Unit for BOUVRY. Men billeted in shed. Weather - very wet indeed	NSL
BOUVRY	26/9/15		Found sleeping accommodation for men in cafe. Men busy preparing sanitary conveniences as for own Unit searched H.L.I. & Field Ambulances in same.	NSL
BOUVRY	27/9/15		Men detailed for duty at SAILLY LA BOURSE and useful work such as's rather hopeless being here before going into action	NSL
BOUVRY	28/9/15		Men detailed for duty among troops at same from as yesterday also BOUVRY. Left this village at 9pm for ANNEZIN in pouring rain. Men billeted in barn near railhead. During the last 4 days have experienced great difficulty in knowing rations owing to lack of information as to breadth of Supply Column. The same remark applies to correspondence. Received 165 frs. from Field Cashier for payments to men.	NSL
FOUQUERQUIL	29/9/15		Very wet day. Left here at 4.30 south F.A.N.U. for St HILAIRE. Received very good billets for men in two barns.	NSL
"	30/9/15		Men detailed for duty at HQrs chiefly water testing - water found to be very good. Paid out 165 frs. with R.B.'s to Unit.	NSL

Appendix 1

Ablution Bench.

Section through one of nine compartments.

Trough for waste water.

Plug

Grease Trap.

To another Grease Trap.

Support for Grease Trap.

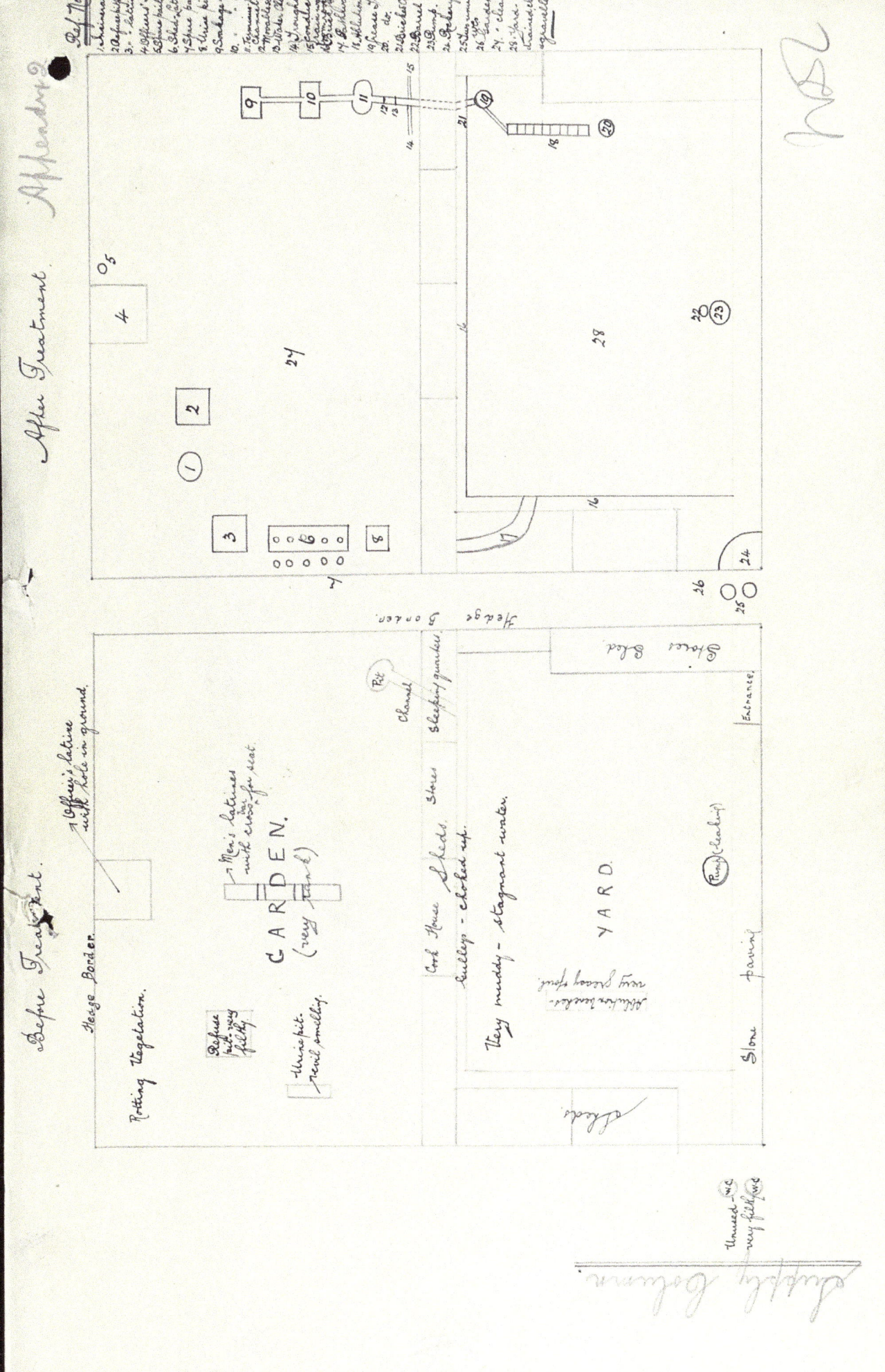

S

Summarised but not copied

24th Division

Oct 1915

121/7431

CONFIDENTIAL

WAR DIARY
OF
41ST SANITARY SECTION

FROM 1st Oct./15 TO 31st Oct./15.

VOLUME 2.

W D Carruthers
Lieut RAMC T
OC

Page 1. 41st Sanitary Section   Army Form C. 2118

WAR DIARY
or
INTELLIGENCE SUMMARY.
(Erase heading not required.)

Place	Date	Hour	Summary of Events and Information	Remarks and references to Appendices
St HILAIRE	Oct. 1st		Section expected to move but orders cancelled. N.C.O + 2 Men tested water & repaired water cart for 2nd Battery. 3 Men attended to sanitary arrangements at 3½ div field Received Summary of Intelligence – 24th Div. SIQ 30/9/15	NSL
	2nd		Left St HILAIRE at 4 p.m. with 24 J.A W.h for STEENVORDE arriving there 7.30 p.m. Men billeted in comfortable barn – Sergeants on hire in the town Rec'd. D.R.O. 2nd October 1915. Note 149 – Div HQrs	NSL
STEENVORDE	3rd		Men at liberty to attend Divine Service at local church Sanitary arrangements made for Section. Received from Field Cashier 165 frs paid while sum to Section. Rec't. b.g.(O. 2/X/15 No 144+5.	NSL
	4th	9 a.m.	Physical Drill for Section. Received Routine Orders by Gen Sir H.C.O. PLUMER. K.C.B. 2/X/15. Note Part. 208 – 9 – 10 – 11 – 13 – 14. Order No 210 "Discipline – Sleeping on Post" will be read out on parade three times as requested by 3 Sergt. Lieut. Newborn 2 R3 A. S/Sgt. suffering from flea.	NSL
	5th	A.M.	Disinfected clothing of 740 men of 34 San.	
		P.M.	4 Men went to RENINGHELST, S/Sgt. took over officers camp site from 34 San Sec: L/Sgt + 2 Man put in charge of Hospital pending arrival of R.A.M.C. 2 Men left in charge of Baths & Laundry pending arrival of same Unit	

Page 2.

Army Form C. 2118.

WAR DIARY
or
INTELLIGENCE SUMMARY.
(Erase heading not required.)

Place	Date	Hour	Summary of Events and Information	Remarks and references to Appendices
STEENVOORDE	5/X/5			NSL
RENINGHELST	6/X/15	P.M.	Recd. DRO HqGs 3/X/5. Note Par 150 & 155 - "Casualties" & "Supplies" in new area. Received order fr ADMS re water duties.	
		A.M.	N.C.O. + 5 Men detailed for Water Duty at BOESCHEPE - returned for 36 hrs - arrangements for reaching destination made by ADMS - party left at 9 a.m. N.C.O. + 4 Men detailed for Water Duty at DICKEBUSCH - arrangements same as former section - party left at 1.30 p.m. Recd. Map "Road Controls 2nd Army Area"	
		2 p.m.	Remainder of Section left with 24 t.S.A.W.U. for RENINGHELST. Tents pitched arriving at 4 p.m.	
		6.30 p.m.	Party in charge hospital relieved. Party in charge Baths re will remain for the present.	NSL
	7/X/15	9 a.m.	Rations for two days sent to section at DICKEBUSCH + BOESCHEPE. 2 Men detailed for journey - latrines seats re. Cpl + 2 Men detailed for duty at HqGs G.O.C. constructing wire pit, latrines, &c. 2 Men still on duty at Baths.	
		P.M.	Received 2nd D.R.O. HqGs 4th Oct. 1915. Note Par 180 "Postal Service". Visited Y.M.C.A. hut at the request of Director of same made arrangements by which this section will be responsible for sanitation of hut & surroundings. Visited D.A.D.O.S. re Shoes, Officer i/c Water Control re Water in village respecting districts A.D.M.S. re urgent Sanitation requirements. Detailed Duty Section for to-morrow.	NSL

Page 3

Army Form C. 2118.

WAR DIARY
or
INTELLIGENCE SUMMARY.
(Erase heading not required.)

Place	Date	Hour	Summary of Events and Information	Remarks and references to Appendices
RENINGHELST	6/10/5	A.M.	Capt. & 2 Men detailed for duty at Hd Qrs G.O.C. 2 Men detailed for duty at Y.M.C.A. hut. Sgt. in charge of 17 fatigues from Corp. Curtis on road & house sanitation duties. Sgt. GOODING detailed for Stores duty with special reference to men at BOESCHEPE — one man to be recalled from this point for duty here. Visited D.A.D.O.S. re stores — timber, tar, canvas &c. A.D.M.S. such parade heating & tent note discussed. 9 a.m. ① Officer i/c Parks — 2 men recalled; question of general sanitation & removal of refuse manure. ② O.C. Divisional Signal Company re general sanitation & removal of refuse manure.	
		P.M.	① Officer i/c Water re duties at BOESCHEPE & DICKEBUSCH. From the former place 3 Men are to be re-called & the remaining men will be stationed by the 92nd F.A. from the morning of the 9th inst. The other section will be relieved in the course of a few days. Work done at Hd Qrs G.O.C. — whole sanitary arrangements overhauled — plans prepared for separate latrines & for orderlies. Work done at Y.M.C.A. Fixed up 3 soil latrines with seats — screen fixed — pit for excreta dug by E. Surreys. Supplies of creol. latrine paper left. Town duties — Roads near important offices scraped & brushed. Incinerator built of bricks in own yard, & a similar one at Gen. H.Q. Clothes infected with scabies disinfected at baths. In future this disinfector to be in charge of O.C. Baths.	WSC

Page 4

WAR DIARY
or
INTELLIGENCE SUMMARY.
(Erase heading not required.)

Army Form C. 2118.

Place	Date	Hour	Summary of Events and Information	Remarks and references to Appendices
RENINGHELST	9/10/15	A.M.	3 Men withdrawn from Water Duties at DICKEBUSCH. Report received from N.C.O in charge there taken to men at BOESCHEPE for duty at H.Q. 3 days rations	
			Work done during day.	
			4 SGT DINNIS – Stoves & huts – 2nd Div Sig RE – unit wired – supervised fatigues on roads. – built large turf incinerator for same unit.	
			CORPL LOTT – 2nd HQ Office – new pit made. Latrine erected & old one removed – empties released all latrines	
			G.H.Q. – erected latrines urinal for warehouse	
			Div H.Q. – erected 2 urinals for camp.	
			Woodworth – 2 men – made 2 stationery trays for A.D.M.S., 2 for D.A.D.M.S. & 2 for own use – 2 Urine pails for Div H.Q, & 1 for G.H.Q. – trench latrine for G.H.Q. – Made & erected screen round full length one smaller size for overflow G.H.Q	
			Roads – work on main roads continued from 3-4 pm. a cart was available for removal of refuse. This cart will not be available on Sundays.	
			Billets – arrangements made for Section to billet in a barn ¼ mile from H.Q. Sent to visit the Church to-morrow when take possession of new billets	

T2134. Wt. W708–776. 500000. 4/15. Sir J. C. & S.

Army Form C. 2118.

Page 5

WAR DIARY
or
INTELLIGENCE SUMMARY.
(Erase heading not required.)

Instructions regarding War Diaries and Intelligence Summaries are contained in F.S. Regs., Part II. and the Staff Manual respectively. Title pages will be prepared in manuscript.

Place	Date	Hour	Summary of Events and Information	Remarks and references to Appendices
RENINGHELST	9/10/15	7pm	Received Circular Memorandum No. 106 "Prevention of Water freezing in radiators of Motor Cars, Motor Lorries" – circulars given to Motor Drivers with instructions to carry out all necessary precautions.	NSL
	10/10/15	A.M.	Received Corps Q.O. No. 417-422 dated 9/X/15. Rec. 24th D.R.O. No. 193-203. Note par. 201-2-3. Re 194 Tents – colour wash indented for from D.A.D.O.S. Re 201 – drew 330 Jts from Field Cashier – paid same num. to Section. Par. 202 – Baths. O/c Baths has arranged for men under my command to bath 3 at a time every ½ hour from 8 a.m. – Par. 203 'Fuel & Light' – have written Stationery Depot HAVRE for copy of Allowance Regulations – re 252(3) D have reported two fireplaces – one for office one for billet O Recd D.R.O. 25th Sep 1915 Nos 1167 & 1174. Work done. Roads – work by fatigues from 6 Survey coy. Woodwork – latrine seats const Cap LOTT – continued work in field opposite billet – latrines, incinerators &c The field is used by various troops. Sgt DINNIS apprehended removal of camp to a farm ¼ mile nearer POPERINGHE – latrine area re arranged. Received 24th D.R.O. 10/10/15 Nos 204-5; also Routine Orders Nos 216-221.	NSL

WAR DIARY
or
INTELLIGENCE SUMMARY.
(Erase heading not required.)

Army Form C. 2118.

Place	Date	Hour	Summary of Events and Information	Remarks and references to Appendices
RENINGHELST.	11/10/5		Inspection of Camps. Billets &c. Reports received from NCOs & Men as follows:-	Sgt DINNIS
			Queen's :- have permanent sanitary squad - sanitation good	
			Suffolks - left camp this afternoon. Having had no incinerator a large amount of refuse was left in many places. Latrines in bad condition. Buffs have now arrived. They have a sanitary squad.	
			Surreys - have Sanitary Squad. Sanitation - Very good. Large incinerator built & several more being made.	
			2 & Div. Lt. Gr. - no latrines. A field now unoccupied, has been left in very foul condition. O.C. will investigate same at once	
			Corpl LOTT (in charge of 3 fatigues)	
			G.H.Q - latrines cleaned, & all refuse burnt in both latrine areas.	
			Y.M.C.A " " " " " " "	
			Div H.Q " " " " " " " in both areas. Tiny incinerator built	
			R.E. prepared site for incinerator.	
			Pw. BLACK (in charge of 4 fatigues) D.A.D.O.S yard - long trench latrine & refuse pit commenced. Black there very foul - kitchen &c left dirty by previous occupants - latter cleaned.	

WAR DIARY or INTELLIGENCE SUMMARY

Army Form C. 2118.

Page 1

Place	Date	Hour	Summary of Events and Information	Remarks and references to Appendices
RENINGHELST	1/10/15		Officers' billets requiring attention — Camp Commandant — latrines & ground cleaning. A.D.V.S. — latrine pit requires emptying. C.R.E. — sea foot seems blocked — work put in hand for to-morrow. S/GOODING — in charge of new camp, stores, sanitation, & C. Private MARTIN appointed Post Orderly. Camp Orderly from 13th inst. lorry — officer's old wine pail for D.A.D.O.S. a one for own camp. both whitewashed — says fresh for storage pit made & fixed. 2 wine pails made for stores. OC — visited water buckyleaders at BOESCHEPE — everything satisfactory — also own camp & camp where fatigue squads are working. Received DRO HQ No 11/10/15 No 210-216	
	10/10/15		S/ DINNIS commenced work of cleaning field opposite R.E. Div. Sig. O. Corpl LOTT — in charge of 2 fatigues (8 survey) G.H.Q. Y.M.C.A; Div HQ — similar work to yesterday Built Turf Incinerator at R.E (Signal) Camp used by G.H.Q. Guard to burn refuse Dug urine pit and filled urinal at Army Omnibus Park Private Black Meani + Morflatt at Army Omnibus shed with 4 fatigues (8 survey) = all refuse in billet burned — walls sprayed with Ascol. In yard urine pit latrines, grease trap completed. Cleared waterway along cookhouse & latrine screens.	NSC

WAR DIARY or INTELLIGENCE SUMMARY

Army Form C. 2118.

Place	Date	Hour	Summary of Events and Information	Remarks and references to Appendices
RENINGHELST	12/10/15		Rec. Report from S/Cpl in charge at DICKEBUSCH. Water Cart 106, 99 & 101 for Oct. 9, 10, 11. One cart belonging 9th R.F.A. in poor condition & only half filled. D.D.M.S. visited 11 F/15. Took sample of water & of bleaching powder. A leakage in tank is to be reported to O.C. Works Patrol. Lorries – 4 Printed Notices for D.A.D.O.S. 2 Latrines – wooden bar system; 1 Urine Pail for G.H.Q. & 1 for own Camp; 1 Stool for Office. Wood supplied for work at O.B. Received 2nd DRLS 12 min. NS 216 & 225; also Circular 2nd Div. No A104 re Age, & also Circular 2nd Div. No A192 re N.I.V. Stores from M.T. Dept.	NSL
	13/10/15	8 A.M.	S/D INNIS continued work of clearing field Capt. LOTT cont routine work at G.H.Q., Q.H.Q., Y.M.C.A. At Office grease trap provided & soakage pit dug – all refuse burnt & ground cleared. At O.B. the cordite cylinder ordnance shed cleared & put into serviceable condition. Incinerator bound round w/ thin/wire supplies & stakes. Quarry over incinerator & latrines commenced. Lorries – 12 pipkins for incinerator — for roof, & bndles reeds for latrines – D.A.D.O.S. – 2 latrine pails for Orderly Room staff. G.H.Q. 2 Latrine seats. DICKEBUSCH – report 105santh. These men will be relieved in a few days, the work being taken over by San. Sec. 20 att/5 9th Div. Reserve Cavalry. Rec'd LOOS + D.R.O. MP. 226 – 231. Note 226-7 re or-1. Return for Period Sep 25-28 Sir J.C. & B.	NSL

WAR DIARY or INTELLIGENCE SUMMARY

Army Form C. 2118.

Page 9

Place	Date	Hour	Summary of Events and Information	Remarks and references to Appendices
RENINGHELST	14/10/5	7am	Received request to supply Canadian Division with oxygen. Have notified A.D.M.S. that we do not possess any apparatus for this.	

Sgt GOODING :- Visited No III Mess had heap of refuse removed & burnt. Flies are very troublesome so left fly papers & chloride of lime. Built incinerator on roadside right B CAMP opposite No III Mess. Dug refuse pit 3 feet cube in field next B CAMP. COMMANDANT's billet wiped some round. Ground round this billet to be cleared. Sump pit to be made - Corpl LOTT to be responsible for this.

Corpl LOTT :- routine work at some places as on previous days. Commenced work on spread by Sgt GOODING. (see above)

D.A.D.O.S :- shoes Latrine screens completed. Incinerator roped over. Ditch cleaned. yds - - Bottom laid with tins & broken bricks. Material prepared for concreting. One fatigue prepared timber for spouting re. flooring :- 2 lengths guttering 14'3".10'. 1 trough 4 supports 3'. 1 front 9'6" x 1'. 1 brace trap aspout - for O.B's fittings for Latrines notices Y.M.C.A.

Regs Circular 204 Div No A.190 re rifles; also Routine Orders St Qr. 14/5/5 No. 232 - 243. Supplied Camp Cmd. Return N. 232. Note par. 243 u Sacks. Answer to 240 THATCHING is in the negative. No 242 will be communicated to the whole of the men under my command. WSL

WAR DIARY or INTELLIGENCE SUMMARY

Page 10. Army Form C. 2118.

Place	Date	Hour	Summary of Events and Information	Remarks and references to Appendices
RENINGHELST	15/10/15		Capt. LOTT - usual routine work at G.H.Q., Y.M.C.A., R.E. Dump, Camp, Q. Branch, Camp Commandant's billet.	
			Dry soakage pit made at rear of Camp Commandant's billet.	
			D.A.D.O.S. yard — cement laid in ditch, travel drain made of used tins to back of cook house; gutterings fixed to eaves of cook house; ablution bench surroundings clean. [a new ablution bench with compartments will be made forthwith]	
			Lorries — Hot latrine, urine pail, entries for Officers, Supply (Dummy), BOESCHEPE — sump pit over for Camp Commandant's billet. Said notices for steel.	
			Plans for new drainage & filtering of water at the Baths commenced.	
			Received Corps Routine Orders No. 68 d/10/10/15, also C.R.O. No. 89 d/13/10/15.	
			Roads from G.H.Q. & A.D.M.S. Office cleaned. Rubbish disposed of on cultivated fields.	NSL
	16/10/15		Capt. LOTT — usual routine work. Pit for refuse dug at G.H.Q. Sump pit at Camp Commandant's completed, cover for same made, gutters cleaned &c.	
			D.A.D.O.S. — work on ditch completed. Spouts fixed. Ground under shed prepared for opening of drain to morrow. Wooden grease trap fixed.	
			Lorries — pump pit covers (2), grease trap — cover, fittings, urinal — notices	
			Water Sply. — barrel cleaned. 52 gals water brought in petrol tins from BOESCHEPE	

WAR DIARY or INTELLIGENCE SUMMARY.

Army Form C. 2118.

Place	Date	Hour	Summary of Events and Information	Remarks and references to Appendices
RENINGHELST	17/X/15		Officer's charge missing from camp.	
			Cpl LOTT - usual routine work at G.H.Q., Y.M.C.A., "Q" office, R.E. Signal Camp, Section H.Qrs.	
			DADOS - guttering completed, rain water tub fixed, prepared tunnel drain & yard	
			commenced cleaning operations. Site on roadway closed temporarily until	
			6 A.M. to-morrow. Drew clean before leaving off for the day	NSC
			Recd. D.R.O. No. 271-4. No. for 273 re clothing demands.	
	18/5		Cpl LOTT - routine work. Large refuse pit burnt at Y.M.C.A., No. II Mess inspected - refuse removed,	
			inspected R.E. Signal Camp - being cleaned at time of visit.	
			Road cleaning continued. A Belgian Officer has arranged for loan of cart from 8-12 daily	
			4/S. DINNIS - Supply Column - Officers' latrines, Men's latrines, Urinal made & fixed	
			complete with screening	
			Sgt. GOODING - opened up drain at Re Baths. Work temporarily suspended pending	
			arrival of sand for filters	
			Jomy - DADOS - took dimensions of stand for rain tub, & a bath, also ablution bench	
			Stand for tub made & fixed. Propping & strutting up of shed. Supplied three	
			rafters & new roof plate. To Supply Column - made one box latrine & in lines	
			entries for same. 1 Urine pail, 5 Tent pegs, 5 Eny. Blocks & holes for screens	NSC
			40 French Latrines with rests, also supplied to 17th Infantry Brigade.	

Page 12

Army Form C. 2118.

WAR DIARY
or
INTELLIGENCE SUMMARY.
(Erase heading not required.)

Place	Date	Hour	Summary of Events and Information	Remarks and references to Appendices
RENINGHELST	19/IX/15		G. GOODING - Own camp - constructed covered eathouse with brick chimney, oven, &c. Erected tent for bathing, washing & drying purposes & constructed grease trap & channel for waste. Roads - from No 3 Mess to G.H.Q. dump - have gravel available so sweepings deposited at new dump. D.A.D.O.S. - bridge 8'6" + 2' over ditch, yard studding spiked finished, work on new office fr Sergt Major commenced, details cleaned & a commencement made with bottoming - tins being used. being painted Cpl. LOTT - routine at usual place. Gravel latrines at "Q" office & No II Mess treated with foul. Joinery - made bridge for D.A.D.O.S., filter 6'4"x4" for bath (with partitions), - commenced latrine covers for G Mess & A.D.M.S. offices. 9 Gravel latrines supplied to H Northants. Recd. D.R.O. d/19/10/15 Nos. 284-293, Circular A/144 "Gravel Stores", Circular Q406+18/5/5 re Men on leave & infestation by lice, Memorandum No A/326 "Honours & Rewards", Circulars D.M.S./2nd Army/2820 + 2805/5 re Booklet on Lice, + A.F.B. 117 respectively. - Circular d/17/IX/15 HQ. I.G.C. re Water testing Notice re winding charges appeared in D.R.O.	MSC

T2434. Wt. W708-776. 500000. 4/15. Sir J. C. & S.

Army Form C. 2118.

WAR DIARY
or
INTELLIGENCE SUMMARY.
(Erase heading not required.)

Page 13

Instructions regarding War Diaries and Intelligence Summaries are contained in F. S. Regs., Part II. and the Staff Manual respectively. Title pages will be prepared in manuscript.

Place	Date	Hour	Summary of Events and Information	Remarks and references to Appendices
RENINGHELST	20/3/5		L/Sgt. DINNIS – Visited camp of Surrey Middlesex – constructed large Urine pit for latter Coy – The latrines left by previous occupiers of this camp were in a very foul condition.	
			Baths – channel 20' x 2' x 1' dug to divert flow of water from channel to ditch at baths.	
			Water sand removed from filter pit. Hole 6'x4'x3' prepared to accommodate filter.	
			Headquarters & Road – usual routine work carried out	
			D.A.D.O.S. – new office for Sgt/Major commenced. Work on ditches commenced continued as regards cleaning, trimming & bottoming with tin cans.	
			Joinery – Improvements to filter box – unearthing & extra partition. Latrine screen -2.	
			Repaired 2 forms & 2 tables for Y.M.C.A. Commenced ablution bench for D.A.D.O.S.	NSC
			Received D.R.O. d/20/3/5. N°. 294 - 303 N°. 297, 298, & 302 specially noted.	
	21/3/5		Received Circular 24th Div. No. A/412. Subject – Rations, Curry Powder; Circular 24th Div" No. A/473 re M.T. Transfers; Circular 24th Div. No. A/415 re Losing of Passes; Circular from D.A.D.O.S. re Ordnance Indents; D.R.O. d/21/3/5. N°. 394 - 304; Circular 24th Div. No. A/310 being Extract from letter No 39/17 dated 14/10/5 from D.D.O.S. Q.M.G to 2nd Army re "Tube" Helmets; also Circular D.D.O.S. 2/Army, 18/4/20, re same. Indents for double supply to men of my Unit & fatigues attached will be submitted at ones. As do not possess army helmets of this pattern	

Army Form C. 2118.

WAR DIARY
or
INTELLIGENCE SUMMARY.
(Erase heading not required.)

Place	Date	Hour	Summary of Events and Information	Remarks and references to Appendices
RENINGHELST	2/5/15		Baths – completed hole for filter, had some with bricks, hot fixed filled with coke. Continued removal of head stones from filter pit – found underground pipe conducting water into pit – placed wooden trough in position to conduct water to stream	
			D.R.D.O.S. – work on ditch completed – ditch has been cleaned out, trimmed, given a proper fall, sides bottomed. Work on shed continued. Office for D/Major continued. Repaired truck footing on centre pillar supporting roof of eating shed.	
			Roads – cleaned from Windmill to Hospital. Good party arrived at Baths in afternoon.	
			Caplett – routine work at various Shops – " " " " "	
			Camps – Sherwood Foresters – sanitary squad at work – everything but state of ground satisfactory. This was attended to during day.	
			x 13" Middlesex (transport) – no urine pit so superintended construction of one –	
			x 7 Northants – everything satisfactory	
			x 9 R.B. Surreys – " " – good sanitary squad.	
			x each unit complains of shortage of water	
			Joinery – completed ablution bench for D.A.D.O.S., trough 11" x 5" for baths, notice boards for Y.M.C.A (2) & orderly room.	

Army Form C. 2118.

Page 15.

Instructions regarding War Diaries and Intelligence Summaries are contained in F. S. Regs., Part II. and the Staff Manual respectively. Title pages will be prepared in manuscript.

WAR DIARY
or
INTELLIGENCE SUMMARY.
(Erase heading not required.)

Place	Date	Hour	Summary of Events and Information	Remarks and references to Appendices
RENINGHELST	22/7/15		BATHS - work on pit continued.	
			D.A.D.O.S. - Overflow chamber cleaned out. Proceeded with boarding up of sides & roof of office for S.M. Completed shed except for the fixing of tarpaulin. Pillars supporting old shed pointed at the brick footing & made secure.	
			Camps - Surrey Regt. (9th Royal) - built brick incinerator. 13th Middlesex left late this afternoon leaving a huge amount of discarded clothing which was burnt in heaps owing to the smallness of the incinerator. Two men only were left to bury the burnt refuse. The remainder will have to be buried by next unit to occupy this camp as the heaps were burning very late. Camp F - generally satisfactory. M.M. Golie cookhouse - refuse not burnt regularly. 1st Staffs (: transport) - only one man left to look after sanitary arrangements. Self promised proper urine pail & funnel to be prepared. Capt. LOTT - routine work at various stages - demolished incinerator at No. III Mess - cleared ground - removed all refuse to Y.M.C.A. incinerator. Roads - as usual. Joinery - repairs to Boards pump, letter box for Staff, urine pail stench latrine for stores. Received D.R.O. 27/7/5 Nos. 398 - 405 & lef. (Vrens.) Circular 24th Div. No G. 507/n Undercook Fur. G.R.O. 1202 - 1210. Winter Clothing indented for.	

T2134. Wt. W708—776. 500000. 4/15. Sir J. C. & S.

Page 16

Army Form C. 2118.

WAR DIARY
or
INTELLIGENCE SUMMARY.
(Erase heading not required.)

Place	Date	Hour	Summary of Events and Information	Remarks and references to Appendices
RENINGHELST	23/5/15		BATHS - Diverted flow of water from baths to ditch, removed all pipes preparatory to relaying making watertight. Filled in pit emptied underground waste pipe drains	
			D.A.D.O.S. - Proceeded with the boarding in of window openings & ceiling of shed adjoining roadway. Completed fixing of tarpaulin on roof of new shed. Pillars supporting old shed now made safe. The pointing & setting of new bricks being finished. Excavated foundations for pillars of the large shed. Commenced to prepare the uprights & wall plates for fixing. Erected finger posts with fitting rivets of details.	
			Roads - Usual routine. Loads deposited at new dump.	
			Cpl LOTT - Routine work at various H.Q⁽ˢ⁾. Collected bricks, iron &c. Commenced building new incinerator at Y.M.C.A.	
			Joinery - Latrine box (tin-lined) for O Tech, fixed ablution bench at D.A.D.O.S. Also connections with grease trap &c; commenced the fixing of a guard rail around top of stairs at O.B.; unrepaired furniture.	
			Camps - Now that permanent allotment of camps is made commenced detailed reports on special forms (Appendix 1) Camp C. general condition "good" as regards 9" trench but not good in case of No thank. Great problem in all camps is disposal of ejecta as burying has already been carried too exced.	1

Page 17

Army Form C. 2118.

WAR DIARY
or
INTELLIGENCE SUMMARY.
(Erase heading not required.)

Place	Date	Hour	Summary of Events and Information	Remarks and references to Appendices
RENINGHELST	24/2/15	7 A.M.	Received Circular 5th Corps No. V.A. 555 "Instructions for Training in the use of the Tube Helmet".	
		5 P.M.	Received Circular on "Water Supply" 2nd Divn. No. A. 236. A map has been drawn by one of the section showing the 2nd 6th Divn Water Area. This will be of considerable value.	
			Received Letter 2nd Divn. No. A. 570 – War Office reply re Promotion of Officers to Lieuts. Marked Commander-in-Chief. B.E.F. Received Circular 24th Divn A/572 re Brutal Staff – temporary assistance from 6th Dec. to 1st Jan. No. member of this section possesses the necessary qualifications. Received D.R.O. No. 417 to 429. – Nos. 419, 421, +427 noted.	
			Baths, Roads, Inspection of Billets – all continued to 12.30 P.M. Incinerator at Y.M.C.A. – continued.	
			Joining – completed guard rail at O.B., made fixed cover to pump-hole at O.B., made fixed door frame at O.B., trench latrine for stash.	
			D.A.D.O.S. – excavated foundations for selected fine posts with footings, nail plates attached; filled in + fixed temporary stays. Window opening in the shed.	
			Camps – 13th Staff, Q.M. Kents (transport) + Sherwood Foresters inspected.	
			O.C. visited with A.D.M.S. (Sanitation) + D.A.D.M.S. (Sanitation). Condition far from satisfactory. Instruction section will proceed there from here à mortyour	N52

Army Form C. 2118.

WAR DIARY
or
INTELLIGENCE SUMMARY.
(Erase heading not required.)

Place	Date	Hour	Summary of Events and Information	Remarks and references to Appendices
RENINGHELST	25/7/15	3 PM	Received D.R.O. 1/23/7/15. Nos 407-416, also War Office letter W.O. No 24th Div. A/580.	
		7 PM	Confidential letter re Parade on 29th inst.	
			Weather very wet indeed all day & time table disorganised in consequence. Road sweeping work on Baths suspended for the day. Routine work at Staff carried out. Camp drainage improved. Slab for D.A.D.O.S. continued. 3 Urine Pails further completed	NSC
"	26/7/15	4 PM	Received instructions from D.A.D.M.S. that the 71st Brigade will indent on us for Hypochlorida for Vermoral sprayers. Received D.R.O. d/26/7/15 No 417-424. No 430 "Returns" - no A.3. B.231 Field State in future.	
			Camp inspected - 2nd London - Comdg D - General condition "Fair" Routine work contd at Staff Spr. D.A.D.O.S. - roof commenced to shed. Work held up owing to scarcity of timber. cement, Baths - bottom of pit cleaned recovered with clay and retried. Channel cleaned slimed ready for Joinery - men arrived in construction of shed at O.S. Used flag poles around isolation camp, took dimensions for Triangular box for filter. Sizes 5 broomheads ready for road sweeping to morrow prior to parade	NSC
			O.C. waited Sanitary Section at BAILLEUL	

Army Form C. 2118.

WAR DIARY
or
INTELLIGENCE SUMMARY.
(Erase heading not required.)

Page 19

Place	Date	Hour	Summary of Events and Information	Remarks and references to Appendices
RENINGHELST	27/5/5		Visit of H.M. the KING. Work during the morning suspended in honour of the visit. Survey - notices for H.Qrs; commenced triangular outlet for filter at Baths; made new handle for chisel sharpened tools.	
		J.P.N.	Copplestitt - routine inspection of various H.Qrs Roads cleared by special fatigue party. Remainder of section employed on camp drainage, hut building at the camp. Received Circular 24th Div. No. Q/504 re Undercoats - furs; Circular 24th Div. No. A/1044; D.R.O. of 27/10/1915 No. 432 - 434 + After Order No. 435; R.R.O. 1223 - 1228. No. 1223 read to the Section, No. 1224 noted "Straw." Forwarded to Officer i/c Base Hygienic Laboratory BOULOGNE two samples of water to be tested for the presence of zinc (One sample was taken from a government tank near ABEELE station - the other from a stand pipe in RENINGHELST. Received D.R.O. No. 436 - 446 No. 436, 442, 445 & 446 duly noted; also Circular 24th Div. No. A/652 re transfers; also Index of Water Supply. Sheet. Inspection of men's outfit at 8.30 A.M. very wet day. Cleaning of latrines at H.Qrs, was cleaning bath, camp drainage, aided building at Q.8. all continued. Commenced fixing of latrine screen tarpaulin at Y.M.C.A.	J.N.C.
	28/5/5			

WAR DIARY
or
INTELLIGENCE SUMMARY.
(Erase heading not required.)

Army Form C. 2118.

Page 20

Place	Date	Hour	Summary of Events and Information	Remarks and references to Appendices
RENINGHELST	29/9/15	9.30 AM	Received Circular 2nd Div No. Q/135 "Salmus Breaking Apparatus."	
			Baths - pit filled with ashes, channel cleaned & filled with clinker, upper portions lined with concrete.	
			Lavatory re-covered, Y.M.C.A. latrines (wooden posts & tarpaulin). Seat also for A.D.M.S. also fitted above.	
			Private KILBURN visited Sanitary Section at BAILLEUL where he was shown various types of successful incinerators. He copied plans & details & will begin work on one of his new type to-morrow.	
			Relais Camp.- Ineffective incinerator demolished - new circular one built of turf, prepared grease trap to sewage pit, made pit for burnt refuse from incinerator,	
			cleared ditch for better passage of water, made grease trap for ablution bench.	
			Constructions - 2nd Lynn & Coy R.E. & 2nd London R.E. (Transport only); detailed reports to be sent to A.D.M.S.	
			GIPLOTT - routine work at staff - continued the building of Y.M.C.A. incinerator	
			Ordnance Stores :- Shed building continued - work not proceeding very fast because of lack of timber.	
			Received D.R.O. N° 447 - 459 of 29/1/15. N° 447, 451, 452, 453, 454, & 457	
			" " C.R.O. N° 449 - 455 of 28/9/15 " " 449, 452, 454	
			Roads - cont'd cleaning of main road. Same party cleaning out culvert near G.H.Q.	
	30/9/15		Received 2nd Div - Return of Casualties, Officers Sep 25-26.	

Army Form C. 2118.

WAR DIARY
or
INTELLIGENCE SUMMARY.
(Erase heading not required.)

Place	Date	Hour	Summary of Events and Information	Remarks and references to Appendices
RENINGHELST	30/3/15		Received D.R.O. d/29/3/15 N.os 447, 459 Note N.o 447, 451, 452-3-4; +57; also C.R.O. d/28/3/15 N.o 449 - 455. Note N.o 449, 452 -n° 3, -4. G. channel. Baths - continued the concrete linings. Roadway - work cont. Cleaning of ditch drain near G.H.Q. Destructor - 2 men engaged on burying refuse rtm at G 34 b. Mch 28 "Ypres" 1'45,000. Inspection of Staff commenced cont. Y.M.C.A. incinerator completed. Commenced framing of Y.M.C.A. latrine. Ordnance Shed - completed roofing, strutting & puling in connection with shed. Hung & fixed doors on rpt end of shed. Covering of holes completed by nailing strips of canvas with. A.D.M.S. - Clerks Office - hut at first time. Isolation Camp - new urine pit constructed, also kit for burying of human excreta. Camps - instructed party of fatigues on camp sanitation at the 6 divisional Transport lines. Destructor - Pte KILBURN commenced burying of destructor in Rest Camp D. The destructor is being made of petrol tins filled with mixture of clay & ashes found with mire from direction of Capt Rhoden, Sanitary Officer, Railway	M.S.E.
	31/3/15.		Roadway - Opened up drain for 12', cleaned thoroughly & flushed (men engaged at 6.30 A.M. because of traffic) Baths - continued. O.L. - fixing of aide to pumbing cont. Destructor - work continued. Inspection of H.Q. cont Continued burying of refuse at G. 34 B. Pay Parade - 2 pm. Received D.R.O. d/31/3/15 N.os 467 - 475, also D.R.O. d/29/3/15	M.S.E.

T2134. Wt. W708-776. 500000. 4/15. Sir J. C. & S.

Unit _____ M.O. _____ Stationed at _____

1	2	3	4	5
Field Kitchen	Ablution Place	Sanitary Area	Water Supply	Huts or Tents
				Special Remarks

1. Field Kitchen
- Situation.
- Cleanliness
- Storage
  (a) Food
  (b) Refuse
- Grease Trap
- Incinerators
  (a) No.-
  (b) Type -
  (c) Use -
  (d) Refuse -
- Disposal of Waste Water

2. Ablution Place
- Character
- Situation
- Cleanliness
- Facilities for Washing Clothes
- Baths
- Disposal of Waste Water

3. Sanitary Area
- Sanitary Squad
  (a) No.-
  (b) Perm. or Temp.-
- Latrines
  (a) No.-
  (b) Type-
  (c) Situation-
  (d) Sanitation-
- Urine Pit
  (a) Type-
  (b) Situation-
  (c) Condition-
  (d) Night Urine-
- General Sanitation

4. Water Supply
- Source
- Purification
- Water Carts
  (a) Care of pumps-
  (b) Clarifier-
  (c) % of Cloth-
  (d) Valves-
  (e) Alum-
  (f) Chloride of Lime-
  (g) Horrock's Case-
  (h) Foram Cabinet
- Water Duty Men
  (a) No.
  (b) Perm. or Temp.

5. Huts or Tents
- Huts.
  (a) No. completed -
  (b) " being constructed -
  (c) Condition -
- Foul Ground
  (a) Quantity
  (b) If marked
  (c) Situation
- Disposal of faeces
  " " urine manure -

Re-VISITS.

S

24th Hussars

Summoned but not acted

41st Hus: Sect.
Vol 3

121/7678

Nov 15.

Nov 1915

CONFIDENTIAL.

War Diary

of

41st Sanitary Section

From 1st Nov./15. to 30th Nov./15.

Volume 3

No 41 Sanitary Section
Nov. 1915

App. I has been
detached & filed
under "Sanitation"
Baths

Army Form C. 2118

WAR DIARY
or
INTELLIGENCE SUMMARY.
(Erase heading not required.)

Instructions regarding War Diaries and Intelligence Summaries are contained in F. S. Regs., Part II. and the Staff Manual respectively. Title pages will be prepared in manuscript.

Page 1

Place	Date	Hour	Summary of Events and Information	Remarks and references to Appendices
RENINGHELST	1/11/15		Received C.R.O. d/31/X/15 N.os 456-460. N.ch N.os 457 "Paris" & 459 "Leave"; also D.R.O. d/1/XI/15 N.os 474-483. N.ch N.o 479 "Correspondence", 481 "Respirators", 483 "Demand Sprayers"; also "Extracts from 2nd Army letter N.o A/3814. re Casualties Strength Returns. Sewing of work done. Instructor Camp D – fourth course almost completed. " – 6.35b. M.op 27 – burning of refuse completed. Inc. removed to Hd. Qrs. for soakage pits &c. Ordnance Stores – tarpaulin fixed on new shed; gutters toured; water channels in yard boarded. A.D.M.S. Office – fireplace &c completed. Isolation Camp – sanitary conveniences &c completed. Sanitary Squad instructed in their duties. Camps visited – 6 Surreys – grease trap made complete; Queen's – latrines & urine pail not quite completed. E Transport mly.] Roads – owing to heavy rain, in bad condition. No sait available so work hampered. Various Hd. Qrs. – cleaned as usual all latrines &c. Commenced work on metal cover for Y.M.C.A. incinerator to be made of biscuit tins. Well cleaning – One well, Camp C, emptied. Being "All Saints' Day" the Belgian workmen were not available so that work was not fully completed. Coal well is to the bottomed, & covered with wooden lid. [Posted War Diary - Volume 2]	NSC

Army Form C. 211

WAR DIARY
or
INTELLIGENCE SUMMARY.
(Erase heading not required.)

Page 2

Instructions regarding War Diaries and Intelligence Summaries are contained in F. S. Regs., Part II. and the Staff Manual respectively. Title pages will be prepared in manuscript.

Place	Date	Hour	Summary of Events and Information	Remarks and references to Appendices
RENINGHELST	2/10/15		Very wet day. Road cleaning, inspection of Billets & camp drainage all continued. Ordnance stores - Brackets & shelving fixed to back of hut. Gutters fixed in front of shed & stores. Isolation Camp - cleaning superintended. Camp - Queen's - latrines erected until timber is available for continuation of permanent ones. Urinal fixed. Well cleaning - Being "All Souls Day" Belgian civilians not available as no progress made with woodwork. ✗ / Destructor - Camp D - much progress made ✗ Baths - work of cementing delayed by rain. Watershower partition completed with urine partition completed. Received C.R.O. d/1/11/15 No[s] 461-5. No[s] 461 "Leave", 462 "Road control", & 464 "Clothing - Issue & Officers repayment". duly noted; also D.R.O. d/2/11/15 No[s] 484-493 No[s] 484 "Location of Units", 485 "Fuel", 492 "Fallen hostile aircraft", 493 "R.E. Stores"; also C.R.O. No[s] 1236-1242 d/31/10/15; also Circular 9/527 "Rations & Forage"; C/g Confidential "Issue of Rum" 19/9/950 re C.R.O. 1194 - facilities for drying clothes &c. Received Circular A/562 "Leave" - Nil return forwarded.; D.Q.O. d/3/11/15 No[s] 494-499	NB 7
	3/11/15		Very wet day. Road cleaning, Billets inspection & continued. Men engaged on making tops for incinerators corners. Ordnance Stores & Destructor Camp D completed. Baths - additional help arranged so work much further advanced. Well - little progress made. Camps - visited all rest camps re new arrangement with regard to senior Q.M. & sanitary squad (D.R.O. 454). Arranged for distribution of 80 latrine buckets among the various camps B & G. Queen's (Transport) - latrines, box seats, urine pit, & grease trap all completed. Received "Secret" Circular C.21	NB 2

T2134. Wt. W708-776. 500000. 4/15. Sir J. C. & S.

Page 3

Army Form C. 2118

WAR DIARY
or
INTELLIGENCE SUMMARY.
(Erase heading not required.)

Place	Date	Hour	Summary of Events and Information	Remarks and references to Appendices
RENING HELST	4/VI/5		HdQrs inspected as usual. Roads cleaned - cart used all day. Destructor at 6 s.m.b - work completed.	
			Wells - 4 Belgian & 1 R.E. existing - well emptied, mud removed, boarding commenced	
			Destructor - Camp D - burning all day - men present to remedy any noticeable defects - left in excellent condition - man from Middlesex Regt left in charge.	
			Baths - screen of petrol tins trended, washers made placed to spread water equally over pit.	
			- cementing continued in channel repaired further until etc.	
			Received D.R.O. d/4/VI/15 Nos 500 to 506. Note No 503 "Straw" 505 "Lecture (Courts Martial).	NSC
			Camps inspected :- C Battery, 109th R.F.A. - fairly satisfactory. D Battery - not so satisfactory.	
	5/VI/5		Hd Qrs - usual work carried out. R.E. refuse removed. New cart available. Roads - continued	
			Wells - pump installed in C camp - forring completed too.	
			Camps - incinerator demolished & new one built in C camp. D camp - 109 R.F.A. inspected	
			Destructor - (Camp E III) - 2 layers completed. Water Patrol bullet disinfected	
			Baths - cementing continued. Cleaning of wire commenced. Its drum to be lowered.	
	6/VI/5		Received D.R.O. d/5/VI/15 Nos 507-511 Note No 509 "Returns" burial tail & 510 C.E. Service	NSC
			D.R.O. d/6/VI/15 Nos 512-520. Note 515 Petrol Turnuli; R.O. Nos 229-236. d/4/VI/5	
			C.R.O. d/4/VI/5 Nos 466-470.	

Page 4

Army Form C. 2118

WAR DIARY
or
INTELLIGENCE SUMMARY.
(Erase heading not required.)

Instructions regarding War Diaries and Intelligence Summaries are contained in F. S. Regs., Part II. and the Staff Manual respectively. Title pages will be prepared in manuscript.

Place	Date	Hour	Summary of Events and Information	Remarks and references to Appendices
RENINGHELST	6/11/5		Baths - large filter covered with removable lid, small filter cleaned, partitions removed, drain left in good order.	
			Camps - D Battery 109 R.F.A - urine pit constructed, latrines of the box seat deep pit type partially constructed. Ammn. Col. - grease trap complete, latrines urine pit commenced.	
			Stables & Roads - work continued as usual	
			Destructor - Camp E. Ill. Shrwards continued using & second course filling to of bins for this course	NSC
			Wells - Camp D - one well emptied released. Top to be re-made.	
	7/11/5	2.30 P.M.	Section attended Divine Service in 72nd Inf. Brigade Recreation Hut at 2.30 P.M.	
		10.15 A.M.	This morning one of the 9th to Surreys engaged in stoking the Y.M.C.A. incinerator was wounded over the left eye by a bullet from a cartridge exploding in the incinerator. The man received 1st Aid. treatment and was removed to the 1/2nd F.A. hospital at mid.	
		4 P.M.	Received D.R.O. 6/4/11/5 No. 521 - 535.	
			Baths - lowering of outlet pipe completed, experimented with sawdust in the distributing trough.	
			Roads - cleared as usual; ditches near shwns sprinkled with chloride of lime. Stables - usual routine work.	
			Destructor - Camp D - third course completed.	
			Camps - 109 R.F.A. D battery - completed latrines urine pit. Incinerator completed for Ammn. Col.	NSC

Page 5

Army Form C. 2118

WAR DIARY
or
INTELLIGENCE SUMMARY.
(Erase heading not required.)

Instructions regarding War Diaries and Intelligence Summaries are contained in F. S. Regs., Part II. and the Staff Manual respectively. Title pages will be prepared in manuscript.

Place	Date	Hour	Summary of Events and Information	Remarks and references to Appendices
RENINGHELST	8/11/5	4 pm	Received D.R.O No 536-540; also G.R.O No 1243-1250. Note No 1247 "Bounds" 9-12-45.	
			Despatch of Documents & Records to Base.	
			O.C. arranged with O.C. Baths for the whole section to bathe each Monday morning at 8 A.M.	
			Well - Camp F. cleaning commenced. Timber prepared. Camp D completed except plug in connection with this well.	
			Camp Inspection - Whole of 109th Brigade - detailed reports prepared for A.D.M.S.	
			Roads - Traffic inspection - usual routine work	
			Baths - ashes in one corner of filter pit replaced by clay; wooden basin placed between	NSC
			Destructor - Camp "E" - much progress made - will be completed to-morrow.	
	9/11/5		Received Traffic Orders - 2nd Army 2/9/11/5; also D.R.O No 542-544 Special D.R.O No 541-544 of 9/11/5	
			Well - Camp F - well completed. Commenced cleaning of well in Transport lines	
			Camp Inspection - 106th Brigade - detailed reports prepared; also 104th Brigade	
			Roads - Traffic inspection - usual routine work.	
			Baths - filter top made impervious to passing water to which alum had been added through small coke. A new scheme using sedimentation tanks is being tried	
			Destructor - Camp "E" completed - very successful since completion this destructor to-day has burned 20 pails of latrine refuse !!	NSC

WAR DIARY or INTELLIGENCE SUMMARY

Army Form C. 2118

Page 6

Place	Date	Hour	Summary of Events and Information	Remarks and references to Appendices
RENINGHELST	10/XI/5	3 pm	Received "Scale of Rations Storage", 24th Divl. Summary of Casualties, C.R.O. a/4/11/5 No 98 Pars 495-498; Circulars 24th Divr A/99/4; C/28 re Engrs. Duties for Cons Drainage Companies R.E.; D.R.O. a/10/11/5 No 545-549 Pars. 541 "Service for Jewish soldiers" Y.M.C.A. hut Sunday 14 inst. 2.30 p.m. — facilities will be granted in this Section. Letter A/993 "System of Shutting"	
			Baths — commenced two new pits 8' x 56' x 3' for sedimentation tanks	
			Wells — Transport lines near Camp F completed	
			Camp Inspection — H.Qrs. field + Divisional Bombing School.	
			Latrines — all tins, urine, etc. prepared for erection of new urinator in Camp F.	
			All other routine work continued as on previous day.	
	11/XI/5		Received Circulars 24th Divr No A/1025 re Temporary Commissions; also D.R.O. No 550-562. Specially note No 551 "Remounts", 553 "Service Dress Jackets", 555 "Boots", 559 "Dinner Service", 560 "Speed of Motor Vehicles" + 562 "Defensive Works" — necessary action taken in all necessary inclines.	N.L.
			Roads — continued. Six men made two journeys to Y.P.R.E.B. for rubble.	
			Baths — finished one pit made ease to be fitted in the same. Staffs usually emptied + cleaned + cleanup of fields.	
			Camp Inspection — A.B.C.D. Batteries 108th Bde., Am. Column, + H.Qrs. lately occupied by H.Q. guards	
			Urinators — Camp F — 3 bottom layers completed. Other urinators burning well.	
			Wells — Camp F — a shallow well examined + dealt with. In N. Staffs. Camp well completed.	N.L.

Page 1.

Army Form C. 2118

WAR DIARY
or
INTELLIGENCE SUMMARY.
(Erase heading not required.)

Instructions regarding War Diaries and Intelligence Summaries are contained in F.S. Regs., Part II. and the Staff Manual respectively. Title pages will be prepared in manuscript.

Place	Date	Hour	Summary of Events and Information	Remarks and references to Appendices
RENINGHELST	12/11/5	—	Received G.R.O. d/10/11/5 N.os 1251-1254; C.R.O. d/11/11/5 N.os 479-485; + D.R.O. d/12/11/5 N.os 563-573. Very wet & very windy. Work at H.Qrs. Baths. Destructor continued. Remainder of men engaged on road making at the camp. Sanitary Squads in Camp A instructed by O.C.	NSL
	13/XI/5	—	Received D.R.O. d/13/11/5 N.os 574-7. N.o 577 "Letters noted, also Circular 2nd Div. N.o S/1056 re Making footpath in Camp + Billets. Destructors in Sherwood's Camp completed. Instruction in Camp A continued. Road making continued. At the Baths another precipitation tap constructed + turned into its place. Inspection of H.Qrs. as usual. Furnished detailed summarised Reports on 104th & 109th Brigades R.F.A. to the A.D.M.S.	NSL
	14/XI/5		Various sections of the Unit attended Divine Service at 9AM on 10.45 A.M. on 11 A.M. on 2.30 P.M. Road work at various H.Qrs. continued as usual [struck through] Received R.O. d/12/11/5 N.os 234-245; C.R.O. d/13/11/5 N.os 486-491; + D.R.O. d/14/11/5 N.os 578-580 Camps inspected – BOESCHEPE – A Squadron 11th Hussars Yeomanry, N.o 3 Div. Am. Column, N.o 2 D.A.C., Cyclist Company, + N.o 1 D.A.C.	NSL
	15/11/5		Wells – continued work on well in Queen's Camp. Roads – usual work [crossed out] Sick Parade + O.C. H.Qrs. Baths – sedimentation tanks completed in position, alum tray fixed, on but drain commenced. Received - D.R.O. d/15/11/5 N.os 581-589.	NSL

T2134. Wt. W708–776. 500000. 4/15. Sir J. C. & S.

Page 7

Army Form C. 2118

WAR DIARY
or
INTELLIGENCE SUMMARY.
(Erase heading not required.)

Place	Date	Hour	Summary of Events and Information	Remarks and references to Appendices
RENINGHELST.	16/11/5	—	Roads - usual routine. Drain cleaning at G.O.C. HdQrs - culvert cleared & grating fixed over mouth of it. HdQrs inspection cleaning as in previous days. Well - work on Queen's Camp continued - this well should be completed to-morrow. In Camps D, F, & G rough surveys were taken & accurate levels made in connection with the erection of ablution benches - the supply of water thereto & the drainage away of the waste water. Baths - work on drain completed. Camp Inspection - BOESCHEPE area - 192nd Tunnelling Company R.E., Supply Column. Received D.R.O. 2/16/11/5 No. 590-600. No. 590, 595, & 598 duly noted; also C.R.O 2/15/11/5 No. 492-497. Note 496 3/ice of ground for horse lines &c; - Letter No. A/1092 d/15/11/15 re "Chiller feet".	NSL
	17/11/5	4/A.M.	Received instructions from D.A.A. & Q.M.G. to move from present camp to the Divisional Baths. With the exception of the men engaged on HdQrs inspection &c all men were employed in this work, viz the work of moving the tent equipment &c of the three men at BOESCHEPE to their new quarters near ABEELE station. Tent Dro No? 601-4	NSL
	18/11/5		Work continued at HdQrs on Roads &c. Work connected with removal of camp completed. Work at Baths continued. Received D.R.O. 2/18/11/5 No. 605-610 also After Order 611.	NSL

WAR DIARY
or
INTELLIGENCE SUMMARY.
(Erase heading not required.)

Army Form C. 2118.

Page 9

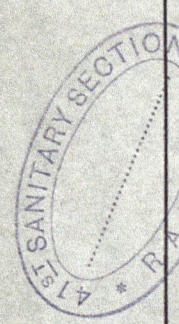

Place	Date	Hour	Summary of Events and Information	Remarks and references to Appendices
RENINGHELST	19/11/5		Inventory taken of all stock to be handed over to the O.B. Sanitary Section, 3rd Division. Baths drainage completed. Other routine duties continued as usual. Received D.R.O. No 612-8, 2/19/15; C.R.O. No 498-501 2/18/15; Circular 24th Divr No Q. 1208 re "Locks"; Q.1204 re "Tents: Tent Bottoms"; A/924 re "Leave"; also Q.144 2/16/15.	NOS2
	20/11/5		Preparations made for "Move". The 16th Coast Surveys who have been attached to us for Sanitary duties returned to their battalion this afternoon. Received C.R.O. No's 1258-1264, & "A" G.R.O. No's 945 + 6.; D.R.O. No's 619 - 622.; Circulars A 1215, & 1251.	NOS7 NOS7
	21/11/5		Advance party moved to STEENVORDE. Received Circular re "Bully Beef" S.A. A. 2/19/15.	NOS7 NOS6
	22/11/5		Remainder of section moved to STEENVORDE - billeted in barn occupied by San: Sec: 3rd Divn.	NOS7
	23/11/5		Whole of section moved to LEDERZEELE - billeted in barn.	
	24/11/5		Advance party moved to TILQUE - billeted in barn.	
TILQUE	25/11/5		Whole of section re-complete establishment moved to TILQUE - all the men billeted in empty house near Chateau.	NOS2
	26/11/5		Work done - whole of sanitary conveniences constructed, billets cleaned & disinfected, & portion of blankets disinfected in steam disinfector. Received D.R.O. No's 623 - 6 2/23/11/5, a. 627 - 632 2/24/11/6; a 633 - 638 2/25/11/5. C.R.O. No's 1265 - 1274, R.O. No's 246 - 253. C.R.O. No's 502 - 5 d/20/15; 506 b/22/15; 504 - 51 D 2/25/15; Circulars Q 1233, X 01266. A/1275, A/1320, 1339, V.0/1990, & Confidential 38 + 55. A. D.R.O. No 639 - 642 2/26/15. also	NOS2

Page 10

Army Form C. 2118

WAR DIARY
or
INTELLIGENCE SUMMARY.
(Erase heading not required.)

Place	Date	Hour	Summary of Events and Information	Remarks and references to Appendices
TILQUES	28/11/5		Forwarded reply to Circular No V/1990 to the effect that the water bottles belonging to the men of the Section are beginning to rust. This to the A.D.M.S. Also reply to Circular C/35 to A.A. & Q.M.G. to the effect that there is in this Unit no shortage of cooks which, what no men sell any of their clothing.	NSC
"	29/11/5		Received D.R.O. Nos 643-8. Note 643 "Divine Service", 644 "Refitting". Section attended Divine service at G.O.C. Headquarters. Received D.R.O. Nos 649-654. Note 650 "Field Cookers vans", 654 "Warm Clothing" Men have insufficient underclothing for the present so that this Section can wait for Woollen Vest. Received Circular 24th Div. No1 A/1225 re Warambre for men proceeding on leave & A/1083 re self inflicted wounds.	NSC
"	29/11/5		Received D.R.O. Nos 655-661. Note 655 "Hours of returning to billets", 657 "Repairs to Vehicles", 659 "Leave Train" & 660 "Letters".	NSC
"	30/11/5		Received Office Order 662 re N.C.O's School & D.R.O No 663-670; also 2nd Div Circular A/1309 & A/1390 re minor Staff Appointments & A/1394 re Candidates for Commissions. During the time the Section has been in present Rest Area special attention has been paid to the physical development of the men - Swedish Drill being regularly taken by Sgt GOODING.	NSC

A.D.S.S./Forms/C. 2118.

San: Sect: 41
Vol: 4

131/3874

24th May

S

Dec. 1915

41st. Sanitary Section - Dec. 1915.

Many plans of Sanitary Appliances
    detached and filed with
    Plans under "Sanitation"

CONFIDENTIAL.

WAR DIARY

OF

41ST SANITARY SECTION

FROM 1st Dec./15 TO 31st Dec./15

VOLUME ----

W Carruthers Lieut. Ramc.
O.C. 41st San. Sec.

Army Form C. 2118.

WAR DIARY
or
INTELLIGENCE SUMMARY.
(Erase heading not required.)

Page 1.

Instructions regarding War Diaries and Intelligence Summaries are contained in F. S. Regs., Part II. and the Staff Manual respectively. Title pages will be prepared in manuscript.

41st SANITARY SECTION — R.A.M.C.(T)

Place	Date	Hour	Summary of Events and Information	Remarks and references to Appendices
TILQUES	1/XII/15	9 AM	Kit inspection. All unserviceable articles noted & indents forwarded for replacement of same. Gas helmets of the pattern exchanged for Tube pattern.	
		4 PM	Received G.R.O. No's 1275-1282; D.R.O No's 641-647. Note 642 "Field Cashier" & 643 "Religion". C. of C. Return made out. Circular 2nd Div. No. Q/1431 "Notes on supervision of Billets". The contents of the latter communicated to the men.	NSL NSL
	2/XII/15	4 PM	Received D.R.O. No's 648-653. Note 680 "Bounds"; + C.R.O No's 512-514. Note 512 "Leave"	
	3/XII/5		Received R.O. No's 254-266. Note 254 "Leave"; 256 copy of "Cash for payment of Companies"; 258 "Hours of Work", 265 "Local Purchases – AFW 3313 to be used for purchase of vegetables"; "266 "Exchange" –5 ½ – 3/4. Received D.R.O No's 684-690. Note 685 "Leave"; 686 "Supervision of Leave Parties"; 689 "Estaminets – use for Recreation purposes"; 688 "Material for making Standings"; + 689 "Billeting – all Billeting Certifs in this area to be sent to G.H.Q. 2/Lt Brittan proceeded on "leave"	NSL
	4/XII/5	4 PM	Received G.R.O. No's 1283-1293. Note 1283 "Double names of River Envelopes"; D.R.O. No's 691-699. Note 693 "Washing Tub" – one indented for for use of Section; 695 "Divine Service".	NSL
	5/XII/5.	4 PM	Received D.R.O. No's 700-705. Note 703 "Material for making Standings – change of kiln. Section attended Divine Service at 9.30 in ground of O.C. Headquarters.	NSL
	6/XII/5.	4 PM	Received D.R.O. 706-7. No. 706 "Identity Discs communicated to the men".	NSL

WAR DIARY or INTELLIGENCE SUMMARY

Army Form C. 2118.

Place	Date	Hour	Summary of Events and Information	Remarks and references to Appendices
TILQUES	6/VII/15	—	Whole of Section engaged on special work for a lecture & demonstration by O.C. at the Divisional Technical School to-morrow. The following were built :- Incinerators :- turf, brick, "Arnold's"; Latrines - long, short trenches, & deep pit covered by 3 hands middle one acting as moveable cover. Urinepits - complete in section. Grease Traps - four types shewing improvium from anything at hand. Received Circulars No P.1450 & D. of T.'s Circular Memo No. 113 re Equipment of Mot. Lorries.	NSL
	7/VII/15	—	Received Instructions in Circular Q.1534 that in future all changes in position of unit are to be telegraphed to D.D. of S.T. 2nd Army direct; also D.R.O. 408 "Care & Preservation of Stores" - these while communicated to the whole of the Section. Received Circular 2nd Div. No. A/1499 re A.S.C. Clerks. One man is available from this Section. Received Q/1538 of 5/7/15 re Bonnet Covers. An effort will be made to provide one made of straw. Section completed the models commenced yesterday & O.C. lectured to the students at the Technical School.	NSL
	8/VII/15	—	Received D.R.O. Nos. 409-414. Indent for Rations forwarded to Deputy Officer in accordance with No. 411.	NSL
	9/VII/15	—	Received D.R.O. Nos. 415-418. Note that Stationery Indents are to be forwarded to BOULOGNE not to HAVRE as heretofore (-/18); also to D.R.O. Nos. 515-4 & Mapt - Road Control issued with same - map amended in accordance with instructions; also Circulars A/900 re Specialist Officers & A/583 re A.F.B. 213.	NSL

Army Form C. 2118.

WAR DIARY
or
INTELLIGENCE SUMMARY.
(Erase heading not required.)

Page 3

Instructions regarding War Diaries and Intelligence Summaries are contained in F. S. Regs., Part II. and the Staff Manual respectively. Title pages will be prepared in manuscript.

Place	Date	Hour	Summary of Events and Information	Remarks and references to Appendices
TILQUES.	10/12/5	1	Received D.R.O. No.s 419-421, also Circulars A/612 re Lubricating Oil for Motor Lorries, C/79 re Surplus Stores, A/605 re Skilled Labour (D.R.O. 442 & 31/10/5), Q/1588 re honoured Lorries on the "Move", & A/1588 re Adjutants.	HSC
			Arrangements made for disinfection of clothing of men infected with lice at the Technical School. This work will be done to-morrow afternoon. Considerable inconvenience has been caused in the work of treating infected clothing by the non-supply in the field of Vermigelli + N.C.I. Powder. Wood-preserving Oils to be tried together with a soft soap & Creol.	HSC
	11/12/5		Clothing of twenty men infested with lice disinfected at the Technical School. Received D.R.O. No.s 722-729. S/Sgt. Brittain returned from leave (midnight). Section attended Divine Service at G.O.C. Headquarters.	HSC
	12/12/5		Received D.R.O. No.s 730-732 also Circular A/616 re Supply of Magnetos.	HSC
	13/12/5		Section went for Route March. Received D.R.O. No.s 1294-1306. No 1302 re Field Service Post Cards, & D.R.O. No.s 733-7.	HSC
	14/12/5		Received D.R.O. No.s 738-740, & Circular No A/835 with respect to the special trades S/Sgt. Gooding went on "leave".	HSC

WAR DIARY or INTELLIGENCE SUMMARY

Army Form C. 2118.

Place	Date	Hour	Summary of Events and Information	Remarks and references to Appendices
TILQUES	14/12/5 15/12/5 16/12/5	— — —	On these three days a thorough inspection of all camps, billets in the Division was made & full reports together with epitomes of the same were forwarded to the A.D.M.S. Taken as a whole the sanitary condition of the Division is quite satisfactory. Many units do not seem to appreciate the necessity for incinerators ordered are to be issued by the A.O.C. on the subject. Grease traps for cookhouse water, for ablution water, for water from washing clothes are not found in every camp, but the advantages of having one have been pointed out to the responsible Officers. In some villages where water is drawn from pumps wells care is not always taken to see that the water is tested ≡, while in some few instances it is not treated at all before consumption. Few units boil their water in the absence of chemicals. The units are to be advised through the A.D.M.S. Office to see that the water is either boiled or chlorinated before use. With regard to lice the following substitute for Sinigell is being circulated throughout the Division by the Field Ambulances who will obtain it from this section :— Proportion { 4 llbs. Soft Soap 2 pts. Water Refining Oil ¼ pt. Cresol ¼ pt. Paraffin. }	NSL

Page 5

Army Form C. 2118.

WAR DIARY
or
INTELLIGENCE SUMMARY.
(Erase heading not required.)

Place	Date	Hour	Summary of Events and Information	Remarks and references to Appendices
THIQUES	15/12/15		Received C.R.O. Nos 263-5; & C.R.O. Nos 266-269, & D.R.O. Nos 941-943. With regard to "Tube Helmets" every man in this section now possesses 2 Helmets of this pattern. All are properly dated & the men have been instructed as to their use.	
	16/12/15		Received G.R.O. Nos 1304-1319. No 1309 "Court-Martial for handing ration meat to a Frenchwoman" read out on parade; D.R.O. Nos 942-946; Circular A/16/12/15 re A.F.B.213.	
	17/12/15		Route March for whole of Section. Received C.R.O. 270-2; D.R.O. Nos 947-953. With reference to No 951 "Smoke Helmets" those remaining on hand will be handed over to O.S. forthwith	
	18/12/15		Route March. Received C.R.O. Nos 273-276; D.R.O. Nos 954-961; Circular Q. 1909 re Drying of Men's Clothing. No difficulty is being experienced in this Section at present, as Circulars A/4/73 & one with reference to G.R.O. 1295 regarding Headlights.	
	19/12/15		Section attended Divine Service this morning. Received copy of G.R.O. 1295, D.R.O. Nos 962-969. No. 964 Gas Attacks & 969 Hardships of Winter Campaign read out on parade; C.R.O. Nos 277-282.	
	20/12/15		Whole of Section employed at the Technical School preparing exhibition as on 6th inst. Received Confidential Circular No 90 re Smoke Helmets. D.R.O. Nos 968-972; C.R.O. Nos 283-5	

Page 6.

Army Form C. 2118.

WAR DIARY
or
INTELLIGENCE SUMMARY.

Place	Date	Hour	Summary of Events and Information	Remarks and references to Appendices
TILQUES	21/12/15		Section completed the exhibition models at the Technical School, QC. lectured at the same in afternoon. Received C.R.O. No: 1318-1330; C.R.O. No: 286-288, D.R.O. No: 445-447. Circular Q. 1456 together with the Map showing the Road referred to in Circular.	NST
	22/12/15		Received Circulars Q. 1659 re Transport & Disposal of Stores prior to moving Q. 1319 re House Return; D.R.O. No: 448-483; + C.R.O. No: 289.	NST
	23/12/15		Section employed in the making of Sermigelli substitute. Section had short route march. Received D.R.O. No: 484-490; also Circulars Q/544 re Stores; A/1461 re Disposal of kits of wounded deceased soldiers with Instructions + Copy of Army Form W. 3190. No difficulty will be experienced in carrying out these instructions in this Section; also Circular Q/1824 re Local Purchases, also C.R.O. No: 290-1	NST
	24/12/15		Commenced disinfecting of clothing at 129th Field Company, R.E. but work hindered by lack of suitable fuel. Received D.R.O. No: 491-4; C.R.O. No: 292-7; + Circular No: A/1464 Q. 1585 "Supply System generally in the Field"	NST
	25/12/15		Xmas Day. Received Q. O No: 264-244. Note specially No: 267 "Courts-Martial"; 265 "Discipline" + 269 "Ink Helmets"; D.R.O. No: 494-5; +C.R.O. No: 298-9	NST
	26/12/15		Disinfection of bundles of clothing at Headquarters of 19th Royal Fusiliers. Received D.R.O. No: 496-499; + C.R.O. No: 300-1	NST

Page 4

Army Form C. 2118.

WAR DIARY
or
INTELLIGENCE SUMMARY.
(Erase heading not required.)

Place	Date	Hour	Summary of Events and Information	Remarks and references to Appendices
TILQUES	27/12/15		Disinfected billet of Royal W. Surrey - case of measles. Received D.R.O. Nos 800-5, & C.R.O. Nos 302-306.	WSC
	28/12/15		Inspection of Gas Helmets with lecture by O.C. on use, care & preservation of the same. Examined boots of every man. The re-soled boots from the Base do not seem to be very lasting in many cases. Received D.R.O. Nos 806-811 Return re D.R.O. 806.' Re-issue of Gases' forwarded to 'Q' office.' C.R.O. Nos 307, & 308-311. & G.R.O. Nos 1351-40	WSC
	29/12/15		Lecture taken for route march. Received D.R.O. No 812 All old helmets have already been returned to D.A.D.O.S.	WSC
	30/12/15		Forwarded Report on Billet to "Q" Office. Section taken for route march. Received no orders to-day	WSC
	31/12/15		Received D.R.O. Nos 813 - 820. Note 820 'Billeting Certificates'.	WSC
			Attached is a set of Drawings (duplicate) of Grease Traps, Latrines, &c found useful in various parts of the Field.	WSC

24th Division

41st Inf. Sans Section

Jan
Feb 1916
Mar

Sam: Sect: 41
Vol: 5

Tan

24

CONFIDENTIAL.

War Diary
of
41st Sanitary Section.
from 1st Jan: to 31st Jan. 1916.

(Volume 5.)

Page 1

Army Form C. 2118.

41/M/ Sanitary Section

WAR DIARY
or
INTELLIGENCE SUMMARY.
(Erase heading not required.)

Place	Date	Hour	Summary of Events and Information	Remarks and references to Appendices
TILQUES	1916			
	1st Jan.		Received DRO No. 167.	WSC
	2nd Jan.		Section attended Divine Service. Received DRO No. 8.	WSC
	3rd Jan.		Camp Inspection – Whole of Headquarters inspected also part of 73rd Brigade. Reports forwarded to ADMS. OC visited new Area. Received Circular No. A/1492re A/1492 re Drunkenness. Also Shorthand writers – Nil return forwarded; A/1943, & A/1492 re Drunkenness. Also DRO No. 9-13. Billet at Bombing School disinfected after case of Cerebro-spinal Fever	WSC
	4th Jan.		Inspection of 73rd Brigade & 14th Brigade completed. In a few instances some camps have been left in an untidy state – all these camps have been cleaned by this Section. Received DRO Nos. 14-15; CRO No. 587– 589.	WSC
	5th Jan.		Advance Parties left to takeover the new Water Duties in new Area. Received DRO Nos. 16-18; Circular Q 1735 re "Move"; CRO No. 540 & CRO 5th Corps 518-521	WSC
	6th Jan.		Preparation for "Move" made.	WSC
	7th Jan.		Advance parties left to take over Headquarters & Sub. Section Billets from 34th San. Sec. Received G.R.O. Nos. 1341-1349; D.R.O. Nos. 19-23; CRO No. 541.	WSC
	8th Jan.		Remainder of Section left for New Area by 8.50 A.M. train from St OMER to POPERINGHE. Day spent in rendering camps more habitable – drainage, new latrine area &c.	WSC

WAR DIARY or INTELLIGENCE SUMMARY

Army Form C. 2118.

Page 2.

Place	Date	Hour	Summary of Events and Information	Remarks and references to Appendices
Map 28. G.15.c.5.9.	9 Jan.	—	Work in camp continued. 4 Men engaged on roads, remainder headquarters at Divisional Headquarters. All sub-stations rationed.	NSC
	10 Jan.	—	All work of yesterday continued. Received provisional Location of Units. O.C. visited C.R.E. & also York huts in G.11 re a report that four cases of the enteric group had occurred in the vicinity since the 21st ult. Received D.R.O. No 84-394 & R.O. 2nd Army No 248-283 & R.O. No 542-3.	NSC
	11 Jan.	3 PM		
		11 A.H.	Received instructions from A.A. + Q.M.G. to supply Brigades with carbonate of soda & sodium hyposulphite for Kernmel Spraying solution until such times as they can secure same from the Divisional Train. Also received D.R.O. No 440 & 44. Circular Q/151 re Smoke Helmet eye-pieces, & Q/125 re "Leave-rations of men". Return required by D.R.O. No 40 forwarded to G/H.Q. Workshop constructed in camp.	
	12 Jan.	—	O.C. visited sub. section at G.18.a.3.y and made arrangements for camps A, B, C, D & G. he inspected & sgt. visited Water Tanks at H.14.a. Found everything satisfactory. Sgt. GOODING in charge of squad cleaning up Divl. H.Qtrs. Two men engaged in making Office-table for A.D.M.S.	NSC

Page 3   Army Form C. 2118.

WAR DIARY
or
INTELLIGENCE SUMMARY.
(Erase heading not required.)

Place	Date	Hour	Summary of Events and Information	Remarks and references to Appendices
Map 28 G.15.c.5.9.	13 Jan	—	Received reports from advanced water pipe at H.22.a. — average no. of carts since Jan 5th is 20. Sgt. visited all sections with rations & to render assistance re organization. Two men sent to assist at Sub Section G.18.a.3.y. O.C. & Sr. Black visited Divisional Baths at POPERINGHE to draw up plans for a better system of supplying the hot water and also for dealing with the soapy effluent. Good progress made with tables for Section Headquarters where A.D.M.S. the cleaning up re of Divisional Headquarters almost completed.	
		IDAM	Received D.R.O. Nos 52 – 60. No. 53 "Passes to enter POPERINGHE, 54 "Rubble", 56 "Field Cashier" & 57 "Baths".	hSC
		4 P.M.	Received D.R.O. Nos 61 – 72 all of which are specially noted. No. 66 "Comn from Div" will be included in the Orders issued to the Section; also C.R.O. Nos 544 – 5; Circular A/1942 re Transfers to Royal Flying Corps; A/725/2 re Leave for Officers; Circular Q/1636/1 re E.F.C. POPERINGHE	hSC
	14 Jan		Work of yesterday continued at all points. Received D.R.O. Nos 73 – 78; Circulars No. Q/2108 re G.R.O. No. 880, A/2078 re Defensive Chemical Cyls – "nil" return forwarded to A.D.M.S. Q/2112 enclosing Road Control Map. A.C.O.'s Waterworks G.18 reported damage to waterpipes presumably by shells. Matter is being dealt with by O.C. Water Patrol.	hSC

Army Form C. 2118.

Page 4.

Instructions regarding War Diaries and Intelligence Summaries are contained in F. S. Regs., Part II. and the Staff Manual respectively. Title pages will be prepared in manuscript.

WAR DIARY or INTELLIGENCE SUMMARY.

(Erase heading not required.)

Place	Date	Hour	Summary of Events and Information	Remarks and references to Appendices
Mar 28 G.15.c.5.9	15 Jan		O.C. visited all sub-sections to day. The stand-pipe in H 22a has been heavily shelled and the pipes have been damaged. The men on duty there have proceeded to H.14.a. Water Tanks until the damage has been repaired. All routine work proceeded as usual. Received D.R.O. No 49-88, Note No. 79 "Tube helmets"- necessary Indent + Certificate forwarded 5 DROs; 81 "Baths- change in time; 86 "Re-filling Points"- change in location & time; list of Grouped Units for re-fillingrequired with DRO 86, of "Drainage of Camps" No 88. L/Cpl. returned from Leave 8-15 Jan/16. Cpl. 1077 sent to take charge at H.Q. to attend to all sanitary arrangements. O.C. visited all sub-sections. The two men in charge of standpipe in H 22 brought back to section's H.Q. + will join the sub-section in G.18 for Camp Inspection. Full preparations made for commencing of incinerator (special design-drawings to accompanies last two volumes of War Diary) at D.w. H.Q. Received G.R.O. No 1358-1364; Summary of Information No 255, DRO 90-94 & After Order No. 89. Sgt GOODING sent to take charge of Sub. Section at G.18. During the next few days this section will make complete inspection of all camps in the vicinity. The Reports will be dealt with by H.Q.O.C. on his return from Leave - 12.6.17 inst.	WSC WSC WSC
	16 Jan			
	17 Jan			

Page 5

Army Form C. 2118.

WAR DIARY
or
INTELLIGENCE SUMMARY.
(Erase heading not required.)

Place	Date	Hour	Summary of Events and Information	Remarks and references to Appendices
G.15.c.6.9	14th Jan	—	Commenced destructor at Div. H.Q. Routine work on roads, latrines &c at D.H.Q. continued. Received D.R.O. Nos. 95 - 104.	WSL
	15th Jan		No. 102. The standpipe at H.22.a.5.9 referred to above is closed until further orders. O.C. visited all sections & made full arrangements for carrying on the work during his absence on "leave".	
	16th Jan		O.C. & one L/Cpl proceeded on "leave". Lieut. S.R. JOHNSTON, R.A.M.C. 74th Field Ambulance took charge of the Section until the O.C.'s return. A well constructed new stream in camp - to ensure a clean & constant supply of ablution water. A commencement made with further drainage of camp which is in a very muddy state. An effort is being made to obtain timber for paths, also timber & roof felt to construct a drying tent. All sections visited by S/Sgt.	WSL
	18th Jan		Received D.R.O. No. 105, Curdled A/2200 to N.C.O.'s & transfers.	WSL
	19th Jan		Received D.R.O. Nos. 106-112, Daily Wireless News of 18/1/16 & Letter G.949 re Lecture on "Sanitation" to be given by O.C. on the 29th inst.	WSL
	20th Jan		Drainage continued, also work on destructor & at D.H.Q. S/Sgt visited 24th Div. Loyal N. Lancs Company at the request of O.C. 74th Fld Amb stated the drinking water there. This was found to be quite satisfactory.	WSL

Army Form C. 2118.

Page 6.

WAR DIARY
or
INTELLIGENCE SUMMARY.
(Erase heading not required.)

Instructions regarding War Diaries and Intelligence Summaries are contained in F.S. Regs., Part II. and the Staff Manual respectively. Title pages will be prepared in manuscript.

Place	Date	Hour	Summary of Events and Information	Remarks and references to Appendices
G 15 c 5 9	20th Jan	—	Sgt. BLACK was sent to the same Company to advise O.C. regarding damaged rifles but found that it had been sent to the Base, C.O.O. Received D.R.O. Nos. 113 - 116. "Re" return forwarded re No. 113 "Lorry Company". G.R.O. Nos. 1365 - 1395. "Daily Wireless" of 19/1/16.	NSC
	21st Jan.		S/Sgt. visited Camp Commandant regarding housing & rationing of the fatigues provided by him at D.H.Q. The men will work under the instruction of Corp. LOTT but for administration purposes will be under O.C. Destructor. Sketch of destructor for burning of horse manure (see accompanying sketch) is to be constructed. Work in camp suspended owing to heavy weather. Incinerators built at camp of 36th Mobile Vet. Section. Received R.O. Nos. 284 - 292, C.R.O. Nos. 546-8, D.R.O. Nos. 117 - 127, & Daily Wireless of 20/1/16.	1 / NSC
	22nd Jan		S/Sgt. visited Sub. section at G. 18 for purpose of advising re disinfection of billet; also 24th Div. Baths to obtain coke sand for experimental purposes. Received Circular G. 23 "Graffiti in Forward Area", "Daily Wireless" of 21/1/16.	NSC

Army Form C. 2118.

WAR DIARY
or
INTELLIGENCE SUMMARY.
(Erase heading not required.)

Place	Date	Hour	Summary of Events and Information	Remarks and references to Appendices
G.15.c.5.9.	22nd Jan.		Received "Amendment to List of Location of Units"; D.R.O No. 125–133.	NSC
	23rd Jan.		Routine work of every sub-section continued. Horse manure destructor commenced near Div. H.Q. (see accompanying sketch). Drainage of camp continued. Routine work at H.Q., Y.M.C.A. &c continued. Sub-section at G.18 continued inspection of Infantry camps. Received Circular No. Q/22444 re "Rations"; Daily Wireless News 2/22/16; CRO No. 549–553; Note No. 550 "Salubia"; D.R.O No. 134–6. As a drying room is being erected application will be made for stove in accordance with No. 135.	NSC
	24 Jan.		All work referred to yesterday continued. Much progress made with drying room. Received D.W.N 2/23/16; D.R.O Nos 134–140. Note No. 139 "Empty Jam tins"—order will be carried out. Sgt visited all sub-sections.	NSC
	25th Jan.		All work continued. As insufficient material was provided for drying room this cannot be completed at present. Received D.W.N 2/24/16; D.R.O No: 141–145; Note No. 143 "Marking of Vehicles"; Circular No. Q/2028 re Return of Shoes; Circular M 52/16 (A.D.M.S.) re Correspondence.	NSC
	26 Jan.		45 Reports received from Sub-section at G.18. These will be classified & forwarded to A.D.M.S. Sgt visited Poperinghe Baths re Scheme for improving water supply, & Water tanks at H.14. Received D.R.O No. 146; Circular A/2303; & D.W.N 2/25/16.	NSC

2352 Wt. W2544/1454 700,000. 5/15 D. D. & L. A.D.S.S./Forms/C.2118.

Army Form C. 2118.

WAR DIARY
or
INTELLIGENCE SUMMARY.
(Erase heading not required.)

Page 8

Instructions regarding War Diaries and Intelligence Summaries are contained in F. S. Regs., Part II. and the Staff Manual respectively. Title pages will be prepared in manuscript.

Place	Date	Hour	Summary of Events and Information	Remarks and references to Appendices
G 15.c.6.9.	27/Jan	—	Received D.R.M. 9/26/1/16. All Routine work continued. House manure destructor at Div H.Q. completed. In order to assist in the thorough sanitation of the Div H.Q. & the cleaning of roads & fatigues have this day been attached to us. Received 信 Reports from the Sub-Section. The main Brigade, Transport, Companies have now been inspected leaving a few detached Units. From the reports received it is evident that the last occupants of the area left it in a very insanitary condition & much hard work has had to be done in the way of cleaning away burning refuse of all kinds, stacks of horse manure, drainage of inhabited areas & camps, locating & marking of foul ground. The most serious defects noted during the inspection are lack of grease traps, insufficiency of strong incinerators, the non-chlorination of water taken from purely local sources, & the lack of properly constructed ablution places. In few cases is any attempt made to deal with waste water of a greasy or soapy nature. This is most important in the area where the soil is very heavy & the water lies about for considerable periods. Attention has been drawn to these points. Received D.R.O. 90' 144-151; Circulars Q/23/6 re Billeting Certs.; Q/2112 re Roads;	NFC

2353 Wt. W2544/1454 700,000 5/15 D.D.&L. A.D.S.S./Forms/C. 2118.

Army Form C. 2118.

WAR DIARY
or
INTELLIGENCE SUMMARY.
(Erase heading not required.)

Page 9.

Instructions regarding War Diaries and Intelligence Summaries are contained in F. S. Regs., Part II. and the Staff Manual respectively. Title pages will be prepared in manuscript.

Place	Date	Hour	Summary of Events and Information	Remarks and references to Appendices
G. 15. c. 5. 9	28th Jan		OC & 2/Lt. Edwards returned from "leave". OC visited all sections. Roofs are to be erected over the detonator refuse dumps at H.Q. As the water stand pipe at H.22.a is not yet re-opened the men who were there will continue to be engaged in camp inspection. Routine work continued. Received D.W.R. a/27/16; G.R.O's 1376 – 1383; D.R.O. 152 – 162	hsc
	29 Jan		OC visited POPERINGHE to arrange for soap effluent purification scheme to be carried out forthwith. The work will be carried out under the supervision of an officer of the R.E.'s. From to-day this Unit will make supply the baths at POPERINGHE & OUDERDOM with Sennigelli substitute at the request of the A.D. & Q.M.G. & D.M.S. Supplies (about 5 gallons) will be taken every other day. The S.S.O. has been asked to supply the ingredients regularly. Routine work continued. Received D.R.O N°s 163 – 168; D.W.R. a/28/16; & C.R.O. N°s 554 – 556. Circular A/956 re Cemetery at I.9.d.3.4.	hsc
	30th Jan.		Pay Parade. Owing to the lack of utensils paint the lorry belonging to the Unit will not bear its distinguishing mark to-morrow. Steps have been taken to expedite supply. 2/Lt. Dinnis relieved by 2/Lt. Edwards at the water tanks at H.14.a. All Routine work continued. Sgt. Gooding instructed to arrange for the bad camps to be re-visited as early as possible. Received Circular A/2354 re striking off of Officers. D.W.R. a/29/16. No "Orders" received.	hsc

Army Form C. 2118.

WAR DIARY
or
INTELLIGENCE SUMMARY.
(Erase heading not required.)

Page 10

Instructions regarding War Diaries and Intelligence Summaries are contained in F.S. Regs., Part II. and the Staff Manual respectively. Title pages will be prepared in manuscript.

Place	Date	Hour	Summary of Events and Information	Remarks and references to Appendices
G.15.c.5.9	31/1/Jan	—	Received D.W.J. of 30/1/16. The original Reports epitomes of same forwarded to A.D.M.S. this day. Pte BLACK reported for duty at the Ordnance Stores this morning to advise as to the erection of suitable sheds. Ptes KILBURN & LANHAM engaged at the A.D.M.S. office making structural alterations with a view to improving the lighting of same. Routine work continued. New incinerator in camp constructed. Received D.D.O.M.S. Nos. 169-173; C.R.O. Nos. 554-8; Circular Q.2364 re Cptes Mackintosh.	WSC

2353 Wt. W2514/1454 700,000 5/15 D. D. & L. A.D.S.S./Forms/C. 2118.

Appendix I

MANURE DESTRUCTOR.

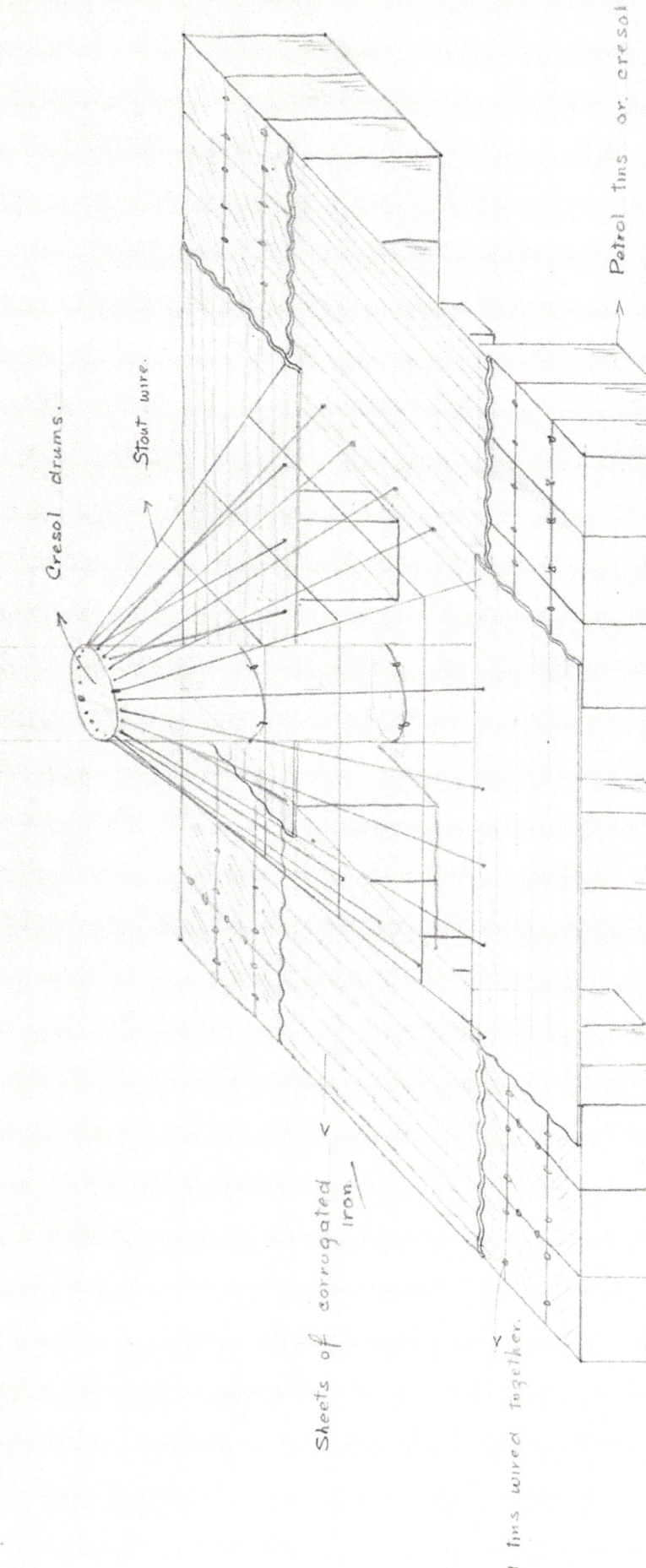

SCHOOL,

Name
Subject
Teacher
Assessment
Date when work was set

Name
Subject
Teacher
Date when work was set
Assessment

Army Form C. 2118.

WAR DIARY
or
INTELLIGENCE SUMMARY.
(Erase heading not required.)

41st Sanitary Section

Volume 6

From 1st February 1916 to 29th February 1916

Private & Confidential.

Page 1.

Army Form C. 2118.

Volume 6

WAR DIARY
or
INTELLIGENCE SUMMARY.
(Erase heading not required.)

SANITARY SECTION R.A.M.C. (T)

Place	Date 1916	Hour	Summary of Events and Information	Remarks and references to Appendices
Map 28. G.15.c.5.9	FEB. 1st		Received D.W.M. of 31/1/16. The duck boards are now available four men will be employed for two or three days rendering camps & approaches to same more convenient to walk about in. The whole of the ground will be levelled & proper drainage trenches continued. Routine work at H.Q. Water tanks &c all continued. Work at Ordnance stores & Div H.Q. (A.D.M.S. officers) continued. Both these works will be completed this week. O.C. met O.C. Water Patrols, V Corps & discussed the question of adequate water supply to all camps for ablution purposes. Received D.R.O. N° 194-6; C.R.O. N° 559-561;	
	2nd		Received D.W.M. of 1/2/16. Received instructions from A.D.M.S. to send two men to report to Town Major, YPRES by 12 noon for sanitary duty. Ptes. HALDANE & LANHAM were sent. OO. LANIGAN & Pte. JOHNSON proceeded on leave — will leave France tomorrow. Received D.R.O. N° 197-181; C.R.O. N° 1384-1386; & 2nd Army P.O. N° 293-297.	NST
	3rd		O.C. met O.C. Water Patrol V Corps visited all Infantry camps + Transport Lines & provision of ablution water (see 1st inst). Reports forwarded to A.D.M.S. All routine work continued. Received D.W.M. 4/2/16; Circular N°. A/1166; D.W.M. 4/3/16; + D.R.O. N° 182-3.	NST
	4th		Routine work at all points continued. Received Casualty Return for January; D.R.O. N° 184-189 & Circular Q. 1030 re Rents, & C.R.O. N° 562-568.	NST NST

WAR DIARY
or
INTELLIGENCE SUMMARY.

(Erase heading not required.)

Page 2

Place	Date	Hour	Summary of Events and Information	Remarks and references to Appendices
Map 28				
G.15.c.5.9	5th Feb	—	O.C. & S/Sgt visited M.O. i/c 2nd Divisional Train re disinfection of a hut occupied by a case of measles which was removed to 4th Field Ambulance yesterday. S/Sgt visited 106th Omnibus Column to instruct as to the construction of a suitable incinerator & grease trap. S/Sgt visited Belgian chateau hut as the place was being hourly shelled at the time no proper inspection was possible. Routine Work continued everywhere. Received DWR of 4/2/16; DRO's No's 188-190; Circular No. 9/106 "New pattern wire cutter."	NOSC
	6th Feb		Received DWR of 5/2/16. Much progress made with laying of duckboards, digging of drains in our camp. The BLACK still engaged at the Ordnance Stores. The KILBURN erecting corrugated iron roof over manure destructor at H.Q.; Divisional Train inspected usual routine work continued at Div H.Q. O.C. with Drainage Officer Capt. MAULE, O.C. Water Patrols visited Div H.Q. re drainage of camp surrounding fields also half the Transport Lines. Received DWR of 6/2/16. Continuation of Circular Q.2112. necessary alterations made to map; DRO No's 191-196; & one copy of "Defence Measures against Gas attack".	NOSC
	7th Feb		Received CRO. No's 1387-1390; All work of yesterday continued. Received no "Orders" on this day.	NOSC

WAR DIARY
or
INTELLIGENCE SUMMARY.

(Erase heading not required.)

Page 3

Place	Date	Hour	Summary of Events and Information	Remarks and references to Appendices
Sh 28 G.15.c.5.9	8th Feb	—	All routine work continued. S./Sgt. visited Disb. Section at G.18 inspected neighbouring billets. OC interviewed ODMS AA+QMG re Sanitary Squads in Camps - see DRO 209 of even date. Pte KILBURN completed roof at Dn H.Q. Received 1000 bricks with which to pave the Cookhouse surrounds. Received DWR of 1/2/16; Circular No A/2+80 re Latrines; DRO Nos 194-204 of 4/2/16 + Nos 205-209 of 5/2/16; CRO Nos 540-574. Circulars Q/2463 re Use of Carbide, Q/181 re PH Tube Helmets + M.86/16 re change of command.	NFSC
	9th Feb.		All routine work continued. Huts of Royal Sussex, Camp F that have been occupied by a case of measles contacts disinfected this afternoon. OC inspected all camps with SSO + MO + fixed sites for permanent destructors of brick to be erected forthwith. OC visited camps occupied by 104th Brigade RFA Received D.G.O Nos 210-3; DWR 9/2/16.	NFSC
	10 Feb.		All routine work continued. Pte KILBURN + BLACK have completed their work at Dn HQ + Ordnance stores. Section's cook house + works left floor paved with bricks, drying room with exception of drains completed. OC visited ODMS re disinfection of blankets of 8th Queens - no stuch is available. Received DWR d. 9 + 10/2/16; DRO Nos 214-219; CRO Nos 575-578.	NFSC

2353 Wt. W2544/1454 700,000 5/15 D. D. & L. A.D.S.S./Forms/C. 2118.

Page 4.

WAR DIARY
or
INTELLIGENCE SUMMARY.
(Erase heading not required.)

Army Form C. 2118.

Instructions regarding War Diaries and Intelligence Summaries are contained in F.S. Regs., Part II. and the Staff Manual respectively. Title pages will be prepared in manuscript.

Place	Date	Hour	Summary of Events and Information	Remarks and references to Appendices
Map 28. G.15.c.5.9	11 Feb	—	Drainage of Section's camp continued. Sgt BLACK & KILBURN commenced building destructors at No.1 Con. Div.Train Camp. Four of which are to be erected for the Grain Cp. Cpl. LOTT took charge of water tanks at Hitta Glacis. Sgt EDWARDS took charge of Div H.Q. Routine work "Camp Inspection continued. Received Burn. of 11/2/16, DRO N° 220 - 223. "Circular No A/2496 regarding promotion; G.R.O. No 1891 - 1400. DWR of 11/2/16	WSC
	12 Feb		Received CRO N° 579-582; WarOffice letter No 29/41/1916; "DRO N° 224 - 229. All work continued as yesterday. Sgt JOHNSON returned from leave.	WSC
	13 Feb		Capt FLANIGAN returned from leave having been detained at Large Rest Camp, BOULOGNE. Gas schools Sun Schools of every member of Section inspected & new one to replace deficiencies indented for. In Section camp a commencement made to new sump pits for treatment of greasy scrap water. The results of this experiment are to be communicated to all the M.O.s of the Division for their consideration & trial.	Appendix 1.
	14 Feb		Received DWR of 12/2/16; DRO N° 230 - 233; + 2nd Army RO N° 300 - 5. Received DWR of 13/2/16. OC + S/Sgt made inspection of Div H.Q. All work in progress yesterday continued. A supply of P.H. Gas Helmets received today - one per Officer & man. Received D.R.O. N° 234.	WSC

WAR DIARY
or
INTELLIGENCE SUMMARY

Army Form C. 2118.

Page 5

Place	Date	Hour	Summary of Events and Information	Remarks and references to Appendices
G.15.c.5.9.	15/7/16		Received D.W.D. d/14/7/16; & D.R.O. No. 255-6. Certificate as to the completion of men's kits, gas helmets & iron rations forwarded to the A.D.M.S. This is to be forwarded every Sunday. Commencement made to destruction in No. 2 Company Dis. Train. The other destructor is burning very well. Careful instruction as to stoking given to man in charge. All other work continued.	NDSC
	16/7/16		In spite of the very wet weather the camp is remarkably dry owing to the efficiency of the drainage pits completed. Sgt. GOODING is to supervise a drop effluent scheme (Appendix 1) in "B" Camp. This is to be commenced at once. Exercise detailed reports on 9 B.L. Survey & 9 F.G. Surveys. Other work continued. Received D.R.O. No. 237-8. C.R.O. No. 583-585 - D.W.D. d/15/7/16.	NDSC
	17/7/16		Received D.W.D. d/16/7/16, D.R.O. No. 239-242; C.R.O. No. 1401 to 1411. Particular note made of No. 1405 "Anti-gas Helmets" - tapes removed from helmet cases; & No. 1408 re notification to C.O's when soldiers are attacked, & 1411 "Anti-gas Goggles"- preservation of eye pieces by flannelette. Received information that "leave" suspended on 15th will be resumed on the 18th. Routine work as usual. Destructor in No. 2 Coy. Camp. Dis. Train completed. Received "Dull" helmet.	NDSC

Page 6

WAR DIARY
or
INTELLIGENCE SUMMARY.
(Erase heading not required.)

Place	Date	Hour	Summary of Events and Information	Remarks and references to Appendices
G.15.c.5.9	18 Feb.	—	All routine work continued. Commencement of Ablution place in H.Q. camp. made case of measles in Camp F. necessary disinfection carried out of R. Sussex Regiment.	N/C
	19"	A.M.	Received D.R.O. No. 243-244; 2nd Army R.O. No. 306-311; C.R.O. No. 587-8; Circular No. C/181 re Economy.	
		P.M.	Received D.R.O. No. 19/36; D.R.O. No. 248-251; + Continuation of Circular No. A/955. O.C. inspected Camp 6/13th Field Ambulance found everything in a highly satisfactory condition. Ablution place completed. Arrangements made with G.A.S to supply necessary pump & pipes for well. what is now completed.	N/C
	20/2/16		Ptes BABB, BLACK, & PHILLIPS proceeded on leave - will return on the 28th inst. O.C. visited Camp A, Our Drainage Officer called & made strong complaints about the condition of the Camp of the 108th S.A.C. Received Circular A/2629 & M.100/16 re Sewerage work. With regard to this - this Section is responsible for the carrying out of D.W.H.G. only. We are aware of no general agreement for the carrying out of this work.	N/C
	21/2/Feb.		Received D.R.O. No. 252; Circular No. A/2 & 42 re forwarding of Casualty Reports. Received D.W.H. of 24/2/16.	N/C

Army Form C. 2118.

Page 4.

WAR DIARY
or
INTELLIGENCE SUMMARY.
(Erase heading not required.)

Instructions regarding War Diaries and Intelligence Summaries are contained in F. S. Regs., Part II. and the Staff Manual respectively. Title pages will be prepared in manuscript.

[Stamp: 41st SANITARY SECTION R.A.M.C.(T)]

Place	Date	Hour	Summary of Events and Information	Remarks and references to Appendices
Map 28. G.15.c.5.9	21st Feb		O.C. visited Camp "A" at the request of the M.O. 3rd Rifle Brigade & found camp in a very unsatisfactory condition - having been left so by previous unit. Several suggestions were made for the improving of the conditions especially the drainage & disposal of urine, sawdust being obtainable from the R.E. siding. Report forwarded to A.D.M.S. Latrine work continued. New latrines commenced at Y.M.C.A. The tanks at H.14.a. are now dealing with about 100 carts per day some of which cannot be filled "full" owing to some obstruction in pipes at the DICKEBUSCH end. Received D.R.O. No. 253.	NFL
	22nd Feb		O.C. visited 108th B.A.C. Camp at request of Div. Drainage Officer & found the camp in a very bad condition. The Camp is in a very flat one & O.C. had asked the D.D.O. to again advise the O.C. regarding the drainage. L/Sgt. DINNIS of this section visited camp & superintended the construction of grease traps. Arrangements made with D.A.D.O.S. for the supply of a dozen latrine buckets to this camp. Much progress made with brick destructor for No. 4 Cav. Div. Train. Received DRO No. 254-254'; GRO No. 1412-1426; V Corps R.O. No. 589-593 & 2nd Army Traffic Order Circular.	NFL

2353 (Wt. W2544/1454 700,000 5/15 D. D. & L. A.D.S.S./Forms/C. 2118.

WAR DIARY
or
INTELLIGENCE SUMMARY.
(Erase heading not required.)

Page 8

Place	Date	Hour	Summary of Events and Information	Remarks and references to Appendices
G.15.c.6.9 Map 28	23rd Feb		Received D.W.M. of 22/2/16, D.R.O. No. 258-265; O.C. visited Camp of 106th B.A.C. The weather has turned very severe & the building of the brick destructors has had to be discontinued for the present. Informed by A.D.M.S. that the two men now at YPRES are to be withdrawn this week. Work at other points proceeded as usual. Arrangements made for commencement of new Soap Wash Scheme in Camp "C". This will be carried out at once. Received D.W.M. of 23/2/16. Interview with O.C. Sanitary Section 6th Division with regard to exchange of men at YPRES.	WSL
	24th Feb		Weather still very severe — Pte KILBORN engaged on construction of models for forthcoming Sanitary exhibition at HAZEBROUCK. Received report that the conditions in "A" Camp are still very bad. Sgt GOODING instructed to visit & render all available assistance. No of cart at the Tanks H.14 a average 105. No of cart at C.R.S. No 589 Para 7 "Hostile Aircraft." Received D.R.O. Nos 266-271, & a copy of C.R.S. No 589 Para 7. This will be sent round to all the sub-sections for compliance.	WSL
	26th Feb		Received D.W.M. of 24/2/16; also wire to say that all "Leave" is suspended until further orders. Pte KILBURN completed models of three Manure Destructors loop Waste Scheme for the Sanitary Exhibition. Received D.R.O. Nos 272-279, & C.R.O. Nos 594-6.	WSL

WAR DIARY
or
INTELLIGENCE SUMMARY.
(Erase heading not required.)

Army Form C. 2118.

Place	Date	Hour	Summary of Events and Information	Remarks and references to Appendices
May 28 G.15.C.5.9	26 Feb	—	Received DWR a/25/2/6; DRO No 280-282, Confidential Circular re drunkenness. Weather much less severe. Routine work at Div. H.Q. Sub. Section + H.Q. continued.	NSL
	27 Feb	—	Received DRO No 283 (After Order re Baths) + No 283/27/6; Circular 2nd Division No A/2739, DWR a/26/6; Routine Work at all points continued. McCHISNALL No 747 removed to 4th F.A.-sick.	NSL
	28 Feb	—	Received DRO No 284-6, DWR a/25/2 New refuse pit in camp commenced	NSL
	29 Feb	—	Received DWR a/28 Vo, CRO No 594-599, + DRO No 287-290; DWR a/29 Vo. Received 600 bricks from C.R.E. Ptes BABB, BLACK, + PHILLIPS returned from "leave." Weather is now much milder more outside work can now be undertaken. for new destination in camp.	NSL

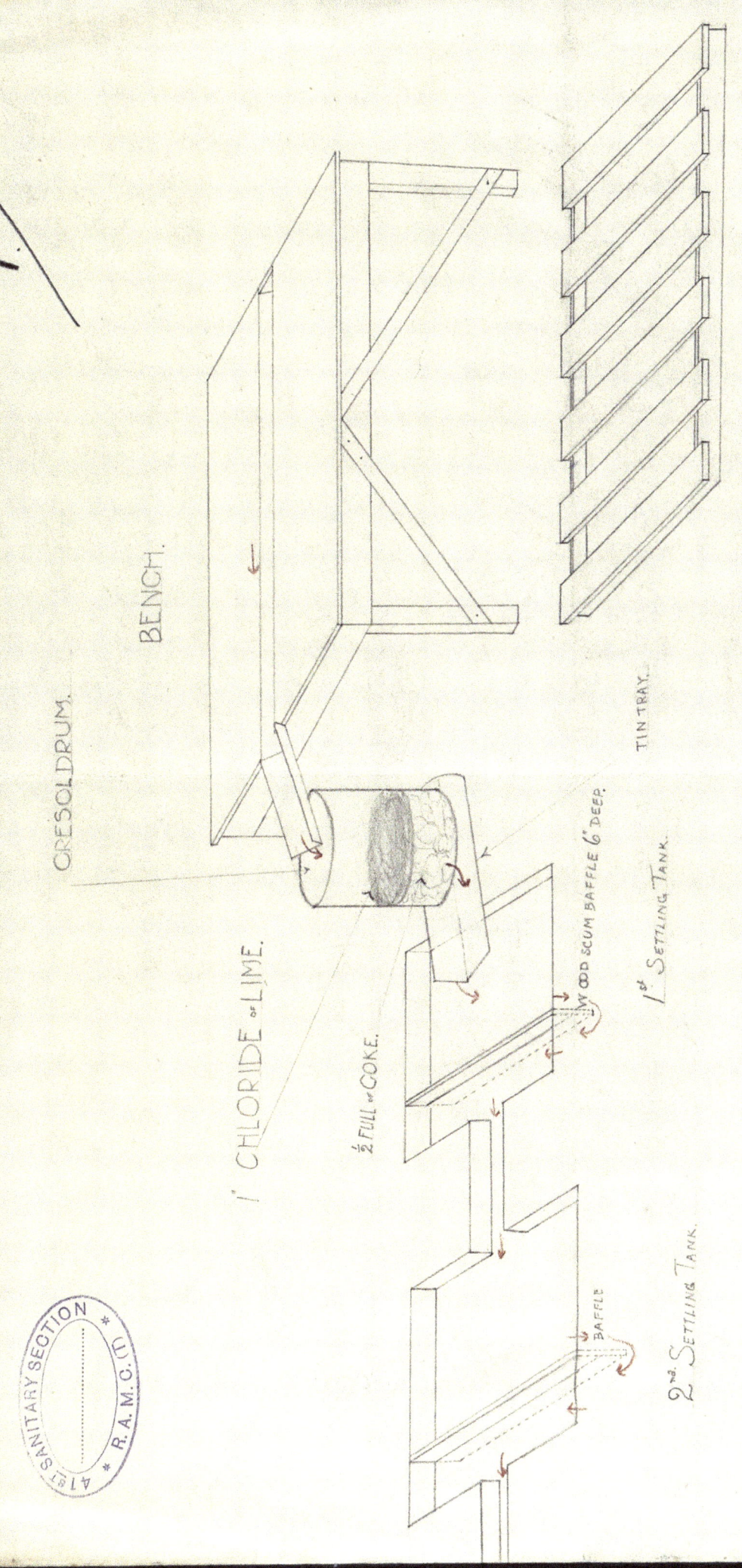

41 San Soc
Vol 7

War Diary
of the
41st Sanitary Section
Volume 7

From 1st March to 31st March, 1916.

Confidential.

WAR DIARY
or
INTELLIGENCE SUMMARY.

(Erase heading not required.)

Army Form C. 2118.

Volume 4

Page 1

Instructions regarding War Diaries and Intelligence Summaries are contained in F. S. Regs., Part II. and the Staff Manual respectively. Title pages will be prepared in manuscript.

1ST SANITARY SECTION
R.A.M.C. (T)

Place	Date	Hour	Summary of Events and Information	Remarks and references to Appendices
Map 28 G.15.c.5.9	MARCH 1st	—	Men are still distributed as follows:— Sgt., L/Cpl., + 2 Privates — at G.17 — in charge of Camp Inspection + the Y.M.C.A. sanitation L/Cpl. + 2 Privates — at Div. H.Q. — in charge of all the sanitary arrangements. Cpl. + 3 Privates in charge of the Water Tanks in H.14.a. + responsible for the testing + chlorination of the water at the bomb-site in H.22.a. Remainder of section at Camp in G.15.c.5.9. Ptes. BLACK + KILBURN continued construction of brick destructors for the Div. Train — the one at No. 3 completed to-day. Received D.R.O. No. 291-5; 2d Army Routine Orders No. 312-316; + D.W.N. 24/1/3/6.	WST
	2nd		The O.C. made the following "local" appointments:— L/Cpl. LANIGAN, Ptes BLACK, GAWTHORPE, KILBURN to be Acting Corporals; Pte. LANHAM to be Acting L/Corporal. Attention of all men drawn to the C.R.O.s with regard to saluting + care of arms & rations. The destructor in No. 2 Coy. Camp. Div. Train proceeded with to-day will be completed to-morrow. Other work proceeded on usual lines. S/Sgt. visited all sections. O.C. interviewed M.O. 106th Brigade R.F.A. relative to the unsatisfactory state of the three lines in "B" Battery. The manure is to be spread over the land, any left-over will be covered with earth + the ditches Ypres are to be specially refreshed. Lab. section went to BRANOUTRE. C.R.O No. 1426-1435; C.R.O. Yr. 600-1; + D.W.N. of usual date.	WST

2353 Wt. W25444454 700,000 5/15, L. D. & L. A.D.S.S./Forms/C. 2118.

WAR DIARY or INTELLIGENCE SUMMARY

Army Form C. 2118.

Page 2.

Place	Date	Hour	Summary of Events and Information	Remarks and references to Appendices
May 28 G.15.c.5.9	3rd March		Received information regarding some cases of cerebro-spinal meningitis, paratyphoid "B", & scarlet fever in A.D.V.C. Camps respectively. Made arrangements for immediate disinfection with formaldehyde. Corpls BLACK & KILDOW R.N. engaged on boot destructor for Div. Train. Commenced a trial scheme for dealing with urine by process of fermentation & filtration. If successful full details will be given in Appendix. All other work continued on usual lines. L/Cpl LANHAM & Pte HALDANE returned from YPRES having been relieved by members of the Sanitary Section attached to VIth Division. Received D.V.R. Q/3/3/16. D.R.O. N°s 300-304, & C.R.O. N°s 602-5	NST
	4th March		L/Cpl LANHAM assisting in construction of Div. Train destructor. Weather very severe & little progress made with outside work. Disinfection (we yesterday) carried out. In the case of cerebro-spinal meningitis we found that during the night the whole Regiment (including contacts) had gone to the trenches & a new Regiment occupied the Camp including the infected hut. The incoming M.O. was given full information by us. Received instructions from D.D.M.S. though A.D.M.S. to disinfect all huts in the Rest Camps. This will be done forthwith commencing tomorrow. Received D.R.O. N°s 305-310, & C.R.O. N°s 606-612.	NST

Page 3

Army Form C. 2118.

WAR DIARY
or
INTELLIGENCE SUMMARY.
(Erase heading not required.)

Place	Date	Hour	Summary of Events and Information	Remarks and references to Appendices
Met 28. G.15.c.5.9	5 Mar	—	17 C.O. + 1 O.R. proceeded to Infantry Camps A, B, & C to disinfect every hut with creol. Work abandoned at 2:30pm owing to A.D.M.S. having cancelled the instructions received yesterday. The weather continues to be very wet & now are frequent. The destructor Div. Grain completed. Fry parade for all - 3pm. Received D.V.N 2/4/3/6; D.R.O. No's 311-313. B.R.O. No's 4136-4146. Circular 24th Divn. No. Q/2865 re examination of American oats	WSL
	6 Mar	—	Capt. BLACK proceed to the 8th BUFFS to examine & report on damage to the large new incinerator there. Capt. KILBURN proceeded with the brick destructor in own camp. 2/Lt. LANHAM took over the stores from Pte. MARTIN who will 2/Lt. visited all sections. 4Cpl. LANHAM to proceed for duty at the tanks in H.14.a. 2/Lt. JOHNSON to return to H.Q. Received D.V.N 2/5/3/6; D.R.O. No's 314-320; + C.R.O. No's 314-322.	WSL
	7 Mar	—	Capt BLACK repaired incinerator referred to yesterday. Camp destructor almost completed. Snow fell all day which interfered with outside work. Boxes made for disposal of urine scheme. O.C. visited the Camp of "D" Battery 107 R.F.A. with regard to complaint that water obtained from tanks in H.14.a. is being too highly chlorinated. Received D.V.N 2/6/3/6.	WSL

Army Form C. 2118.

WAR DIARY
or
INTELLIGENCE SUMMARY.
(Erase heading not required.)

Instructions regarding War Diaries and Intelligence Summaries are contained in F. S. Regs., Part II. and the Staff Manual respectively. Title pages will be prepared in manuscript.

Page 4

Place	Date	Hour	Summary of Events and Information	Remarks and references to Appendices
Map 28 G 15.c.5.9	8 March	—	Destructor in own camp completed. Much progress made with urine disposal scheme. Routine work as usual. Received D.W.R. 11/3/16 & D.R.O. No 326-8; C.R.O. No 615-8; Circular No A/2749/1 re Road Control Officers.	NS
	9 March		O.C. visited MAPLE COPSE I.28.d Map 28 to investigate the case of cerebro spinal meningitis (see 4 March) where contacts had proceeded straight to the trenches. On arrival found that the Company had left for the BELGIAN CHATEAU two days previously. O.C. made full investigation there & reported afterwards to A.D.M.S. Routine work as usual. Received D.W.R. 11/3/16, & D.R.O. No 329-331	NS
	10 March		Extensive alterations made to Section's cookhouse with a view to improving ventilation & heating thereof. Urine disposal scheme much more forward. Disinfection now of measles in Camp "C" – 1st Royal Fusiliers. All other work as usual. Received D.W.R. 2/9/3/16 & D.R.O. No 332-5.	NS
	11 March		Work on cookhouse almost completed. Routine work continued at all points. Received complaint from O.C. Water Patrol re nuisance in Camps of 2nd Entrenching Battalion & 8th Buffs Transport Lines. Corp. LANIGAN will investigate & report. Received D.W.R. 2/10/3/16 & D.R.O. No 336-341	NS

Army Form C. 2118.

WAR DIARY
or
INTELLIGENCE SUMMARY.
(Erase heading not required.)

Page 5

Instructions regarding War Diaries and Intelligence Summaries are contained in F. S. Regs., Part II. and the Staff Manual respectively. Title pages will be prepared in manuscript.

Place	Date	Hour	Summary of Events and Information	Remarks and references to Appendices
Map 28 G 15. a. 5. 9.	12 March	—	Received information regarding case of Scarlet Fever in Camp B - Cpl Lucey, Corp. LANIGAN visited during afternoon but was unable to disinfect at the time. The necessary disinfection will be carried out early to-morrow morning. Contacts have been segregated in tents away from the main camp. All other work progressed favourably. Received D.W.M. 11/3/16, D.R.O. No 342-3, Circular Q.2947 re Chapel Helmets.	NSL
	13 March		The weather to-day has been of a summery nature much outdoor work in the way of camp drainage & the like has been possible. The disinfection mentioned yesterday was carried out this morning the necessary reports forwarded to A.D.M.S. Work to Staffs... re carried on as usual. Received D.W.M. 12/3/16; D.R.O No 344-7.	NSL
	14 March		New ablution place erected in camp & a commencement made to a new workshop. Routine work as usual. Received D.W.M. 13/3/16 & D.R.O No 348-9; Routine Orders No 325-330.	NSL
	15 March		O.C. visited Camps A, B, & C in company with Capt. SCOTT, D.A.D.M.S. to-day suggested several improvements in the sanitation being Workshop in Camp completed. Urine scheme completed. In about a week's time it will be possible to investigate its value. Routine work carried out. The swop [swab?] wash disposal schemes are complete in all Rest Camps but H. Received D.W.M. 14/3/16; D.R.O. 350-6.	NSL

Page 6.   Army Form C. 2118.

Instructions regarding War Diaries and Intelligence
Summaries are contained in F. S. Regs., Part II.
and the Staff Manual respectively. Title pages
will be prepared in manuscript.

WAR DIARY
or
INTELLIGENCE SUMMARY.
(Erase heading not required.)

Place	Date	Hour	Summary of Events and Information	Remarks and references to Appendices
Mar 28 G.S.C 59	16th March		Received information regarding case of cerebro spinal fever in ZILLEBEKE dug-out. S/Sgt. Copp. went to carry out the necessary disinfection but after waiting 1½ hrs east of KRUISSTRAAT were obliged to return owing to the heavy shelling by the enemy. Do the surveys are going up to-night the M.O that company will see to this work. All Camp + A/fx work carried on as usual. New Years Greetings fixed at Y.M.C.A. No.1650, Pte. SALTERS, A.G. joined the Section 6-day being transferred from the Sanitary Section, VIth Division. Received D.R.O. N°. 357, 359, + D.U.R. 2/5/3/16.	NSL
	17th March		No.684, Pte. JOHNSON, Pl. removed to 44th F.A. this morning suffering from Pyrexia. Corp. LANIGAN is visiting every camp frequently now to see that the soap made is being properly dealt with. It is most important that the time is renewed daily. Routine work as usual. Received D.R.O. N°. 360-5; + S.U.R. 2/16/3/16.	NSL
	18th March		No. 684, Pte JOHNSON, Pl. returned from 44th F.A. this afternoon. O.C. visited the new area with Capt. SCOTT, D.A.D.M.S. Received word that leave is reopened - two places allotted for the 23rd inst. Routine work continued. Received D.R.O. N°. 364 "to" 370 (really 366-372 inspectors) + C.R.O. N°. 632-6, also a copy of Field Almanac from A.D.M.d of "G" office.	NSL

2353 Wt. W2514/1454 700,000 5/15 L.D. & L. A.D.S.S./Forms/C. 2118.

Army Form C. 2118.

WAR DIARY
or
INTELLIGENCE SUMMARY.
(Erase heading not required.)

Page 1

Instructions regarding War Diaries and Intelligence Summaries are contained in F. S. Regs., Part II. and the Staff Manual respectively. Title pages will be prepared in manuscript.

Place	Date	Hour	Summary of Events and Information	Remarks and references to Appendices
Map 28 G.15.c.5.q	19th March		Routine work only. Received DWR a/18/3/6. DRO N° 271-4, & CRO a/18/3/6 N°s 145-69	NSL
"	20th March		Gas parade. Routine work continued. Received DWR a/19/3/16, & DRO N°375-7, & CRO N° 634-6+8.	NSL
"	21st March		Advance party of 3rd Canadian Sanitary Section arrived. OC visited all pub. sections. Received no return this day owing to removal of Div H.Q.	NSL
"	22nd March		Remainder of 3rd C.S.S. arrived & took over the Sub-Section work in G.15 & the Water Tanks in H.14.a. Advance parties from this section left for new quarters in Rest Area at FLETRE. Received N° other	NSL
FLETRE	23rd March		Remainder of section travelled to FLETRE. The reserve billets here has been claimed by R.E.s so this section will move to billets in Marie's premises to-morrow. Received DRO's 378-9 & 380-5. DWR a/22/3/16. Location of Units & R.A.M.C. Operation Order N° 3	NSL
"	24th March		Section H.Q. changed to Marie's premises. Men engaged in manufacture of Serenzelli substitute. Received DRO N° 386-8. CRO N° 331-3.	NSL
"	25th March		O.C. investigated case of ? measles at X.18.a.9.9. Slept 27 - case proved the interim do - no disinfection was carried out. Received Circular 6/16yy re gas helmets & DRO N°s 389-393. The L.A.W. N°709. Removed to 42nd J.A. Magnbie figeuil & Pl. Flevis.	NSL

2353 Wt. W3514/4454 700,000 5/15 L. D. & L.   A.D.S.S./Forms/C. 2118.

Army Form C. 2118.

WAR DIARY
or
INTELLIGENCE SUMMARY.
(Erase heading not required.)

Sheet 8

Instructions regarding War Diaries and Intelligence Summaries are contained in F. S. Regs., Part II. and the Staff Manual respectively. Title pages will be prepared in manuscript.

Place	Date	Hour	Summary of Events and Information	Remarks and references to Appendices
FLETRE	26 March		Case of measles in Officers billet, 3rd Rifle Brigade. Men sent to disinfect but found case not removed. The patient was removed later in the day & the room closed until to-morrow morning when the necessary disinfection will be carried out. Received information that R.O. 709. Pte L.A.W.V.J. was removed to 1st Canadian C.C.S. yesterday. Received D.R.O. Nos 389-394.	NSC
	27 March		Disinfection referred to above carried out early this morning. Station taken for route march. Received D.R.O. Nos 400-11.	NSC
	28 March		O.C. visited new area at St JANS CAPELLE. Disinfection carried out in Officers servants billet, 3rd Rifle Brigade. Received D.R.O. Nos 402-407 & C.R.O. Nos 648-9	NSC
	29 March		Case of measles reported from 13th Middlesex Regt. Disinfection not carried out owing to presence of a second case not removed. Received D.R.O. Nos 408-413. Case of cerebro-spinal fever reported from D.A.C at GODWAERSVELDE. Necessary disinfection carried out.	NSC
St JANS CAPELLE	30 March		Section removed to St JANS CAPELLE where camp of 1st Canadian Sanitary Section was taken over.	NSC
"	31 March		Case of measles reported from 3rd Rifle Brigade in Bulford Camp - disinfection carried out. Received Circular Q.2395 re Return of Winter Clothing. D.R.O. Nos 413-8, E.R.O. Nos 1480-1490 & R.O. Nos 334-7.	NSC

Vol 8
24th Dec

41st SANITARY SECTION
WAR DIARY
(CONFIDENTIAL)
VOLUME 8.
from 1st April to 30th April 1916.

COMMITTEE FOR THE
MEDICAL HISTORY OF THE WAR
Date 9 - JUN.1916

Army Form C. 2118.

WAR DIARY
or
INTELLIGENCE SUMMARY.

(Erase heading not required.)

41st SANITARY SECTION — R.A.M.C. (T.)

Page 1.

Place	Date 1916	Hour	Summary of Events and Information	Remarks and references to Appendices
ST JANS CAPELLE	11th April		Case of members affected fever measles reported from D.A.C. at GODWAERSVELDE. Barn disinfected. Straw burnt - contacts bivouced in adjoining field. To-morrow the unit is moving to the new camp the contacts will be segregated in tents. O.C. with D.A.D.M.S. visited the south eastern part of the new area. Section divided into parties under superintendence of members of the Section relieved by us toured the main Infantry Camps. A sub-section will again have charge of the sanitary arrangements in this village. To-day the various headquarters messes have been stocked. New incinerators built to dispose of bulk of refuse. Received D.R.O. No. 419-429. Specially noted 422 "Hurricane Lamps" & 429 "Tents". Nil returns in both cases. Also Circular No A/3063 re Leave.	NFC
	12th April		Disinfection in KORTEPYP huts - billet occupied by contacts of measles. See 29 of ult. Case of scarlet fever reported from Canadian Camp at T.18.a. On our men's arrival there it was found that one hut had been destroyed by shell fire & another one left vacant. This was disinfected. Contacts removed to T.25.b.6.10. Fatigue until the 8th inst. when the hut in the Grenade school will be disinfected. O.C. visited sub-section at DRANOUTRE & afterwards the various ambulances & the advanced dressing stations. Received Location of Units. D.R.O. No. 430 - 3. C.R.O. 650-4. L/Cpl LANHAM & Pte BRADLEY returned from "leave"	NFC

Army Form C. 2118.

WAR DIARY
or
INTELLIGENCE SUMMARY.
(Erase heading not required.)

Page 2.

Instructions regarding War Diaries and Intelligence Summaries are contained in F. S. Regs., Part II. and the Staff Manual respectively. Title pages will be prepared in manuscript.

41ST SANITARY SECTION * R.A.M.C.

Place	Date	Hour	Summary of Events and Information	Remarks and references to Appendices
ST JANS CAPELLE	3rd Ap.	—	O/c with A.D.M.S. & D.A.D.M.S. visited 1st Inf. Bde. H.Q. to arrange for the disposal of house manure. Satisfactory arrangements are to be carried out by the units. O/c visited the advanced H.Q. at the A.P.M.'s request regarding the manager sanitation generally of the farm. An incinerator will be built here by this section & the drainage will be improved by the D.D.O. Information received from M.O. 8th Queens that a case of measles had occurred in officers' billet at TEA FARM situate in N.34.d.0.6. Party sent to disinfect but on arrival found that the 8th Queens had left & their places taken by the R.W. KENTS who knew nothing of the case so no disinfection could be carried out. Ditches in village cleaned out – notices in three languages printed & erected in various places regarding sanitary cleanliness. Routine work in H.Q. carried out as usual. Received D.R.O. Nos. 434–6. L/Cpl. EDWARDS made Acting Corporal.	NFC
	4th April		Ditches cleared in the village. All the various Staffs are now in a very satisfactory condition. To-day all the water posts have been visited & the water tested. In every case the water is satisfactory & little bleaching powder is needed. Vermigelli substitute supplied to all the Field Ambulances. Received D.R.O. Nos. 439 – 443.	NFC

WAR DIARY
or
INTELLIGENCE SUMMARY.

(Erase heading not required.)

Army Form C. 2118.

Place	Date 1916	Hour	Summary of Events and Information	Remarks and references to Appendices
ST JANS CAPELLE.	5 Ap.		Routine work at Div HQ continued. More work done on ditches which are now almost completed. Div Baths at DRANOUTRE inspected. The three large soakage pits are not satisfactory, the stream receiving the effluent is becoming contaminated. The ground in the vicinity is becoming fouled. OC will personally investigate this. Notice boards for the various water-points printed. Received D.R.O. No's 444 – 452, & 544 – 5.	NFL
	6 April		Routine work continued. OC visited DRANOUTRE. Pts HALDANE, WHITTAKER, & WOOLF proceeded on leave until the 14th inst. Pts Cpl. Grice Canteen & Y.M.C.A. at DRANOUTRE inspected. The supervisor of both these will be the work of the sub section but each will provide the necessary fatigues. Received D.R.O. No's 546 – 551, C.R.O. No's 1491 – 1502, R.O. No's 338 – 340, & C.R.O. No's 655 – 654.	NFL
	7 April		Routine work at D.H.Q. as usual. Disinfection of two tents – 8th Entrenching Battn – case of query measles. The contacts were found to be on duty – he M.O. examines each every night & morning. This will be remedied by OC. Pte BABB sent to Sub. Section. Received D.R.O No's 552 – 564. The Artillery Groups will be inspected to-morrow	NFL

Army Form C. 2118.

WAR DIARY
or
INTELLIGENCE SUMMARY.
(Erase heading not required.)

Instructions regarding War Diaries and Intelligence Summaries are contained in F. S. Regs., Part II. and the Staff Manual respectively. Title pages will be prepared in manuscript.

Page 4

41st SANITARY SECTION * R.A.M.C.(T.) *

Place	Date 1916	Hour	Summary of Events and Information	Remarks and references to Appendices
ST JANS CAPELLE	8th April		D.HQ.- All latrines cleaned, trench latrines fills in at rear of H.Q. Guard billet & Engineers billet & pails substituted in lieu thereof. Streams & ditches cleaned. Grease traps & incinerators emptied & the former renewed. Camp Inspection - The following Camps were inspected:- Artillery - 106th Bde, 109th Bde (eacpt 110 Bty), 108th Bde, + 109th Bde (eacpt "A" Battery). On the whole the camps are in a satisfactory condition. A large quantity of manure left by the 1st Canadian Division is to be found all over the area. Means will be devised to dispose of this. Grannette - Summary of work done since last report. Y.M.C.A. - Latrines, covered urine pit, covered grease trap, + incinerator constructed. D & G Canteen - urine pit in process of construction. Camps visited - Infantry - 9th Surreys + Grenade School. ", 8th R.W. Kents, 1st Rdliffs, + 8th Queens. Artillery - 108th Bde - "B", "C" Batteries, + B.A.C. R.E. - 103rd Field Company.	

Received D.R.O 558 - 561

2353 Wt. W2514/1454 700,000 5/15 D. D. & L. A.D.S.S./Forms/C. 2118.

Page 5

Army Form C. 2118.

WAR DIARY
or
INTELLIGENCE SUMMARY.
(Erase heading not required.)

Place	Date	Hour	Summary of Events and Information	Remarks and references to Appendices
ST JANS CAPELLE	9th April		Disinfection — 1st Royal Fusiliers — measles — Cpl. SIMMONDS, Pte. GARDNER + WOODAGE (No 4+4 + 7931 + 9522). 12th Devon Fusiliers — erysipelas — Pte. HOLMES. In the case of measles the hut + the blankets were disinfected, in the case of GARDNER the tent was disinfected. 3 contacts in all were segregated. In the case of erysipelas the hut was disinfected, the blankets had gone with the man to the hospital; the contacts were not segregated. Church Parade - all available men attended Divine service at 9 a.m. Received D.R.O. No. 562-3, + Admd. No. 4+38 re Cerebro-Spinal meningitis. Camp Inspection — The following camps were inspected. Transport — 17th Bde Machine Gun Corps, 1st R. Fusiliers, 8th Buffs, 3rd Bde, 12th R. Fusiliers. Miscellaneous — 8th Lowr Battn, 2nd Lindens (Dokeyphis), 12th R. Fusiliers (Belfast Hut), 17th Inf. Bde HQ, 195th Coy A.S.C., 12th Devon Fusiliers (Aberdeen), 14th Inf. Bde General Mortar Battery.	N.F.C.
	10th April		S.H.Q. — Routine work continued. Pails provided now for all chief billets messes. Disinfection — 12th Devon Fusiliers— measles — No. 20505 Pte. WABY, + 14202 Pte. WATERHOUSE. Hut disinfected — blankets taken to hospital — contacts removed to another hut. H.Q. Hussars — measles — No. 13035 Pte. DELLOW, 12 Middlesex Regt — usual precautions. Received D.R.O. No. 564-5, + M 50/6 re Gas — C.O. inspecting.	N.F.C.

Army Form C. 2118.

WAR DIARY
or
INTELLIGENCE SUMMARY.
(Erase heading not required.)

Place	Date	Hour	Summary of Events and Information	Remarks and references to Appendices
ST JANS CAPELLE	11th Apr		Very wet day & much outdoor work impossible. Yesterday O.b visited DRANOUTRE took plans & specification made for sedimentation & filtration tanks for dealing with the bath water & laundry water. Corp¹ KILBURN drew all necessary material from R.E. Park at STEENWERCK & the R.E. Hutting Dump at NIEPPE. Routine work as usual O.b visited 14th Fd Ambe Machine Gun Company with regard to para-typhoid case reported to-day. Full investigation made report forwarded to A.D.M.S. Received D.R.O. No. 566-541.	1  N.O.V
	12 Apr		Corp¹ LOTT visited the 14th Brigade Machine Gun Company H.Q. to instruct the men responsible for the sanitation of the camp in construction work. Owing to the heavy rainfall it was impossible to build an incinerator or make grease traps &c but full explanations were given. Disinfection :- 12th Sherwood Foresters - German measles - No 15925. Pte L CLARKE - a hut & tent disinfected - blankets had accompanied patient to hospital. Contacts - nil. The Serg¹ Major who occupies a separate hut. 24th Div. Supply Column - measles - No. M.2/098592. Pte H. BAGOT - room disinfected also blankets. Contacts - two - now segregated. 3rd Rifle Bde - two cases No. 893. Pte GREEN. No. 1036. Pte WATMORE - measles were reported to us this morning but on visiting the camp we found that the M.O.Y attending has was applied the M.O.11 - had had the necessary disinfection carried out. The contacts are occupying seven dug-outs three in each one.	N.O.V

WAR DIARY or INTELLIGENCE SUMMARY

Army Form C. 2118.

Place	Date	Hour	Summary of Events and Information	Remarks and references to Appendices
S'TJANS CAPELLE	12 Apr		**Bath Scheme** - The boxes for laundry scheme partly prepared to day. The sides are being made watertight by putting pieces of tarred felting between the various boards - the whole sides will also be tarred. The actual fitting together of the boxes will be done at the Bath.	N S L
			Routine - at D.H.Q as on previous days.	
			Received D.R.O. No's. 542 & 543-7. & Circular A/746 re writing to Base for reinforcements	
	13 Apr		Corpl LOTT & Pr. MARFLEET from to day are to be in charge of the water-supply in Bulford Camp. For disciplinary purposes & rations they will be under Lieut WIGALL, R.A.M.C. O.C. NEUVE EGLISE baths. For duty they are still under O.C. this Section. Fatigue parties will see to the filling of the tanks & the water duty men in charge of the carts will themselves attend to the water under the Corporal's instructions. Water Carts - 34	N S L
			Bath Scheme - much progress made with boxes.	
			Routine - at D.H.Q. especially work on ditches - carried on as on previous days.	
			Received D.R.O No's 578-582	
	14 Apr		**Disinfection** - measles - Capt HAYES, G.J.P. 1st Royal Fusiliers - Bulford Camp - necessary disinfection re carried out this morning	N S L

Page 8.

Army Form C. 2118.

WAR DIARY
or
INTELLIGENCE SUMMARY.
(Erase heading not required.)

Place	Date	Hour	Summary of Events and Information	Remarks and references to Appendices
S'TJANS CAPELLE.	14th Apl. 1916.		Bath Scheme - The boxes are now ready for fitting & work at DRANOUTRE will be commenced to-morrow	N.S.L.
			Routine - work as usual. Pay Parade.	
			Received no "Orders" this day.	
	15 Apl		Bath Scheme - filter pit dug & boxes partly fitted.	
			O.C. visited DRANOUTRE & arranged new billet for sub. section there. Water Carts - 33	
			Sub Sector. Received summary of work done since last report, as follows:-	
			Camp Inspection - 8th Queens - Infantry Camp	In every case men have been sent to remedy any defects noticed during the inspection.
			— 108th Bde R.F.A. - H.Q.	
			— 72nd Bde. Machine Gun Company	
			— " H.Q. Transport.	
			— 143rd A.A. Company	
			— revisits to all town billets	
			— " " units re elimination of water	
			Disinfection - measles - 2/Lt. FOSTER R.D. - 6/7th R.G.A. Battery - Chips - work carried out this day. Contacts - 3 Officers, 2 Servants 2 Signallers who will carry on but will remain isolated when off duty.	N.S.L.
			Ditches - arrangements made for cleaning of all civilian ditches,	

Page 9.

Army Form C. 2118.

WAR DIARY
or
INTELLIGENCE SUMMARY.

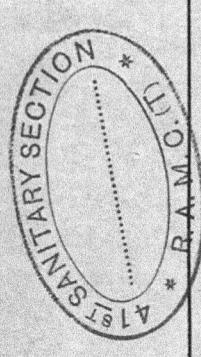

Place	Date	Hour	Summary of Events and Information	Remarks and references to Appendices
S JANS CAPELLE	15/4/16		Routine work carried out as usual. Received allotment of accommodation in BAILLEUL. Water Carts - 39 " D.R.O. No. 582 - 8 d/4/16, + 589 - 595 d/14/16. " C.R.O. No. 1503 - 1515. No. 1503 " Correspondence and Strangers" included in to-day's Orders for the Unit. Much progress made with Bath scheme at DRANOUTRE	NS2
	16/4/16 cont.		Disinfection - 12th Sherwood Foresters - 16932, Pte H MALTBY - measles. Disinfection of hut carried out. Man's blankets accompanied him to hospital. Contacts number 14 + those are sleeping in a hut by themselves. 9th R Fusiliers - 3911, Pte D ANDERSON - measles. The loft occupied by patient thoroughly sprayed. Man's blankets were roped with many others to all blankets were hung out in the strong sunshine for the day. Contacts number 34 and are segregated. 24th Div Supply Column - S. 4109 + 509, Pte REYNOLDS - measles - contacts 18 in number occupying the room - visited too late to disinfect same day. 24th Div Train - T.S./9441 - Wheeler S F STEPHENS - measles - contacts 6 in number. Received D.R.O. No.s 596 + 599. Routine work as usual at D.H.Q. Water Carts - 32. Still occupying same tent which will be sprayed to-morrow.	NS2

WAR DIARY or INTELLIGENCE SUMMARY

Army Form C. 2118.

Place	Date	Hour	Summary of Events and Information	Remarks and references to Appendices
St JANS CAPPEL	17th April		Baths - first scheme almost completed. All media for filters obtained & fixed in position. Disinfectors - 9th Durham Reg.t - Pte W. CARLWHITE - case of enteric. Sgt. GOODING sent to investigate & report on the movement of the patients for last 3 weeks. Found that case was removed from trenches on 14th inst. M.O. will report to A.D.M.S. re movements as they will take a little time to discover. 2nd Supply Column & Div. Train (see 16th inst) - full disinfection re carried out. Case of measles reported from ENGLISH FARM. As O.C. & all N.C.O's men were out of camp engaged on duty no transport was available. It was impossible to visit case to-day. It will receive attention early to-morrow.	
	18th		Routine work at D.H.Q. continued as usual. Water Carts - 38. Received movement orders for to-morrow. D.R.O. No. 600-2 & R.O. No. 341-5. Headquarters of section moved to BAILLEUL this afternoon Distribution of Section is shewn on following page :-	MSL

WAR DIARY or INTELLIGENCE SUMMARY

Army Form C. 2118.

Place	Date	Hour	Summary of Events and Information	Remarks and references to Appendices
BAILLEUL	18/4/		Distribution of Section at present is as follows:-	
			H.Q. - 28, RUE des MOULINS - N.C.O. in charge	
			ASYLUM - L/Sgt. + 4 men - camp inspection &c in southern portion of Div Area	
			S! JANS CAPPEL - 6 N.C.O's + 3 Men - to continue preparations for Bath Scheme, No. 2	
			WATER POST - N.C.O. + man	
			DRANOUTRE - N.C.O. + 6 men - camp inspection &c in northern portion of Div Area.	
			Disinfection - 4th Norhants Regt: - 1488th Co. RUTHERFORD - measles - stationed at ENGLISH FARM	
			- disinfection of hut, cookhouse, + blankets. Contacts (all cooks) number	
			5 have been segregated will remain so until 5th inst:	
			24th Div. Supply Column - M/2/099365 Driver BARNES, + Pte REYNOLDS - both	
			measles - blankets disinfected to day	
	19/4/		D.H.Q. - removed. All places left in a satisfactory condition.	N/SL
			Received no Orders this day. Water Report - 35 carts	
			Baths - work almost completed as regards first scheme.	
			D.H.Q. In GOC's quarters all rubbish collected removed also from Q offices Latrines behind	N/SL
			various offices cleaned. New latrines erected for officers & men at GOC's, C.R.E's.	

WAR DIARY
or
INTELLIGENCE SUMMARY.

Army Form C. 2118.

Page 12

Place	Date	Hour	Summary of Events and Information	Remarks and references to Appendices
BAILLEUL	19 Ap.	—	Disinfection - of Mr Roberts - 17621. Sgt NICHOLAS- cerebro-spinal meningitis - disinfected hut. 15 contacts segregated in hut but will be removed to tents when we shall be informed.	NSL
			Sub-section - Disinfection - civilian named DELEFORTRIE - measles - rooms 3 disinfected - 8 contacts warned not to move abroad until 5th prox. when rooms will be again disinfected. Waterloo - 38.	
			Received D.R.O.s Nos 603-611 but not V Corps Orders Nos 666-669 (see DRO 607)	
	20 Ap.		Baths - scheme for dealing with laundry water completed with exception of sludge pieces. Work will be commenced on scheme for dealing with bath water to-morrow the necessary material having been drawn to-day.	
			Disinfection - WH refuses to case of cerebro-spinal meningitis of yesterday Sgt. GOODING superintended removal of 15 contacts from hut to tents - hut & thoroughly disinfected.	
			Corp LANGAN informed of case of measles in DRANOUTRE for immediate disinfection.	NSL
			D.H.Q. - all latrines & cleaned. Nuisance at CRE's office & at ADMS office dealt with. Waterloo 39	
			Received D.R.O. 612-614 (b)	

Page 13

Army Form C. 2118.

Instructions regarding War Diaries and Intelligence Summaries are contained in F.S. Regs., Part II. and the Staff Manual respectively. Title pages will be prepared in manuscript.

WAR DIARY
or
INTELLIGENCE SUMMARY.
(Erase heading not required.)

Place	Date 1916	Hour	Summary of Events and Information	Remarks and references to Appendices
BAILLEUL	21/4	—	Baths - work commenced at H.Q. on second scheme to deal with the bath water.	
			DHQ - routine as follows - HQ - yard rooms thoroughly cleaned nullah cleared. All latrines cleaned surplus tins removed.	
			G.O.C's quarters, Messes + Stables - all refuse removed.	
			Cesspools arranged with Sanitary Dept for the emptying of cesspools at C R E's office + Div H.Q. + A.D.M.S' office.	
			A.D.M.S' office - cleaned urinal latrines &c.	
			Disinfection - 1/2 Royal Fusiliers - 8564 Pte. H. STRATTON - measles - M.O. had already had the hut + tent thoroughly scrubbed out. All the patient's blankets had been mixed with others all blankets were hung out to be aired. Received D.R.O. № 616-622. Circular 9.3362 w.f and.	NFS
			Water Report - 34 carts.	
	22 Ap.		Baths - much progress made with woodwork for filters.	
			DHQ - similar to detailed scheme above.	
			Disinfection - 108th R.E. - D... COUNSEL - scarlet fever - hut disinfected - contacts - 13 - isolated - food being prepared separately. A case of measles removed from same hut to-day before disinfection.	NFS
			Water Report 31 carts. Circular A.D.S.S. 628.6.	

2353 Wt. W2544/T454 700,000 5/15 D.D. & L. A.D.S.S./Forms/C. 2118.

Army Form C. 2118.

Page 14.

WAR DIARY
or
INTELLIGENCE SUMMARY.
(Erase heading not required.)

Place	Date	Hour	Summary of Events and Information	Remarks and references to Appendices
BAILLEUL 	22/6/16 cont'd		Sub Section - Report of work done since last entry. Camp Inspection - R.W. Kents, "A" & "D" Batteries, 108th Bde R.F.A. Reinits to Transport of R.W. Kents, N. Staff, E. Surreys, 8th Queens, M.G. Company 42nd Bde H.Q, 17th A.A. Company, "C" Battery, Am. Col., & H.Q. of 108th Bde R.F.A.	
			Constructional work completed as follows.	
			8th Queens Transport - incinerator	
			R.W. Kents " & grease trap.	
			N. Staff " " "	
			Inf Camp M.35.d (28) - new latrines	
			42nd Bde H.Q. Transport - incinerator refuse pit.	
			"C" Battery 108th Bde R.F.A - ablution bench.	
			103rd Field Coy. R.E. " ", incinerator for burning excreta.	MFL
	2.30p		Camp Inspection - 24th D.A.C - 3 Section "H.Q. - all in good condition. Water Testing - 4 sources in Camp of Glasgow Yeomanry - on the whole satisfactory - detailed Report sent to A.D.M.S.	MFU

WAR DIARY
or
INTELLIGENCE SUMMARY.
(Erase heading not required.)

Army Form C. 2118.

Page 15

Place	Date	Hour	Summary of Events and Information	Remarks and references to Appendices
BAILLEUL	23rd A. Oct 17		Disinfection – 1st N. Staff Transport – Pte PERCY, J – measles – have disinfected patient's blanket, sprayed contacts numbering 9 segregated in two tents at a satisfactory distance from horse lines. Water Report – 41 tents. To day I have forwarded to ADMS a list of four units which have not obtained bleaching powder since the report on 16th inst. Received DRO No 629-634.	MSL
	24 A.		Disinfection – 8th Entrenching Battalion – 25401 Pte ANDREWS, H. – measles – disinfection carried out re 13 contacts segregated in tents. Baths – work on second scheme transferred to DRANOUTRE where much progress was made. Pump No received from NIEPPE for scheme. Routine – carried on under supervision of S/Sgt of Sanitary section for BAILLEUL. The arrangement well held good during our stay here. Construction work – N.C.O. + 2 men commenced brick incinerator for burning of all refuse in KORTEPYPP Camp. Received information that "leave" allotment of two for the 29th inst is reduced to one. also DRO No 635-638.	MSL

WAR DIARY
or
INTELLIGENCE SUMMARY.

Army Form C. 2118.

Place	Date	Hour	Summary of Events and Information	Remarks and references to Appendices
BAILLEUL	25/4/		Disinfection - 103rd Field Company R.E. - Pte EDGE T. - measles - contacts numbering 4/ sleep in one tent - the contacts are all officers servants. Camps - Sgt GOODING visited following units particularly for inaminate ablution places:- 73rd D., 2nd Trench Transport, 9th Devon T., 73rd T.M.B., 8th contending Battn., & 12th Sherwoods - every effort is being made to provide camps with destructors to burn all refuse to see that each camp is also provided with scheme for dealing with soap waste. Sgt GOODING will undertake the latter duty this week. Baths - continued work at DRANOUTRE. Destructors - " " KORTEPYP. Stone refuse pits is being made complete. Water testing - water of 12th Sherwoods & DurGelish tested - 4/sources - report forwarded to ADMS. Water Return - 43 Baths - 6 Units without Bleaching Powder. Duties at various H.Q's continued under new arrangement. Received Circular Q. 3334 re "Instructions for Roads & Paths in Camps" also DRO. No. 639-644.	

WAR DIARY or INTELLIGENCE SUMMARY

Army Form C. 2118.

Place	Date	Hour	Summary of Events and Information	Remarks and references to Appendices
BAILLEUL	26 April		Disinfection - 2nd Div Supply Col. 099457 Driver D SYKES - measles - blankets & kit removed with him - contacts 20 in same hut - which was sprayed. 1st Royal Fusiliers - 2/Lt. VAN GRUISEN - measles - contacts 2 Captains - hut disinfected. The Unit move forward on Saturday night - when the hut will be labelled & again disinfected on Sunday next. Constructive work - work continued at the Baths. - KORTEPYPP Camp (2nd Instructor) Camp Inspection - 1st Q Fusiliers J. (incinerator), 13th Middlesex J., 73rd Bde M.G. Coy, & T.M.B. 936th M.V.S. with reference to incinerators & ablutions. Latrine continued as yesterday Water Testing - KORTEPYPP Camp. 9b visited both sub sectors in KORTEPYPP Camp Received Circulars F 442 re Espionage from A.P.M., M.271/16 (Confidential) re Case of Horses, & D.R.O. nos 658. 653.	NSE
	27 April		Disinfection - final disinfection in billet of 2nd Div Supply Column - M2/095592 Pte BAGOT. . 9 G Lorry - KORTEPYPP Camp - 2/Lt J S CASSIL - measles - thoroughly disinfected - contacts are officers & officers servants.	NSE

WAR DIARY or INTELLIGENCE SUMMARY

Army Form C. 2118.

Place	Date	Hour	Summary of Events and Information	Remarks and references to Appendices
BAILLEUL	27th Ap. cont		Water Testing. - 1/34th M.B. (T&b) - two sources @ farm pump - dark blue in 10 min. @ stream - light " KORTEPYP Camp - old well dying in disuse - blue reaction in 2 min. will be cleaned out & the water re-tested as soon as possible. Received D.R.O. No 654-5 Baths - work continued very well Destructors - 2nd destructor almost completed at KORTEPYP Camp. Routine at D.H.Q. - ordinary duties carried out. Water Cart - 35 carts - 7 units without Bleaching Powder.	MFL
	28th Ap		Sub Section - Pioneers MILLS & PHILLIPS withdrawn from DRANOUTRE for duty at H.Q. Disinfection - 44th Field Ambulance Adv. Dressing Station, Hyde Park Corner & 30160 Pte MCCARTHY & 51540 Cpl FREEMAN - & 12 B.Q Quickes PLOEGSTEERT - 17737 Pte LONGHURST - all men's kit- party went to disinfect but found that the work had been done by M.O. i/c Dressing Station. Constructive work. - Baths continued. Destructors 'C' completed in KORTEPYP Camp. Soap waste scheme for 1st R.E. Transport 73rd Bde. T.M.B. Sub Section - Report received on the Rest Camps after their weekend by N.STAFFS on the 26/27. - forwarded to A.D.M.S. Received D.R.O No 659-664 Routine - continued. Water cart 39 carts.	MFL

Page 19.

WAR DIARY
or
INTELLIGENCE SUMMARY.

Army Form C. 2118.

Place	Date	Hour	Summary of Events and Information	Remarks and references to Appendices
BAILLEUL	29 Ap.	—	Baths - work continued. Another tank is found necessary for the men's bath water will be proceeded with at once.	
			Disinfection - 12th Royal Fusiliers - 14736. Pte. GURNEY - ?Measles - hut disinfected - blankets had been removed with patient - contacts numbering 6 have been segregated.	
			1st Royal Fusiliers - 14734. Pte. LONGHURST - measles - dug out had been thoroughly cleaned out with creol & contacts removed to a vacated extainnet near by.	
			The regiment moves to BULFORD CAMP to-night & contacts will be segregated in hut there for 6 days when the hut will be disinfected.	
			Re-disinfection - 8th Entrenching Battalion (see 7th inst.)	
			Camp visited - 14th Bde. M.G. Company - 14th Bde. H.Q.	
			Routine work in town carried on as before.	
			Water Report - 40 sants. Five units without Bleaching Powder reported to A.P.M.D.	NSR
			Received D.R.O. No 666-690	
30th Ap.	—	Baths - work continued as usual.	
			Removal of billet - with reference to entry under date 19th inst. the men have repaired from Asylum Farm to a farm at S.18.c.5.0 where the whole of the Section will camp in a few days.	NSR

Army Form C. 2118.

WAR DIARY
or
INTELLIGENCE SUMMARY.
(Erase heading not required.)

Place	Date	Hour	Summary of Events and Information	Remarks and references to Appendices
BAILLEUL	30 Ap 1916		Disinfection - Northants - 10149 Pte LEVI, C - measles - left thoroughly disinfected - nothing known of man's blankets - contacts numbering 41 (platoon) will sleep by themselves. R.F.C. - No.7 Squadron. 2nd A.M. HIRONS, L - hut had already been well scrubbed out with xesol - blankets & kit already removed. Contacts segregated. 12th Sherwoods - 28314 Pte THEAKER, H, + 11242 Pte WILLIAMS, E J - ? measles - huts disinfected - blankets & c removed - 19 contacts sleeping by themselves. 108th Bde R.F.A. "B" Battery - Lieut. KING - 3 other officers occupy the same hut which has not been disinfected. Sub Station - work done since last Report:- Inspection - R.M.R.E - aircraft farm. Re visits - all Transport + all R.F.A + R.E. Units in the locality Construction work - Soap wash scheme in both Infantry Rest Camps. 103rd R.E, + "C" + "D" Battery, 108th Bde. R.F.A manure in upcart traps for 174th A.A. Company - B.A.C. 108th Bde. Disinfection - Y.M.C.A. hut. Routine - as usual	

References: DRO 67-3, G.R.O. No. 1529-1548, + Que G.H.9. D/1874

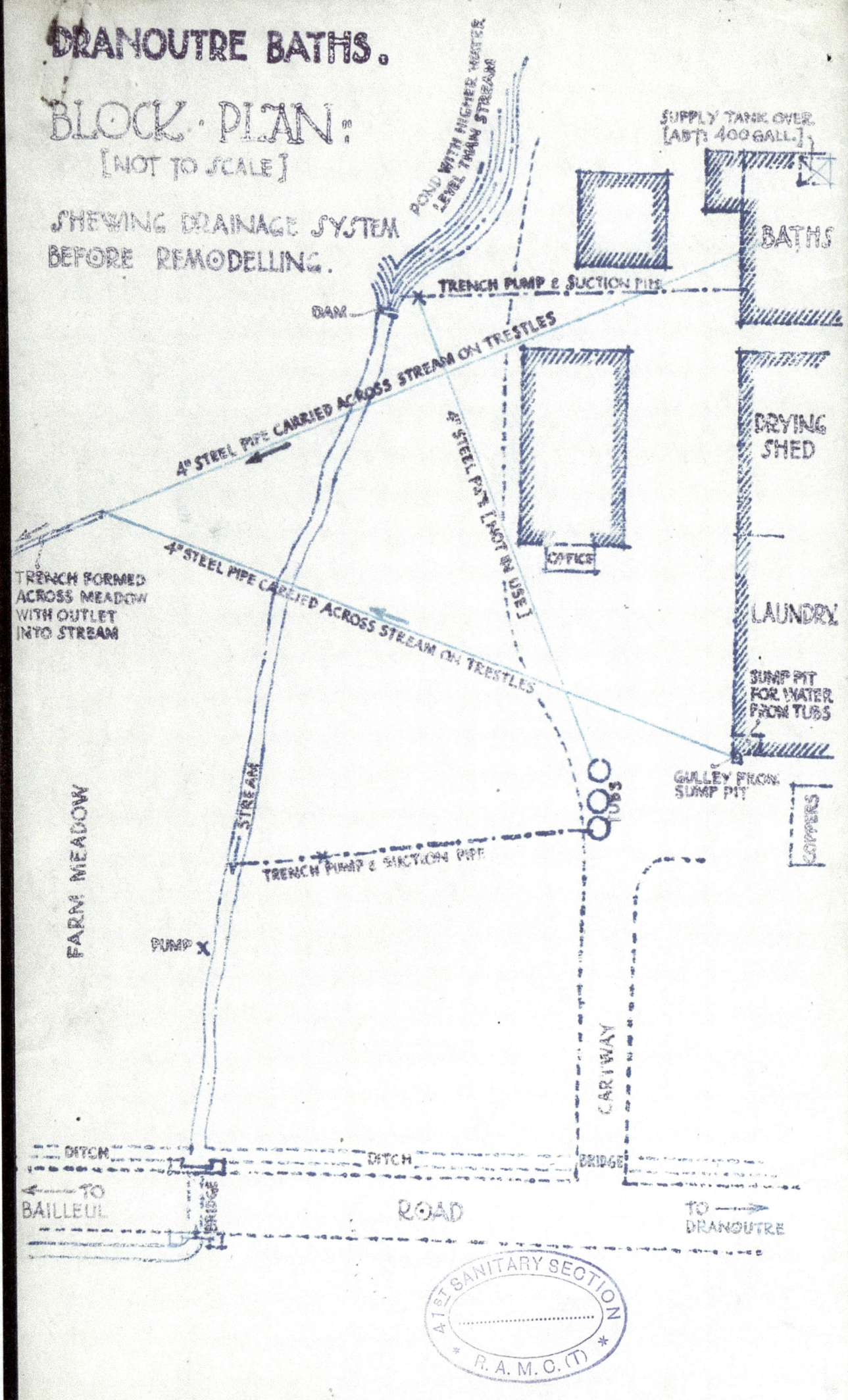

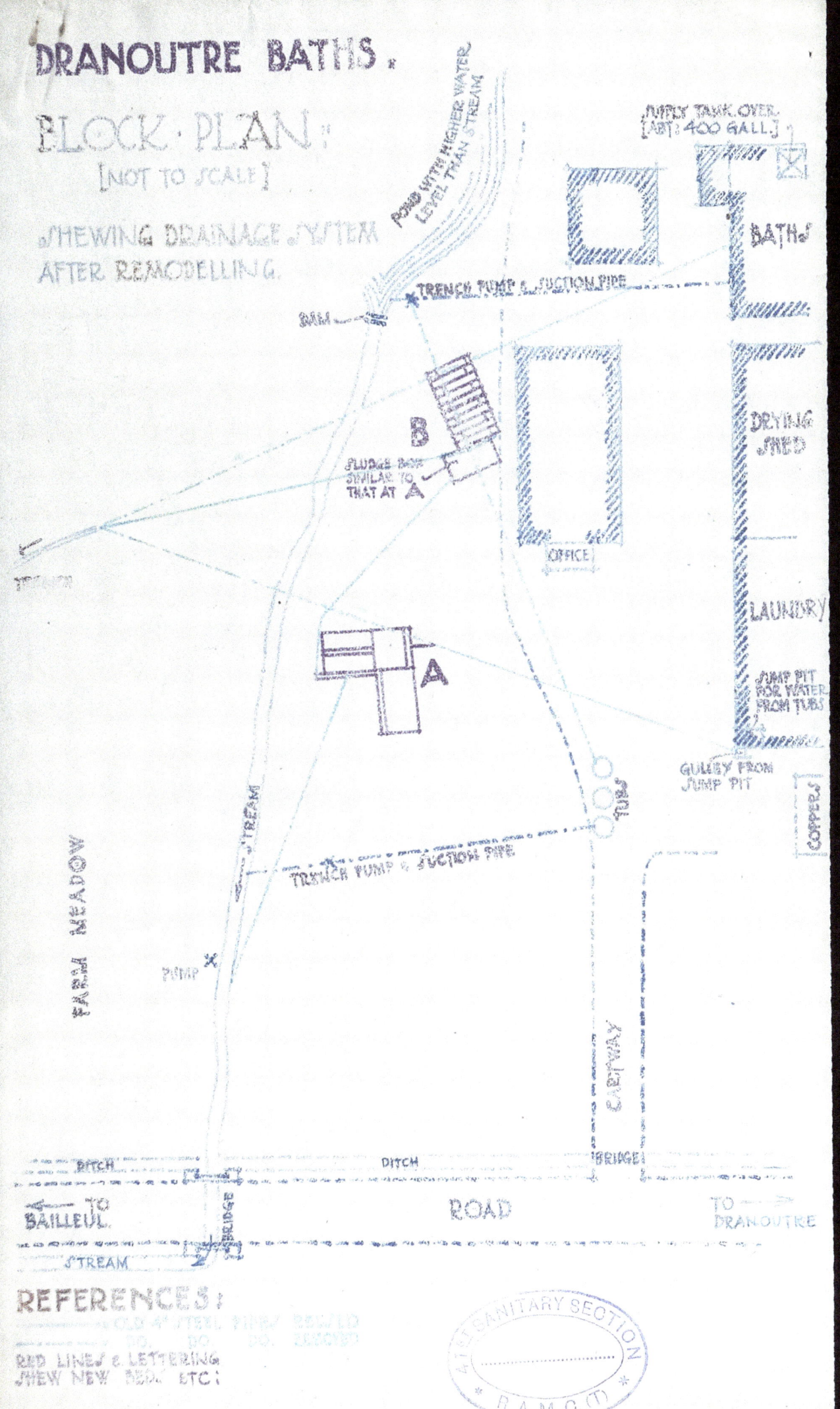

DRANOUTRE BATHS.

DETAILS OF TANKS FOR LAUNDRY WATER.
[INDICATED AT "A" ON BLOCK PLAN].

SCALE: ½" = 1 FOOT.

NOTE:- ALL BOXES COATED WITH TAR & JOINTS FRAMED UP UNDER PRESSURE WITH TARRED BLANKETING BETWEEN.

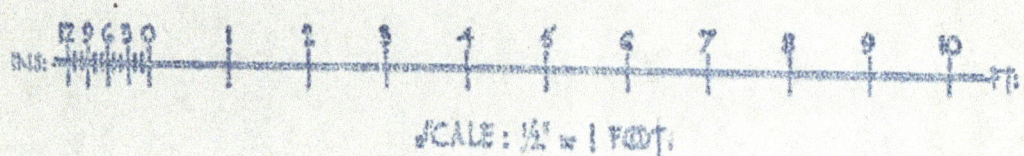

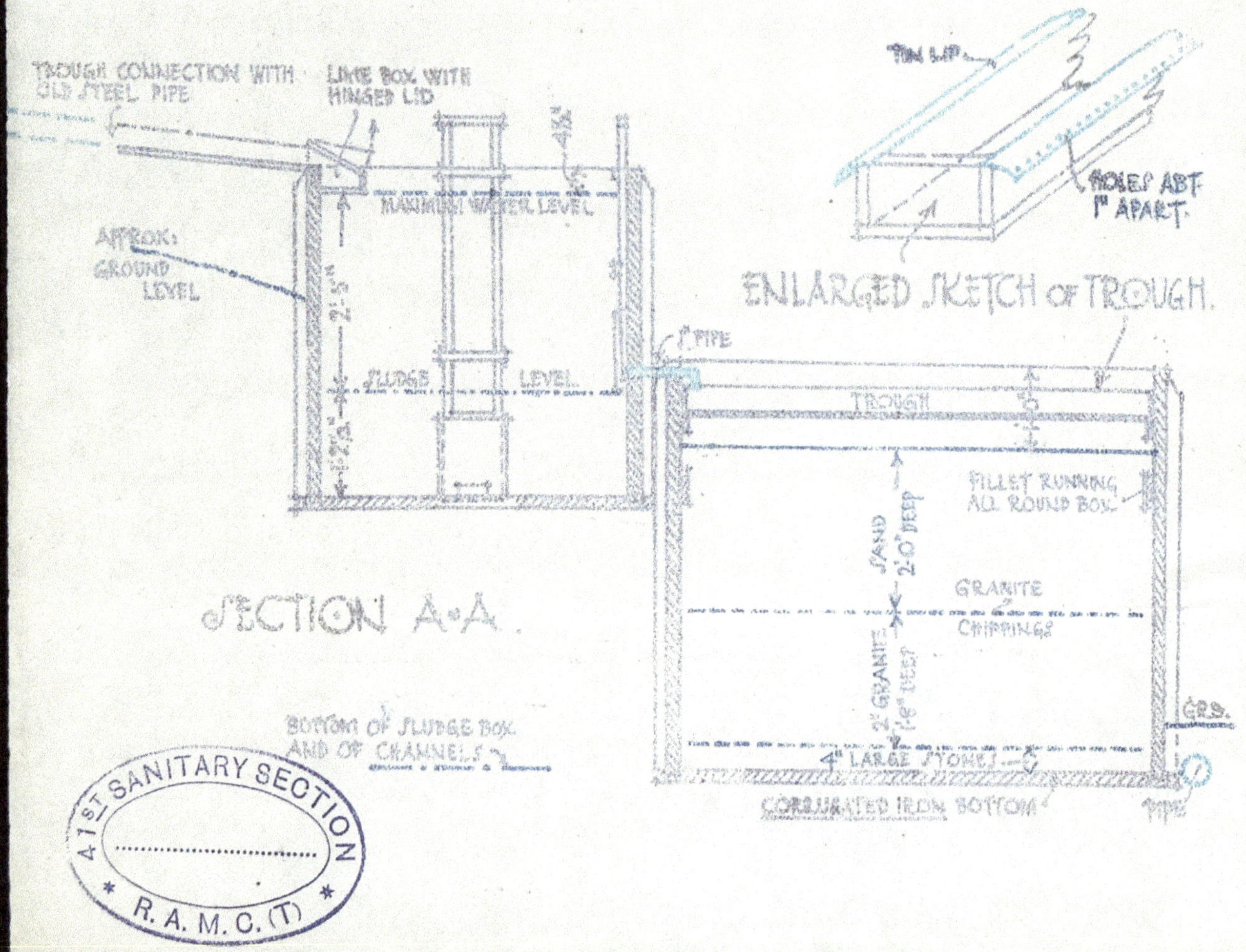

SECTION A-A.

ENLARGED SKETCH OF TROUGH.

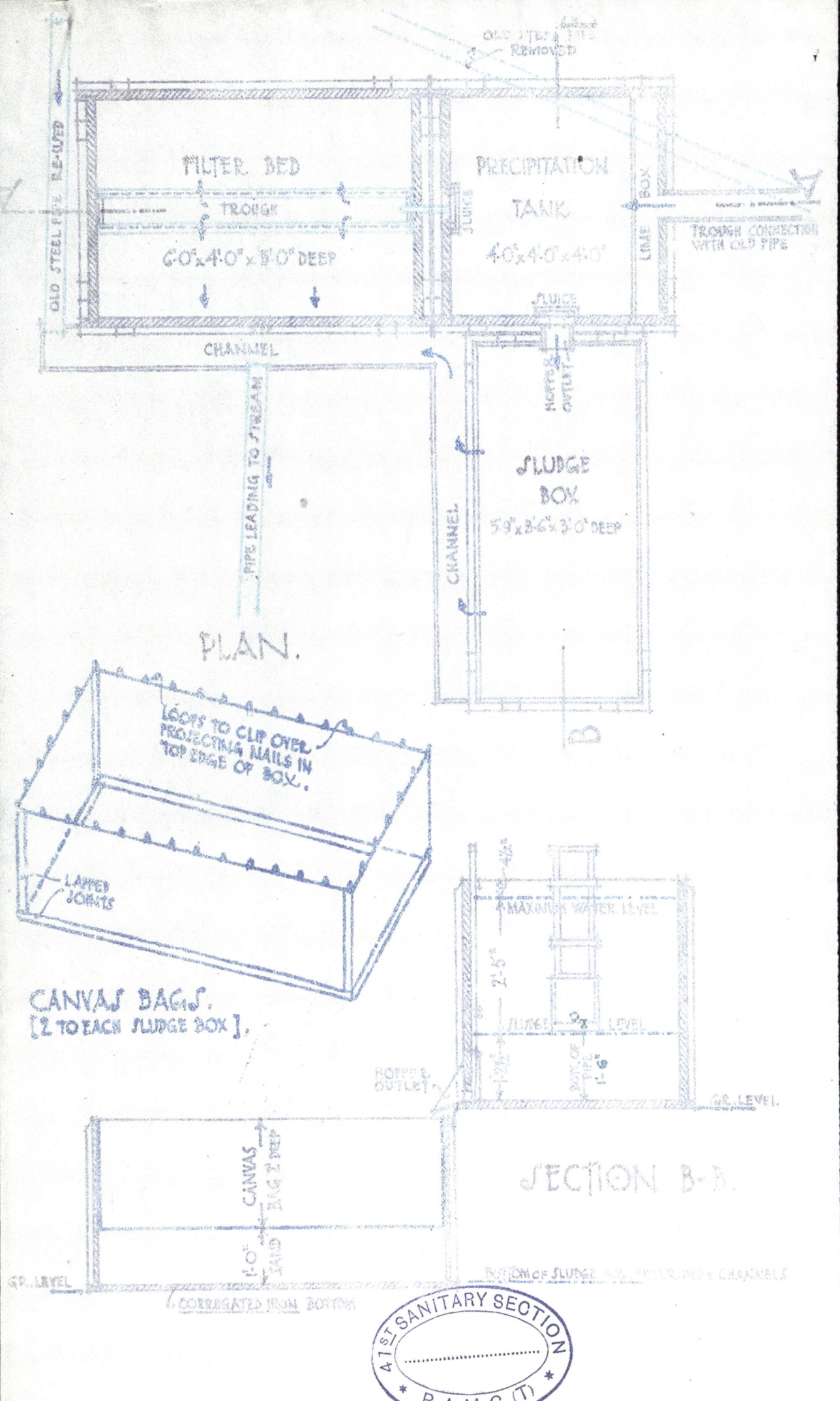

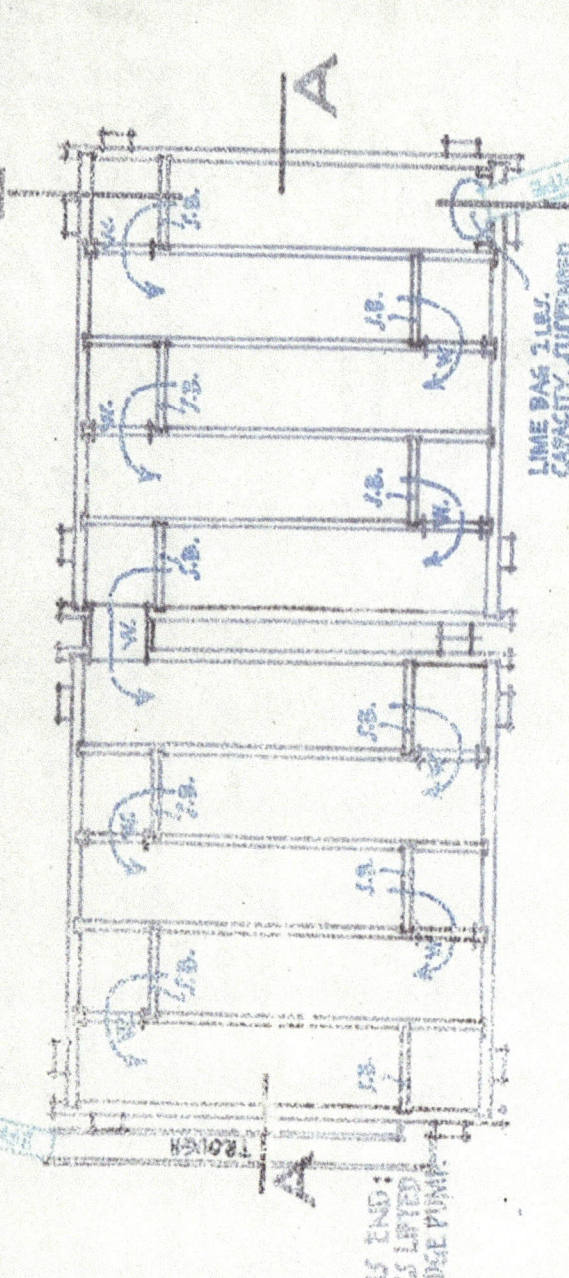

DRANOUTRE BATHS.
DETAILS OF TANKS
FOR BATH WATER.
(INDICATED AT B ON BLOCK PLAN)

SLUDGE BOX AT THIS END :
CONTENTS OF TANKS EMPTIED
INTO SAME WITH SLUDGE PUMP.

SCALE : ½" = 1 FT.

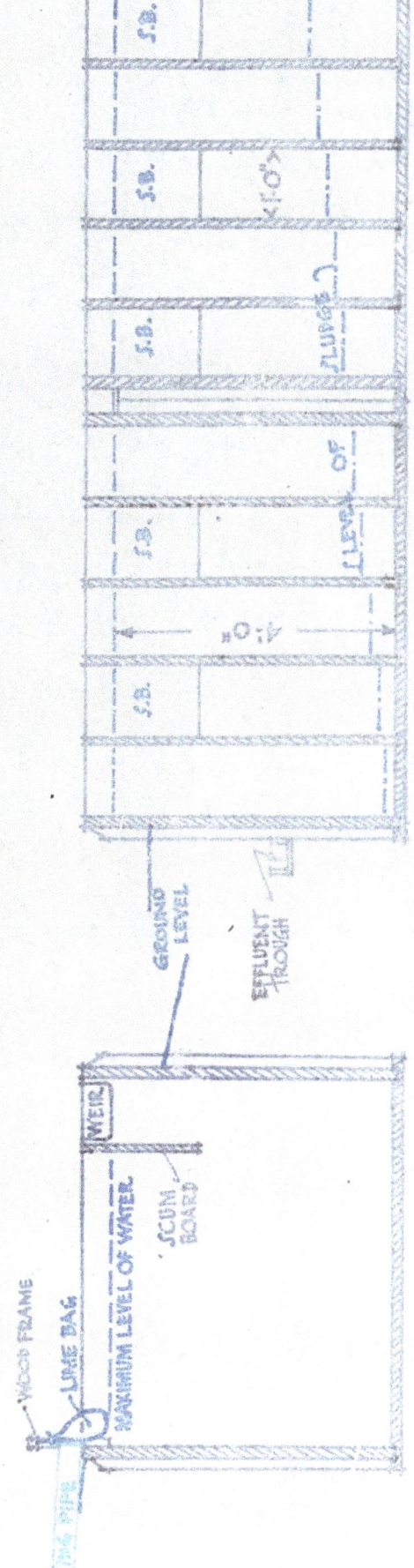

SECTION A-A.

SECTION B-B.

NOTE:— TANKS [2 IN NUMBER] ARE COUPLED. EACH TANK 5'-4" x 5'-0" x 4'-6" INSIDE DIMENSIONS, WITH COMPARTMENTS 5'-0" x 1'-0" SIDES AND BOTTOM, THE DIVISIONS 1" : THE WHOLE COATED WITH TAR & ALL JOINTS FRAMED UP UNDER PRESSURE WITH TARRED BLANKETING BETWEEN.

This tank is only sufficient size to deal with 2000 fellres a day.

Material required for Destructor
(3 ft. wide, 3 ft. broad, & 4 ft. high - inside dimensions)

———————————

750	bricks.
19	iron bars 4' 3" long. 1" x ½". (3 for supporting top, others for grate
8	" " 1' 3" " 1" x ½".
2	" " 2' 0" " 1" x ½".
2	" " 5' 0" " 1" x ½". (turned down at ends 3" to support (rubbish
2	doors. (from oil drums).
1	chimney (complete with base).
4	staples for wire to support chimney.
20	yards of wire " " ".
3	barrow loads of fine ashes
3	" " " clay.

———————————

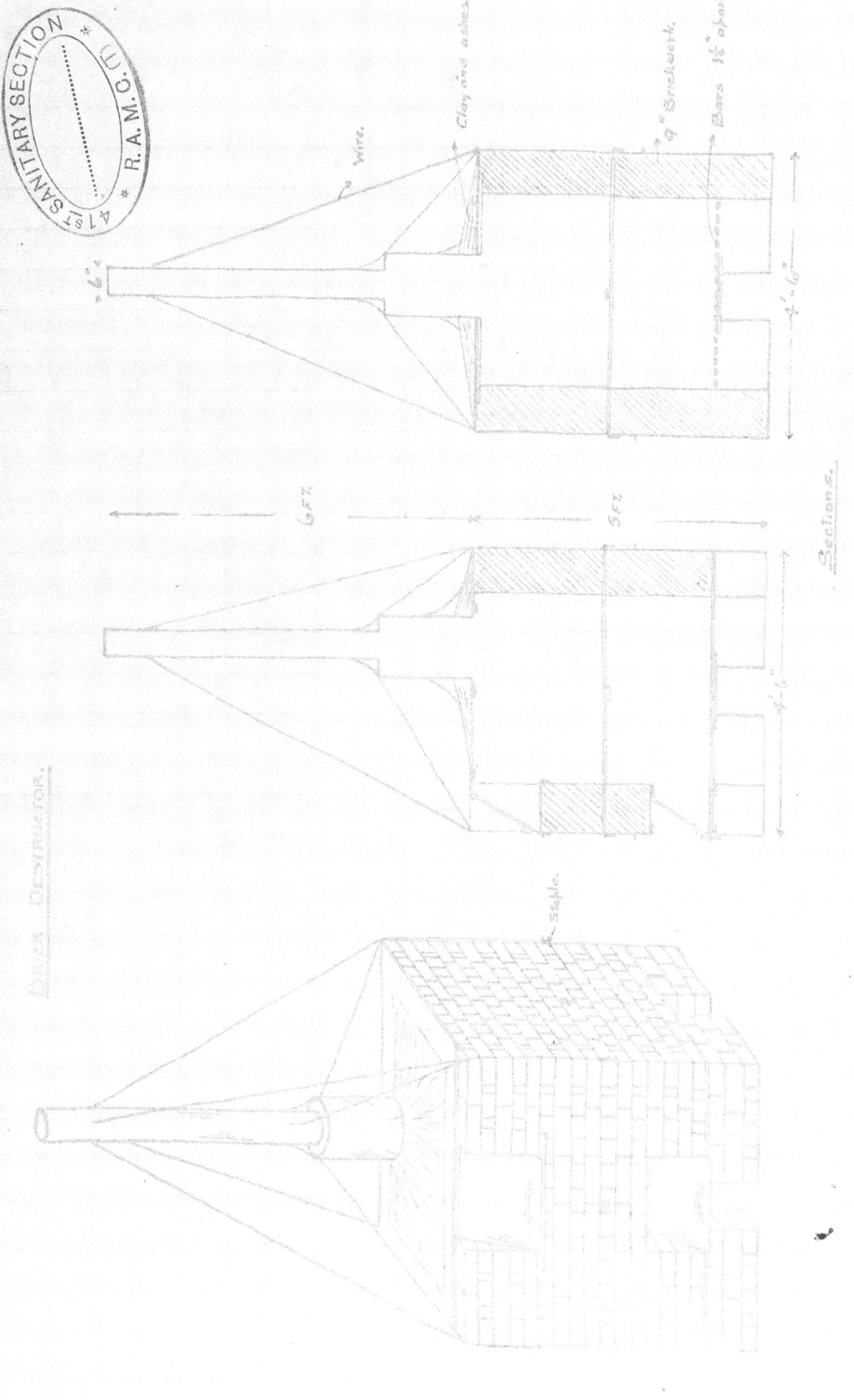

41st Sanitary Section
vol 9

COMMITTEE FOR
MEDICAL HISTORY OF THE W.
Date 26 JUN '25

41ST SANITARY SECTION
WAR DIARY
(CONFIDENTIAL)

VOLUME 9.
from 1st May to 31st May 1916.

WAR DIARY or INTELLIGENCE SUMMARY.

Army Form C. 2118.

Place	Date	Hour	Summary of Events and Information	Remarks and references to Appendices
BAILLEUL	1/5/16	—	Disinfection — Final disinfection in the following cases of measles — 194th Coy Div Train Wheeler STEPHENS " 24th Div Supply Column — Driver REYNOLDS. 1st Royal Fusiliers — disinfection of hut lately occupied by the contacts of Lt. VAN GRUISEN. 12th Sherwood Foresters — impossible to disinfect here owing to the heavy shelling of the camp by the enemy. 108th Bde. R.F.A. — "A" Battery — measles — Gr. A. LUKONS — hut disinfected — 3 contacts segregated. Baths — much progress made with second tank for dealing with bath water. Destructors — material drawn for new one at RED LODGE. U.13.c. (sheet 28) Routine at H.Q. continued Water Cart — 45 carts — 2 Units without Bleaching Powder.	WSC
	2/5/16		Received D.R.O. No⁵ 674-682, Circular 24th Div A/2233, G.R.O. 1529-1548. D.R.O. No⁵ 683-686, R.O. No⁵ 356+357, Circular A/1077 re Earthlets " The Circular will be read to all the members of the section as requested. Routine work & work on Baths proceeded with.	

WAR DIARY or INTELLIGENCE SUMMARY

Army Form C. 2118.

Place	Date	Hour	Summary of Events and Information	Remarks and references to Appendices
BAILLEUL	2nd May		Disinfection - 12th Stewards - final disinfection in case of measles - Pte MALTBY - hut at KORTEPYP Camp. - 8th Entrenching Battn - Lieut SHELLEY - measles - hut & blankets disinfected - no contacts. No 18458 Pte REDFERN - now diagnosed as measles - sent to hospital on 27th ult. suffering from Pyrexia N.Y.D. - hut disinfected - blankets had been removed - contacts 20 will remain in the hut. Water Testing - 3 samples from 8th ENTRENCHING BATTN - 2 good - one unfit for drinking purposes - report sent to A.D.M.S. Water Report - 40 carts - one unit without Bleaching Powder. Lice continues to be a scarcity of water at this point.	No 1
	3rd May		Water Testing - water at UNDERHILL FARM, Red Lodge - faint blue in 4 min. The water will be tested again meanwhile its use is forbidden for drinking purposes. Constructive work - soap waste saline in 14th R.F. Transport & 43rd Bde. T.M.B. working well. Baths ; Desimates at RED LODGE continued	No 1

Received D.R.O. Nos 687, 689.

Army Form C. 2118.

WAR DIARY
or
INTELLIGENCE SUMMARY.
(Erase heading not required.)

41st SANITARY SECTION R.A.M.C.(T)

Page 3

Place	Date	Hour	Summary of Events and Information	Remarks and references to Appendices
BAILLEUL	4 May 1916		Constructive work on Baths & Destructor at RED LODGE continued. Routine work at DHQ continued under direction of Town's Sanitary Officer. Disinfection - 12th Royal Fusiliers - 6080 F/S TAYLOR J - measles - but not disinfected as enteric numbering 15 still occupy it. The Unit moves out of this Camp on 5/6th May 1916 & the necessary disinfection will be carried out on the morning of the 6th inst. All blankets were hung out in the bright sunlight all day. Water Report - 4½ carts Shortage of water reported to ADMS. Received 24 sets of 1914 Pattern Infantry Equipment. Received G.R.O. Nos 1549-1666, D.R.O. Nos 690-694, & C.R.O. Nos 683-5 also Circular No 3489 re Captaincies in the Regular Army.	NOSE
	5 May		Constructive work on Baths & Destructor at RED LODGE continued. Water Testing - most below NEUVE EGLISE Baths tested - blue re-action obtained in 4 such so water will not be used at present. A bacteriological examination will be made. Well near BULFORD CAMP is to be finished up & pipes laid to the new tanks	

Page 4.

Army Form C. 2118.

WAR DIARY
or
INTELLIGENCE SUMMARY.

(Erase heading not required.)

Instructions regarding War Diaries and Intelligence Summaries are contained in F. S. Regs., Part II. and the Staff Manual respectively. Title pages will be prepared in manuscript.

41ST SANITARY SECTION R.A.M.C.(T)

Place	Date 1916	Hour	Summary of Events and Information	Remarks and references to Appendices
BAILLEUL	5th May		Disinfection – final disinfection after measles (18.4.16) carried out at camp of 73rd Bde H.Q. & 24th Div Supply Column	
			8th Entrenching Battalion – measles – 2/Lt MARKHAM – hut & blankets disinfected – no contacts.	
			Water Report – 12 carts	
			Water Testing – well at 40th Brigade Canteen – thus re-action in 2nd exp. At this canteen water (thus re-action in 3rd exp) from an extremist is also being used for lemonade. Instructions given re necessity for boiling same.	
			Routine work as usual. Received DRO. N[o] 695-401 Constructive work – Baths – Destructor at RED LODGE.	HST
	6th May		Inspection of nuisance at billet of C/o. 2/4th Div. Sig. Co. – full cess pit – what will receive immediate attention.	
			Disinfection – 1 Royal Fusiliers – Pte STRATTON – measles (21.5.16) – final disinfection also hut vacated by contacts of a later case.	
			Received no Orders this day.	HST

Page 5

Army Form C. 2118.

WAR DIARY
or
INTELLIGENCE SUMMARY.

Place	Date	Hour	Summary of Events and Information	Remarks and references to Appendices
BAILLEUL	6th May		Received summary of work done by Sub-section since last report:-	
			Camp inspection - "B" & "C" Companies 11th Labour Battalion & 196th Coy Div Trans	
			Re-visits to both Rest Camps, all Transport Lines & all Artillery units.	
			Disinfection - measles - "A" Battery 108th Bde R.F.A. & 737th Field Amb	
			" - fever - " - 64th R.G.A, 1st A.A. Bgy, 41st R.G.A. H.Qrs, 103rd R.E.	
			" - " - scarlet fever - 103rd R.E.	
			Water Report. 43 carts - 2 units without Bleaching Powder	
			Testing - Royal Monmouth Engrs bgy, & 103rd Field Coy R.E. - staying at M.35 central (Sheet 28) - blue re-action in 1st cup until 14½ mns	NSL
	7th May		Capt GAWTHORPE proceeded on "leave" until 14.5. mnt	
			Work at Baths & RED LODGE, & D.W.O, continued	
			Disinfection - 2nd Dr Duffy Column - 100855 Dr HOLT - measles - 18 contacts living apart from them.	
			24th Field Amb Workshops Unit - 116262. Pte HEARD - measles	
			15 contacts (whole of unit) warned re mixing with other units	

WAR DIARY or INTELLIGENCE SUMMARY

Army Form C. 2118.

Place	Date	Hour	Summary of Events and Information	Remarks and references to Appendices
BAILLEUL	7 May		Visited estaminet near H.Q. of 107th Bde R FA where a case of measles was reported. Estaminet placed out of bounds to all troops — as patient was still playing with other children in house no disinfection was carried out. BULFORD CAMP visited by O.C. — no permanent sanitary squad has yet been detailed for this camp & no sawdust is being drawn for destructors as laid down in D.R.O's. A.D.M.S. informed. Water Report — 42 carts. Received D.R.O. N° 702-3. Constructive work. Baths. — destructor at RED LODGE completed.	WSC
	8 May		Disinfection — 8th Entrenching Battalion — 2074 Pte. BLOW — measles — hut disinfected — contacts numbering 10 continue to occupy this hut. Lieut PARKER — measles — hut blankets disinfected — one contact remains in hut. 1/1 WESSEX, R.G.A. — 612 Pte. ADNUM — diphtheria — contacts 12 in number segregated — hut. blankets moving & bowl disinfected. Sedimentation tanks at BULFORD Camp are being deepened. Pte MILLS returned from "leave". Pte MESSENT hospital on leave. Camp removed from ST JANS CAPPEL to site occupied by 243 F.A.W.U.	

WAR DIARY or INTELLIGENCE SUMMARY

Army Form C. 2118.

Place	Date	Hour	Summary of Events and Information	Remarks and references to Appendices
BAILLEUL	8th May		Water Testing at T.25.b. (Sheet 28) - 2 new wells & 2 old wells. Former none of latter gave good blue re-action on 1st exp. The remaining one gave a pale blue on 1st exp. Report forwarded to A.D.M.S. Water Report - 42 sents Received D.R.O. No.s 409-412 & G.R.O. No.s 686-8.	WSL
	9th May		Sanitative work - in Bulfurs Camp - sedimentation tanks & ablution bench require attention. Work on new camp - work at DRANOUTRE suspended meanwhile. Water Testing - supplies at T.25.b. (Sheet 28) again tested - same result. Received D.R.O. No.s 413-419, G.R.O. No.s 1554-1564, & Circular on Patrol Economy. Water Report - 42 sents - one Unit without bleaching powder. New urine pit made at Y.M.C.A. NEUVE EGLISE ROAD.	WSL
	10th May		Work at new camp still proceeding. Water Report - 40 sents - one Unit without bleaching powder. Received D.R.O. No.s 420-5. & Circular on Discipline referred to in D.R.O. No 720. New Water Supply opened at DRANOUTRE - Pres MARTIN & HALDANE sent to Lab. Section to determine the supply.	WSL

WAR DIARY or INTELLIGENCE SUMMARY

Army Form C. 2118.

41ST SANITARY SECTION R.A.M.C.(T)

Place	Date	Hour	Summary of Events and Information	Remarks and references to Appendices
BAILLEUL	11th May		Two men sent to NIEPPE for materials for new destructor at Y.M.C.A. Disinfection - 171st Tunnelling Coy R.E. - Lieut HAMMOND - measles - hut blankets disinfected - one contact not segregated still sleeping in same hut. 2nd Div Supply Column - final disinfection after measles - Pte SYKES (26-4-16). Visited 4th Northants Transport Lines - found that contacts of Lt. NICHOLAS segregated on 19-4-16 had gone up to the trenches & that the tents had been well sprayed with creosol. Constructive work at BULFORD CAMP completed. Work on new camp still proceeding - there is a large accumulation of refuse left by previous occupants which will take some time to dispose of. Received Circular Q.O.S. 4 & 34/A re Clothing of Cadets & R.O. 426-430. Water Reports - Neuve Eglise - 45 carts; Dranoutre - 14 carts - one Unit without bleaching powder. Work commenced on new destructor for Y.M.C.A. & recommenced on Baths at DRANOUTRE.	W.S.L.
	12th May		Water Reports - Neuve Eglise - 41 carts; Dranoutre - 14 carts; 5 Units without Bleaching Powder.	

WAR DIARY
or
INTELLIGENCE SUMMARY.

Army Form C. 2118.

Place	Date 1916	Hour	Summary of Events and Information	Remarks and references to Appendices
BAILLEUL	12 May cont'd	—	Disinfection - 1st Royal Fusiliers - Capt HILL - measles - hut disinfected at 11.30 p.m last night. As the M.O. & O. were not present no information re contacts was available. 8th Entrenching Battn. - Capt. SHIPMAN - measles - no contacts 1055H 2nd Div. Supply Column - Dr. SPEAKMAN - measles - 19 contacts not segregated - hut & blankets disinfected	WSL
	13 May		Received D.R.O. 431-6. & Circular A/2233 re Honours & Rewards. Constructive work - baths at DRANOUTRE, destructor at Y.M.C.A Disinfection - final disinfection in cases of measles (2nd inst) - 8th Entrenching Battalion + 12 Sherwood Foresters. Received D.D.O. No. 737-8. CRO. No. 692-4, & Circular Q.369 re loads for baggage wagons. Routine work at D.H.Q. continued as before. Water Reports - NEUVE EGLISE - 36 carts, DRANOUTRE - 14 carts - 2 Units without leaving.	
	14 May		Constructive work continued at DRANOUTRE baths & the Y.M.C.A. on NEUVE EGLISE ROAD. Materials brought from NIEPPE for destructor at DRANOUTRE.	WSL

WAR DIARY
or
INTELLIGENCE SUMMARY.

(Erase heading not required.)

Army Form C. 2118.

Page 10.

41ST SANITARY SECTION
R.A.M.C. (T)

Place	Date	Hour	Summary of Events and Information	Remarks and references to Appendices
BAILLEUL	4th May cont.		Disinfection – Maid "C" of 42nd Field Amb. – one case of cerebro-spinal meningitis, also disinfected 49 blankets & pillows – final disinfection at camp of 12th Sherwood Foresters – Pte WILLIAMS & THEAKER (30th/4/16) & R.F.C. 2nd A.M. HIRONS – both measles – During the past few days two men have been engaged in the disinfection of the whole of the CONVENT, St JANS CAPPEL there having been much sickness there. Water Reports. NEUVE EGLISE 36 carts, DRANOUTRE 14 carts. Pte MILLS reposted to Sub Section at DRANOUTRE for water duty. Water testing – R.W. KENTS – Grenade School – M 30. C.5 + blue reaction in 1½ cup (Sheet-28) " " Machine Gun Co's " M 30 d 67 faint " " " " " " " " " 14th A.A. Bay – Pump – S.6.6.67 – " " " " " " " " 42nd Bde. H.Q.(T) ; S.6.6.65 – Sub-Section – Summary since last report. Camp Inspection – all units revisited. Constructional work – Horsfall destructor for R.M.R.E. " A Batty 108th Bde R.F.A. Sooty water sedimentation scheme – R.W. Kents – M.G. Company.	

2353 Wt. W2544/1454 700,000 5/15 D.D.&L. A.D.S.S.Form/C. 2118.J

Army Form C. 2118.

WAR DIARY
or
INTELLIGENCE SUMMARY.
(Erase heading not required.)

Page 11

Instructions regarding War Diaries and Intelligence Summaries are contained in F. S. Regs., Part II. and the Staff Manual respectively. Title pages will be prepared in manuscript.

41st SANITARY SECTION R.A.M.C. (T)

Place	Date 1916	Hour	Summary of Events and Information	Remarks and references to Appendices
BAILLEUL	14 May	—	Received D.R.O. No: 939-940. A.D.M.S. furnished with list of Units now having latrine refuse, & also bacteriological therein of all water supplies tested from 23/4/16 to date. Disinfection - 4th Northumberland Fusiliers - measles - case reported to 50th Divl. Sanitary Section.	N.S.L
	15 May		Constructive work continued at DRANOUTRE - baths & destructor. Latters being erected for 9th Surreys & 8th R.W. Kents. Transport. Final disinfection - 12th Sherwoods - PL REDFERN (2nd May/16) 12th Sherwoods - PL REDFERN - Camp continued. O.C. + Capt KILBURN + Rev. CANNON on leave. Routine work at D.H.Q. Camp continued. O.C. + Capt KILBURN + Rev. CANNON on leave. Received D.R.O. No: 941-944 + E.R.O. No: 1565-1546. Water - 41 + 19. Lieut MACPHERSON is acting as O.C. during Capt CARRUTHERS absence on leave.	N.S.L
	16 May		Disinfection - hut at PLOEGSTEERT WOOD strayed after case of measles which passed through 44th. F.A. Dressing Station at ROMARIN. Constructive work on destructor proceeding. Water Reports - 36 + 22. Received D.R.O. No: 941-945 + R.O. No: 363-365.	N.S.L

2353 Wt. W2514/1454 700,000 5/15 D. D. & L. A.D.S.S./Form/C. 2118.

Page 12

Army Form C. 2118.

WAR DIARY
or
INTELLIGENCE SUMMARY.
(Erase heading not required.)

Place	Date	Hour	Summary of Events and Information	Remarks and references to Appendices
BAILLEUL	14th May		Yesterday 8 cases of cerebro-spinal meningitis were reported to us from the 8th R.W. Kents but as the Unit was still occupying the trenches the dug-outs in the first line no disinfection was carried out. Late last night information reached us that the dug-outs in the first line had been vacated & disinfection of the following has been carried out to-day:- 8 dug-outs & dressing station at WULVERGHEM. Ambulance Cars & stretchers used for conveyance of patients. All blankets belonging to all patients destroyed. All contacts	
		Later	many cases have been proved to be negative. All contacts have been segregated near Transport lines of the regiment. Received D.R.O. No. 446-450. + Location of 24th Div. Artillery Wagon Lines. Water Reports - New water supply opened at DRANOUTRE - 43. 10. Yards. Work on disinfection at DRANOUTRE continued. also work at camp & D.H.Q. Water testing - T.19.a.10.b. (28) - well - very faint blue in 14 cups ", DRANOUTRE - 14 " 9 Water Reports - NEUVE EGLISE -	WSU
	15 May		Case of measles reported from 47. Northants - in front line trench 142. Received D.R.O. No. 451-456 & Circular on Petrol Consumption from A.D.M.S.	WSU

2353 Wt. W2511/1454 700,000 5/15 D, D. & L. A.D.S.S./Forms/C. 2118.

Army Form C. 2118.

WAR DIARY
or
INTELLIGENCE SUMMARY.
(Erase heading not required.)

Page 13

Instructions regarding War Diaries and Intelligence Summaries are contained in F.S. Regs., Part II. and the Staff Manual respectively. Title pages will be prepared in manuscript.

Place	Date 1916	Hour	Summary of Events and Information	Remarks and references to Appendices
BAILLEUL	19 May		Desinfector at DRANOUTRE completed.	
			Water Testing - T 19 a 10.4 - reservoir - faint blue re-action in 2nd cup.	
			S 18 a 9 8 - well - " " " 1st "	
			Disinfection - horse ambulance wagon used for conveyance of patient of ?	
			Husband refused to take yesterday.	
			Baths visited with regard to conveyance of patient of ?	
			presumably owing to wrong treatment & use of the bags is perishing	
			Water Reports - NEUVE EGLISE 38, DRANOUTRE 13, 9,	
			Received DRO No.s 454 - 463; & GRO No.s 1544 - 1684.	hS
20 May		Desinfector - truck - commenced in our camp.	
			Water Testing - now well T 26 b. 6.5 - KORTE PYP - blue re-action in 2nd cup.	
			" " " " " - " " " " 1st "	
			T 26 a 4 4 - BULFORD - " " " 1st "	
			Sgt DINNIS went to DRANOUTRE baths to instruct man in charge how to deal	
			with lime (see yesterday) Water Reports - 38 ; ; .	
			Received instruction to send No. 691 Pte MESSENT to HAVRE he having been	
			transferred to the A.S.C. (Field Butchery Dept)	
			Received DRO Nos 464 - 464.	hS

WAR DIARY
or
INTELLIGENCE SUMMARY.

Army Form C. 2118.

Page 144.

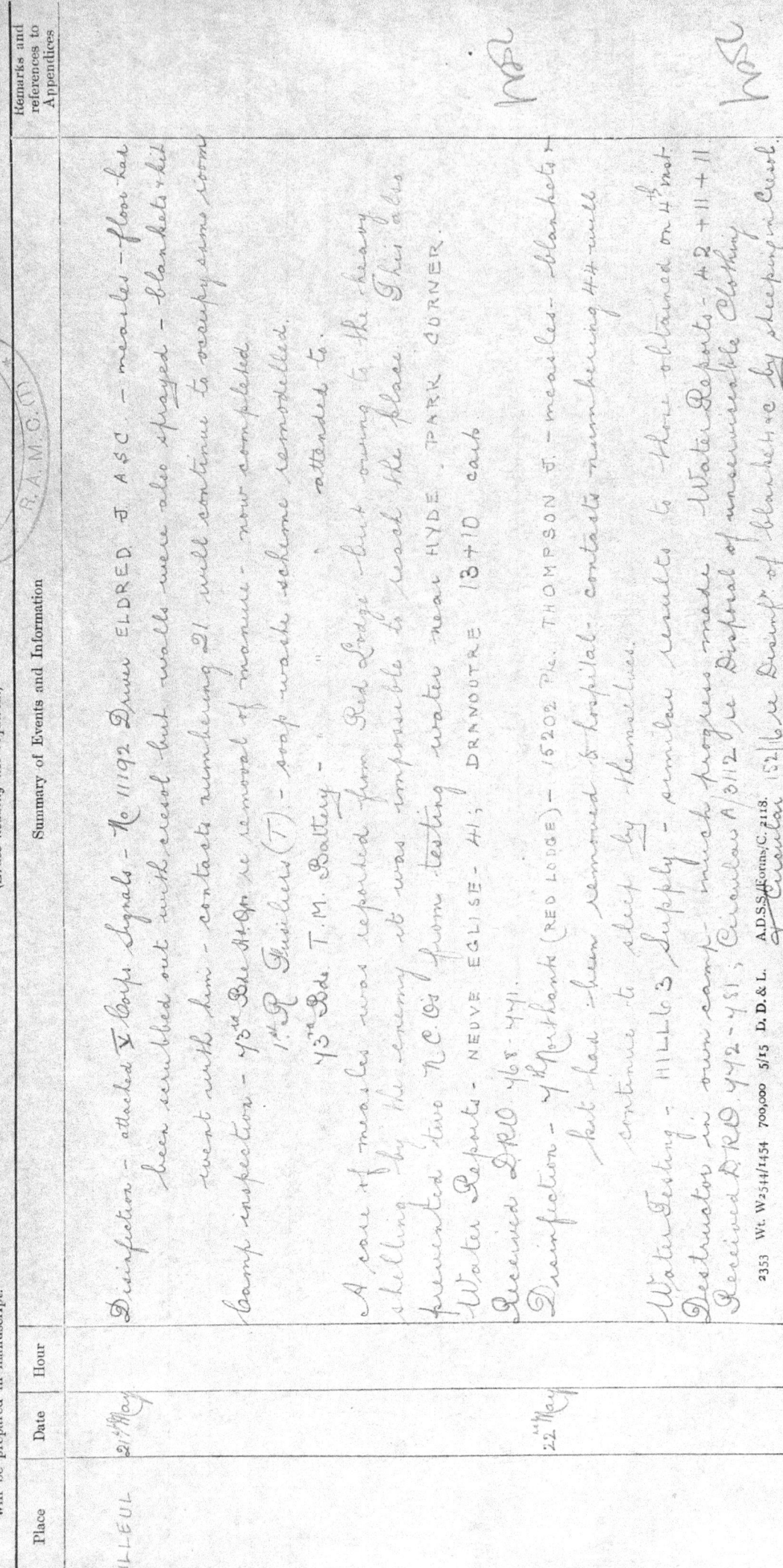

Place	Date	Hour	Summary of Events and Information	Remarks and references to Appendices
BAILLEUL	21st May		Disinfection – attacked V Corps Signals – No 11192 Driver ELDRED J. ASC. – measles – floor has been scrubbed out with creol but walls were also sprayed – blankets will sent with him – contacts numbering 21 will continue to occupy same room.	
			Camp Inspection – 73rd Bde H.Qrs. removal of manure – now completed. 1st R. Fusiliers (T) – soap waste scheme remodelled. 73rd Bde T.M. Battery – " – attended to.	
			A case of measles was reported from Red Lodge but owing to the heavy shelling by the enemy it was impossible to reach the place. This also prevented two N.C.Os from testing water near HYDE PARK CORNER.	
			Water Reports – NEUVE EGLISE – 41; DRANOUTRE 13+10 cas. Received DRO 468-471.	WSR
	22 May		Disinfection – y Northout (RED LODGE) – 15202 Pte. THOMPSON J. – measles – blankets hot had been removed to hospital – contacts numbering 44 will continue to sleep by themselves.	
			Water Testing – HILL 63 Supply – similar results to those obtained on 4th inst. Destructor in own camp making progress made. Water Reports A.2 + 11 + 11. Received DRO 472-481; Circulars A/3/112 re Disposal of unserviceable Clothing 152/16 re Disinft of Blankets by steeping in creol.	WSR

2353 Wt. W2544/1454 700,000 5/15 D.D.&L. A.D.S.S. Forms/C. 2118.

Page 15.

Army Form C. 2118.

WAR DIARY
or
INTELLIGENCE SUMMARY.
(Erase heading not required.)

Place	Date	Hour	Summary of Events and Information	Remarks and references to Appendices
BAILLEUL	23rd May	9.6	S/Sgt visited 194th Company. Dev Train re disposal of manure soak-awake. Nuisance at 2nd Div of P.O. investigated - cellar to be cleared, well in cellar to be emptied. Other routine work continued. Water Testing - T 24 & 6.5 (Dhet 28) - light blue in 3rd Corps. Issued instructions that no water from this source is to be used for drinking purposes at present. Water Reports - 39; 12; 11. Destructor in own camp completed. Received DRO No 482-489, 2O No 369-342.	WFU
	24 May		Disinfection - cases of measles reported from 4th F.A. Dressing Station at ROMARIN - the ambulance men will carry out the necessary disinfection re - case of ? typhoid reported by M.O. 3rd Rifle Brigade. Water Testing - tank on N side of road just W of HYDE PARK CORNER - distinct - 1st Corps ditto - 1st " ditto " well at RED LODGE - no blue reaction up to 6.8 cup. - very bad water. Final disinfection - 8th Entrenching Battalion (Lieut PARKER) - 171st Tunnelling Company R.E. (" HAMMOND). Tent occupied by contacts of Pte BLOW (8th Cordg. Bn) has been destroyed.	WFU

Page 16

WAR DIARY
or
INTELLIGENCE SUMMARY.
(Erase heading not required.)

Army Form C. 2118.

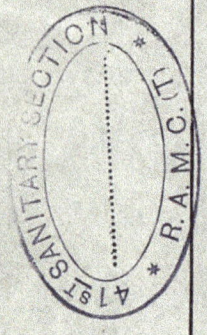

Place	Date 1916	Hour	Summary of Events and Information	Remarks and references to Appendices
BAILLEUL	24th May		Water Reports. NEUVE EGLISE ROAD – Nº1. DRANOUTRE:– 13's. 13 cwt. The water obtained from Well Nº 2 at the first named supply is now requiring 2 scuttles of Bleaching Powder per water cart. Received D.R.O. Nº 490. Cpl KILBURN & Pte. CANNON returned from "leave". Materials drawn for new latrines at GRANDE MUNQUE FARM.	WFL
	25th May		Large soap waste scheme commenced in own camp. O.C. returned from "leave". BATHS. slight alteration made to tanks Destructor (new part) – work commenced. Infectious diseases – case of measles reported from 4th F. Ambulance. 2nd Londons in trenches. In both cases disinfection was carried out by M.O. – case of scarlet fever – B/106/F.A.B – in action – dealt with by M.O. Reinforcement – No. 449. Pte. CHISNALL & family of this Section sent from 14th T.F. Base Depot. ROUEN. Water Reports.- 49; 14's; 12 carts. Routine work – as usual Received D.R.O. Nºs 491–499; G.R.O. Nºs 1585–1591; Circulars 9/3940 permitting Shorts & G.X. 365/1 re Aircraft at night.	WFL

Page 19

Army Form C. 2118.

WAR DIARY
or
INTELLIGENCE SUMMARY.
(Erase heading not required.)

Place	Date	Hour	Summary of Events and Information	Remarks and references to Appendices
BAILLEUL	26th May		Disinfection - 9th R. Sussex - KORTEPYP - 6403 Pte BOWLES - measles - contacts 15 in number not segregated - Sent gone into action to night. Constructive work - 12th RF Grande fort line + 73? Bde. T.M.B. - soap waste schemes over hauled. Dranoutre - baths - work continued. Grande Munque Line - work continued on distribution. Soap waste scheme continued in own Camp. Water Reports - DRANOUTRE - 14; 13; NEUVE EGLISE ROAD - 42 certs. Received D.R.O. Nos 800-807.	MSL
	27th May		Constructive work - at Dranoutre + Grande Munque zone continued. Received complaint from M.O. Div. Train re new brand of milk - "Zealandia" - tin sent to Canadian Mobile Laboratory. Disinfection - 1/1 Wessex R.G.A. - 359. Bomr HARCOURT - measles - 5 contacts segregated. Sgt. GOODING visited all camps pressing soap-waste scheme - all needing attention noted - he will re-visit in a few days. Received D.R.O. Nos 808-811, + G.R.O. Nos 694-701, + Circular M 365/16 on "The Jouriquet". Water Reports - 443; 17; 12 certs.	MSL

WAR DIARY or INTELLIGENCE SUMMARY

Army Form C. 2118.

41st SANITARY SECTION R.A.M.C.(T)

Place	Date	Hour	Summary of Events and Information	Remarks and references to Appendices
BAILLEUL	28 May		Destructor at GRANDE MUNQUE FARM completed. Work in DRANOUTRE Baths continued. Soap-work scheme at own Camp complete. Water Testing. The water in the new wells at BULFORD & KORTEPYP Camps has been tested daily for the past 4 days. The quality of the water in the first well has proved to be consistently good, but in the second the quality has varied a great deal from time to time. Daily reports have been forwarded to ADMS. Disinfectors - 8nd. 5th Entrenching Battalion (8e SHIPMAN) & 2nd Div Supply Column (2nd SPEAKMAN & HARRISON). Received no "Orders" this day. Water Reports - 42, 13, 14 carts	MO2
	29 May		Constructive work - destructor at KORTEPYP is to be pulled down re-built as owing to improper stoking it has got into disrepair. Work on improvement of Baths continued. Sgt. visited chief Camps re condition of soap-work scheme. He will supervise any renovations necessary. Water Reports - 40, 18, 13 carts. Received D.R.O. 812-820; D.R.O N° 702 - 706, & List of Stores made at 2nd Army Workshops.	MO2

Page 18

Army Form C. 2118.

WAR DIARY
or
INTELLIGENCE SUMMARY.
(Erase heading not required.)

Place	Date	Hour	Summary of Events and Information	Remarks and references to Appendices
BAILLEUL	30th May		Summary of work done by Sub-Section at DRANOUTRE. Camp Inspection :- 2 Infantry Rest Camps, all 42nd Bde Transport, all 42nd Bde Transport, 108th F.A.B.- HQr, 'A' + 'B' Amm. Column No 1. C/109/F.A.B. Constructive work:- destructor No 1 Am Col.; pump attached to well at 42nd Bn Canteen + platform at the Public Destructor - all completed. Water Testing - Glasgow Yeomanry - N.31.B. Sgt. visited + reported on condition of all destructors, burning latrines & refuse in 142 + 143 Brigade areas. All defective ones will be repaired or new ones built. Work on KORTEPYP destructor continued. Own destructor repaired. Work on Baths continued. Will reference to milk sent b Laboratory (see 27/B inst.) report received:- "There was nothing wrong with the tin of milk - the contents of which were shewn." Forwarded to M.O. + S.S.O. Div Train Water Reports = 46; 10; 19 carts - one Unit without Bleaching powder. Routine work at D.H.Q. continued. Received D.R.O. No 821-826.	MF

Page 19.

WAR DIARY
or
INTELLIGENCE SUMMARY.

Army Form C. 2118.

Place	Date	Hour	Summary of Events and Information	Remarks and references to Appendices
BAILLEUL	31st May 1916		Camp Inspection – 73rd Bde M.G. Company, 13th Middlesex Transport, 2nd Lincolns Transport, 4th/3rd Authorits Transport – all visited by Lt. GOODING who will visit daily until chief defects have been remedied. Constructive Work – much progress made with destructor in KORTEPYP Camp. Divisional Baths – experimenting with anthracite duff in laundry filter. Materials drawn from NIEPPE for new destructor in Camp of B/106/F.A.B. D.H.Q. visited & cleaned as usual. Received D.R.O. No. 827 – 830.	WFL

41 San Sec
vol 10
June

COMMITTEE FOR THE
MEDICAL HISTORY OF THE WAR
5 AUG. 1916
Date

41ST SANITARY SECTION
WAR DIARY
(CONFIDENTIAL)

VOLUME 10.

from 1st June to 30th June 1916.

Page 1

Army Form C. 2118.

Instructions regarding War Diaries and Intelligence Summaries are contained in F. S. Regs., Part II. and the Staff Manual respectively. Title pages will be prepared in manuscript.

WAR DIARY
or
INTELLIGENCE SUMMARY.
(Erase heading not required.)

Place	Date	Hour	Summary of Events and Information	Remarks and references to Appendices
BAILLEUL	1st June 1916		Water Testing - stream called "BOLLENBEEK" on KEMMEL HILL tested - pale blue re-action in 1st Cup - good re-action in 2nd Cup. The water, however, was muddy as there has been no rain now for some days. The O.C. will investigate the source & course of stream to-morrow.	N.O.C.
			Disinfection - B/106/F.A.B - Lieut. CORQUODALE - scarlet fever - 3 contacts segregated - all blankets disinfected.	
			Camps visited - "43rd Bde M.G. Coy, 13th Middlesex T, 13th Rohart T, & 13th Bde Hd Qrs - all defects will be followed up by Lt. GOODING	
			D.H.Q. :- The following report is typical of work done daily by N.C.O's Helpers: All latrines attached to Billets, Messes & cook houses scrubbed.	
			2. Refuse removed from some all cook houses. Yards swept & cleaned	
			3. Stables, yards swept manure removed.	
			4. Chloride of lime placed where necessary.	
			5. After above was done men went on road sweeping & one to the destructor.	
			Destructor :- KORTE PYP Camp - completed, B/106/F.A.B. - everything obtained for the Baths :- work continued. Received D.R.O. 831-5; G.R.O. 1592-1609; Special G.R.O.	

T.M11. W. W708-776. 500000. 4/15. Sir J.C. & S.

Army Form C. 2118.

WAR DIARY
or
INTELLIGENCE SUMMARY.
(Erase heading not required.)

Page 2.

Instructions regarding War Diaries and Intelligence Summaries are contained in F. S. Regs., Part II. and the Staff Manual respectively. Title pages will be prepared in manuscript.

Place	Date	Hour	Summary of Events and Information	Remarks and references to Appendices
BAILLEUL	2nd June		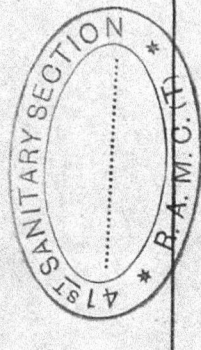 Disinfection - 12. K.O. Fusiliers - 19529 Pte ELKINS G. & BULFORD CAMP - Pose measles - hut disinfected. Blankets & kit had been packed on lorries as Unit moves forward to-night. Contacts - 18 - will be kept isolated in the trenches as far as possible.	
			Destructors - B/106/F.A.B - completed 8th June - base fired HYDE PARK CORNER - material drawn	
			Baths - Laundry scheme - new sludge bed & box made. Anthracite duff is to be used as an extra filtering medium	
			Camp Inspection - 14/1 T.M. Battery, 9th R. Sussex T., 473rd Bde M.G. Coy for a few days attention will be confined to 9th R. Sussex T. who are without a satisfactory ablution place, grease trap incinerator destructor &c. Lt. GOODING will have all these erected forthwith.	
			Water Testing - 06 found that the BOLLANBEEK stream receives the sewage washed from LOCRE; also that another stream on KEMMEL HILL which it was intended to use runs parallel with a proposed new road so both streams were condemned.	
			Received D.R.O. 836-839, B.R.O. 404-409, & Circular G.S. 615/2 re Gas Helmet Construction.	Nov

Page 3

WAR DIARY or INTELLIGENCE SUMMARY
Army Form C. 2118.

Place	Date	Hour	Summary of Events and Information	Remarks and references to Appendices
BAILLEUL	3rd June	—	Constructive work:- Destructor for 13th Middlesex Transport- site chosen arrangements made to draw materials for same to-morrow. Wire cage set up for burning of horse manure. Destructor - B/106/F.A.B.- bottom door fixed & bricks to 13th course laid. - HYDE PARK CORNER - commenced - 10 courses laid. Bath - drying bed 9'×5'×2' of anthracite duff laid for laundry water. Routine work continued at D.H.Q. Shortage of ablution water reported from DRANOUTRE Infantry Rest Camp. Will investigate same to-morrow morning. Water Reports 5, 6, 14; 3. 14.	Received D.R.O. N°'s 40 - 1. WSL
"	4th June		Constructive work:- Destructor - 13th Middlesex Transport - materials drawn. B/106/F.A.B. - 4 more courses laid & top door fixed. HYDE PK CORNER - completed except for pointing. The step in front & place for stage will be made to-morrow. Baths - cleaning of pits &c carried on. 96- visited DRANOUTRE re ablution water suggested sites for wells to the punb. Water testing - 4 wells - B. + b. vicinity of 129th Tun'lg Company R.E.= one +h, one 2nd + two others gave - blue re-action in 11th Cup. Received D.R.O. 84 2-6	WSL

T.M51. Wt. W708-776. 500000. 4/15. Sh J.C. & S.

WAR DIARY
or
INTELLIGENCE SUMMARY.

Army Form C. 2118.

Page 4

Place	Date	Hour	Summary of Events and Information	Remarks and references to Appendices
BAILLEUL	5 June	—	Constructive works:- Destructors:- B/106/F.A.B & HYDE PARK CORNER - both completed. 9th R. Sussex Transport - 5 courses laid. Baths:- working of scheme superintended. Routine work at D.H.Q continued - S/Sgt inspected everywhere to-day, found everything satisfactory. Summary of work done by Sub-section at DRANOUTRE :- Revisits to all Units - Infantry & Artillery in the Area. " " " " " Instructors in the Area - all burning well.	
	6 June		Received D.R.O. N° 847 - 850. Water Reports:- 48 ; 14 ; 4 . A very wet day, consequently outdoor work did not progress very much. Constructive work :- Destructor - 9th R. Sussex Transport - 4 courses laid at Seabridge removed into wood - 4 courses laid Baths - both efficients dealt with as usual. Disinfection - final - 2nd Leinsters Transport after case of measles brought down from the trenches, 25th ult. " Methents - hut & tent - after case of suspicious typhoid - KORTE PYP Camp. Received D.R.O. 851 - 856 ; G.R.O. 70,910 ; & R.O. 378 - 383.	NFC

WAR DIARY
or
INTELLIGENCE SUMMARY.

Army Form C. 2118.

41st SANITARY SECTION R.A.M.C.(T)

Place	Date	Hour	Summary of Events and Information	Remarks and references to Appendices
BAILLEUL	5th June		Disinfection - final - E. boys "signals" - measles - first disinfection on 21st ult. Constructive work - Destructor - 9th R Sussex - 16 courses laid	
			2nd " - bottom door & grid laid, also 9 courses near Rest Lodge	Brickwork
			Camp Inspection - 164th Field Company R.E. H.Q 109/F.A.B. D/109/F.A.B. } 43rd DIVN 18.	
			Baths:- experiment made with regard to burning of sludge from laundry water. 2/3 will burn easily in one of camp destructors	
			Received information from D.M.S 2nd Army that 10969 Qr G.W. BROWN, 8th R.W. Kents, M.G. Section 42nd Bde. is suffering from typhoid. Enquiry at the 43rd F.A. Dressing Station elicited the fact that he was inoculated on 4.5.16 diagnosed 'Gas Poisoning'	
			Received no "Orders to-day."	NIL
	6th June		Constructive work:- Destructor - 9th R Sussex T - completed, 2nd one near Rest Lodge - top field; D/109/F.A.B. - 9 courses of brickwork laid	
			Baths - material drawn for alterations (see later page) Routine work continued Received D.R.O's 854-863; L.R.O's 1610-1617. 2 Special L.R.O.'s	NIL

Army Form C. 2118.

WAR DIARY
or
INTELLIGENCE SUMMARY.
(Erase heading not required.)

Place	Date	Hour	Summary of Events and Information	Remarks and references to Appendices
BAILLEUL 	9th June		Constructive work :- Destructors :- 43rd Bde Machine Gun Company - building commenced. D/104/F.A.B. - completed except for pointing mixing place. 2nd one at Rid Lodge completed & burning. Baths :- drying bed for sludge completed. D.H.Q. - usual routine work in addition to which soap work scheme almost completed for R.E. Signals. Camp - much progress made with shower bath scheme. Received b.q.o 40 411-414.	
	10th June		Destructors :- 43rd M.G. Company - twelve courses of brickwork, bottom door & grid finished. D/104/F.A.B. - finally completed. Camp Inspection - C/104/F.A.B. + A/104/F.A.B. - both have destructors working. Disinfection :- 14th Bde M.G. Company (Count Drew) - 6949 Pte BYWATER. W. - measles. loft disinfected - contacts numbering 30 occupy loft. Baths - routine work. Outlet to settling tank to be lowered. Camp - work continued on shower bath scheme. Received D.R.O. 864-872; Circular re use of Petrol tins; Special Order of the Day by the C. in C. relating to the great naval battle off Jutland.	NSC

Page 1.

Army Form C. 2118.

WAR DIARY
or
INTELLIGENCE SUMMARY.
(Erase heading not required.)

Instructions regarding War Diaries and Intelligence Summaries are contained in F. S. Regs., Part II. and the Staff Manual respectively. Title pages will be prepared in manuscript.

Place	Date	Hour	Summary of Events and Information	Remarks and references to Appendices
BAILLEUL	1/11 June		Constructive Work:- Destructors - 98th M.G. Company - completed.	
			Camp - work on shower bath & soap scheme attached continued.	
			Baths - outlet lowered - Laundry scheme.	
			24th Signals: soap trap completed	
			Camps visited - "A", "C", "D"/106/F.A.B.; B/109/F.A.B.; 9th R. Surrey (T) & 13th Middlesex (T)	NFL
			Received no "Orders"	
	12 June		Constructive Work:- Commenced to repair Destructors (3) - Canadian type - in Bulford Camp.	
			A/106/F.A.B. - old destructor demolished; 6 courses of new one laid	
			Baths - routine work	
			D.H.Q. - in addition to usual work the rain water well, another small well & cesspool under F.P.O. pumped out to try remedy the nuisance there.	
			Disinfection:- 4th Northants - 22826 Pte BRAY. A. - measles - contacts 22 - the Unit moved forward last night.	
			4th R.M.R.E. - 6090 Spr. WHITWORTH. H. - suspected typhoid - suspected typhoid - hut & blankets disinfected - contacts 14 placed in 3 tents & segregated.	
			Camps visited - Transport - 6th Buffs, 1st R.F., 12th R.F., 14th M.G. Coy, 3rd R.B., 13 T.M. 4th Northants.	NFL
			Received D.R.O. 1615-1631; Q.R.O. 885; Special Order re death of Lord Kitchener.	

WAR DIARY or INTELLIGENCE SUMMARY

Army Form C. 2118.

Place	Date	Hour	Summary of Events and Information	Remarks and references to Appendices
BAILLEUL	13th June	—	Constructive work :- Destructors - A/106/F.A.B. - 9 covers & fruit doors fixed.	
			" - Bulford - large incinerator repaired	
			" - Baths - outlet made water tight.	
			D.H.Q - routine & cesspools at R.E. HdQrs thoroughly cleaned out &c.	
			Camps visited :- "13th Bde T.M Battery, 1/1 R. Lincolns (T), 8th Buffs (T), Bulford & Aldershot camps with regard to soap waste - all but the Unit in Bulford have scheme in good working order.	NSC
			Received D.R.O. No. 886 - 892. L/Sgt. went to Defensive bar class until 15th inst.	
	14th June		Constructive work. Destructors - A/106/F.A.B. - completed.	
			" - Bulford - "	
			" - 1/1 Northants - materials drawn.	
			" Grease traps - 2 on R.E.'s premises.	
			Water testing - Transport lines of 4/2nd F.A. - pond - S.15.d.3.8 (28) - 6th Cup.	
			Brick lined moat - S.15.d.1.2. (") - 3rd "	
			The case of Typhoid (see 12th inst) has been proved to be negative. Water on KEMMEL HILL tested - 2nd Cup. New latrines &c are to be erected here at once.	NSC

Page 9

Army Form C. 2118.

WAR DIARY
or
INTELLIGENCE SUMMARY.
(Erase heading not required.)

[Stamp: 41ST SANITARY SECTION R.A.M.C.(T)]

Place	Date	Hour	Summary of Events and Information	Remarks and references to Appendices
BAILLEUL	15 June		Constructive work: Destructors - Ploegsteert Woods - material drawn 4th Gurkhas - service door transfixed.	NSC
			Water testing - wells above Nieue Eglise Baths - in two of the four water is very good.	
			Baths & D.H.Q. - routine work as usual.	
			Received D.R.O. 898-9.	
	16th June		Constructive work: Destructors - Ploegsteert Woods - 12 covers, door, bars fitted. 4th Gurkhas - 9", top door "	NSC
			Covers to latrines at rear of C.R.E's office.	
			Meat safe & store for Sub-Section.	
			Camp Inspection - 12th R Fusiliers, 14th Bde M.G. Coy, 14th & 43rd Bde Transport HQrs.	
			Received D.R.O. 900-904.	
	17th June		Constructive work - Destructors - Ploegsteert Woods - brickwork completed. 4th Gurkhas - completed.	NSC
			New sludge bed at the Baths.	
			Camp Inspection - all the Transport of 14th Brigade.	
			Received Circular 222/16 (Romd) re Gas alert.	

Page 10.

Army Form C. 2118.

WAR DIARY
or
INTELLIGENCE SUMMARY.
(Erase heading not required.)

Place	Date	Hour	Summary of Events and Information	Remarks and references to Appendices
BAILLEUL	18th June	—	Constructive Work:- Destructions - Ploegsteert Woods - fixed & & finished brickwork. Material drawn for H.Q./109/F.A.B.	
			Camp visited - 17th Bde H.Qrs	
			Baths - tanks cleaned, also stream.	
			In the afternoon a lecture on Gas & how to combat it by L/Sgt. who has just completed a course at the Defensive Gas School. The lecture was followed by a thorough inspection of gas helmets & goggles. The same lecture will be given to the Sub. sections	NDL
			No "Orders issued to-day	
	19 June	—	Constructive work :- H.Q. 109/F.A.B - 8 courses of brickwork & bars fixed. 14th M.G. Coy - preliminary work done. Ploegsteert Woods - completed.	
			Baths & D.H.Q - routine work continued	
			Camps visited - "A" & "B" - D/106/F.A.B, B/104, & A/109.	
			Received D.R.O No 905-914; & R.O. 1632-1642. In connection with R.O. 1639 necessary Indent forwarded for "Tyreine.	NDL

WAR DIARY
or
INTELLIGENCE SUMMARY.

Place	Date	Hour	Summary of Events and Information	Remarks and references to Appendices
BAILLEUL	20th June		Constructive work - Destructors - 17th M.G. Company - 11 covers grid + door fixed. HQ/109/F.A.B. - 10 " + top door " "	
			Baths & DHQ - routine work continued	
			Camps visited - HQ/109, "A" + "C"/107, B/109/F.A.B.	
			Water Testing - 12, Ruelle d'Ypres where HQrs M.T. A.S.C. men are billetes - pale blue in 4th cup - Sanitary Officer of the town informed + supply sealed.	
			Received DRO No 918-9	NDL
21st June			Constructive work - Destructors - 17th M.G. Company - almost completed. HQ/109 F.A.B. - completed.	
			Baths - supports fixed for pipe from laundry tank to bath tank	
			Camps visited - DAC Section I; C/106; D/107/F.A.B, & Bulford Camp	
			D.HQ - routine work only	
			Lecture on Gas (see 18th inst.) given to Inh. destroyed at DRANOUTRE.	
			Received D.R.O. Nos 920 - 923 + Special After Order re Gas attack 16/17	
			New Camps - BADAJOZ + WAKEFIELD at LOCRE - visited by OC	NDL

Army Form C. 2118.

Page 12

Instructions regarding War Diaries and Intelligence Summaries are contained in F. S. Regs., Part II. and the Staff Manual respectively. Title pages will be prepared in manuscript.

WAR DIARY
or
INTELLIGENCE SUMMARY.
(Erase heading not required.)

Place	Date	Hour	Summary of Events and Information	Remarks and references to Appendices
BAILLEUL	22 June	—	Constructive work - two urine pits provided at the Div Train H.Qrs. Destructor - 14th M.G. Company completed. Baths - routine work. Camps visited - 194th, 195th, & 197th Companies, A.S.C., H.Qrs D.A.C. D.A.C. Section II; 36th Mobile Vet. Section; D/106; D/108/F.A.B. Received circulars 9/11/16 "Camp" & "Trench Stores" Q 4260. "Guides to Rifilling Point" M/430/263 "Precautions against Gas Attack". D.R.O. No 924-928 Infectious Diseases reported to us - 4th Bde, 24th Batts Australian Inf. Bde. - measles - KORTEPYP Camp. - disinfection to ensue. 1st Royal Fusiliers - 89th! The Johnson R. - suspect typhoid	NSC
	23rd June		Constructive work - superintended new forms of grease trap for BULFORD - necessary notice boards made. Destructor - WAKEFIELD HUTS - materials drawn. Disinfection - measles - KORTEPYP - Pte BOULTON No 3026 - 19 contacts - hut disinfected Camps visited - 14th T.M. Batteries, H.Qrs/106/F.A.B; 8th Entrenching Battalion Received D.R.O. No 929-933.	NSC

Page 13

Army Form C. 2118.

WAR DIARY
or
INTELLIGENCE SUMMARY.
(Erase heading not required.)

41ST SANITARY SECTION
R.A.M.C. (T)

Place	Date	Hour	Summary of Events and Information	Remarks and references to Appendices
BAILLEUL	24 June		Constructive work. Destructors - Help of 5the Australian Infantry - ENGLISH FARM - sources & grid fixed.	
			Camps visited - 1491st Travelling Coy R.E.; 2nd Divl T.M. Batteries; D.A.C. Section 4. The second named is to have a destructor.	
			D.H.Q. - Baths - routine work. Received D.R.O. No. 933-9	NSL
	25 June		Constructive work - Destructors - ENGLISH FARM - destructor completed.	
			Incinerator - 1st N. Staffs	
			Urinal - Infantry Rest Camp. DRANOUTRE	
			Baths - filters re cleaned & renewed	
			Camps visited - all Units having chloride of lime purification scheme for slop waste. The majority were being used indifferently.	
			Received D.R.O. No. 940-1.	NSL
	26 June		Constructive work - Destructors - ENGLISH FARM - destructor pointed - making chamber finished	
			WAKEFIELD HUTS - materials drawn - foundations	
			Camps visited :- Hodspyp, 93rd H.Sp, Red Lodge, 13th Middlesex & 9th R. Sussex (T). - new sanitary squads had all work well in hand.	
			D.H.Q. - soap filler renewed.	NSL

Page 114.

WAR DIARY
or
INTELLIGENCE SUMMARY.
(Erase heading not required.)

Army Form C. 2118.

Place	Date	Hour	Summary of Events and Information	Remarks and references to Appendices
BAILLEUL	27 June		Constructive Work: - WAKEFIELD HUTS - destructor almost completed.	
			D/108/F.A.B. - materials for destructor partly drawn	
			D.H.Q. :- special attention to drain - R.E. Mess - 110, Rue d'Ypres.	
			Received D.R.O. Nos 942-947; C.R.O. Nos 718-722; R.O. Nos 394-396	NSC
	28 June		Constructive Work: - WAKEFIELD HUTS - destructor completed.	
			Destructor } D/108/F.A.B - mixing chamber & first few courses completed. Iron	
			} work will be ready to morrow morning.	
			D.H.Q. :- work on drains continued. Baths - routine work only	
			Received D.R.O. Nos 948-953.	NSC
	29 June		Constructive work - D/108/F.A.B. destructor almost completed	
			Routine work continued at D.H.Q. + Dranoutre	
			Received D.R.O. Nos 954-8	NSC
	30 June		Destructor for D/108/F.A.B completed.	
			Preparations made for 'move' to C.R.E. Work at D.H.Q. + Baths continued	
			Received D.R.O. Nos 959-961.	NSC

Appendix

Treatment of Waste Water at DRANOUTRE BATHS

To Volume 8 of the War Diary for April 1916 detailed drawings of the proposed method of dealing with the waste were appended. This scheme has been carried out in part, experience having shown that the following alterations were necessary:—

(a) Effluent from Bath House. The original capacity of the tanks proved inadequate, the effluent passing through too quickly to allow of sufficient sedimentation, so another tank was made, making the total capacity equal to half a day's flow, viz 2000 gallons. The chloride of lime is mixed in a vessel drum having a small hole near the bottom so a man has to constantly stir the mixture so that a stream of the solution flows on to the effluent as it passes into the tank. The water as it leaves the tank is quite clear.

(b) Effluent from the Laundry. The opening from the tank to the side filter had to be lowered 1 foot, as it was found that when the chloride of lime was mixed with the effluent & stirred vigorously most of the deposit became mixed with air bubbles & rose to the top of the tanks, only a small amount sinking. The method of allowing the sludge to fall into a canvas bag was abandoned owing to the corrosive action of the lime destroying the bag.

WSR

Army Form C. 2118.

WAR DIARY
or
INTELLIGENCE SUMMARY.
(Erase heading not required.)

Place	Date	Hour	Summary of Events and Information	Remarks and references to Appendices
			<u>Appendix continued</u>	
			The sludge is now spread upon a bed of coal slack when nearly dry & burned in a Destructor.	
			The amount of chloride of lime used is roughly equal to the amount of soap used so that it is essential to know both the volume of liquid to be treated & the soap used when preparing a similar scheme.	
			The present one has now been working satisfactorily for a week. The only objection to it is the amount of supervision necessary.	NSC

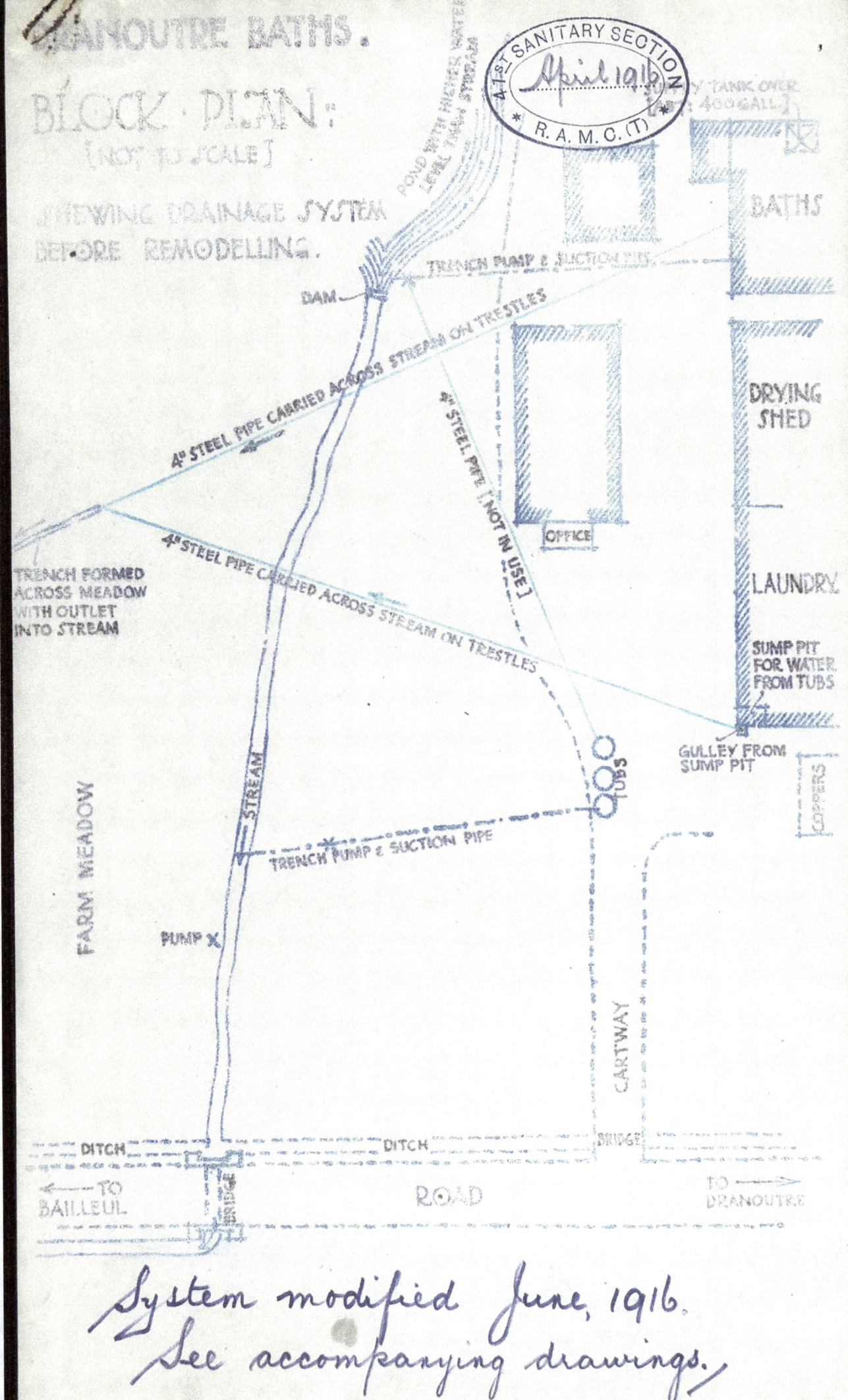

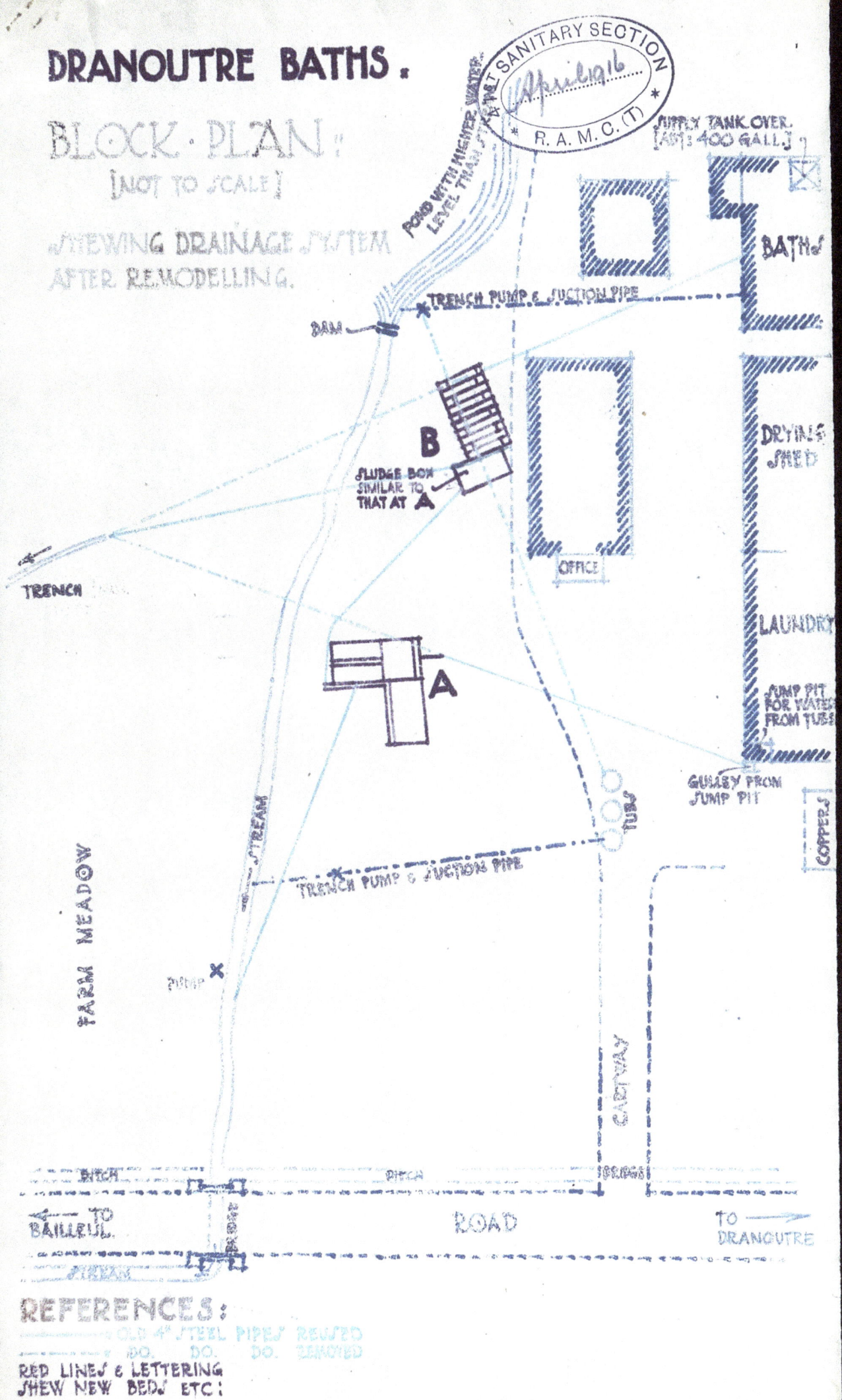

DRANOUTRE BATHS.

DETAILS OF TANKS FOR LAUNDRY WATER.
[INDICATED AT "A" ON BLOCK PLAN].

SCALE: ½" = 1 FOOT.

NOTE :- ALL BOXES COATED WITH TAR & JOINTS FRAMED UP UNDER PRESSURE WITH TARRED BLANKETING BETWEEN.

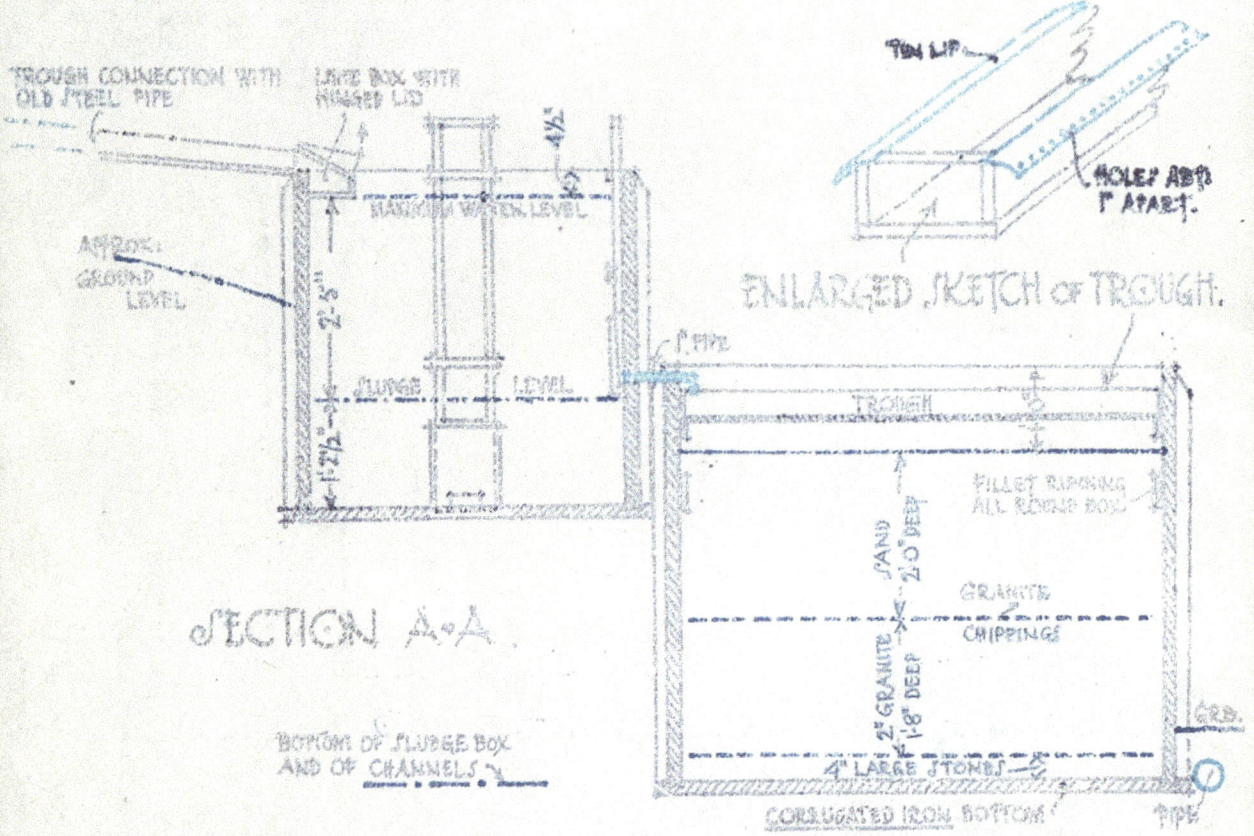

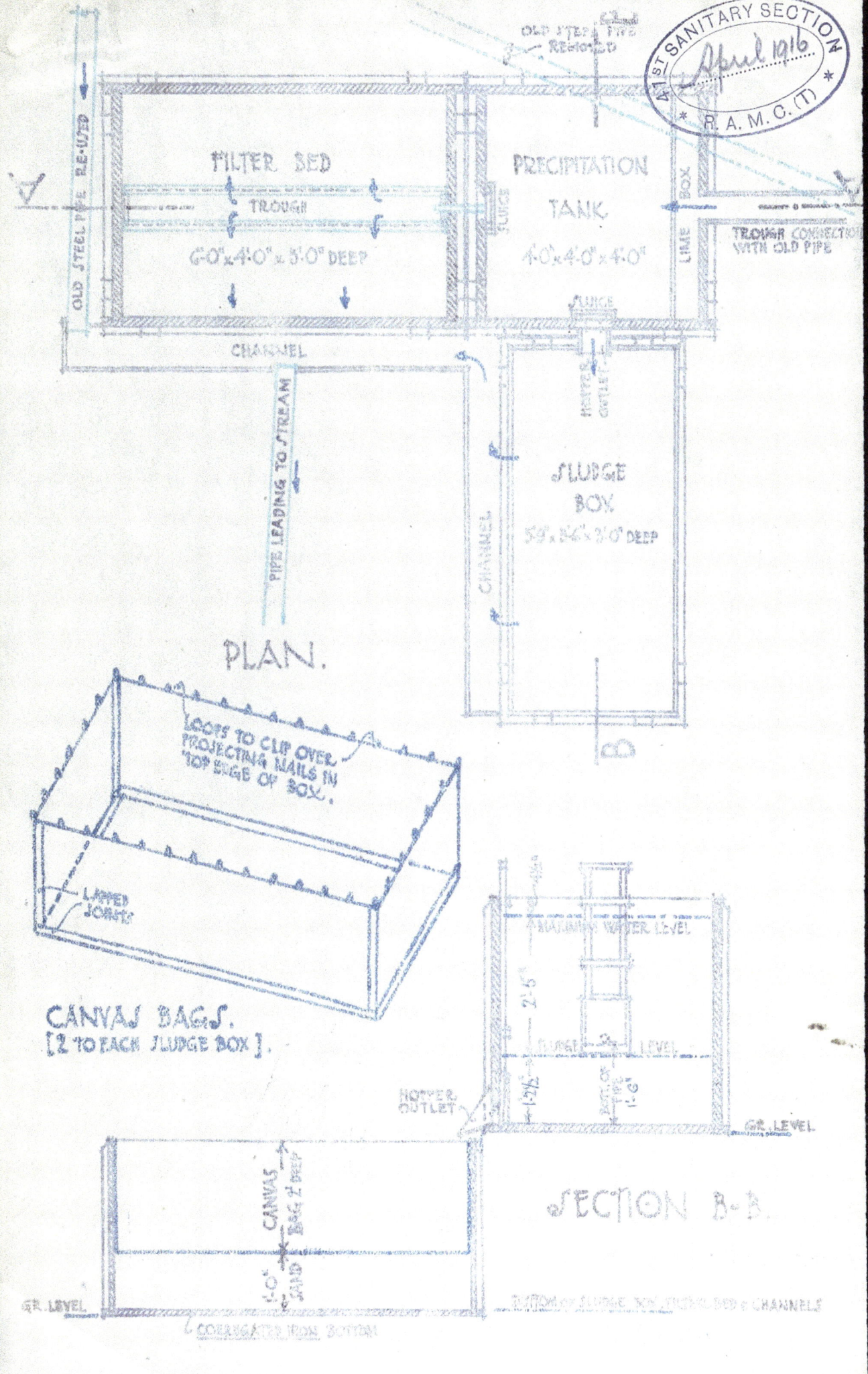

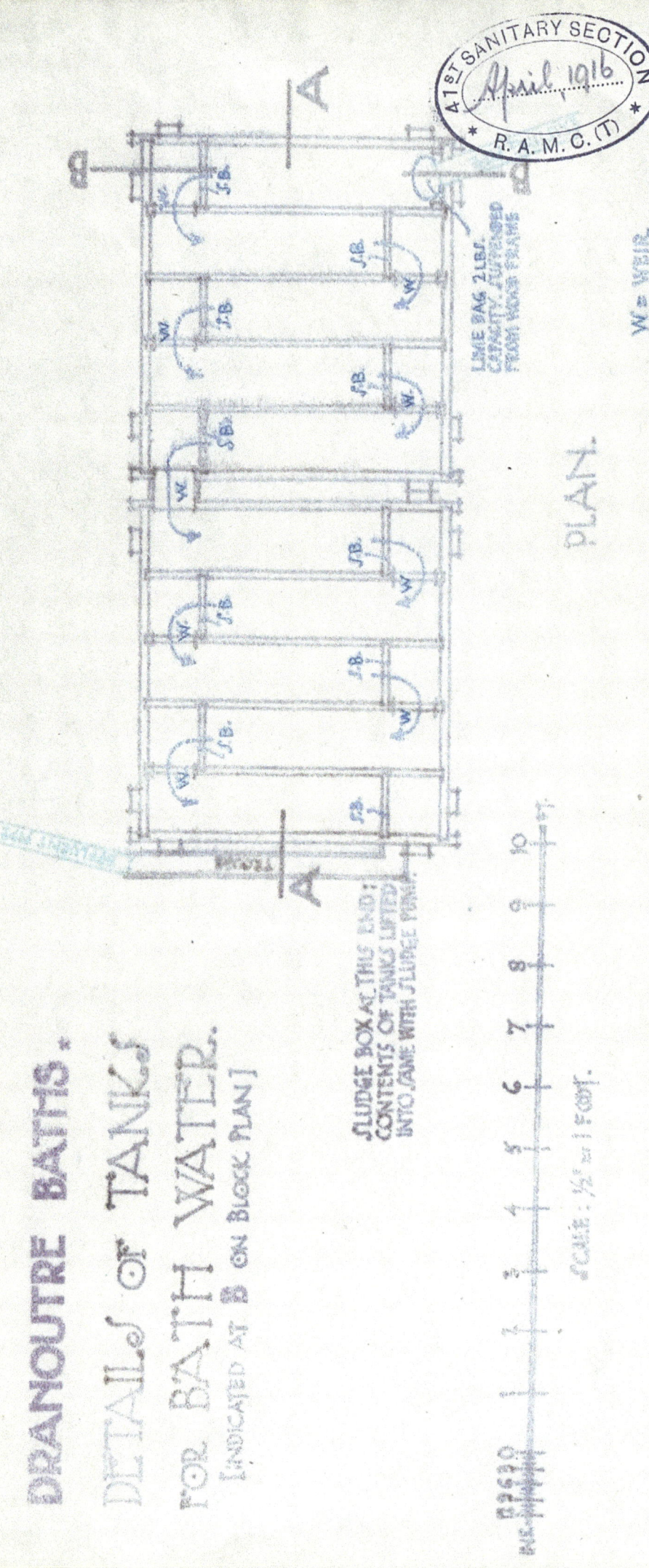

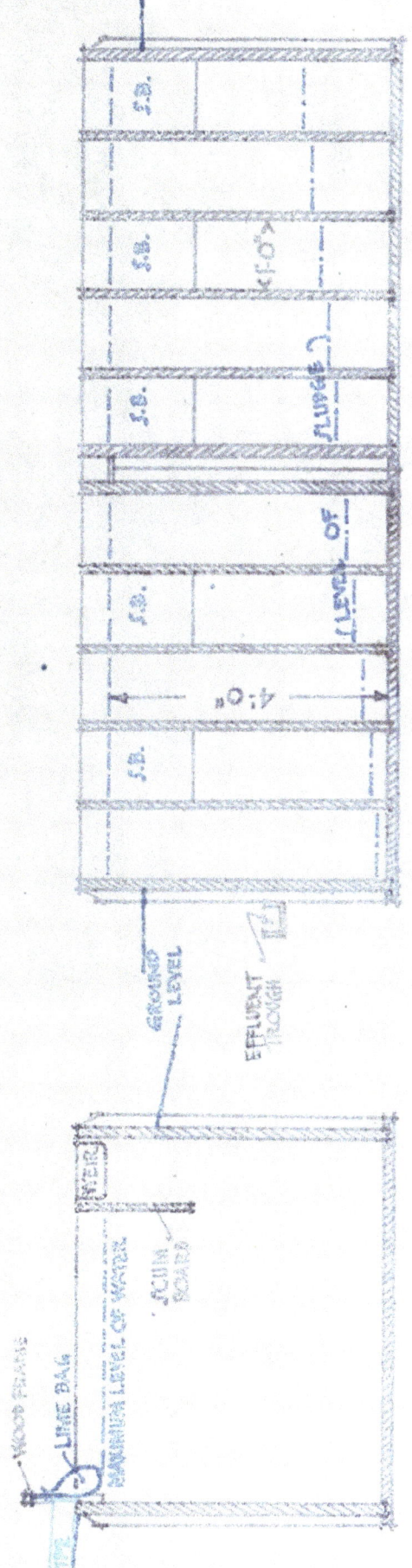

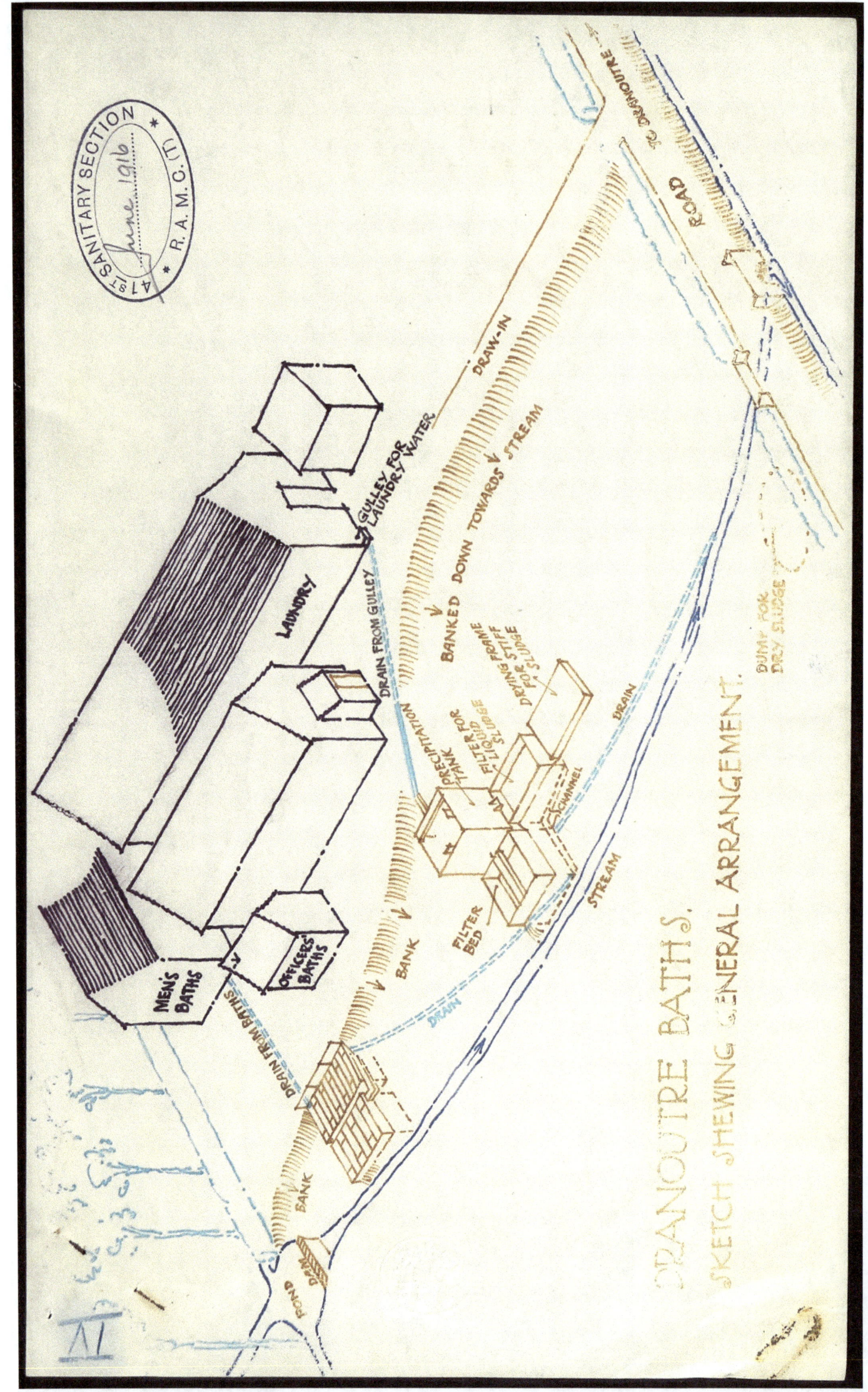

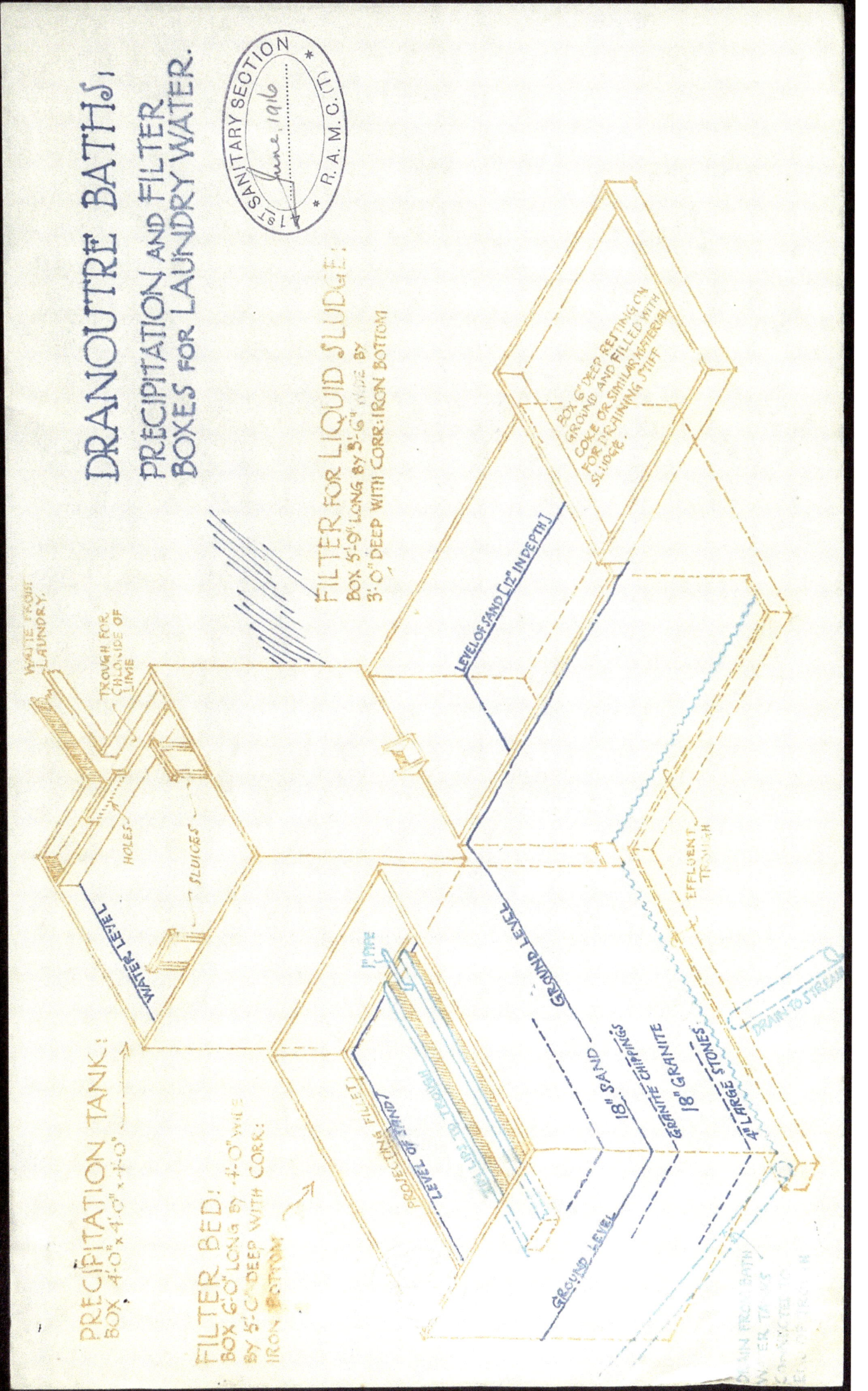

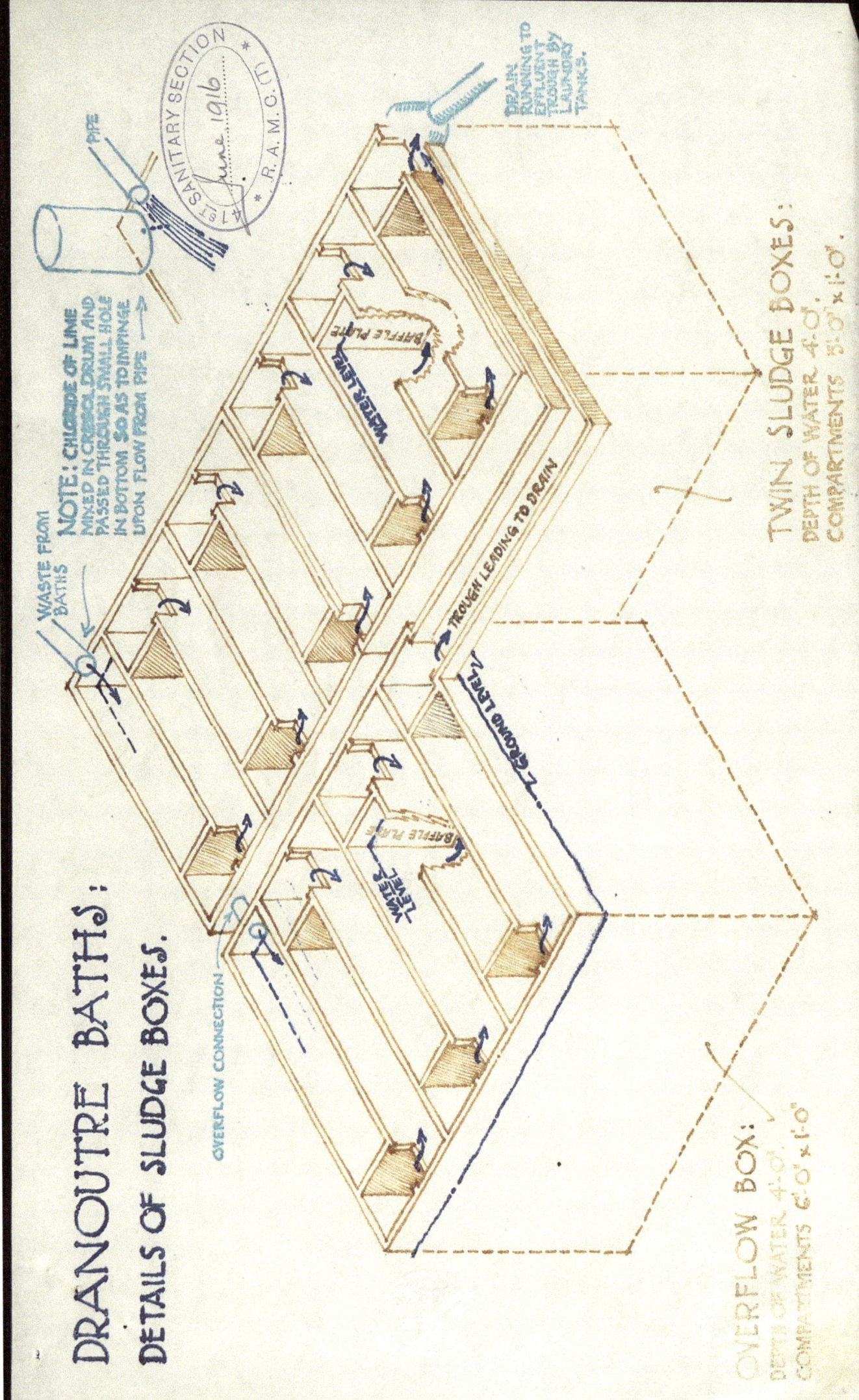

MANURE DESTRUCTOR.
SIZE: 10 FEET SQUARE.

- STOUT WIRES SUPPORTING NETTING
- 3/4" WIRE NETTING: DOUBLE
- CORR. IRON SHEETS
- TINS FILLED WITH EARTH: ALL WIRED TOGETHER.
- SUPPORT
- TWO DRUMS FILLED WITH EARTH OR CLAY

41ST SANITARY SECTION — R.A.M.C.(T) — June 1916

GREASE TRAP:

CONSISTS OF 2 COMPARTMENTS EACH 2'-0" x 2'-0" CONSTRUCTED OF 4½" BRICKWORK AND HAVING BRICK DIVISION WITH 3 OPENINGS AT BOTTOM. THE WHOLE RENDERED IN CEMENT INTERNALLY, AND COVERED WITH HINGED FLAPS FOR CLEANING.

Army Form C. 2118.

WAR DIARY
or
INTELLIGENCE SUMMARY.
(Erase heading not required.)

Confidential

41st Sanitary Section

Volume XI

From 1st July 1916 to 31st July 1916.

24 July
41. San Se

Vol
II

COMMITTEE FOR THE
MEDICAL HISTORY OF THE WAR
Date 5 - SEP. 1915

Page 1.

Army Form C. 2118.

WAR DIARY
or
INTELLIGENCE SUMMARY.
(Erase heading not required.)

Instructions regarding War Diaries and Intelligence Summaries are contained in F. S. Regs., Part II. and the Staff Manual respectively. Title pages will be prepared in manuscript.

Place	Date	Hour	Summary of Events and Information	Remarks and references to Appendices
BAILLEUL	1st July		Received instructions to send advanced party to new camp at 28. M. 29. a. & 8. Sub-section of N.C.O. + 5 Men still to remain at DRANOUTRE for the present. Routine work at D.H.Q. + Dranoutre Baths continued. Received D.R.O. Nos 962-4.	WSL
	2nd July		Remainder of camp moved to new location. H.Qrs. of the Section to remain in this town pending further instructions. Received information from Medical Officer, 9th R Sussex regarding 52246 Pte BROOKS diagnosed as suffering from Infectious Diseases. Received information from A.D.M.S. regarding L.6939 Pte EWINS, 8th Queen - diagnosed Paratyphoid A. Received information from A.D.M.S. regarding L.6939 Pte EWINS, 8th Queen - diagnosed Paratyphoid A. Received D.R.O. Nos 965-967. + G.R.O. 1651-8.	WSL
	3rd July		Day spent in preparing permanent sanitary arrangements in new camp. Sgt GOODING detached this day for duty with IX Corps, 2nd Army. Received instruction that H.Qrs of the Section are to move to-morrow to M. 29. a. 7. 8. Received D.R.O. 968-940.	WSL

T.M34. Wt. W708-776. 500000. 4/15. Sir J. C. & S.

Army Form C. 2118.

WAR DIARY
or
INTELLIGENCE SUMMARY.
(Erase heading not required.)

Page 2

Instructions regarding War Diaries and Intelligence Summaries are contained in F.S. Regs., Part II. and the Staff Manual respectively. Title pages will be prepared in manuscript.

Place	Date	Hour	Summary of Events and Information	Remarks and references to Appendices
Sheet 28 M.29.a.8.8.4 July & 5.			H.Qrs. moved to new location. Owing to heavy rain little outdoor work was possible. Received instructions to take over two water supplies from 50th Divl Sanitary Section. Received D.R.O. No 941–944 + 945–7.	WSC
	6 July		Water Supplies — N.C.O. + 2 Men took over tanks at S.3.6.9.9. " " 1 Man " " KEMMEL SHELTERS D.H.Q. + LOCRE — N.C.O. took over sanitary work from N.C.O. 50th Div San Sec. Destructor commenced in own camp. Camp now however greaseshrap (brick cement) — drawing forwarded with last month's Diary. Permanent latrines, shower bath, + ablution shelter D.R.O. No 948–982. Infectious diseases — @ No 6454 Pte SMITH.F. 8th R.W.Kent. admitted 8th C.C.S. 4th inst. — diagnosed as suspected enteric. @ 4 fausible paratyphoid carriers have been collected from Q.te Q. Survey at 28.M.29.c.8.7.	WSC
	July		Destructor completed. Material for long standing sawdust for urine pits in WAKEFIELD HUTS drawn. The pits are to be filled + the sawdust burned. Received D.R.O. No 983–4.	WSC

Page 3

Army Form C. 2118.

WAR DIARY
or
INTELLIGENCE SUMMARY.
(Erase heading not required.)

Instructions regarding War Diaries and Intelligence Summaries are contained in F. S. Regs., Part II. and the Staff Manual respectively. Title pages will be prepared in manuscript.

Place	Date	Hour	Summary of Events and Information	Remarks and references to Appendices
Sheet 28 M.29.a.8.8	8th July		Long standing made. Men were sent out to all Transport Lines & Wagon Lines with a view to reporting as to the shortage of ablution benches & destruction but as all these had received a "Movement Order" for to-day or to-morrow an inspection was impracticable. Many were already on the move. Received notice that this Unit is to return to camp at BAILLEUL. Received D.R.O. No. 988-993.	WSC
15.14.a.07	9th July		Section moved to BAILLEUL. Received D.R.O. No. 988-993 & No. 9/16 ; E.R.O 1st & 4/6 Special Order from H.M. the King. Disinfection — D.A.C. — Section III — 50939 Gunner LEITCH F. suspected cerebro-spinal fever — tent & kit disinfected — contacts segregated. Estaminet — COV de CORC-DRANOUTRE. girl DURIZ removed from Convent at St JANS CAPEL - diphtheria - report forwarded to O.R.Md. who reported to to Belgian civil authorities who will take necessary action. Appointment — Sho BABB. W. 70 441. to by Lines Corporal, & to take charge of LOCRE Water Supply — Corp LOTT & Pte SALTER took over Water Supply this afternoon.	WSC
	10th July		NEUVE EGLISE ROAD Received D.R.O. No. 992-994 + Z Corps Area Orders.	WSC

T.J.M. W1. W708-776. 500000. 4/15. Sir J. C. & S.

Page 4.

Army Form C. 2118.

WAR DIARY
or
INTELLIGENCE SUMMARY.

(Erase heading not required.)

Instructions regarding War Diaries and Intelligence Summaries are contained in F.S. Regs., Part II. and the Staff Manual respectively. Title pages will be prepared in manuscript.

Place	Date	Hour	Summary of Events and Information	Remarks and references to Appendices
Sheet 28 S.14.a.0	11th July		Work in Camp:- completed latrines(2), ablution place, shower bath, cookhouse, workshop. Brick cement grease trap commenced. Materials drawn for destructor.	WSE
	12 July		Received no Orders to-day. Infectious disease – 4th Northants – WAKEFIELD HUTS – 1351 Pte BUSHBY – measles. Unit had moved out on 11/12th & no information could be gained by us as to the hut occupied or the contacts. With reference to case of diphtheria at DRANOUTRE (see 10th) the patient has now been removed by the civil authorities. Constructive work:- destructor almost completed in own camp. " " " " " " grease trap.	WSE
	13 July		Received D.R.O. No: 998-1005, C.R.O. No: 4-6. Constructive work:- destructor in own camp completed " " " at DRANOUTRE repaired. Infectious disease:- 42nd M.G. Coy – case of cerebro-spinal fever investigated. Report Received D.R.O. No: 1006-1010 forwarded to A.D.M.S.	WSE

WAR DIARY
or
INTELLIGENCE SUMMARY.
(Erase heading not required.)

Army Form C. 2118.

Page 5.

Instructions regarding War Diaries and Intelligence Summaries are contained in F. S. Regs., Part II. and the Staff Manual respectively. Title pages will be prepared in manuscript.

Place	Date	Hour	Summary of Events and Information	Remarks and references to Appendices
S.14.a.0.7.	14 July		New well sunk in camp for ablution water. Arrived Field Ambulance in some field to clean up & burn rubbish after fire of 12th inst. Received D.R.O. No.s 1011-1019 - List referred to in D.R.O. No.1017. With reference to No. 1016 "Camp Stores Form" this Unit took over one left over in the "moves" of the 4th & 10th inst. "Nil" returns not required by A.D.m.d.	WSE
	15 July		Men engaged on cleaning up & burning as yesterday. Received D.R.O. No.s 1020-1026.	WSE
	16 July		Load of sand brought from MALO-LES-BAINS (NORD) for filter grease traps. Disinfection - of hutments "Grampetulus" T.27.c.6.3 (28) - scarlet fever - dug-out sprayed - contacts numbering 3 will be segregated in a tent.	WSE
	17 July		Sgt. GOODING returned from IX Corps for duty with the Section. Received IX Corps D.R.O. No.s 7-12; + D.D.O. No.s 1027-1036.	WSE
			Baths:- pits cleaned out & new beds laid using sea-sand. O/6 visited all sub-sections. Received D.R.O. No.s 1037-1043.	WSE
	18 July		Further work on Baths with regard to filter beds. Bathing Camp visited. Received Circular G.444/16 relating to further grease trap to be put in working order. Received Circular Gas; D.R.O. No.s 1044-1049; D.R.O. No.s 403-408.	WSE

T:MH. W¹. W708—776. 500000. 4/15. Sir J.C.&S.

Page 6

Army Form C. 2118.

WAR DIARY
or
INTELLIGENCE SUMMARY.
(Erase heading not required.)

Instructions regarding War Diaries and Intelligence Summaries are contained in F.S. Regs., Part II. and the Staff Manual respectively. Title pages will be prepared in manuscript.

Place	Date	Hour	Summary of Events and Information	Remarks and references to Appendices
S 14 a 0.7	19th July		Work on Baths continued. Sgt GOODING sent to LOCRE to take charge of the sanitation of the village. 4 T.Vs detailed by O.C. 133rd Field Ambulance for this work. Received D.R.O. Nos 1048-1051, & Special Morning Order No. 165.	NSL
	20 July		Section moved to field at R.36 b.4.1 - Sheet 27.	NSL
R 36 b.4.1	21st July		Camp taken over by 33rd Sanitary Section. Camp form completed forwarded to A.D.M.S. Received D.R.O. Nos 1052-5. Our men withdrawn from LOCRE, NEUVE EGLISE Rd & LOCRE Water Supplies and	NSL
			BRANDHOEK. Received D.R.O. Nos 1056-8. Latrine work at D.H.Q.	NSL
	22 July		Preparation of our camp. refuse pits, latrines &c. & usual routine work in village.	NSL
	23 "		Further work in camp & at D.H.Q.	NSL
	24 "		Preparations for move. Gay Pieter.	NSL
	25 "		Section moved to CAVILLON - 8 N.C.Os & 12 O.R. proceeded by train, the remainder by road.	NSL
CAVILLON	26 "		Work in village - latrines for H.Q., messes as one public one. Destruction for village built. Refuse pits to filled in. Received D.R.O. Nos 1075-7 & R.O. 409-411	NSL
	27 "		Continued scavenging of village. Received Circulars re AMIENS & Circular No A.4795, Creation of Unit, & D.R.O. Nos 1078-1082.	NSL
	28 "		Work in village continued. Received D.R.O. Nos 1083-1090	NSL

Page 7.

Army Form C. 2118.

WAR DIARY
or
INTELLIGENCE SUMMARY.
(Erase heading not required.)

Place	Date	Hour	Summary of Events and Information	Remarks and references to Appendices
CAVILLON	29th July	—	Further work in village. Received D.R.O. Nos 1091–1095	WD
	30"	—	Work in village & adjoining woods & fields continued. Empty houses cleaned & made ready for troops	WD
	31st		Section moved to CORBIE.	WD

41st SANITARY SECTION

WAR DIARY

(CONFIDENTIAL)

VOLUME 12.

From 1st August to 31st August, 1916.

COMMITTEE FOR THE
MEDICAL HISTORY OF THE WAR
Date -9 OCT. 1916

Army Form C. 2118.

WAR DIARY
or
INTELLIGENCE SUMMARY.
(Erase heading not required.)

Instructions regarding War Diaries and Intelligence Summaries are contained in F. S. Regs., Part II. and the Staff Manual respectively. Title pages will be prepared in manuscript.

Place	Date	Hour	Summary of Events and Information	Remarks and references to Appendices
CORBIE	1st Aug		Closing of billet of Divisional Ammunition Column. Cleaning of all billets, offices & messes of D.H.Q. Received D.R.O. No.d 1105-1120	WSC
	2d.		Moved to sheet 62.D. F.25.b.6.1. Received D.R.O. No.d 1121-1128	WSC
F.25.b.6.1	3rd		D.H.Q. constructed incinerator, urinal, latrine & usual routine work. Plans prepared for the Camp to be re-modelled & made complete at Headquarters.	WSC
			Own Camp: constructed latrine, garbage pit, &c. Received D.R.O. No.d 1129-1133.	
	4 Aug		D.H.Q. continued constructive work.	WSC
			Section engaged in salvage work in "Happy Valley" materials to be used at D.H.Q. & own Camp. Received D.R.O. No.d 1134-5.	
	5 Aug		Disinfector - 24 b Supply Column - Lieut BUTLER - chicken pox - officers servant's blankets & kit disinfected removed to 13th Corps Rest Station - tent disinfected - one contact - officers still occupies the tent.	WSC
			Section moved to 62.D. F.26.c.5.3. Work at D.H.Q continued. Received D.R.O. 1136-1145	WSC
F.26.c.5.3	6th Aug		Received D.R.O. No.d 1146-1150, & C.R.O. No.d 332-339	
			Disinfection - 2d Londons - Happy Valley - 1156 Pte WHEBLE S.H. - measles - tent changed & contacts - 9 - occupy same tent.	WSC
			Construction - incinerators at the Citadel, room Camp, cookhouses at D.H.Q. & our own Camp	

Page 2

Army Form C. 2118.

WAR DIARY
or
INTELLIGENCE SUMMARY.
(Erase heading not required.)

Instructions regarding War Diaries and Intelligence Summaries are contained in F. S. Regs., Part II. and the Staff Manual respectively. Title pages will be prepared in manuscript.

Place	Date	Hour	Summary of Events and Information	Remarks and references to Appendices
62 D.				
F.26.0.5.3	7 Aug		Disinfection:- all tents bivouacs in own Camp sprayed because of fly nuisance. Constructional work:- cookhouse, grease trap, urine pit, cum-bump work on fire cookhouses at D.H.Q. cont.	MSC
	8 Aug		Received D.R.O. 1151 - 1158 + A.O. 1159. Ref. 1158 = this Order - Hair Cutting - has been carried out. Constructional work:- cookhouses at D.H.Q. completed - 3 grease traps " "	MSC
	9 Aug		Received D.R.O. Nº 1160 - 1164. Constructional work - 3 urinals complete made. " materials (part) drawn for destructor	MSC
	10 Aug		Received D.R.O. Nº 1165 - 1167 + Special Orders of the Day by Gen. Sir D. Haig d/4+5/8/16. Constructional work:- work commenced on destructor (petrol cans) at D.H.Q.	MSC
			Received D.R.O. Nº 1168 - 170 + Fourth Army Routine Orders Nº 173 - 7.	MSC
	11 Aug		Constructional work:- destructor at D.H.Q. completed - all other work " "	
			- grease-trap urinals incinerator " at Battle H.Qr.	MSC
			No Orders received to-day.	MSC

Page 3.

Army Form C. 2118.

WAR DIARY
or
INTELLIGENCE SUMMARY.
(Erase heading not required.)

Place	Date	Hour	Summary of Events and Information	Remarks and references to Appendices
62D				
F.26.c.5.3 Citadel	12 Aug		Section moved to Citadel F.21.b.	WSC
	13		Sgt. GOODING will be responsible for sanitation of that part of the Citadel occupied by D.H.Q. of this Division. Corpl. EDWARDS for MINDEN POST. These N.C.O.s will have the assistance of 14 T.U.s supplied by Camp Commandant. Remainder of Section constructed our Camp. Received letter from A.D.M.S. re bourse in Water Testing at PONT NOYELLES - No 685 Corpl. LOTT & No.758 Pte. MILLS will attend; also Circular re things done by long return to be rendered by 5 p.m. Saturdays; also D.R.O. No 1176 - 1181.	WSC
	14		D.H.Q. work continued. Our camp completed. Signs for trenches relating to Drying Station &c made & lettered. Road for water main for D.H.Q. two men detailed for PONT NOYELLES however this to-day. Party of men engaged on transport of stretchers from D.O.Q. to DIVE COPSE. Received D.R.O. No' 1187 - 1194. G.R.O. No' 1721-1734.	WSC
	15		D.H.Q. sanitary work continued. More signs painted & taken to BRONFAY FM E. More stretchers transported to DIVE COPSE. Men engaged in taking down D.H.Q. & removing same to another site at the Citadel. Received D.R.O. 1195 - 1201.	WSC

Army Form C. 2118.

WAR DIARY
or
INTELLIGENCE SUMMARY.
(Erase heading not required.)

Place	Date	Hour	Summary of Events and Information	Remarks and references to Appendices
Citadel	16 Aug		D.H.Q. "B" Mess constructed also grease traps for cookhouses. Lined (tin) meat safe for this mess. MINDEN POST - cookhouses, mess rs are now sprayed nightly to prevent diarrhoea - formalin being used. Own camp - tents dug outs &c sprayed with formalin solution. Received D.R.O. 1202-4.	M.S.C.
	17 Aug		D.H.Q. - latrines for Officers & men erected also urinals. More signs for trenches made & delivered. Party of men engaged in transport of blankets from D.Q.Q. to DIVE COPSE. Received D.R.O. N°. 1205-6.	M.S.C.
	18 Aug		D.H.Q. ablution place & cook house tables &c made & fixed. Tents darkened with cutch. More blankets (2040 in all) taken to DIVE COPSE. Further supplies of notice boards written & delivered to BERNAFAY WOOD. Received D.R.O. N°. 1207-1212.	M.S.C.
	19 Aug		D.H.Q. - work completed. Cleaning up of area. Received D.R.O. 1213-17. 4th Army Circular Memo N°. 16 re Purification of Water.	M.S.C.

Page 5

Army Form C. 2118.

WAR DIARY
or
INTELLIGENCE SUMMARY.
(Erase heading not required.)

Instructions regarding War Diaries and Intelligence Summaries are contained in F. S. Regs., Part II. and the Staff Manual respectively. Title pages will be prepared in manuscript.

Place	Date	Hour	Summary of Events and Information	Remarks and references to Appendices
Sheet 62D				
Citadel	20 Aug		Divine Service. Section attended open air service at 9 a.m. D.H.Q — routine work continued at both centres	
			Sign — new trench signs painted. Received D.R.O. No. 1218 – 1221	WSC
	21 Aug		Routine work & sign writing & flying continued. Received D.R.O. No. 1222 – 1225. Also R.O. No. 1725 – 1744. No. 1736 & 1737 included in Section's orders.	WSC WSC
F.26.c.5.3	22 Aug 23 "		Section moved from "Citadel" to "Forked Tree" camp F.26.c.5.3. Section employed in moving D.H.Q from "Citadel" to "Forked Tree Camp". Every tent, hut, mess tent & cookhouse sprayed with formalin because of fly nuisance. Separation of plot near D.H.Q. for parade purposes.	WSC
	24 "		Preparation of own camp. Eyes & flyproof windows most essential in various H.Q. messes. R.O. S.326 attached. Quarantine from the date.	WSC
	25 "		Section moved to D.28.d.8.5. assisted in removal of D.H.Q. Received D.R.O. No. 1283 – 1285.	WSC
D.28.d.8.5	26 "		Made & fixed latrines in new D.H.Q. & prepared own camp. Received D.R.O. 1236 – 1242.	WSC

Army Form C. 2118.

WAR DIARY
or
INTELLIGENCE SUMMARY.
(Erase heading not required.)

Page 6

Instructions regarding War Diaries and Intelligence Summaries are contained in F.S. Regs., Part II. and the Staff Manual respectively. Title pages will be prepared in manuscript.

Place	Date	Hour	Summary of Events and Information	Remarks and references to Appendices
Sheet 62D D.28.d.8.5.	27 Aug	10.30 a.m	Church Parade at 10.30 a.m. Very heavy downpour of rain interfered with this. Outdoor work impossible. Received D.R.O. No: 1243-1249, G.R.O No: 1749-1763, & Circular A/4752/4 "Strength Return".	WDSC
	28 Aug		Heavy rain prevented much outside work being carried out. Usual routine work in own Camp & D.H.Q. continued.	WDSC
	29 Aug		Received D.R.O 1250-1255	
	30 Aug		Received D.R.O No: 1256-7. Usual routine work. L/Cpl. DINNIS on duty with Dumpster.	WDSC
			" No: 1258-60. Ditto.	WDSC
	31		" No: 1261-1266, Extracts from XV Corps Standing Order	WDSC
			" moved to E.II.C. Mess & Office at new D.Q sprayed with Formalin. Ablution benchmade fitted at D.H.Q.	WDSC

140/1734

24/1/10

41ST SANITARY SECTION
WAR DIARY
(CONFIDENTIAL)
VOLUME 13.
from 1st Sept. to 30th Sept. 1916.

Sept. 1916

COMMITTEE FOR THE
MEDICAL HISTORY OF THE WAR
Date 30 OCT. 1916

WAR DIARY
or
INTELLIGENCE SUMMARY.
(Erase heading not required.)

Army Form C. 2118.

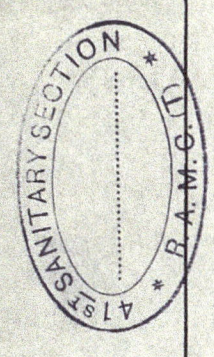

Place	Date	Hour	Summary of Events and Information	Remarks and references to Appendices
Sheet 62 D				
E.11.c	1st Sep.		Distribution of section is as follows:-	
			FRICOURT:- Corp. LOTT, Ptes Mills, Moffett, Cannon, Haldane - 3 on Water Duty, 2 to supervise work of sanitary squads working under Town Major. This Sub-Section took over from 33rd Division on 30th ult.	
			BECORDEL:- L/Corp. BABB, Ptes Dalton & Smith - all on Water Duty	
			H.Q.:- all remaining members.	
			An inspection of Divisional Hdqrs. resulted in finding that the following constructional work was necessary:-	
			Ablution bench workage fit for servants.	
			Urinal near offices for clerks.	
			Latrines - flyproof for N.C.O.s.	
			Grease trap workage fit for "C" Mess; new ones required for "A", "B", & Div. Train St-Qr. Messes.	
			Covered boxes for refuse.	
			Manure destructor	NSC

Army Form C. 2118.

Page 2

WAR DIARY
or
INTELLIGENCE SUMMARY.
(Erase heading not required.)

Instructions regarding War Diaries and Intelligence Summaries are contained in F. S. Regs., Part II. and the Staff Manual respectively. Title pages will be prepared in manuscript.

41st SANITARY SECTION * R.A.M.C.(T)

Place	Date	Hour	Summary of Events and Information	Remarks and references to Appendices
62 D E 11 c	1st Sep. cont.		The Signal Company required the following :- Latrine - fly proof Urinator Refuse pit Grease trap + soakage pit Covered refuse boxes for field kitchen Manure destructor The Ordnance required the following :- Incinerator Grease trap + soakage pit This work was undertaken by the Sanitary Section assisted by 4 T.U. men who are doing general sanitary duties at Steppes during the next three days Fly-sticks :- one man engaged in making these from wire used daily for binding hay + straw dipped in resin & castor oil in the proportion of 1 pint of oil to 2 lbs resin - 75 required per day at D.H.Q.	HDC

Page 3

Army Form C. 2118.

WAR DIARY
or
"INTELLIGENCE SUMMARY."
(Erase heading not required.)

Instructions regarding War Diaries and Intelligence Summaries are contained in F. S. Regs., Part II. and the Staff Manual respectively. Title pages will be prepared in manuscript.

41ST SANITARY SECTION
R.A.M.C.(T)

Place	Date	Hour	Summary of Events and Information	Remarks and references to Appendices
62D				
E.11.c	1st Sep contd		Disinfection:- In order to combat the fly nuisance the various messes, cook houses, tents will be sprayed with a solution of formalin (1½ ozs to the gallon) on every fine day. To-day the following were disinfected:-	
			Tents - ORml DRml, 96, 3 section tents. – inside + outside	
			Messes:- "B", C.R.E., C.R.A. " "	
			Huts:- G.O.C. (outside), Camp Commandant's annexe – inside + out	
			Received D.R.O. 1269-1273, G.R.O. 464-470: a letter from DDMS XV Corps (through ADMS) re elimination of water at FRICOURT, BECORDEL	NSC
	2nd Sep		Constructive work:- the following were completed to-day.	
			Manure destructor:- DHQ Transport + "Signals" Transport.	
			Latrines:- DHQ R.E.O's (2 fly proof seats, urinal, soap), one opposite DHQ re-	
			-ceived a new urinal fixed; DHQ men's latrine repaired	
			Incinerator:- "Signals" Camp.	
			Grease Traps:- " , Div Train Ordnance, "flowing Messes - A, B, C, CRE Signals	
			Received D.R.O. 1274-6; a Sanitation Orders No A/4914/2 dated 2.9.16.	6 NSC

T.131. Wt. W708–776. 500000. 4/15. Sir J. C. & S.

Army Form C. 2118.

WAR DIARY
or
INTELLIGENCE SUMMARY.
(Erase heading not required.)

page 1
Instructions regarding War Diaries and Intelligence Summaries are contained in F. S. Regs., Part II. and the Staff Manual respectively. Title pages will be prepared in manuscript.

Place	Date	Hour	Summary of Events and Information	Remarks and references to Appendices
62 D				
E 11.c	1st 3/Sep		The following administrative arrangements for supervising the sanitation of the Area were made. The front area of the Corps was divided into Right & Left Divisional Areas, the 2nd Division being made responsible for the Right Area as shown in red on the accompanying map. This was sub-divided into 3 sub-sections each of which was to be patrolled daily by members of the Sanitary Section reports sent in at the end of each day. This work was put in hand at once & 29 camps were visited reported on to-day. Constructive work:- Manure destructors in D.H.Q. Transport & Signal Transport Lines were doubled in size to-day. Sgt GOODING made responsible for supervision of sanitary fatigues at D.H.Q. He is responsible for thorough cleanliness of the whole of the area occupied by Div. H.Q. received D.R.O. 1247-1282.	1 WSC

Army Form C. 2118.

WAR DIARY
or
INTELLIGENCE SUMMARY.
(Erase heading not required.)

Place	Date	Hour	Summary of Events and Information	Remarks and references to Appendices
62 D				
E.11.c	6/9/16		The Corps having decided that the 24th Division should now supervise the Left Area, the scheme was finally elaborated as follows:-	
			(1) The Area for which the 24th Division has been made responsible in matters of sanitation is shown in the attached sketch map	2
			(2) The division of this area into sub-areas is also shown on the map.	
			(3) For each sub-area an Inspector is detailed:- Areas 1, 2 & 3 - an officer of the R.A.M.C. Area 4 (marked in brown) - Town Major, FRICOURT.	
			(4) The duty of the officers detailed in (3) is to see that the Sanitation Orders issued on 2/9/16 (q.v.) are carried out & they will report any failure to comply with these orders to the A.D.M.S. 24th Division, who will investigate the matter without delay	
			(5) The Sanitary Officer, 24th Division, will detail trained men to patrol the Sub Areas & report to the Sub-Area Inspector anything affecting efficient Sanitation	
			(6) The officers detailed in (3) will be responsible that copies of Sanitation Orders	NSL

Page 5

Army Form C. 2118.

Instructions regarding War Diaries and Intelligence Summaries are contained in F. S. Regs., Part II. and the Staff Manual respectively. Title pages will be prepared in manuscript.

WAR DIARY
or
INTELLIGENCE SUMMARY.
(Erase heading not required.)

Place	Date	Hour	Summary of Events and Information	Remarks and references to Appendices
62 D				
E. 11. c.	4. Sep. cont.d		are handed to the Commanding Officers of Units camped in the Area, who do not normally receive copies of 24th Division Orders. (4) Where work is required on ground not actually occupied by troops the Sub. Area Inspector will call upon the nearest Unit to take the necessary steps this order is the authority for his doing so. FRICOURT:- O.C. visited Town Major, & went over Area No 4. This Sub-Area is to be again sub-divided into 4 areas instead of which a member of the Sanitary Section is to be responsible. In order to carry this out efficiently the Sub section will be increased from 5 to 8. Camps inspected to-day - 44.	
	5. Sep.		Received orders to withdraw all men from FRICOURT & BECORDEL-Key being relieved by members of the San. Section, 55th Division. Reports on camps visited 3rd & 4th inst. together with 49 made to-day were handed over to O.C., San. Sect., 55th Divn who will continue all work as outlined above, the general scheme having been adopted by this Division. Received D.R.O. No 1284-6.	WSC

Page 6

Army Form C. 2118.

WAR DIARY
or
INTELLIGENCE SUMMARY.

(Erase heading not required.)

41ST SANITARY SECTION
R.A.M.C.(T)

Place	Date	Hour	Summary of Events and Information	Remarks and references to Appendices
62 D				
E 11 cent.	6 Sep		The Division having received orders to move into the Rest Area the whole of the Section was engaged in assisting the various sanitary squads to clean ground to in D.H.Q and the surrounding camps as the various units moved off.	1 NSC
	7 Sep.		The Section moved to AILLY le haut clocher. Received DRO 1287-1292	3 NSC
AILLY	8" " 9" "		An inspection of the village revealed the fact that a public destructor & several latrines were necessary. The following work was done at D.H.Q :- Scrubbing of seats of public latrine; incineration of refuse from mess kitchens &c; Built Leaf incinerator at transport lines; made urinal at same location; also long trench latrine; removed large heap of rubbish from rear of GOC's billet; & improved Officers' latrine behind "Q" office At Div Ordnance :- a grease trap, a box latrine over trench, a urinal, & incinerator partly completed In village :- public incinerator of bricks In workshop :- Complete fly proof latrine (box seep) for officers & framework almost completed Our camp :- soakage pit, grease trap, urinal, refuse pit & incinerator Received DRO 1293-1301 & 1302-1312	NSC

Army Form C. 2118.

WAR DIARY
or
INTELLIGENCE SUMMARY.
(Erase heading not required.)

Instructions regarding War Diaries and Intelligence Summaries are contained in F. S. Regs., Part II. and the Staff Manual respectively. Title pages will be prepared in manuscript.

41st SANITARY SECTION
R.A.M.C. (T)

Place	Date	Hour	Summary of Events and Information	Remarks and references to Appendices
AILLY	9 Sept		Water Testing :- 1 well past BUIGNY cross roads :- distinct blue in 3rd cup	3.
			2nd " " " " " " 2nd "	
			Well on St. RICQUIER road :- medium " 3rd "	
			On Long Road :- pump at Gendarmerie - pale " 1st "	
			Well opposite " " " 1st "	
			" in M.V.S. billet " " " 1st "	
				NSC
			In village :- Officers' latrine & men's latrine at Signal Office - both flyproof seats erected round men's latrine; grease trap cleaned & enlarged.	
			Div Ordnance :- incinerator completed; refuse pit dug; canvas screen erected round men's latrine; grease trap cleaned & enlarged.	
	10 Sept		Div HQ :- Latrines - Officers' latrine outside Townhall thoroughly cleaned, seats of public latrines, latrines at Officers' billets, messes all scrubbed with cresol solution. Latrine at rear of car park dismantled.	
			Grease traps :- all messes - cleaned & changed.	
			Incinerators :- all tended, relined. One at rear of car park dismantled.	
			Scavenging :- all messes, billets, - refuse burned. Roads also cleaned.	NSC
			Received D.R.O. No. 1313 - 1319	

WAR DIARY
or
INTELLIGENCE SUMMARY.

Army Form C. 2118.

Place	Date	Hour	Summary of Events and Information	Remarks and references to Appendices
AILLY	11 Sept		D.H.Q.:- Latrines - all cleaned seats wiped with creol. Incinerator " " re-lit; one circular drum removed near Ordnance Camp for instruction purpose. Cross-traps - all cleaned & changed; pit dug behind Sgt's Mess bullet. Urinals - all washed with creol. Disinfection:- 2 rooms r left occupied by Graffo control sprayed with creol - said to be verminous. Scavenging &c:- fields in several latrines found in various orchards, vicinity of all messes, billets, & O. cleaned. Constructional work:- turf manure destructor built at H.Q. transport lines. Divisional Advance:- 1 bay latrine made &pits dug; urinal provided for Officer's latrine; canvas screen erected. In workshop - Sentry box for A.O.C.'s guard. Instruction Class: 107 R.E.O.'s reported here for a 3 days' course of instruction. Work will commence to-morrow. Received D.R.O. No. 1320 · 1322.	WS

WAR DIARY or INTELLIGENCE SUMMARY

Army Form C. 2118.

Place	Date	Hour	Summary of Events and Information	Remarks and references to Appendices
AILLY	12th	-	Instruction Class. N.C.O. from 9th Q. Sussex reported here this morning. Total number of students is now 11, three men being in charge of the Sanitary Squad of each Infantry Battalion in the Division (excepting 1st M. Staff). The course of Instruction to extend over three days will be entirely practical work in the field, the men being divided into four groups in charge of N.C.O. of this Section. No.1 building incinerators, No.2 building fly proof latrines of long trench pattern, No.3 Sanitary arrangements of kitchen areas, No.4 manure destructors. As each batch finishes the work in hand the men pass to the work of the next batch. To-day the structures were partly finished, the materials used being fly proof latrines found in every camp. Divisional Ordnance:- incinerator or "urinal completed, 2 fly proof latrines (deep trench pattern) completed, ablution bench made & fixed, with soakage pit. Signals Camp:- Fly proof latrine (deep trench pattern) made complete, also usual D.H.Q:- ordinary routine work as for previous days, special attention being paid to burying of manure at transport Lines.	# 5 NSC

WAR DIARY or INTELLIGENCE SUMMARY

Army Form C. 2118.

Place	Date	Hour	Summary of Events and Information	Remarks and references to Appendices
AILLY	13 Sept	to	Instruction Class:- all appliances mentioned on previous day completed. D.H.Q :- latrines re-scrubbed as on 11th inst., & other routine work continued. At Transport Lines following sanitary appliances made & fixed:- incinerator (turf); manure destructor - outer walls of turf, flow of wire netting; circular one of expanded metal; urinal, & latrine - fly proof, - long deep bench pattern. Own Camp :- new grease trap & soakage pit dug	WSC
	to 14 Sep		Instruction Class :- The class was shown manure destructor actually in use, special attention being paid to lighting & stoking. As well men were in charge of regimental sanitary squads a lecture was given on Chlorination & chlorination of water. Thirman of the simplest character but sufficient detail was given to enable them to understand what the duties of the water details are. The men were examined by the D.A.D.M.S. the O.C. San. Sect. being asked the following questions :-	WSC

P.T.O.

WAR DIARY
or
INTELLIGENCE SUMMARY.
(Erase heading not required.)

Army Form C. 2118.

Page 1

Place	Date	Hour	Summary of Events and Information	Remarks and references to Appendices
AILLY	12th Sep cont.	—	Instruction class contd.	

Examination questions :-

1. What is the first duty of a sanitary squad on going to another camp?
2. What type of latrine is authorised in this area. How is it made fly-proof?
3. How would you make a urinal?
4. Explain what your daily duties are in connection with latrines & urinals.
5. What materials can be used to make an incinerator? What is the best size & shape? Where should it be erected?
6. Why is it dangerous to allow manure to collect in a camp? How should it be dealt with? What materials are required for a manure construction.
7. What sanitary arrangements are necessary in a field kitchen? Why should these be covered?
8. Why should it be necessary to allow food to be taken at one spot only in a camp? What steps should be taken by the sanitary squad to keep this place sanitary.
9. Give a list of the daily duties of a sanitary squad.
10. Why should men be allowed to wash at one place only in a camp. What sanitary arrangements must be made there?

NSC

Army Form C. 2118.

Page 12

WAR DIARY
or
INTELLIGENCE SUMMARY.

(Erase heading not required.)

Instructions regarding War Diaries and Intelligence Summaries are contained in F. S. Regs., Part II. and the Staff Manual respectively. Title pages will be prepared in manuscript.

Place	Date	Hour	Summary of Events and Information	Remarks and references to Appendices
AILLY	14 Sept. cont'd		All candidates passed this test, the best being Corp SWIFFIN, 7th N'hants, Cpl McGREGOR, 6th Queens, & L/Cpl CRONIN 8th Buffs. Constructive work:- Police Billet:- Grease Trap. Signals Camp No 1:- incinerator, 2 manure destructors, grease trap.	NSC
	15 Sept.		" " - Flyproof latrine (approved pattern), urinal, refuse pit. Div Ordnance - incinerator (brick) re-built as brick lid & returned to previous site by sentry. Traffic Billet :- grease trap. A.P.M.s " " :- Latrine (bucket) & urinal fixed.	NSC
	16 Sept.		Constructive work:- Sgts Mess Billet :- grease trap. H.Q. Guards " " , ablution bench, soakage pit. Car Park :- urinal Signal Transport - manure destructor. Signs for various sanitary appliances erected in village	NSC

T:131. Wt. W708—776. 500000. 4/15. Sir J. C. & s.

Page 13

Army Form C. 2118.

WAR DIARY
or
INTELLIGENCE SUMMARY.
(Erase heading not required.)

41st SANITARY SECTION
R.A.M.C. (T)

Place	Date	Hour	Summary of Events and Information	Remarks and references to Appendices
AILLY.	16 Sept		Routine work at D.H.Q. now supervised by Lg Dinnis. Commenced Billet notices	NSL
	contd 17/9/15		The Section has been instructed to number all Billets & to erect notice boards stating no. & accommodation on each. The work of preparing, writing & fixing of boards has been carried out & completed to-day.	NSL
	18/9/15		Scavenging of village - burning of manure &c - preparation for move have occupied the Section to-day. Very heavy rain all day interfered with plans for burning. Complete kit inspection this morning - all surplus kit, stores, &c eliminated. Section moved to BRUAY.	NSL
BRUAY	19th		The following camps were visited :- 129th Field Company R.E.; 1st Northants; "Signals" camp; 13th Middlesex; Div. Train; 2nd Londons; 194th Company A.S.C.	NSL NSL
	20"		Div. H.Q :- provided refuse tins with lids, & greasetraps for all messes urinal for "G" "Q" clerks; fitted up officers latrine behind D.H.Q	NSL

Army Form C. 2118.

Page 14

WAR DIARY
or
INTELLIGENCE SUMMARY.
(Erase heading not required.)

Instructions regarding War Diaries and Intelligence Summaries are contained in F. S. Regs., Part II. and the Staff Manual respectively. Title pages will be prepared in manuscript.

41st SANITARY SECTION R.A.M.C. (T)

Place	Date	Hour	Summary of Events and Information	Remarks and references to Appendices
BRUAY	1916			
	21st Sep.		Constructive work	
			Incinerator - for 194th Company, A.S.C. - turf reinforced with wire netting	
			Destructor (public) - central - fitted chimney to this destructor - seated with cement & wire - wired to encircling wire guides with 12 wires	
			Signs - made, wrote, & fixed signs on latrine rinsed completed yesterday	NSC
			Received D.R.O. Nos. 1356-7. 1458-1464.	
	22nd		Constructive work	
			Destructor - converted brick incinerator off RUE de CENTRE into a destructor - made typed cover, two door, chimney etc	
			Urinal - near above destructor - made & fixed two new stands	
			Received D.R.O. Nos. 1466-1472. O.C. visited Sani. Section at LA GORGUE.	NSC
	23rd "		Constructive work	
			Latrines - fitted seat with 8 sittings to central latrine near incinerator	
			made & fitted seat with 9 sittings to same latrine	
			Received D.R.O. Nos. 1493-1498.	NSC
	22nd "		Men sent to take over new areas at CAUCHIN LEGAL, ESTRÉE CAUCHIE, GOUY SERVINS & CAMBLAIN L'ABBÉ	NSC

Page 15

WAR DIARY
or
INTELLIGENCE SUMMARY.
(Erase heading not required.)

Army Form C. 2118.

Place	Date	Hour	Summary of Events and Information	Remarks and references to Appendices
BRUAY	24 Sept.		Men sent to sub sections at following locations, personnel now as under:—	
			CAUCHIN LÉGAL — Corp LANIGAN + 3 Men — responsible for all units in neighb'd	
			GOUY SERVINS — S/Sgt DINNIS + 6 — " " " " " "	
			also GOUY SERVINS, PETIT SERVINS, CHATEAU de l'HAIE,	
			ABLAIN ST NAZAIRE	
			respectively	
			CARENCY — Corp EDWARDS — " for village camps around him at	
			VILLERS au BOIS — L/Cp BABB — " " " " " S.H.Q.	
			ESTRÉE CAUCHIE — Corp LOTT — " " " " " "	
			Constructive work:—	
			Latrines:— made & fitted seat with 5 sittings to latrine off Rue Marmottan	
			Disinfection — M.M.R — scabies — P139b of Corp HOOKER,I — room, lainera, washing	
			utensils & washed with wool solution — blankets & kit sent to	
			hospital — contacts — all medically examined.	
			Received D.R.O Nos 1480–1488	NOC
	25 Sept.		Section (remainder) removed to CAMBLAIN L'ABBÉ in charge of	
			Sgt GOODING, O.C. remaining in BRUAY until to-morrow. S/Cp.	
			LANHAM in charge of S.H.Q. sanitation, visited all officers' billets, messes,	
			in the village	NOC

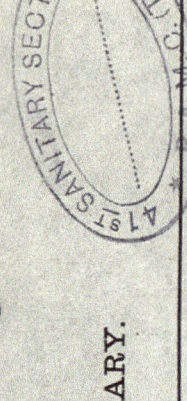

Army Form C. 2118.

WAR DIARY
or
INTELLIGENCE SUMMARY.
(Erase heading not required.)

Page 16.

Instructions regarding War Diaries and Intelligence Summaries are contained in F. S. Regs., Part II. and the Staff Manual respectively. Title pages will be prepared in manuscript.

Place	Date	Hour	Summary of Events and Information	Remarks and references to Appendices
CAMBLAIN L'ABBÉ	26th Sept.		Constructive work	
			Reinforcement Camp BRUAY :- cooking place, grease trap with cover, Officers' latrine complete with screens – 2 fly proof seats & covers, urinal.	
			Camp Inspection	
			VILLERS au BOIS :- Divisional A.T.C. R.E's; Sherwood Foresters (latrine accommodation poor). 9th R. Suss., 129th R.E.s - camps in fairly good condition	
			CARENCY :- 7th Northants, 129th Battery R.G.A, Anti-aircraft Battery - camps found in good condition	
			CAMBLAIN L'ABBÉ - all troops in village visited. The number of latrines in the village seems too high. The whole question of conservancy will be considered at once. Manure has been stacked hitherto – destructors will be made in various transport lines to dispose of same by burning.	
			GOUY SERVINS :- Sgt. GOODING visited this sub-section to-day, the number of preliminary inspection of the area was well in hand.	NSC

T.134. Wt. W708-770. 500000. 4/15. Sir J. C. & S.

Page 17

Army Form C. 2118.

WAR DIARY
or
INTELLIGENCE SUMMARY.

Place	Date	Hour	Summary of Events and Information	Remarks and references to Appendices
CAMBLAIN L'ABBÉ	1916 27th Sept.		Constructive work:- Reinforcement Camp. BRUAY:- men's latrine complete with screening, 5 fly-proof seats & covers, & 2 urinals. CHATEAU de la Haie:- 2 large latrines demolished & 1 new one erected on new site. 2 grease traps & pits completed, another in process of construction. Div. Canteen - 1 large urinal, & 1 latrine for orderlies only. ADMS office - soakage pit dug & strainer attached for soapy waste. San. Sect. - 2 grease traps, flyproof gauze fixed to office windows. A.P.M. " " " " Disinfection:- San. Sect. office, APM office, G.O.C's stables, APM office. Camp Inspection:- 137 M.G. Company, Grandcourt 129 R.E.s, 20th Div. Section " " 129th R.E.s, & 9 R. Surrey Received G.R.O. № 1814-1825	WSL WSL
	28th Sep		Constructive work. 3 manure destructors - H.Q. Transport Lines GOUY SERVINS - 3 grease traps (Chateau), incinerator & extra latrine at Div. Canteen.	

WAR DIARY or INTELLIGENCE SUMMARY.

Army Form C. 2118.

Page 18

Place	Date	Hour	Summary of Events and Information	Remarks and references to Appendices
CAMBLAIN L'ABBÉ	28th Sept		Camp Inspection:-	
			CAMBLAIN L'ABBÉ:- all camps, offices, billets, messes etc. Trench Warfare School & Divisional Gas School. The sanitary arrangements in both need renewal.	
			MAISNIL BOUCHÉ:-	nil
	at 2pm Sept		Received D.R.O. No. 1518-1532.	
			Constructive work:-	
			CAMBLAIN L'ABBÉ - 1 latrine complete including fly proof seat & urinal for A.D.M.S.	
			repaired men's latrine & urinal.	
			made latrine box for D.A.D.O.S.	
			Camp Inspection	
			CAMBLAIN L'ABBÉ:- a list of latrines has been compiled to day showing character, situation etc. Buckets & destructors for burning are to be provided	
			GAUCHIN LÉGAL:- This sub-section has been occupied in disposing of refuse left & also safeguarding water supplies. Steps will be taken to prevent the bathing water at GAUCOURT from fouling the stream for horses	nil
			Received A.O. No. [illegible] 475-481. D.R.O No. 1534-6	

Page 19

Army Form C. 2118.

WAR DIARY
or
INTELLIGENCE SUMMARY.
(Erase heading not required.)

Instructions regarding War Diaries and Intelligence Summaries are contained in F.S. Regs., Part II. and the Staff Manual respectively. Title pages will be prepared in manuscript.

41st SANITARY SECTION * R.A.M.C.(T)

Place	Date	Hour	Summary of Events and Information	Remarks and references to Appendices
GAMBLAIN L'ABBÉ	30th Sept		Constructive work :- Destructor :- manure for 17th M.G. Company. Urinal :- new one made & fixed behind Sanitary Section camp. Latrine :- completed latrine for Bq. D.O.S. " new seat fixed for "D" & H.Q. latrine & re-arranged urinal screen. Ablution bench - moved & re-fixed at 173rd M.G. Company Disinfection - On 28th inst :- Measles - 29th T.M. Battery - No 62495 Gunner STREETLY W.T. - hut disinfected history of the case - Left trenches on 15th for 4 days rest - again to trenches 19th inst - reported sick on 19th, 23rd & 25th inst being evacuated on the 27th. He was quartered at Colburg Clanouse Road, Vimy Ridge when in action. His movements in the village are not accurately known the source of infection has not yet been ascertained. Camp Inspection :- Trench Warfare & Gas School. O.C. visited all Sub-sections.	WSC WSC WSC WSC

Received L.R.O. 1826-1836, D.R.O. 1537, 1542. Circulaire Unurinies de vieille clothing.

T.134. Wt. W708-776. 500000. 4/16. Sir J. C. & S.

Appendix 1.

Sheet 62 D.

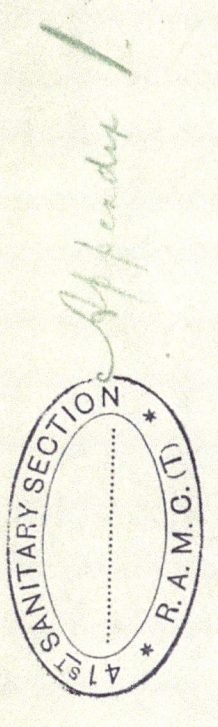

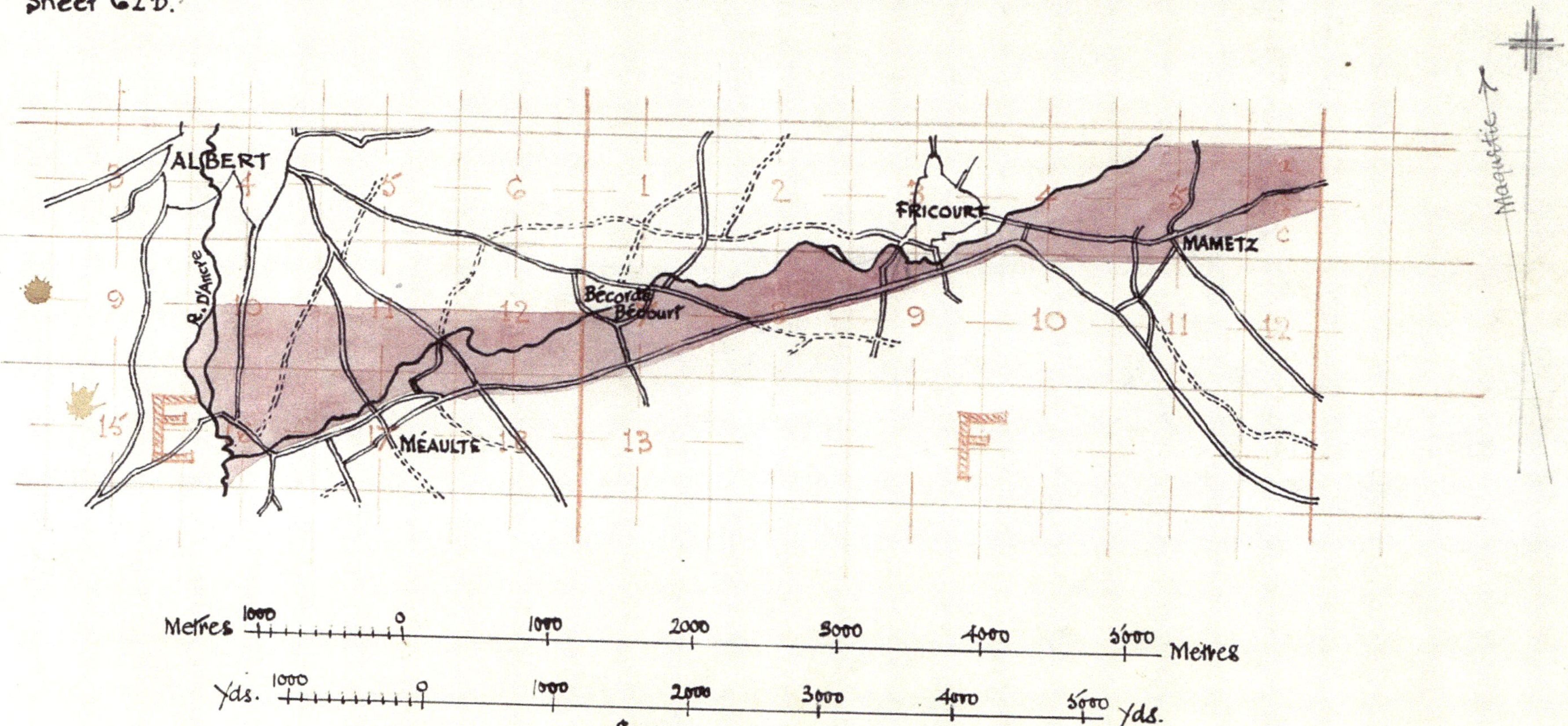

Scale - 1: 40,000.

G2d NE

24th DIVISION. Appendix

SANITATION ●●●●●●●●●●
ORCHIDS. ●●●●●●●●●

Bécourt Wood
Red Cottage
FRICOURT
Cemetery
Bécordel Bécourt
Hospital
Cemetery

41ST SANITARY SECTION
R.A.M.C.(T)

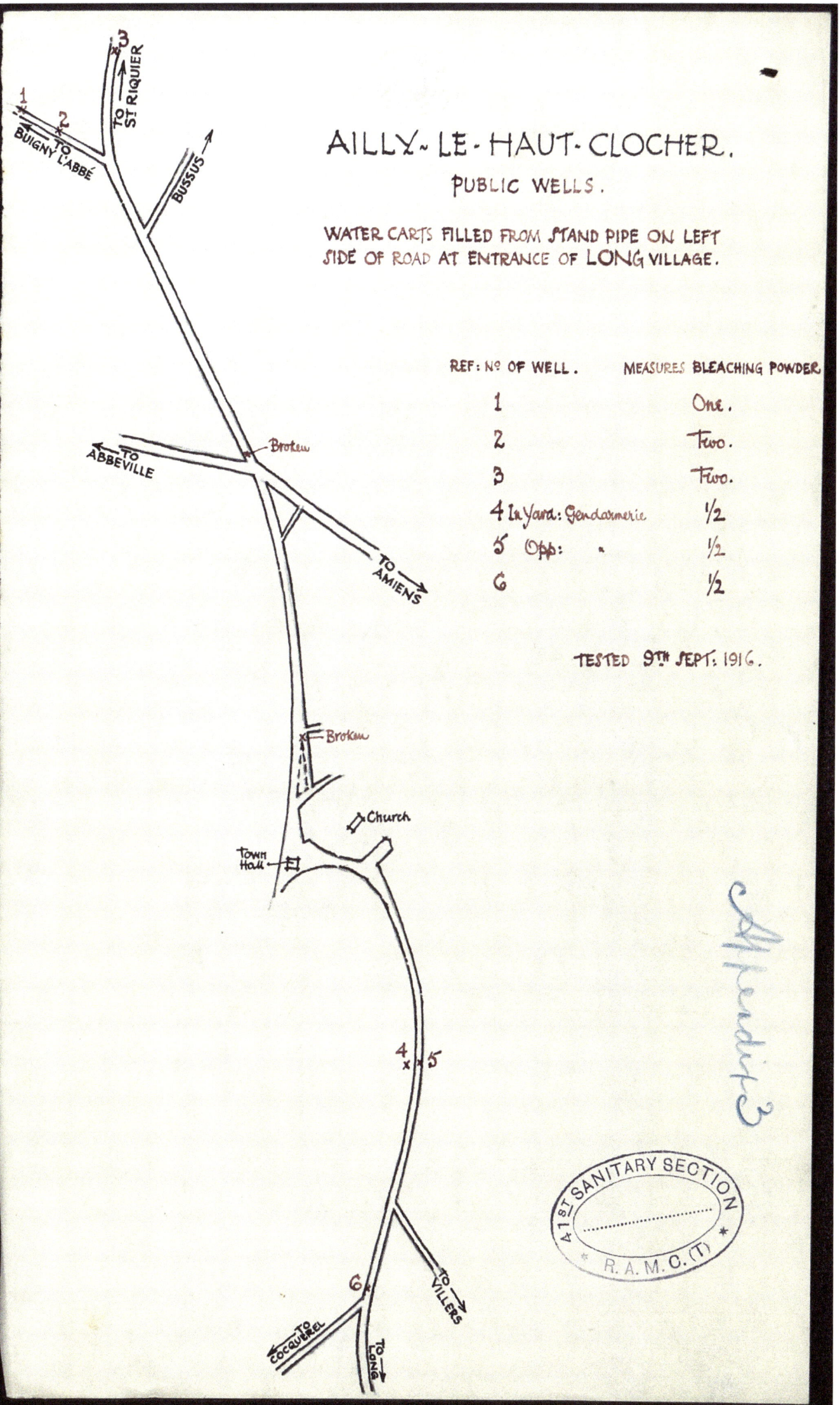

MAP OF REST AREA.

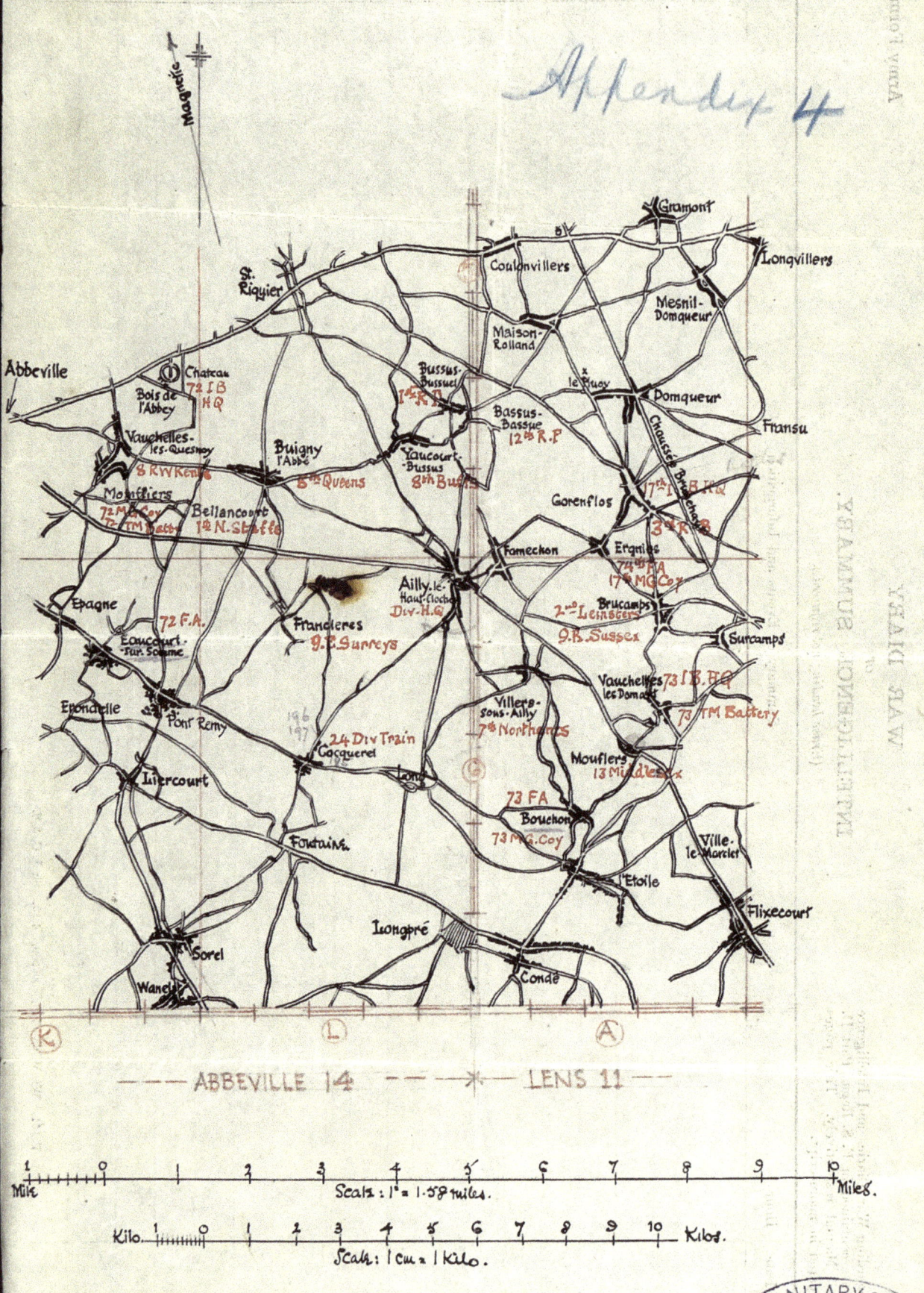

Appendix 4

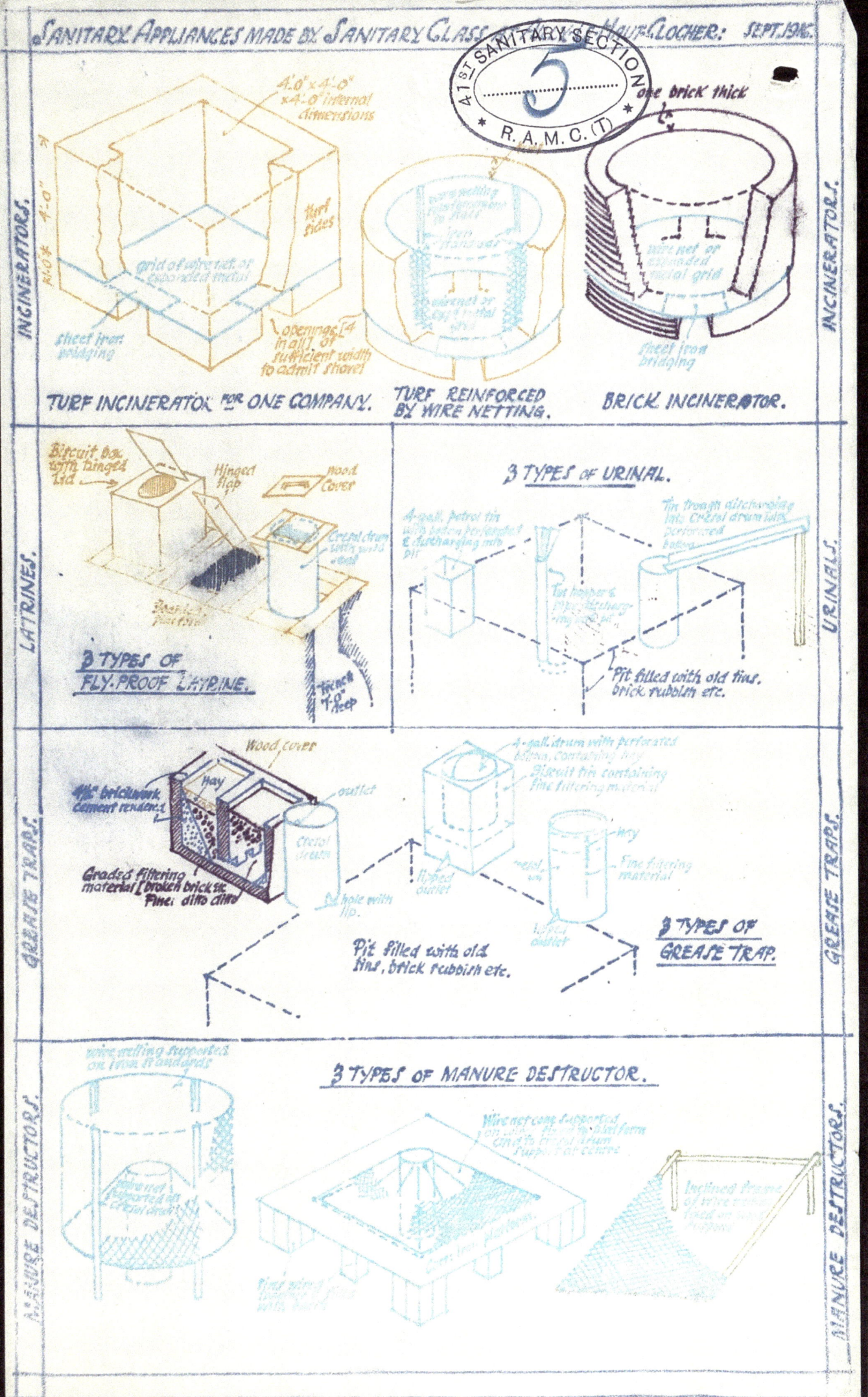

24th Division No.A.491½/2.

SANITATION.

(1) **SANITARY PERSONNEL.** Every Unit will have personnel told off, whose duty it will be to see that Latrines, Urinals, Soak-Pits are constructed and kept in proper order, that incinerators are erected and made full use of, and that camps etc. are kept tidy and free from litter.

(2) **LATRINES.** Must be looked to by personnel told off for the purpose at regular intervals every day.

Toilet paper can be obtained from Ordnance and should be fixed up in a box or by some other improvised means which will prevent it from blowing about.

The seats of latrines must be inspected and kept scrupulously clean. In the inside of the woodwork or box of the seat should be sprayed regularly with Creosol Solution.

Chloride of Lime, or Creosol Solution should be used freely in cleansing operations. Proportions for Creosol mixture should not exceed 1½ ozs. to a gallon of water.

(3) **URINALS.** Similarly to the latrines, Urinals must be looked to regularly and Chloride of Lime, or Creosol Solution, should be used daily in cleansing operations. The ground round the urinals should be sprayed with Creosol Solution or sprinkled with Chloride of Lime.

(4). **SOAK-PITS.** A portion of ground must be marked off in each Unit area for washing purposes, and stringent orders must be issued to ensure that all washing is confined to this area.

Soak-Pits must be dug, into which all water used for washing must be emptied. These pits will be fitted at the top with a perforated biscuit tin, filled loosely with straw or grass through which the water will filter, leaving all soap suds in the straw- the straw or grass should be burnt as often as necessary and replaced by fresh.

Chloride of Lime should be freely used by sprinkling over ground where washing is permitted.

(5). **INCINERATORS.** All refuse must be burnt. Incinerators must be kept going and made the utmost use of.

Tins, after being burnt clean, should be separated and placed tidily in heaps and utilised for pathmaking, urine pits, etc as required.

(6). **MANURE.** Immediate and active measures must be taken to deal with manure which has been allowed to collect in small heaps all over the area.

All manure must be burnt and, where no care or trouble has been taken in the past to systematically collect manure in dumps some distance away from the ground occupied by the Troops, action must NOW be taken and places selected where manure can be dumped, and burnt.

Existing dumps must be burnt at once. In order to facilitate burning, trenches should be cut through the dumps to form wind lines and be set fire to in many places on the windward side.

(7). **RATION BOXES.** Ration boxes, in which to keep cheese, sugar, jam, etc. are to be improvised at once. This can easily be done by Units, out of biscuit boxes fitted with a cover.

All Quartermasters' Stores and places where rations are divided and meat cut up, should be provided with muslin to keep rations and meat covered, whilst they are in process of being divided up for issue. Muslin can be obtained through the Ordnance.

It cannot be too strongly impressed on those responsible for the cutting up of meat, how vitally important it is, to keep scrupulously clean that which they cut it on, and the meat waiting to be cut must be kept COVERED.

The fly is not particular as to what he alights on and devours, and thus conveys filth to the food of the Troops, which is a sure source of illness.

P.T.O.

SANITATION ORDERS (Continued).

(8). **MEALS.** Attention is drawn to the delay which is noticeable in the clearing up of bits, etc., after meals. Places in which meals are to be taken should be allotted wherever possible and retained for such purpose only – immediately a meal is finished, a thorough cleaning up should be made and thus prevent flies from congregating.
Metal receptacles for refuse should be placed conveniently near cook-houses and the places allotted for meals, the contents of these being burnt at intervals during each day.
It is sound, adds considerably to cleanliness, and can be arranged for under almost any conditions, for cooks to be provided with a basin or bucket, soap, towel and water for the purpose of washing their hands.

(9). **WATER.** On no account is water to be drunk from any source other than that detailed for drinking purposes.

(10). Patterns of LATRINES, URINALS, INCINERATORS and SOAK-PITS may be seen at E.11.b.3.3, Headquarters, Sanitary Section, marked by a yellow flag.

(11). Any difficulties experienced in complying with these instructions, should be referred to the A.D.M.S.

(12). The above instructions, and particularly the REASONS for such instructions, are to be explained to the Troops.

It is the duty of every soldier to do his utmost to assist in the carrying out of these instructions, disregard or neglect of which will affect the health and fighting efficiency of the Troops, and thus directly influence the result of operations against the enemy.

(13). It must be clearly understood that all Latrines, Urinals, Incinerators, meat-safes, etc., erected, are to be considered as permanent fixtures in the area and must be kept in good repair and serviceable condition, and handed over to an incoming Unit, or left standing in the area if the Unit leaves and no-one to hand over to.

(14). When a Unit leaves, it is incumbent on it to ensure that the area is left scrupulously clean with fixtures in good order.

2nd September 1916.

Lieut-Colonel,
A.A. & Q.M.G., 24th Division.

140/8/1
24

24 A. Dn.

1st Oct 1916

4th AUST SANITARY SECTION
WAR DIARY
(CONFIDENTIAL)
VOLUME 14.
from 1st Oct: to 31st Oct: 1916.

COMMITTEE FOR THE
MEDICAL HISTORY OF THE WAR
Date -9 DEC. 1916

ESTRÉE·CAUCHIE.
KEY PLAN OF VILLAGE [NOT TO SCALE].

NOTE:
BLACK ■ SHOWS POSITIONS OF OFFICES, MESSES ETC.
RED ■ " " " CAMPS & BILLETS.
GREEN ■ " " " LATRINES.

OCTOBER: 1916.

Estée Bouche

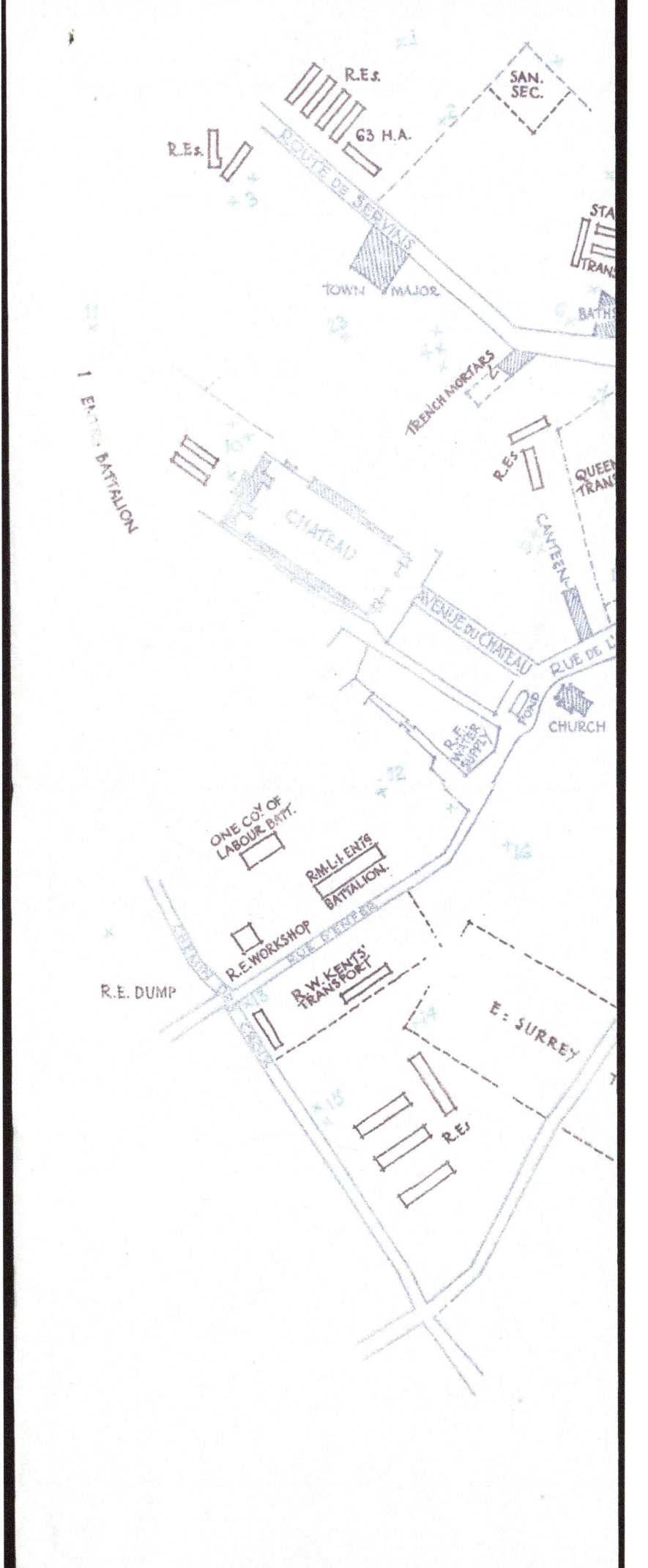

Gouy Sievers

Camblain l'Abbé

[Stamp: 1ST SANITARY SECTION R.A.M.C.]

Unit	Personnel Officers	NCOs	Men	Map No.	Latrine for Officers	Latrine for NCOs	Latrine for Men	Type Closed trench	Type Bucket	Type Biscuit tin	Type Open trench	No. of Seats	Kind of Seats	If roofed	Remarks
d Machine Gun Coy. Transport	-	2	24	48	✓					✓		1	Box with lid	✓	To have buckets
				49			✓	✓				1	ditto		ditto
				50			✓				✓				Has no seat. To be filled in
d Machine Gun Company	4	10	140	38	✓				2			2	Circular	✓	Officers share
				39			✓		5			5	Half circ.	✓	with Inf: Comp?
d Trench Mortar Battery	5	8	112	15			✓	✓				3	Box with lid		To have buckets
				15A		✓		✓				1	ditto		ditto
				15B	✓			✓				1	ditto	✓	ditto
				16			✓		3				Cross bar		To be demolished
				2			✓	✓				2	Box with lid		To have buckets
Sanitary Section 41	1	8	7	3			✓	✓				3	ditto	✓	To be demolished
				46	✓			✓				1	ditto	✓	
nch Mission + O Mess	-	-	-	18	✓			✓				1	ditto	✓	
Canteen	-	-	-	23			✓	✓				2	ditto		To be demolished
				52			✓		2			2	Box without lid	✓	To be reconstructed
d Battn - 1 Company	7	12	220	40			✓		4				Crossbar		To be demolished
				47			✓		1						To be reconstructed. Has no seat.
				41		✓			1				Crossbar		To be demolished
ditto	7	12	220	42			✓	✓				2	Box without + with lid		ditto
				43			✓	✓				2	Box with lid		ditto
				44		✓			1			1	ditto		To be reconstructed
ditto	7	12	220	29			✓	✓				5	3 board system		To be demolished
Quartermaster's Stores	1	2	29	29a		✓			2						ditto
				6	✓				3			3	Half circ:	✓	
				7	✓				2			2	ditto	✓	
				8	✓			1				1	Box without lid	✓	
Inf Battalion	15	26	469	9		✓			2			2	Box with lid	✓	
				10			✓					9	3 board system	✓	To be demolished
				11		✓			4			6	Half circ:	✓	2 buckets to be provided
				51			✓	✓				3	Box with lid		To be demolished
Signals	3	7	113	27			✓				✓				Demolished
				28			✓	✓				4	Box with lid		To be demolished
Pioneers Transport	1	6	54	45			✓	✓				3	ditto		ditto
				53	✓			1				1	ditto	✓	
R.E.	-	3	19	30	✓				1			1	Box without lid	✓	To have 1 bucket
				31	✓				2			2	Box with lid	✓	ditto
R.F.A.	4	6	74	32			✓	✓				2	1 ditto 1 3 board system		To be demolished
				34			✓	✓				2	Box with lid		ditto
C.R.A.	-	-	-	33			✓	✓				1	ditto	✓	ditto
				35	✓			1				1	ditto		To be reconstructed
Div. Hdqrs	-	-	-	4			✓	✓				2	1 box with lid 1 3 board system		To be demolished
				5	✓			1				1	Box with lid	✓	
Traffic Control				12			✓		2			2	Half circ:	✓	To have new seats
				13	Not in use			1				1	ditto		To be demolished
Public Latrines				17			✓		16			16	Box with lid	✓	
				19			✓		8			8	ditto	✓	
Chateau				20	✓				3			3	ditto	✓	
				21		✓			3			3	ditto	✓	
B Mess				25		✓		✓				1	Box with lid	✓	To be reconstructed
				26		✓			1				ditto		
Public Latrines behind Brewery				36			✓	✓				6	3 board system	✓	To be demolished
				37	✓				2			2	Box with lid		ditto

Camblain L'Abbé

Army Form C. 2118.

WAR DIARY
or
INTELLIGENCE SUMMARY
(Erase heading not required.)

41ST SANITARY SECTION
R.A.M.C. (T)

Place	Date	Hour	Summary of Events and Information	Remarks and references to Appendices
	1916			
Camblain L'Abbé	1st Oct.		Constructive work:- Manure destructor extended - 14th M.G. Coy Transport Lines Latrine - Camp Commandant's Office - flyproof box cover made & fixed. Sanitary Section Office - Officer's latrine complete with flyproof box seat, roof & made fixed. Camps visited:- VILLERS au BOIS:- 9th R. Sussex - camp very satisfactory 20th Field Section - incinerator completed & corrugated iron 129th R.E's - new grease trap & refuse pit constructed incinerator being re-constructed 14th Bde H.Q. - grease trap needed. 43rd M.G. Coy - camp not very tidy. In all necessary unsatisfactory conditions notified to N.C.O. responsible of Northants, 50th Bde R.F.A., 126th Bde R.G.A. & A.A. Battery - all in good order. CARENCY:- usual routine work & road sweeping. Received D.R.O. Nos 1544 - 1549.	1 & 4

WAR DIARY
or
INTELLIGENCE SUMMARY

Army Form C. 2118.

Place	Date	Hour	Summary of Events and Information	Remarks and references to Appendices
Camblain L'Abbé	2nd Oct		Constructive work:- Own camp - cookhouse fireplace, cookhouse table, & stove fitted together; fixed in men's messing room. Camp inspection:- VILLERS au BOIS:- 13th Middlesex - 2 new grease traps. 43rd T.M. Battery; - conditions not very good - no urinal - no grease trap, & a good incinerator not in use. 1st K. Staffs - quite good. 109th R.E.s - in good condition. Routine work:- D.H.Q.:- urinals, latrines, incinerators, grease traps & manure destructors visited & where necessary put in good condition. Road sweeping & ditch cleaning continued. Summary of work at ESTRÉE CAUCHIE from 28/9/16 to date:- Div. Ordnance - midden in yard drained, new urinal & new latrine for men; floors swept daily; all units visited daily. Received D.R.O. No. 1560.H.	5

WAR DIARY or INTELLIGENCE SUMMARY

Army Form C. 2118.

(Erase heading not required.)

Place	Date	Hour	Summary of Events and Information	Remarks and references to Appendices
Camblain L'Abbé	3rd Oct.		Constructive work:- Ablution bench repaired for 73rd M.G. Company. Soakage pit made " " " " Urinals - two complete made for stock. Sermigelli:- four men engaged in making vermigelli for the various infantry units. Camp Inspection.- MAISNIL BOUCHÉ - Guard Warfare School - new latrine erected for N.C.O's & Men; another latrine provided with four box seats; one disused latrine to be filled in. New sanitary squad instructed in their duties. D.H.Q. - routine work continued. Sign Writing:- "Grease Trap" & "Foul Ground with Divisional sign made & lettered - 22. Received D.R.O. Nos. 1565 - 1570.	NSC
	4th Oct.		Constructive work:- soakage pit for own camp. box seat latrine for D.A.D.O.S. ablution bench made & fixed in own camp. MAISNIL BOUCHÉ:- Supervision of new sanitary squad in their routine duties	NSC

WAR DIARY
or
INTELLIGENCE SUMMARY
(Erase heading not required.)

Army Form C. 2118.

Place	Date	Hour	Summary of Events and Information	Remarks and references to Appendices
Coamblain L'Abbé	4th Oct. cont.		Sign Writing:- "Foul Ground", "Grease Trap", "Urinal" notices with Divisional Sign - 30 made & written to-day. D.H.Q.- routine duties. The third manure destructor in signals camp stacked & lighted to-day. New soakage pit for 43rd M.G. Company almost completed. Received D.R.O. No. 1571-3.	NSC
	5th Oct.		Constructive work:- Inv. for electrical apparatus for D.A.D.V.S. GOUY SERVING:- ⓐ Grease trap for 72nd M.G. Coy. ⓑ 103rd R.E.s, 42 T.M. Battery, 104th R.E.s Transport Lines. ⓒ Soap waste scheme (chloride of lime) for 103rd R.E.s, 42nd T.M. Battery, Chateau. Signs:- "Gas Alert-On" & "Gas Alert-Off" made & partly painted. Hebuterne - 8 more gallons made. D.H.Q.- soakage pits for San. Sec., & 43rd M.G. Company completed. Camp Inspection - VILLERS au BOIS:- 42nd Div. H.Q., 129th R.E.s, 20th Rifle Section (new grease trap vermalised), 13th Middlesex. Received D.R.O. No. 1574-6.	6, 2, 4. NSC

Army Form C. 2118.

WAR DIARY
or
INTELLIGENCE SUMMARY
(Erase heading not required.)

Page 5

Instructions regarding War Diaries and Intelligence Summaries are contained in F. S. Regs, Part II. and the Staff Manual respectively. Title Pages will be prepared in manuscript.

Place	Date	Hour	Summary of Events and Information	Remarks and references to Appendices
Camblain L'Abbé	6th Oct.		Constructive work:- public latrine behind Jan See bullet completed except for canvas screen down the centre. Three star shell stands for 1st R.G. Signs "Foul Ground" with Div. Sign. 12 made to-day. Camp Inspection:- MAISNIL BOUCHÉ:- one new latrine urinal erected for C.O. new ablution place for troops is being erected here by R.E.'s. Latrine accommodation - ESTRÉE CAUCHIE - village surveyed, recommendations forwarded to D.H.Q. Routine work continued at D.H.Q. Received D.R.O. No. 1577 - 1583.	WSC
	7th Oct.		Constructive work:- public latrine (see 6th inst.) - screen fixed. Destructor:- sample chimney made for R.E.s. Latrines wa kage pits completed at Div. Ad. Stores. Latrine accommodation - this village - plans & specifications prepared. The work will be commenced as soon as material & men are available.	WSC

WAR DIARY
or
INTELLIGENCE SUMMARY

(Erase heading not required.)

Army Form C. 2118.

Place	Date	Hour	Summary of Events and Information	Remarks and references to Appendices
Camblain l'Abbé	7th Oct. cont'd		Camps visited:- VILLERS au BOIS:- 12th Royal Fusiliers, 129th R.E., 14th M.G. Coy - everything here is receiving the necessary attention, the village continues to be very clean. CARENCY:- one Company 2nd Leinsters, 7th Northants, & 129th R.G.A. - camps village fairly clean. D.H.Q:- mess, latrines &c all in good condition - road sweeping & ditch cleaning continued. Received D.R.O. No. 1584-88.	WSC
	8th Oct.		Constructing work:- chimney, doors, & bars made for destructor in San Lee camp. GAUCHIN LEGAL:- brick incinerator for D/106/F.A.B. soap wade scheme for D/107/F.A.B. Sign writing - "Foul Ground" & "Salvage Dump" with Div. sign made completed. Camps visited:- MAISNIL BOUCHE:- Trench Warfare & Gas School - new sanitary squads are working satisfactorily. Received D.R.O. 1589-96.	3 WSC

Army Form C. 2118.

WAR DIARY
or
INTELLIGENCE SUMMARY

(Erase heading not required.)

Page 4

Instructions regarding War Diaries and Intelligence Summaries are contained in F. S. Regs., Part II. and the Staff Manual respectively. Title Pages will be prepared in manuscript.

Place	Date	Hour	Summary of Events and Information	Remarks and references to Appendices
Camblain L'Abbé	9th Oct.		Constructive work:- owing to the fact that the buckets supplied for new public latrines are shallow ones tin slats have been made fixed underneath seats for buckets to fit into. Signs:- "Foul Clumal", "Urinal" & signs for trenches (with arrows) made & written to-day. Materials drawn for new destructor. Received D.R.O No's 1594-1603.	NSL
	10 Oct.		Constructive work:- destructor in Sandee camp. Camps:- GAUCHIN LEGAL:- owing to the fact that the camp here are in such a bad condition it is probable that the camps here are 4 cowries land will not take them over except as a temporary measure. Permanent sanitary arrangements will therefore not be made for the present. The whole of the camps require systematic cleaning & permanent sheltered latrines. D/107/F.A.B. have already left for a better site at GOUY SERVINS. CARENCY:- here satisfactory. Sign writing & drainage work at D.H.Q. continued. Received D.R.O 1604-6.	NSL

J2449. Wt. W14957/Mgo 750,000 1/16 J.B.C. & A. Forms/C2118/12.

WAR DIARY
or
INTELLIGENCE SUMMARY
(Erase heading not required.)

Army Form C. 2118.

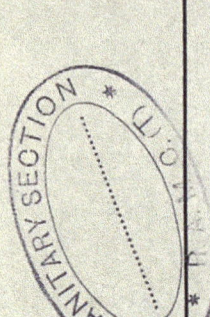

Place	Date	Hour	Summary of Events and Information	Remarks and references to Appendices
Camblain L'Abbé	11th Oct		Constructive work:- Destructor - San. Sea. camp - 12 seines laid. Soakage pit - new - for Urinal near public latrine signs - 14 miscellaneous completed to day. Camps visited - MAISNIL BOUCHÉ - Trench Warfare & Gas School - work done as follows:- new latrine for officers, grease-trap for O.R. cookhouse, new seat for R.E.O's latrine. Old 3 board latrine done away with. Pioneer sgt. instructed in the construction of soap filter & pits for soap scheme for new ablution place put up by R.E.'s, & two new grease-traps for men's cookhouse. D.H.Q. - routine work, road sweeping, ditch cleaning continued. Water testing:- turnip well off Pioneers' Transport, Rue de la Gare - "turbid, offensive smell, pale blue in 6th cup - marked "Not to be used". Depth 150 ft. Possible source of contamination - Urinior closet close by. Buckles of gas plainly seen continuously. Report to C.O.M.S. Received D.R.O. 1607-16/10/16.	WSR well done

Army Form C. 2118.

WAR DIARY
or
INTELLIGENCE SUMMARY
(Erase heading not required.)

Instructions regarding War Diaries and Intelligence Summaries are contained in F. S. Regs., Part II. and the Staff Manual respectively. Title Pages will be prepared in manuscript.

Place	Date	Hour	Summary of Events and Information	Remarks and references to Appendices
Cambrin L'Abbé	12th Oct.		Constructive work:- Destructor - Sambo comp - completed to day. GOUY SERVINS:- grease trap for 9th R. Surrey (none last report) 13th Middlesex 4th Northants soakage pit - 13th Middlesex - 4th Northants. CAMBLAIN L'ABBÉ - soakage pit for public latrine No 2. Water Testing:- all wells in PETIT SERVINS. Camp inspection:- VILLERS-au-BOIS:- new urinals; grease trap have been provided for N.B.9's cookhouse; soap scheme for ablution place almost completed. 13th Bde. H.Q.:- new latrine with two box seats has been provided. 20th Rifle Section:- water duty men instructed in their duties. D.H.Q.:- routine work continued - urinals smeared with oil, latrine seats scrubbed - manure destructors cleaned - roads swept - ditch cleaning continued. Received D.R.O. No. 10/11-13.	WSL

41st SANITARY SECTION * (D.) * R.A.M.C

Army Form C. 2118.

Page 10.

WAR DIARY
or
INTELLIGENCE SUMMARY
(Erase heading not required.)

Place	Date	Hour	Summary of Events and Information	Remarks and references to Appendices
Camblain L'Abbé	15th Oct.		Constructive Work :- Mixing place for destructor refuse in Camblee camp. Ten urine guides fixed to public latrine. Destructor converted into ordinary incinerator. Chimney 2 door table pieces for new destructor. Erected. Soakage pit completed for M.C. Company all supplies in VILLERS au BOIS. One wells in village. Tabulated reports will be compiled on completion of water testing in the whole area. Water Testing :-	No 2
			Camps visited :- CARENCY - 129th R.G.A. - roof screen provided for latrine all other units visited - camps fairly clean.	
			Signs :- 10 signs made & written. D.A.Q. :- routine work continued Received D.R.O. No. 1614-15.	

Army Form C. 2118.

WAR DIARY
or
INTELLIGENCE SUMMARY

(Erase heading not required.)

Page 11

Place	Date	Hour	Summary of Events and Information	Remarks and references to Appendices
CAMBLAIN L'ABBE	14 Oct.		Constructive work:- 3 urinals made & fixed for 1st Merchants Regiment material drawn for detention in Infantry Camp. Water testing:- 20 wells in village. Camps visited - CARENCY, VILLERS au BOIS, & MAISNIL BOUCHÉ. Signs - 10 signs made & finished to show foul ground at CARENCY. Received D.R.O. Nos 1616 - 1619.	N&C
	15 Oct.		Constructive work:- commenced latrine (20 seats) for Infantry Camp. "Grease trap" soakage pit made for "details" attached to "Signals". CARENCY:- one new latrine for Officers. " " " " urinal " " GAUCHIN LEGAL:- all section of D.A.C. visited, also A, B, C, D/104/F.A.B., A.B.C./105/F.A.B. cesspool at Chateau is being cleared out. Foul ground notices placed in every camp. A/108/F.A.B is a new battery from England. Sanitary corporal shown what sanitary appliances are required. The water duty men instructed in chlorination. Received D.R.O. Nos 1620 - 1625.	N&C

Page 12

WAR DIARY or INTELLIGENCE SUMMARY

(Erase heading not required.)

Place	Date	Hour	Summary of Events and Information	Remarks and references to Appendices
CAMBLAIN L'ABBÉ	16th Oct.		Constructive work:- Latrine commenced yesterday continued. Shot for A.D.M.S. repaired. New grease trap soakage pit - San. Sec. camp. "Soakage pit & urinal made for public use" near main Infantry camp. Destructor - walls completed as far as top door & centre bars. Begins:- 18" "Foul ground" & 8" "Urinal" notice boards made & written. Water testing:- in each sub-area this work is proceeding. Camp inspection:- all units in GOUY SERVINS area visited to-day. Received D.R.O. No. 1626-1628 & 1629-1632.	No 1
	17/Oct		Constructive work:- Latrine in Infantry Camp completed, old latrine demolished & timber utilised for making trench boards for new latrine. Destructor completed; also mixing chamber. 2 doors, sills, & chimney made for next "	8 No 2

WAR DIARY or INTELLIGENCE SUMMARY

Page 13

Place	Date	Hour	Summary of Events and Information	Remarks and references to Appendices
CAMBLAIN L'ABBE	14th Oct cont		Construction work continued:- 4 urinals made for GAUCHIN LEGAL. Grease trap soak pit at Signal'billet "Signs: 9 "Grease Traps", 6 "Refuse Pits" made & written to-day. Construction work:- MAISNIL BOUCHE:- new latrine for Officers, two grease traps, cookhouse " " Latrines for GAUCHIN LEGAL commenced.	NSL 
	15th Oct		Water Testing:- 10 more wells tested in village; work is proceeding in other areas. CARENCY invaded also new work as under in VILLERS au BOIS inspected - 2 new hot latrines, ablution place, grease trap incinerator Signs:- new Office sign "Out of bounds" sign for A.P.M., & 4 "Foul Ground signs". Routine work at D.H.Q. by sanitary squad has been continued daily. Reduced D.R.O. No. 1623 - 1638.	NSL

WAR DIARY or INTELLIGENCE SUMMARY

Army Form C. 2118.

Page 14.

Place	Date	Hour	Summary of Events and Information	Remarks and references to Appendices
CAMBLAIN L'ABBÉ	19th Oct	—	Constructive work:- Latrine for 18 buckets made behind N. STAFFS billet. 4 box seats for latrine " for GAUCHIN LEGAL. supports & " " " " Destructors - 4 courses laid, grid fixed. Camp Inspection - CARENCY & VILLERS au BOIS visited - notices to show foul ground fixed. At the former village a new grease trap & urinal fixed. Signs:- 9 miscellaneous signs made & written. Water testing in all areas continued. Received D.R.O 705. 1639 " 1641.	Rose
	20th		Full report of work done in present area up to present date forwarded with maps, tables to A.D.M.S to be handed over to the A.D.M.S of the 1st Canadian Division which is relieving this Division in a few days. VILLERS au BOIS:- comp of 1st R Sussex visited. Cookhouses for officers messes & latrines for cooks in bad condition. Defects pointed out to battalion responsible.	WSR

WAR DIARY
or
INTELLIGENCE SUMMARY
(Erase heading not required.)

Army Form C. 2118.

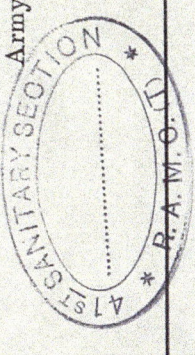

Place	Date	Hour	Summary of Events and Information	Remarks and references to Appendices
CAMBLAIN L'ABBÉ.	20th Oct.		Constructive work:- GAUCHIN LEGAL:- 1 latrine + 1 urinal (both new) completed. 3 new bores fixed in existing one. Public latrine with 6 seats & 2 urinals completed. All signs made Signs:- 5 miscellaneous signs completed. by this section have on them the Dipinople sign. ESTRÉE CAUCHIE during the last few days, the following latrines have been made under our supervision:- 10 pail latrine for men. 8 " " " 1 " " Officers. 2 " " "	WSL
	21st Oct.		Received D.R.O. No.s 1643-1648. & XVII Army Corps R.O. No.s 347-349. Constructive work:- GAUCHIN LEGAL:- new public latrines urinals completed. Latrines at Chateau repaired & bot seats substituted for open board arrangement which previously existed.	WSL

Page 16.

Army Form C. 2118.

WAR DIARY
or
INTELLIGENCE SUMMARY

(Erase heading not required.)

Instructions regarding War Diaries and Intelligence Summaries are contained in F. S. Regs., Part II. and the Staff Manual respectively. Title Pages will be prepared in manuscript.

Place	Date	Hour	Summary of Events and Information	Remarks and references to Appendices
CAMBLAIN L'ABBÉ	21st Oct		Constructive work:- latrine behind N. STAFFS camp completed Water Testing:- completed to day in all areas Signs - 9 miscellaneous completed Routine work continued. Received D.R.O. 1649 - 1652. His Majesty the King has been graciously pleased to award the Meritorious service Medal to No. 924 Sgt. T. KILBURN of this Section.	WSL
	22nd Oct		Sgt. GOODING + Cpl. GAWTHORPE sent to new area LOOS subject to get full information regarding work there + disposition of men. Constructive work: Destruction behind N. STAFFS built by Pioneers under our supervision completed to day. Two urinals made + fixed near new latrine + completed yesterday. Urinal for C/105/F.A.B. " " A/107/F.A.B. Incinerator " " C/105/F.A.B. Signs - 6 completed. "Washing water only." Routine work at D.H.Q. continued. Recd. D.R.O. 1653 - 1658.	WSL

2449 Wt. W14957/M90 759,000 7/16 J.B.C. & A. Forms/C.2118/12

WAR DIARY or INTELLIGENCE SUMMARY

Army Form C. 2118.

Place	Date	Hour	Summary of Events and Information	Remarks and references to Appendices
CAMBLAIN L'ABBE	23rd Oct.		Constructive work:- Latrines for Transport men of main Infantry camp in village commenced. 2 urinals screen fixed at 6th Queen's latrine. CARENCY:- two new refuse pits at H.Q Brigade. 1 new urinal + 1 new latrine in village. Signs:- 10 miscellaneous signs completed. Relieved D.R.Q. 1659-1642.	WSR
	24th Oct.		Commenced to relieve 83rd Sanitary Section. Corp EDWARDS:- took over Clayton disinfector at Divisional Laundry near BETHUNE. Corp LOTT - took over the sanitation of 4008 village + trenches around. Constructive work:- all tools sharpened. Several minor repairs to latrines in village. Latrine commenced yesterday completed. Path to public latrine 102 completed. Work will be undertaken in present area.	WSR

WAR DIARY or INTELLIGENCE SUMMARY

Army Form C. 2118.

Page 16

Place	Date	Hour	Summary of Events and Information	Remarks and references to Appendices
CAMBLAIN L'ABBE.	25th Oct		MOVE :- The MILLS took over Shack disinfector at DROUVIN prisoners' camp. Cpl LANIGAN visited most of area worked from LES BREBIS. Inspection - all men visiting camps especially those of units moving at once - minor defects remedied. Advance party sent to LES BREBIS. Received D.R.O. No 1678 - 1681	
	26th Oct		MOVE :- advance party sent to BRAQUEMONT. Men employed as yesterday. Received D.R.O. No 1682 - 1684.	NSC
	27th Oct		Move to new area completed. Men are now distributed as follows:- Laundry - 1 N.C.O. Drouvin - 1 Man. Braquemont - 1 N.C.O. + 4 Men. Lens - 1 N.C.O. Received D.R.O. No 1685 - 1688.	* Les Brebis - remainder of Section NSC

Page 10.

WAR DIARY
or
INTELLIGENCE SUMMARY
(Erase heading not required.)

Army Form C. 2118.

Place	Date	Hour	Summary of Events and Information	Remarks and references to Appendices
LES BREBIS	28th Oct.		Constructive work:- mess room commenced for attached men. fireplace oven at San. Sec. billet. Two night latrines made at rear of San Sec billet	Nos.
	29th Oct.		Camps:- inspectors located various units. camps re-billets but no detailed inspection was made. Received D.R.O. Nos 1689-1691. Constructive work:- mess room completed. two standard corrugated iron incinerators made complete with grid.	
	30th Oct.		Camps:- a more thorough inspection made of Les Brebis. list of defects made and attention of units drawn to same. BRAQUEMONT visited - this village will be divided into sub areas at once. Received D.R.O. Nos 1692-1694. Arrangements made to day for the removal of the Section from LES BREBIS to BRAQUEMONT. Received D.R.O Nos 1695-9	Nos. Nos.

WAR DIARY or INTELLIGENCE SUMMARY

Place	Date	Hour	Summary of Events and Information	Remarks and references to Appendices
BRAQUEMONT	30 Oct.	—	Constructive work - LES BREBIS. Latrines - 2 flyproof hot seats & urinal behind Billet occupied by O.M. 9th C. Surveys Repaired canvas around latrines opp: billets No's 454, 466, 1554. Constructed officers' latrine (box pattern) ready for fixing for 72nd M.G. Coy's Transport. Repaired brick incinerator in "A" area Fixed new urinal opp. Billet 976 Grease trap } made for 72nd M.G. Company Incinerator (new iron) } Grease trap - 9th C. Surveys Camp inspection - all sub areas in Les Brebis & Braquemont. 10 T.U. men reported for duty in Les Brebis H.Q. of section moved to BRAQUEMONT. Sgt DINNIS will have charge of original section at LES BREBIS.	WDL

Page 21

WAR DIARY or INTELLIGENCE SUMMARY

Army Form C. 2118.

Place	Date	Hour	Summary of Events and Information	Remarks and references to Appendices
BRAQUEMONT	31st Oct.		Constructive work - latrine for officers, urinators, grease trap } 172nd M.G. Company	WSL
			The Divisional Area has now been divided as follows for supervision ie:-	
			LES BREBIS :- 3 men - village divided into 3 areas, to include GRENAY.	
			MAZINGARBE :- 1 man	
			P'T SAINS & FOSSE 2 BETHUNE - 1 man	
			MAROC :- 1 man	
			PHILOSOPHE & QUALITY St - 1 man	
			BRAQUEMONT - 2 areas - 2 men - to include FOSSE 2 DUPONT, RESERVE PARK.	
			DROUVIN & HOUCHIN :- 1 man.	
			Preliminary inspections made in all areas.	

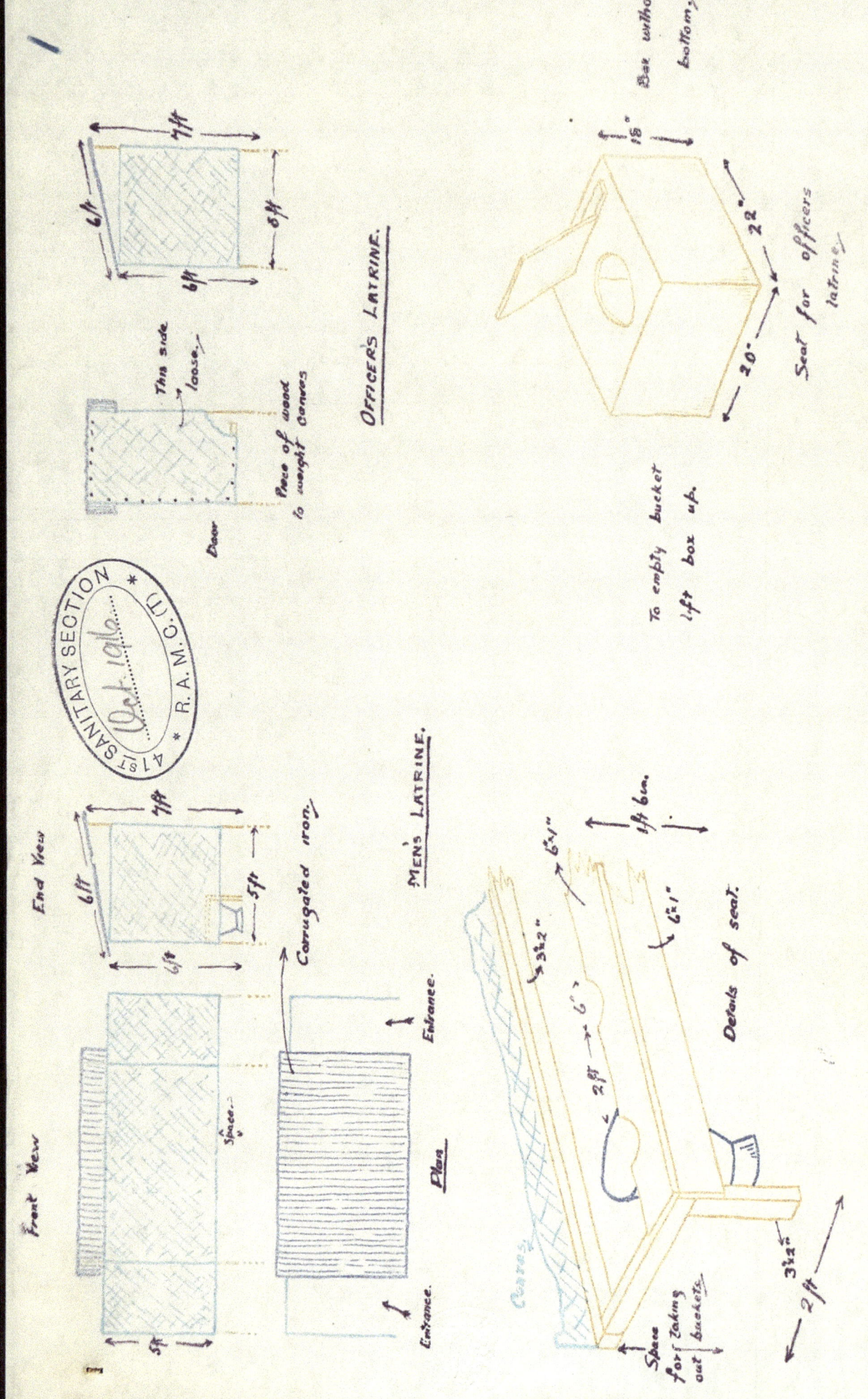

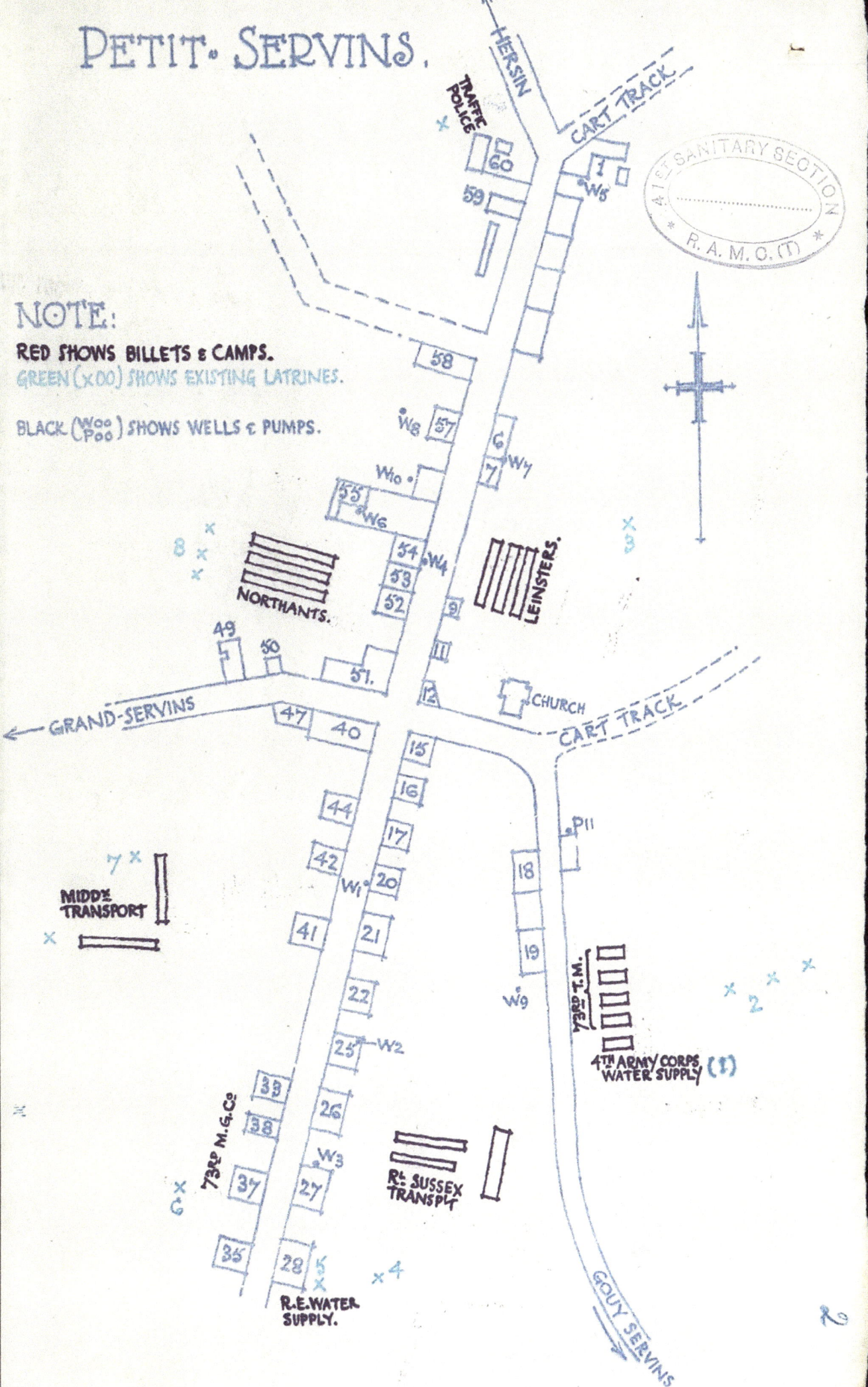

GAUCHIN-LEGAL :: PLAN OF VILLAGE :: [NOT TO SCALE]

41st SANITARY SECTION — R.A.M.C. (T)

NOTE:
RED SHOWS POSITIONS OF CAMPS
GREEN [X] " " " EXISTING LATRINES.
" " " " PROPOSED NEW "

OCTOBER 1916.

GRAND-SERVINS.

41ST SANITARY SECTION R.A.M.C.(T)

→ PETIT-SERVINS
→ VILLERS AU BOIS
← HERSIN
← FRESNICOURT

MANURE DUMP
RIFLE BDE TRANSPORT
TR.MORTAR
33 R.F. 33 LABOUR
No.4 CONTROL POST
POND
1ST R.F. TRANSPORT
123 R.F. TRANSPORT
61ST ANTI-A: BATTERY
QMS
FIELD AMBULANCE
8TH BUFFS.
17TH BDE TRANSPORT

NOTE:

RED SHOWS CAMPS & BILLETS.

GREEN (×oo) SHOWS EXISTING LATRINES.

BLACK (Woo) SHOWS POSITIONS OF WELLS.

Camblain L'Abbé

41st SANITARY SECTION R.A.M.C. (T)

No. of Well	No. of Billet	Well Pump or Spring	Water Drawing apparatus		Source or Depth	Possible sources of contamination	Horrock's Test			
			Nature	Condition			Mug	Colour	Taste	Smell
1.	51.	Well	B & N	Bucket leaks	90 ft.	None apparent	1	Clear	None	None
2.	Adjoining 52.	Pump tank								
3.	52.	Well	B & N	Good	95 ft.	Stables	1	Clear Slightly	None	None
4.	47.	"	"	Good	90 ft.	Surface	1	Turbid	None	None
5.	49.	"	"	"	90 ft.	Manure	1	Clear	"	"
6.	50.	"	"	"	100 ft.	Surface	1	"	"	"
7.	105.	"		"	100 ft.	None apparent	1	"	"	"
8.	45.	Pump	Leaky Out of Order	"	?	Manure	1	"	"	"
9.	44.	"				Manure	1	"	"	"
10.	43.	Well	B & N	"	100 ft.	None apparent	1	"	"	"
11.	42.	"	No bucket	Fair	100 ft.	Surroundings bad	1	"	"	"
12.	on 42.	"	B & N	Good	100 ft.	None apparent	1	"	"	"
13.	38.	"	Not in use		—	—	—	—	—	—
14.	39.	"	B & N	Fair	95 ft.	Surface	1	"	"	"
15.	39 A	Pump	—	—	—	Surface	1	Turbid	"	"
16.	34.	"	—	—	—		1	"	"	"
17.	3.	Well	B & N	Bucket leaks	95 ft.	None apparent	1	Clear	"	"
17A.	4.	"	"	Good	?	"	1	"	"	"
18.	5.	"	"	"	90 ft.	"	1	"	"	"
18A.	1.	"	Not in use		—	—	—	—	—	—
19.	31.	"	Tap and tank		—	—	1	Clear	"	"
20.	29.	Pump	Bad wood structure		—	Surface	1	"	"	"
21.	23.	"	Not in use		—	—	—	—	—	—
22.	19.		B & N	Fair	No cit.	100 ft.	None apparent	1	Clear	"	"
23A.	21.	Well	B & N	Fair	95 ft.	"	1	"	"	"
24.	15 A	"	"	"	100 ft.	Manure	1	"	"	"
25.	13.	"	"	No cit.	95 ft.	"	1	"	"	"
26.	Chateau	Pump	—	Fair	100 ft.	None apparent	1	"	"	"
26A.	" (cookhouse)	"	—	"	"	"	1	"	"	"
26B.	" (kitchen)	"		"	"	"	1	"	"	"

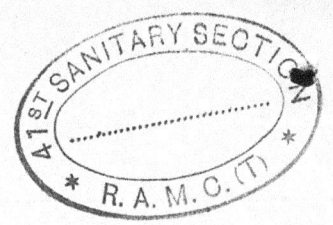

No of Well	No of Billet	Well or Spring	Water Drawing apparatus Nature	Condition	Depth	Sources of contamination	Horrock's Test Mag	Colour	Taste	Smell
27.	7.	Well.	Under	repair.	95 ft.	None apparent.	–	–	–	–
28.	10.	"	B & W.	Fair.	95 ft.	"	1	Clear	None	Non
29.	9.	Pump.	–	Out of order.	–	–	–	–	–	–
30.	12.	Well.	B & W.	No sill.	80 ft.	Surface.	1	Clear	"	"
31.	14.	"	"	Bucket leaks.	100 ft.	Manure. Pig-bowshed. stys.	1	"	"	"
32.	15.	"	"	Windlass needs repair.	100 ft.	None apparent.	1	"	"	"
33.	16.	"	"	Fair.	100 ft.	Pig stys. Privy.	1	"	"	"
34.	22.	"	"	No sill.	95 ft.	Manure.	1	"	"	"
35.	67.	"	"	Good.	100 ft.	None apparent.	1	"	"	"
36.	71.	"	"	No sill.	?	"	1	"	"	"
37.	94.	"	"	Good.	100 ft.	"	1	"	"	"
38.	96.	"	No windlass.		–	–	–	–	–	–
39.	Opposite 88.	"	B & W.	Good.	–	None apparent.	1	Clear	None	Non
40.	87 A.	"	B & W.	"	100 ft.	Manure.	1	"	"	"
41.	85.	"	"	"	?	None apparent.	1	"	"	"
42.	84.	"	"	No windlass.	?	"	–	–	–	–
43.	83.	"	"	Bucket leaks.	95 ft.	Surface.	1	Clear	None	Non
44.	82.	Pump.	–	Not in use.	–	–	–	–	–	–
45.	Near 82.	Well.	B & W.	Bucket leaks.	100 ft.	Surface.	1	Clear	None	Non
46.	80.	"	"	Fair.	100 ft.	None apparent.	2	Turbid	"	"
47.	Near 80.	"	"	No sill.	95 ft.	"	1	Clear	None	Non
48.	Behind 102.	Tap.	–	Not in use.	–	–	–	–	–	–
49.	"	"	"			"	–	–	–	–
50.	101.	Well.	B & W.	Fair.	?	None apparent.	1	Clear	None	Non
50 A.	102.	"	"	No windlass.	?	"	–	–	–	–
51.	78.	Pump.	–	Not in use.	–	–	–	–	–	–
52.	78.	Well.	B & W.	No sill.	95 ft.	Manure.	1	"	"	"
53.	Near 73.	Well.	B & W.	Good.	100 ft.	None apparent.	1	"	"	"
54.	74.	"	"	"	100 ft.	"	1	"	"	"
55.	72.	Pump.	Out of order.		–	–	–	–	–	–

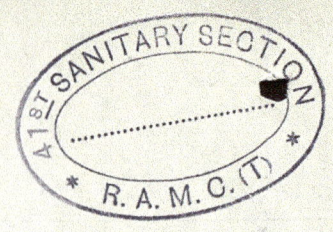

No. of Well	No. of Billet	Well Pump or Spring	Water drawing apparatus Nature	Water drawing apparatus Condition	Source or Depth	Possible sources of contamination	Horrock's Test Mug	Horrock's Test Colour	Horrock's Test Taste	Horrock's Test Smell
56.	68.	Pump.	—	—	—	Surface bad.	1	Clear	None.	None.
57.	66.	Well.	B. & N.	Good.	100 ft.	Manure.	1	"	"	"
58.	63.	Pump.	Not in use.	—	—	—	—	—	—	—
59.	63.	Well.	New washer required for pump.	—	—	None apparent.	1	Clear	None	None.
60.	61.	Pump.	—	Good.	—	"	1	"	"	"
61.	59.	Well.	Windlass needs rep:	—	—	"	1	"	"	"
62.	56.	"	B. & N.	No cvr.	100 ft.	Surface.	1	"	"	"
63.	Mongrel Vesticant	"	"	"	100 ft.	"	2	"	"	"
~~64.~~	~~58.~~									
64.	53.	"	No windlass.		95 ft.	None apparent.	2	"	"	"
65.	14.	Pump.	—	Good.	—	"	2	"	"	"

140/262

24th Divn.

41st Sanitary Section

Nov 1916

COMMITTEE FOR THE
MEDICAL HISTORY OF THE WAR
Date −3 JAN. 1917

Vol 15

41ST SANITARY SECTION
WAR DIARY
(CONFIDENTIAL)
VOLUME 15.
from Nov. 1st to Nov. 30th 1916.

Army Form C. 2118.

WAR DIARY
or
INTELLIGENCE SUMMARY
(Erase heading not required.)

Instructions regarding War Diaries and Intelligence Summaries are contained in F. S. Regs., Part II. and the Staff Manual respectively. Title Pages will be prepared in manuscript.

Place	Date	Hour	Summary of Events and Information	Remarks and references to Appendices
BRAQUEMONT	1st Nov	—	As stated in previous month's Diary the Section is working as follows:-	
			(1) BRAQUEMONT :- divided into two areas - L/Corp LANIGAN & L/Corp BABB } from BRAQUEMONT.	
			(2) HAILLICOURT, DROUVIN, HOUCHIN :- Pte. CANNON.	
			Included in (1) is FOSSE 2 DUPONT & RESERVE PARK.	
			(3) LES BREBIS :- divided into three areas - Ptes JOHNSON, SALTER, SMITH	
			" Workshop - Corp. KILBURN & BLACK & Pte. BRADLEY.	
			(4) MAROC :- Pte. WHITTAKER	} from LES BREBIS.
			(5) MAZINGARBE :- " MARFLEET	
			(6) FOSSE 2 BETHUNE & Pt. SAINS :- Pte. LAW.	
			(7) PHILOSOPHE & QUALITY ST. :- Pte. CHISNALL.	
			(8) D.H.Q. :- L/C. LANHAM	
			(9) LOOS :- Corp. LOTT & Pte. HALDANE.	
			(10) DIV LAUNDRY :- Corp. EDWARDS, %C CLAYTON disinfector.	
			(11) PRISONERS' CAMP, DROUVIN :- Pte. MILLS %C THRESH "	
			Where a man is in charge of an area he visits this area daily, notes any defects & brings them to the notice of the N.C.O. %C San. Squad. Where are reported & board kept of improvements when made.	

Army Form C. 2118.

Page 2

WAR DIARY
or
INTELLIGENCE SUMMARY
(Erase heading not required.)

Instructions regarding War Diaries and Intelligence Summaries are contained in F. S. Regs., Part II. and the Staff Manual respectively. Title Pages will be prepared in manuscript.

Place	Date	Hour	Summary of Events and Information	Remarks and references to Appendices
BRAQUEMONT	1st Nov.		Water Carts:- L/cp DINNIS & Pte MILLS will be the inspectors of water carts will commence duties in a few days. Reports will be made in accordance with Chief Army instructions.	
			Constructive work:- LES BREBIS:- public latrine:- 5 flyproof box seats over new pit. 195 new urinal fixed. 209 grease trap " " " " ; + refuse pit dug (House opp. Baths)	
			Received D.R.O. Nos 1708 - 1714.	
			Infectious disease:- cases of diphtheria in HOUCHIN - CAPPELLE LOUIS & CALOUANNE LEON - houses cleansed or by order of Maire; streets placed "Out of bounds" by TOWN MAJOR, & Mobile Laboratory asked to take swabs of these cases with the contacts also.	
	2nd Nov		Constructive work.	
			LES BREBIS:- 608. urinal removed completed, 362 urinal fixed. 4 M.G.T. - new screen for latrine & new urinal. 212. public urinal, 3 new urinals fixed, screen repaired. 765 grease trap fixed; Rue Carnot:- urinal repaired, 381 do.; 5 grease trap finished	

2449 Wt. W14957/M90 750,000 4/16 J.B.C. & A. Forms/C.2118/12.

Page 3

Army Form C. 2118.

WAR DIARY
or
INTELLIGENCE SUMMARY

(Erase heading not required.)

Place	Date	Hour	Summary of Events and Information	Remarks and references to Appendices
BRAQUEMONT	2nd Nov		Constructive work in LES BREBIS continued.	
			Large house off Baths:- grease trap provided	
			MAZINGARBE:- 181st R.F.A. " " "	
			" " Y.M.C.A. :- hot seat latrine for Staff only	
			" " 186th R.G.A.:- grease trap provided.	
			MAROC :- 821, 814 - latrine seating repaired.	
			PT SAINS. - urinal repaired, y.B. hydrant billets sprayed, grease trap for dressn. T.	
			WORKSHOP:- Urinals, 12 hot seats for latrines	
			In BRAQUEMONT area several minor defects were noted & remedied by Unit.	
			Owing to the fact that one cart less is being supplied for the BRAQUEMONT area,	
			& that carts are not remaining over night at LES BREBIS thus wasting time	
			going to & from the Refuse Dump. the work of scavenging the various areas is	
			not being done as thoroughly as it ought to be. The Town Major of LES BREBIS	
			has been informed & asked to take steps to remedy this.	
			LOOS:- work of supervision well in hand; the work of cleaning billets is being	
			proceeded with.	

Army Form C. 2118.

Page 4

WAR DIARY
or
INTELLIGENCE SUMMARY

(Erase heading not required.)

Instructions regarding War Diaries and Intelligence Summaries are contained in F. S. Regs., Part II. and the Staff Manual respectively. Title Pages will be prepared in manuscript.

Place	Date	Hour	Summary of Events and Information	Remarks and references to Appendices
BRAQUEMONT.	3 Nov	—	Constructive work:—	

LES BREBIS:— 381, 379. Box seat latrine made & fixed; new screen fixed; new pit not necessary

" " — Latrine fixed, 581 ditto.

" " 14th T.M.B — soakage pit; 93rd T.M.B — box seat for Officers' latrine

" 14th T.M.B — screen & frame repaired.

832 latrine screen & frame repaired.

204 & 442 — 3 boxes fixed in each, screening repaired or replaced where necessary

N. Staff Band:— grease trap, incinerator, & latrine screen

Pt SAINS:— N. Hants T. ⎫
             Middlesex T. ⎬ new grease trap
             Sussex T.   ⎭

MAZINGARBE:— Y.M.C.A:— latrine fixed, gangway provided with roof &c.
17th Bde T. — new urinal & grease trap provided
186th R.G.A. — refuse pit " " "
379 x 675 — latrines rescreened

HOUCHIN:— various minor defects remedied; & convenience for ablution provided.
LOOS:— " " " e.g. latrines damaged by weather

Received DRO Nr 1724 - 1427

Army Form C. 2118.

WAR DIARY
or
INTELLIGENCE SUMMARY
(Erase heading not required.)

Place	Date	Hour	Summary of Events and Information	Remarks and references to Appendices
BRAQUEMONT	July 4/16	—	Constructive work:-	

PHILOSOPHE:- R.W.Rnts:- 4 grease-traps, latrine screened, 2 ablution benches provided, soakage pits dug

QUALITY ST:- two lot seats fixed & latrine screen fixed also.

MAROC:- 6/8 latrine screen repaired

MAZINGARBE:- 11th Entrenching Battn R.N.D. - long deep trench latrine with 6 fly proof boxes constructed; pipes sewer needed; trough urinal fixed & is leading into main village sewer; old latrine urinals demolished, foul ground marked.

Tr SAINS. Middlesex T.:- grease soap traps completed
Northants T.:- " " trap completed, new latrine urinal provided

FOSSE 2 BETHUNE:- 12th R.F.T. - grease trap
A new manure dump has been provided for units in two last named

WORKSHOP:- 12 hop seats for latrines, 6 urinals, 32 notice boards

BRAQUEMONT:- M.M.P:- grease-trap;

Infection diseases: two civilian cases of enteric fever in FOSSE 2 DUPONT washes & full report forward to D.M.S.- also one in NŒUX LES MINES - in the case are at local billets there & no source of infection was found

NSL

Page 6.

WAR DIARY
or
INTELLIGENCE SUMMARY

(Erase heading not required.)

Army Form C. 2118.

Place	Date	Hour	Summary of Events and Information	Remarks and references to Appendices
BRAQUEMONT	4th Nov. 5th Nov	—	Received D.R.O. Nos 1728-1734. LOOS:- inspection of billets is proceeding; 4 dirty cellars ordered to be cleaned up today. Constructive work:- LES BREBIS:- Salvage dump - grease trap fixed. 8th Buffs Q.M.S:- " " " 42nd M.G.T:- refuse pit dug 12th Sherwood T- soakage " BULLY GRENAY:- 129th R.E.s - new latrine erected - 3-box seat " " - 1 " seat for officers PT SAINS:- Sussex Band:- soap trap provided MAZINGARBE:- 3rd R.D:- many insanitary conditions remedied by this Unit since last visit. Public incinerators (2) are now being looked after by our P.B. men. WORKSHOP:- 4 non incinerators - square; pattern of ironwork for destructors; sample refuse tin for cookhouse A.181; civilian BRAQUEMONT:- Grease-trap for cookhouse A.181; Well at R. Rue d' ARRAS, Mont Les Mines inspected, found to be in a most insanitary condition. This had given by owner as nuisance was caused by troops of a previous Division. Decision D.R.O. No 1735-1740	N.S.2. N.S.2.

Army Form C. 2118.

WAR DIARY
or
INTELLIGENCE SUMMARY

(Erase heading not required.)

Page 1.

Instructions regarding War Diaries and Intelligence Summaries are contained in F. S. Regs., Part II. and the Staff Manual respectively. Title Pages will be prepared in manuscript.

Place	Date	Hour	Summary of Events and Information	Remarks and references to Appendices
BRAQUEMONT	6th Nov		WATER CARTS:- 3 carts, 195th, 196th, + 197th Companies, A.S.C. examined to-day. Detailed reports forwarded to A.D.M.S. - on all carts many spares are wanting.	
			Constructive work:-	
			PHILOSOPHE:- incinerator renewed for eyelets - now burning satisfactorily. Soakage pit for ablution bench.	
			PT. SAINS:- new public urinal fixed & one repaired	
			" " " latrine - 4 hot seats fixed, canvased in	
			" " " " - 2 " " " " "	
			" " " " - 3 " " " " "	
			" " " " - 3 " " " " + 1 seat repaired	
			" " " incinerator - fixed iron pattern - square	
			Notice boards:- To Manure Dump (2), "Out of Bounds", + "Out of Bounds" on civilian W.C. fixed.	
			LES BREBIS:- Latrine RUE de NICHOLAS - 4 new seats + canvas fixed	
			" " " 159 - new front screen.	
			WORKSHOP:- 12 latrine boxes, 11 refuse tins, 12 signs for refuse tins, + 2 signs	WPL
			HOUCHIN:- new latrine (D.A.C. No.1); grease trap (D.A.C. No.2).	

Army Form C. 2118.

WAR DIARY
or
INTELLIGENCE SUMMARY
(Erase heading not required.)

Place	Date	Hour	Summary of Events and Information	Remarks and references to Appendices
BRAQUEMONT	6th Nov.		Infectious Diseases:- similar case of enteric fever, wife of M. DELATTE, 44, Rue de Cauchy, NOEUX les MINES - patient removed to BETHUNE hospital 14 days ago; the house disinfected 4 days ago. The house is locked up in the daytime while the husband is at work. No endeavour to let it there. Scavenging in both areas is still proceeding under the difficulties previously mentioned. Received D.R.O. Nos. 1441 - 1443. " I Corps Routine Orders Nos. 139 & 140.	WSL
	7th Nov.		Constructive work:- MAZINGARBE. 3rd R.B. - latrine seats & 2 water taps repaired 11th Ent. Bn. :- demolished unused latrine 13th Surrey Co. :- new latrine pit dug. LES BREBIS. 12th Sherwoods - grease trap 129 R.E. Dump - 3-seat latrine erected Rue Cadurna - 4 " " " " 581 - 3 " " " " ; new canvas & new urinal 927 & 683 - Seaters renewed " " " WORKSHOP:- 6 hot seats, 3 urinals, 12 Refuse tins, & one sign	WSL

Page 9

Army Form C. 2118.

WAR DIARY
or
INTELLIGENCE SUMMARY
(Erase heading not required.)

Place	Date	Hour	Summary of Events and Information	Remarks and references to Appendices
BRAQUEMONT	Mar 1/16 cont'd to 31/16		Received D.R.O. Nos 1744-1753. Constructive work:-	WSL
			LES BREBIS:- 42nd T.M.B.- standard pattern corrugated iron incinerator. 129 R.E. (Chateau) - 2 grease traps; ditto 8th Buffs T. & 73rd Bde. T. 3rd Sieg. R.G.A. 1 ", demolition of latrine. Latrines 921 & 945 re-canvassed.	
			MAZINGARBE:- 12 Linwood:- new canvas round latrine urinal, 2 new urinals, new soakage pit, new iron incinerator. dug 8th Buffs:- new iron incinerator fixed, 2 refuse pits filled in & 1 new one dug. foul ground marked.	
			PETIT SAINS:- 3rd R. BT.- grease trap & garbage pit provided. 2nd Leinsters " " " provided. 4th Northants T. soap wash scheme complete.	
			BRAQUEMONT:- H.Q. cook house fire place improved - inside lined - chimney (to rear) handy painted.	
			WORKSHOP:- 3 log seat latines, 4urinal, 1 incinerator, 20 notice boards, 30 notice boards painted.	
			Water Testing:- 170th Tunnelling Company R.E.:- new well sunk by military - good. Chlorine re-action on 1 & 1 cup. Received D.R.O. Nos 1754-1763.	WSL

Army Form C. 2118.

WAR DIARY
or
INTELLIGENCE SUMMARY

(Erase heading not required.)

Place	Date	Hour	Summary of Events and Information	Remarks and references to Appendices
BRAQUEMONT	9 Nov		Constructive Work:—	
			LES BREBIS:— "A" Baths — 3 latrines demolished & pits filled in	
			73rd Bde H.Q. — 3 have seats fixed.	
			42nd " (T) — 2 " " urinal fixed, foul ground marked	
			129th R.E. (bhatow) — ablution bench & soakage pit, new urinal, " "	
			PETIT SAINS:— public latrines — 2 re-canvased, notices fixed, urinal repaired	
			Montcanh T. — ablution bench fixed	
			Qtr Guard T. — " " "	
			FOSSE 2 BETHUNE:— standard incinerator — square — fixed	
			MAZINGARBE:— 12th Field Cay. RE:— soakage pit & grease trap made	
			latrine at X roads:— 5 hot seats fixed, latrine & framework made (part)	
			roofed & re-canvased same, urinal - canvased.	
			LES BREBIS:— fixed 24 refuse tins for civilian use	
			BRAQUEMONT — 4 " " " a new urinal in RUE CANROBERT	
			WORKSHOP:— 19 miscellaneous signs made & painted	
			C.151 R.F.A.:— new grease trap & refuse pit made to day	

WAR DIARY or INTELLIGENCE SUMMARY

Army Form C. 2118.

Place	Date	Hour	Summary of Events and Information	Remarks and references to Appendices
BRAQUEMONT	9 Nov		Water Carts:- In accordance with instructions the water carts of the Division are to be carefully inspected every 10 days. In order to carry out this work effectively L/Sgt DINNIS & Cpl MILLS have been detailed for the work. The following units have been inspected to date:- 42nd M.G. Coy, 9th L. Surreys(2), 1st N. Staffs(2), 12th Sherwoods(2), Div. H.Q. 195th, 196th & 197th Companies A.S.C, Div. Train, 8th R.W. Kents(2), 8th Buffs(2), 8th Queens(2), & 12th Royal Fusiliers. Water supplies:- (a) Testing of the main supplies with a view to labelling each is proceeding in each area. At LOOS a great deal of uncertainty seems to prevail with regard to the taking over of the 3 main supplies so that within units change over the supplies are not supervised for a day or two. In other parts of the area constant supervision is unnecessary - all supplies tested up to now being very good requiring the minimum amount of bleaching powder. Received DRQM 1763-4	

Page 12

WAR DIARY
or
INTELLIGENCE SUMMARY.
(Erase heading not required.)

Army Form C. 2118.

Place	Date	Hour	Summary of Events and Information	Remarks and references to Appendices
BRAQUEMONT	10 Nov		Constructive work:-	

MAZINGARBE:- urinal off Mairie - pipe repaired - new screen fixed on public latrine near hospital.
Officers latrine - new canvas fixed, urinal repaired.
Public " " " " & seat repaired
" " " " & new urinal provided, also canvas for tus [?]
12th Field Coy R.E.- " " " & new standard incinerator supplied, fixed, latrine repaired
" " " " new standard incinerator supplied & fixed for RGA camp

PHILOSOPHE - 9 notice boards & new grease trap provided for 1st Aid Post.

MAROC:- new urinal behind 1st Aid Post.

P⁻ SAINS - " Public latrine - 4 seats canvas - fixed

FOSSE 2 - manure destructor erected.

LES BREBIS:- 9/B Surreys - incinerator built.
12/B Sherwoods - ablution bench fixed
8/B Buffs - 9 mds - new officers latrine erected
120 R.E. - new urinal & four notice boards fixed

WORKSHOP:- 3 bot latrines, 10 notice boards, strainer for grease trap.
Water Testing - all supplies in at HAILLICOURT & HOUCHIN ag used by the military kitchen. Good blue in the 1st Inst.

Received DRO No. 14165/1464

Page 13.

WAR DIARY
or
INTELLIGENCE SUMMARY.

Place	Date	Hour	Summary of Events and Information	Remarks and references to Appendices
BRAQUEMONT	11 Nov		Constructive work:-	

LES BREBIS:- Two areas "A" & "B" are being taken over again by the civilian authorities, placards placed "Out of bounds to troops all military sanitary appliances are being demolished.

1st Div. S.Q.T.- standard incinerator

PHILOSOPHE:- Road & Dig:- Latrine repaired & ash was refixed

FOSSE No 2 R.B.T - soap trap repaired

PETIT SAINS:- 4 notice boards fixed HOUCHIN:- cover screen for No 1 & 3 D.A.C. Latrine

MAZINGARBE:- 12th Field Coy R.E.- incinerator
public ablution bench completed.
" Latrine behind church repaired & new urinal fixed
" one standard incinerator, 40 notice boards, & door for

WORKSHOP:- destructor in MAZINGARBE at present out of use

Water Testing:- DROUVIN - M.V.S. - well - deep blue in 1st cup
Gunners camp - well - " " "
BRAQUEMONT:- grease trap for C 181 F.A.B also new refuse pit, C 175 new urinal

Received D.R.O. No 1 & 08 11/42
A 5834 Wt. W4973/M687. 750,000 8/16 D.D. & L. Ltd Forms/C.2118/13.

WFL

Army Form C. 2118.

WAR DIARY
or
INTELLIGENCE SUMMARY.

(Erase heading not required.)

Page 1A
Instructions regarding War Diaries and Intelligence Summaries are contained in F. S. Regs., Part II and the Staff Manual respectively. Title pages will be prepared in manuscript.

Place	Date	Hour	Summary of Events and Information	Remarks and references to Appendices
BRAQUEMONT	12/1	—	Constructive work :-	

LES BREBIS - Work of demolition continued in "A" & "B" areas.

MAZINGARBE - 12th Coy R.E. - new canvas for latrine screen urinal fixed.

1st Bn SWB T - urinal fixed

1st Bn SWB T - full latrine - A new hopper over pit - 12 feet deep - urinal fixed - structure re-canvased - old urinal demolished.

PHILOSOPHE - Refuse pit filled in, new one dug.

LES BREBIS :- 42nd Bde HQ T. - 6 box seats fixed on latrines.
9th Suff or 965. ablution benches fixed - one for each.
129 RE - incinerator built refuse pit dug.

WORK SHOP :- 5 latrine boxes & 3 grease trap strainers.

BRAQUEMONT :- one brick destructor completed to day. This has been built by two men from the 12th Sherwood Foresters.

HOUCHIN - 1st Army Mining School - incinerator repaired.

Inspection of all areas is proceeding daily.
Alterations are being made to HQ Cookhouse fire to try & prevent smoking.

Received DRO No 2 1773.

A 3834. Wt.W 4973/M687. 750,000 8/16 D.D.&L.Ltd. Forms/C.2118/13.

Place	Date	Hour	Summary of Events and Information	Remarks and references to Appendices
BRAQUEMONT	Nov. 15th	—	Constructive work:-	
			LES BREBIS:- 4th - grease trap fixed	
			9th Surreys - refuse pit dug	
			12th R.F. - public latrine constructed near this camp to-morrow,	
			roof wants complete.	
			Work of demolition in "A" + "B" areas now completed.	
			P^t SAINS:- Officers latrine built for 9th Durm. Transport.	
			PHILOSOPHE:- gauge strainer fixed to grease trap in camp of R.G.A	
			MAROC:- 2nd Leinster - new refuse pit	
			1st Munster Regt R.E:- new latrine urinal erected.	
			WORKSHOP:- tops for D.H.Q cookhouse - work here will be completed to-morrow.	
			BRAQUEMONT:- new grease traps in all Artillery camps	
			HOUCHIN:- No. 3 D.A.C:- breeded latrine converted replenished into a 12 hot Latrine. A new one is being made by 138th R.G.A.	
			Received D.R.O. Nos 1444 - 1444.	

Army Form C. 2118.

Page 16

Instructions regarding War Diaries and Intelligence Summaries are contained in F. S. Regs., Part II. and the Staff Manual respectively. Title pages will be prepared in manuscript.

WAR DIARY
or
INTELLIGENCE SUMMARY.
(Erase heading not required.)

Place	Date	Hour	Summary of Events and Information	Remarks and references to Appendices
BRAQUEMONT	14th Nov.	—	Appointment:- No. 422 A/Corp. GAWTHORPE J. to be A. Staff Sergeant from this date.	WS
			Only routine work possible to-day as every man attended the Divl. Gas School to be fitted with & instructed in the use of the new Box respirator. Received D.R.O. No's 1446 - 1483.	
	15 Nov		Constructive work:-	
			LES BREBIS - Q.tte Durays T:- 2 latrines re-canvased + 1 urinal fixed	
			12th R.F:- new refuse pit	
			3rd Siege R.G.A.:- new latrine erected	
			8th Buffs T:- soakage pit dug + 2 latrines repaired	
			PHILOSOPHE:- gauze trap fixed to grease trap; various notice boards fixed	
			WORKSHOP:- 8 box latrines, 2 shove lids, 12 signs for Water supplies	
			12 refuse tins	
			RESERVE PARK:- showroom here has been remented	
			Sign writing - 23 2nd Ground notices made & painted. Stencil cut for	
			Water DB&L	
			Received D.R.O. No.s 1484 - 1786.	

Received DRO No.s 1484-1786.

Page 14

Army Form C. 2118.

WAR DIARY
or
INTELLIGENCE SUMMARY.

Place	Date	Hour	Summary of Events and Information	Remarks and references to Appendices
BRAQUEMONT.	16 Nov	—	Construction work:—	
			PETIT SAINS :- 2 public latrines & 1 Officers latrine re-covered.	
			2 " urinals fixed	
			ghent T :- new latrine erected & Northants T :- new grease trap	
			FOSSE 2 :- all refuse has now been removed	
			& Field 207 R.E. :- brick incinerator rebuilt, refuse pit dug	
			MAZINGARBE :- 12 & Field 107 R.E. :- brick incinerator rebuilt, refuse pit dug	
			MAROC :- 2 public latrines re-covered.	
			WORKSHOP :- sign making - 28 for water supplies, 14 miscellaneous	
			BRAQUEMONT :- second destructor completed. A shed will now be built	
			in which to store refuse for incineration	
			C 178 - Lat seats (3) fixed, also canvas around latrine	
			Disinfection - blankets for Military Police disinfected this afternoon	
			Inspection - a systematic inspection of cellar dug outs is now being	
			made in MAROC & LOOS - a number of unoccupied billets are in a	
			dirty condition containing refuse that should be burned.	
			Received D.R.O. N°s 1759 - 1793	W.A.

Page 18

Army Form C. 2118.

WAR DIARY
or
INTELLIGENCE SUMMARY.
(Erase heading not required.)

Place	Date	Hour	Summary of Events and Information	Remarks and references to Appendices
BRAQUEMONT	17th Nov	—	Constructive work:—	
			MAILLICOURT:— Supply Column — trench for latrine now completed. A bucket latrine with cement floor is to be erected here.	
			HOUCHIN:— Rect Bomb - latrine is being repaired by the Corps R.E. Section 3. D.A.C. — deep trench latrine — 12 seats, cover, screen — now finished. New cookhouse completed.	
			BRAQUEMONT:— No. 1 Coy A.S.C. — hot seats provided. Reserve Park — " " canvas provided.	
			MAROC:— 2 refuse pits & 2 grease traps provided by R.G.A.	
			MAZINGARBE:— 3 urinals, 11th Entrenching Battn — officers latrine.	
			PETIT SAINS:— Middlesex T. — latrine repaired & re-canvased.	
			Received D.R.O. No. 1794–1799.	NSL
	18th Nov		Constructive work:—	
			BRAQUEMONT:— urinal behind 24th Div. Hqs. Q.M. Stores. " — road made to destructor.	
			DROUVIN:— new refuse pit for Ammunition Column	NSL

Page 19.

Army Form C. 2118.

WAR DIARY
or
INTELLIGENCE SUMMARY.

(Erase heading not required.)

Place	Date	Hour	Summary of Events and Information	Remarks and references to Appendices
BRAQUEMONT.	18 Nov		Constructive work:-	
			PHILOSOPHE:- Y.M.C.A.:- new latrine urinal with screening erected.	
			72nd Bde H.Q. Signals:- incinerator fixed	
			FOSSE 2.:- R.B.(T):- incinerator completed	
			MAZINGARBE:- 168th R.G.A:- refuse pit dug & grease-trap constructed	
			14th Bde H.Q.-(T):- incinerator fixed	
			LES BREBIS:- 72nd M.G. Coy:- new latrine erected.	
			" " "officers":-	
			3rd R.B. workshop:- new ablution place erected.	
			26th R.G.A.:- new latrine erected	WSL
	19 Nov		Received D.R.O. No. 1800 - 1810.	
			Constructive work:-	
			LES BREBIS:- 2 new urinals (with pits) & 1/3 Bde T. latrine re-screened.	
			MAZINGARBE:- standpipe repaired. All water has now been tested.	
			The necessary notices fixed	
			MAROC:- new latrine for D/151/F.A.B, lids for latrine 880, & latrine near school improved.	WSL

Army Form C. 2118.

Page 20.

WAR DIARY
or
INTELLIGENCE SUMMARY.
(Erase heading not required.)

Instructions regarding War Diaries and Intelligence Summaries are contained in F. S. Regs., Part II. and the Staff Manual respectively. Title pages will be prepared in manuscript.

Place	Date	Hour	Summary of Events and Information	Remarks and references to Appendices
BRAQUEMONT	19 Nov	—	PHILOSOPHE:- 103rd Field R.E:- grease trap. LES BREBIS:- 2 notice boards (miscellaneous) fixed. BRAQUEMONT:- shed for refuse near destructor commenced to-day. 200B:- no work possible to-day owing to heavy shelling. Received D.R.O. N̄os 1815 - 1818.	WSC
	20 Nov	—	Constructive work:- BRAQUEMONT:- shed near destructor almost completed. LES BREBIS:- destructor on site of refuse pit almost completed to-day. PHILOSOPHE:- new latrine for 103rd R.E's. MAZINGARBE:- latrine urinal screened. 192 R.G.A:- new " " erected, brick incinerator repaired. MAROC:- several minor repairs to latrines. LES BREBIS:- " " - grease traps WORKSHOP:- 7 hot seats, 9 notice boards, 2 grease traps, 2 grease traps frames, 30 miscellaneous signs. Received D.R.O. N̄os 1819 - 1826.	WSL

A.5834 Wt.W4973/M687 750,000 8/16 D.D. & L. Ltd. Forms/C.2118/13.

Place	Date	Hour	Summary of Events and Information	Remarks and references to Appendices
BRAQUEMONT	21st Nov	—	Constructive work:-	
			MAROC:- Hot seat latrine & urinal fixed.	
			PHILOSOPHE:- new grease trap fixed over new pit, urinal fixed.	
			Pt. SAINS:- Public latrine repaired, much malicious damage is done in this village by civilians, necessitating constant repairing of latrines, urinals, grease traps.	
			LES BREBIS:- notice boards fixed to all water supplies used by troops. 2 covers for soakage pits, new latrine for R.E. Dump.	
			WORKSHOP:- 8 box seats, 5 lids, 1 urinal, 20 notice boards (miscellaneous) made & painted.	
			BRAQUEMONT:- new latrine - Jughs Coy Div Train (40th Division); 2 grease traps in two latrines the three board system has been replaced by 6 box seats.	W52
			Received D.R.O. No 1819-1826, G.R.O. No 1949-1959.	
	22nd Nov		Constructive work:-	
			LES BREBIS:- new "officer" latrine at 1b0, Rue Mazingarbe.	
			PHILOSOPHE:- 2 grease trap strainers, 3 notice boards.	
			Pt. SAINS:- all "un-official" water supplies marked "Unfit for drinking" as they are mostly wells liable to contamination.	W52

WAR DIARY or INTELLIGENCE SUMMARY

Army Form C. 2118.

Page 22

Place	Date	Hour	Summary of Events and Information	Remarks and references to Appendices
BRAQUEMONT	22nd Nov cont.		FOSSE 2 BETHUNE:- 12 office tins made fixed MAROC:- several minor repairs to latrines, urinals, water notices fixed in trenches where drinking water is drawn. WORKSHOP:- 6 box seats; 2 urinals, & 28 water notices. Received D.R.O. No. 1827-1832.	
	23rd Nov		Inspection of water carts is however daily. Majority of carts are not in use consequently there is little to report on. No deficiencies in equipment have yet been made good, but so far as being taken with regard to these. Scavenging in all areas is proving satisfactorily in all areas except PHILOSOPHE & QUALITY ST. where much remains to be done. Constructive work:- FOSSE 2 BETHUNE:- Now that the two brick destructors for the LES BREBIS area have been completed a shed similar to the one in BRAQUEMONT is being made for storage of refuse. LES BREBIS:- A grease trap with strainer & lids &c. been fixed, slag placed on paths near water trough. MAROC:- remainder of 16 water notices fixed.	WSL

Army Form C. 2118.

WAR DIARY
or
INTELLIGENCE SUMMARY.
(Erase heading not required.)

Page 23

Place	Date	Hour	Summary of Events and Information	Remarks and references to Appendices
BRAQUEMONT	23rd Nov contd	-	FOSSE 2 BETHUNE:- 2 latrines re-covered.	
			PHILOSOPHE:- 3 grease traps; 3 latrines re-covered, 2 urinals moved to new site & screened, tins provided for wet refuse at each cooker.	
	Received D.D.O. No. 1833-4.			WSL
	24 Nov		Constructive work:-	
			FOSSE 2 BETHUNE:- shed 18' x 6' completed, together with one small lock-up shelter for tools &c.	
			All refuse from gardens has now been removed.	
			MAZINGARBE:- 2 box seats for 16 W.YORKS, urinal & 2 grease traps constructed, officers' latrine supplied & fixed for 192nd R.G.A., also new refuse pit.	
			WORKSHOP:- 3 box seats for pail latrines; 3 trough urinals.	
			MOUCHIN - new refuse pits are required here as ones being constructed at once, much of the ground round about is fouled & improved grease traps will have to be made to deal with soapy & grease waste. Conversion of 3 board system to box seat latrines is proceeding.	
			New cookhouses are being erected by the R.E's who are also supplying new ablution benches.	
	Received D.R.O. No. 1835-1840.			WSL

Page 24

Army Form C. 2118.

WAR DIARY
or
INTELLIGENCE SUMMARY.

Place	Date	Hour	Summary of Events and Information	Remarks and references to Appendices
BRAQUEMONT	25 Nov.		HOUCHIN :- 1st Army Mining school. a new soapy water scheme is being made to deal with water from new ablution Lane.	
			BRAQUEMONT :- new urinal screen for Review Park	
			WORKSHOP :- 40 miscellaneous signs made & painted. 3 trough urinals, 1 hot seat for bucket, 6 grease trap strainers & 1 experimental grease trap.	
			LES BRE BIS :- work of re-screening public latrines continued.	
			QUALITY ST.:- new officers' latrine + urinal near Batts. H.Qrs.	
			MAZINGARBE :- latrine at H.Q. R.F.A. extended & completed	
			Received D.R.O. Nos. 1843-1850 + Special Order of the Day by C-in-C. Constructive work.	N.S.L.
	26th Nov.		BRAQUEMONT - new urinal shit for D.A.D.O.S. office, new urinal for A.D.M.S. office	
			LES BREBIS :- 299 officers' latrine - seats repaired, partition erected, renewing	
			QUALITY ST :- " " (R.F.) - new urinal erected	
			" " - 14th Bde. advanced H.Q.headquarters	
			WORKSHOP :- 35 miscellaneous signs made & painted, 12 hot seats, & 6 upright urinals	
			Received D.R.O. Nos. 1851-3.	N.S.L.

Place	Date	Hour	Summary of Events and Information	Remarks and references to Appendices
BRAQUEMONT	27 Nov.		Continuative work:-
WORKSHOP:- 8 miscellaneous signs made & painted; 6 upright urinals, 6 lids for hot seats, 4 large notice boards.
LES BRÉBIS:- one latrine fitted with 3 hot seats, 2 latrines re-screened, bath made & fenced to a public latrine, one trough urinal fixed for canteen.
MAZINGARBE:- ablution bench repaired, canvas fixed round officers' mess latrines, officers' urinal constructed.
BRAQUEMONT:- water engines fixed on supplies mostly used by troops. All water supplies in the area have now been examined a second time - no new water suits have now been examined have been provided.
Two new important avenues have been provided.
Received DRO No. 1854-1857. Weekly Army circular memorandum No. 32 re "Leave for Officers & Men".
Disinfection. 12 Sherwood Transport Lines - case of 9 by phd - weening action taken in violation of contacts	

Army Form C. 2118.

WAR DIARY
or
INTELLIGENCE SUMMARY.
(Erase heading not required.)

Page 26

Instructions regarding War Diaries and Intelligence Summaries are contained in F. S. Regs., Part II. and the Staff Manual respectively. Title pages will be prepared in manuscript.

Place	Date	Hour	Summary of Events and Information	Remarks and references to Appendices
BRAQUEMONT	28 Nov		Constructive work:-	
			MAROC:- an exhaustive survey is being made of this area with a view to making all latrines rural in a satisfactory condition.	
			LES BREBIS:- 2 latrines re-sanvased; 1 new latrine (2-bores) erected; 4 new seats fixed in public latrine	
			PT. SAINS:- 4 lids & 2 latrines re-sanvased	
			MAZINGARBE:- camp left in very bad state by 12 K.R.F. has now been put into good condition in every particular by the 8th Queen's. 1 new urinal fixed, 3 grease traps fitted with strainers, minor repairs to a public latrine.	
			PHILOSOPHE:- 1 latrine resaved.	
			Destruction:- 2 new brick ones are to be made in MAZINGARBE – one for burning of excreta from pail latrines, the other for camp refuse. 1 new one is to be built in PHILOSOPHE for the whole battalion area. A cart road is to be made to existing destructor in former village where civilian refuse will be burned.	
	29 Nov		Rectified DRO No 1858-1869 & BRO. No 1960-1940.	WDL

WAR DIARY
or
INTELLIGENCE SUMMARY

Army Form C. 2118.

Page 2

Place	Date	Hour	Summary of Events and Information	Remarks and references to Appendices
BRAQUEMONT	29th Nov cont.		Constructive work:-	
			WORKSHOP:- 36 miscellaneous signs, 9 box seat lids, & 1 corrosion refuse bin made & fixed.	
			PHILOSOPHE:- 4 latrines erected, 4 lids made & fixed on public latrines. - necessary notices fixed.	
			MAZINGARBE } latrines. - necessary notices fixed.	
			MAILLICOURT:- new latrine for No. 6 Oz erected; cover & screen erected over temporary latrine for men.	
		30th Nov	HOUCHIN:- new trench latrine completed (No. 2 DAC) - a new soakage pit is being made by this Unit.	NFR
			Constructive work:-	
			DROUVIN:- new men's latrine & new urinal completed.	
			HOUCHIN:- " urinal constructed, new grease trap (No.2 DAC) new soakage pit referred to yesterday completed.	
			BRAQUEMONT:- D.A.D.O.S. office - new ablution place & pit in process of construction.	
			MAROC:- steps will be taken at once to re-screen all latrines in bad repair when this area will be in a good condition	NFR

Army Form C. 2118.

WAR DIARY
or
INTELLIGENCE SUMMARY.
(Erase heading not required.)

Place	Date	Hour	Summary of Events and Information	Remarks and references to Appendices
BRAQUEMONT	30 Nov.		Scavenging. Owing to the fact that the Reserve Park has moved from the area no scavenging was possible to-day. The streets have been swept & the refuse left in piles ready for removing when carts are available.	WR

140/1902

24th Dec.

4th Sanitary Section

Dec 1916

COMMITTEE FOR THE
MEDICAL HISTORY OF THE WAR
Date 31 JAN. 1917

O.C. 41st. Sanitary Section

Plan of Destructor. detached & loaned to Major Brereton.

WAR DIARY
or
INTELLIGENCE SUMMARY.
(Erase heading not required.)

Army Form C. 2118.

Place	Date	Hour	Summary of Events and Information	Remarks and references to Appendices
BRAQUEMONT	Dec 1st 1916		Constructive work :-	
			WORKSHOP :- 8 upright urinals.	
			LES BREBIS :- new 4 bot seat latrine (deep trench). 2 new urinals + urine pits	
			Pt SAING :- " " " " " . new public urinal continued.	
			BRAQUEMONT :- incinerator (fr DADOS), new ablution place commenced with soakage pit.	
			HAILLICOURT :- new latrine in course of construction; new type grease trap made & fixed.	
			Scavenging in all areas is proceeding under difficulties owing to lack of carts since the Reserve Park moved. This especially refers to BRAQUEMONT, MAZINGARBE,	
			PHILOSOPHE.	
	2 Dec		Received D.R.O. No 1873-1875.	W.S.C.
			Constructive work :-	
			MAROC :- work on improvement of latrines in this area commenced to day & the following work completed :- 4 latrines re-canvased, 2 fitted with new box seats	
			PHILOSOPHE :- 2 new deep trench bot seat latrines commenced & completed	
			QUALITY ST :- new latrines are needed here & boxes have been supplied for both Infantry & Artillery units.	

Place	Date	Hour	Summary of Events and Information	Remarks and references to Appendices
BRAQUEMONT	2nd Dec. 1916.		MAZINGARBE:- This village is in an unsatisfactory condition from a sanitary point of view apparently because the sanitary personnel is insufficient & scavenging carts are not being regularly supplied. Very much work will have to be done to make the village as satisfactory as others in the area. Civilians complain of the wilful damage apparently by civilians, or two great traps made by all the 6th Divn. troops in this area are working parties without special sanitary personnel their billets & camp sites are rarely as satisfactory as they ought to be & considerable difficulty is experienced in getting the places cleaned. All defects are reported daily to the Town Major. WORKSHOP:- 12 box seats made, & miscellaneous signs made rewritten for LOOS. BRAQUEMONT work on soakage pit continued. Received D.R.O. No. 1846-1885; G.R.O. No. 1941-1946.	

Army Form C. 2118.

WAR DIARY
or
INTELLIGENCE SUMMARY.
(Erase heading not required.)

Instructions regarding War Diaries and Intelligence Summaries are contained in F. S. Regs., Part II. and the Staff Manual respectively. Title pages will be prepared in manuscript.

Page 3

Place	Date	Hour	Summary of Events and Information	Remarks and references to Appendices
BRAQUEMONT.	3rd Dec		Constructive work:-	
			LES BREBIS:- 3 box seat deep trench latrine & 4 urinals completed to-day.	
			WORKSHOP:- officers latrine for "B" mess made to-day. This will be erected in the grounds of the house to-morrow morning.	
			BRAQUEMONT:- As the artillery of the 40th Division is moving this week commencing to-day special arrangements have been made to inspect all wagon lines camps as they are vacated.	
			Received D.R.O. No. 1886 - 1888.	WSC
	4th Dec.		Constructive work:-	
			MAROC:- work on latrines continued & following work completed:- one latrine demolished, new 5 box seat deep trench latrine erected one new urinal	
			WORKSHOP:- 10 miscellaneous signs made & painted, 2 fire buckets for billet made & painted.	
			BRAQUEMONT:- With the exception of camp occupied by C/181/F.A.B all artillery lines were left in a sanitary condition	
			Water Testing:- 2 wells at HOUCHIN - good blue 1st cup.	
			Received D.R.O. No. 1889 - 1893.	WSC

Army Form C. 2118.

BRAQUEMONT

WAR DIARY
or
INTELLIGENCE SUMMARY.

(Erase heading not required.)

Instructions regarding War Diaries and Intelligence Summaries are contained in F. S. Regs., Part II. and the Staff Manual respectively. Title pages will be prepared in manuscript.

Place	Date	Hour	Summary of Events and Information	Remarks and references to Appendices
BRAQUEMONT	5 Dec		Constructive work.	
			WORKSHOP:- 11 miscellaneous signs made & painted. 6 box seats completed.	
			BRAQUEMONT:- Latrine for "B" Mess erected, framework for new latrine for No. 12 Examining Post (M.P.) made.	
			In other areas several minor repairs executed.	
			Received D.R.O. No.s 1894-5.	WSC
	6th Dec		Constructive work:-	
			MAROC:- new latrine - 6 box seats, deep trench - remains to be removed	
			WORKSHOP:- 9 box seats for men's latrines, 3 box seats for officers' latrines & 4 miscellaneous signs.	
			LES BREBIS:- new soakage pit.	
			MAZINGARBE:- several minor repairs	
			QUALITY ST.:- Latrine completed for Infantry.	
			BRAQUEMONT:- new one box seat deep trench latrine for No. 12 Examining Post completed, also new urinal.	
			Water Testing: - Lines of 19th Coy O.C. - Pump - good - blue in 1' cup.	
			Received D.R.O. No.s 1896-1904.	WSC

Army Form C. 2118.

WAR DIARY
or
INTELLIGENCE SUMMARY.
(Erase heading not required.)

Page 5

Instructions regarding War Diaries and Intelligence Summaries are contained in F. S. Regs., Part II and the Staff Manual respectively. Title pages will be prepared in manuscript.

Place	Date	Hour	Summary of Events and Information	Remarks and references to Appendices
BRAQUEMONT	1st Dec		Constructive work:-	
			WORKSHOP:- 5 box seats for latrine buckets; office furniture for A.D.M.S. repaired	
			BRAQUEMONT:- ablution shed & chutes of same erected for R.A.O.S. new latrine for N.C.O's erected - C/104; large con: iron incinerator for same Battery; latrine for night use - A/108.	
			MAZINGARBE:- new covered latrine, deep trench, box seats, new urinal, new grease trap - Dunkirk huts.	
			MAROC:- 5 latrines re-canvassed, one new deep trench latrine erected & supplied with box seats. Majority of latrines are roofed with corrugated iron.	WSL
	6th Dec		Received D.R.O. No. 1905 - 1914.	
			Constructive work:-	
			WORKSHOP:- latrine boxes, 3 urinals (upright), 1 trough urinal, 6 refuse tins, 3 grease traps.	
			Ft. SAINS:- new urinal erected received.	
			PHILOSOPHE - ablution benches erected under cover, urinal repaired, urinal soakage pits filled in with unburnable refuse.	WSL

Page 6

WAR DIARY
or
INTELLIGENCE SUMMARY

Army Form C. 2118.

(Erase heading not required.)

[Stamp: 41ST SANITARY SECTION R.A.M.C. (T)]

Place	Date	Hour	Summary of Events and Information	Remarks and references to Appendices
BRAQUEMONT	9th Dec.	—	Constructive work :-	

LES BREBIS :- Officers latrine erected complete, pail system. - Sawn iron refuse bin, several minor repairs.

Sewing iron refuse bin, 3 new ablution bench. In the village the man-holes in the main streets have been cleared out by the sanitary fatigues.

MAZINGARBE :- Shed erected over ablution bench.

PETIT SAINS :- Public latrine - structure canvas repaired.

PHILOSOPHE :- Three urinals (one trough) supplied by us refixed by units all in Quality Street area.

WORKSHOP :- Sawn iron refuse bin, 3 urinals, 1 large seat for bucket latrine. 8 mis. signs.

LOOS :- Officers latrine complete.

BRAQUEMONT :- D/108, cookhouse shed erected, new latrine (without roof) for C/106.

HAILLICOURT - new latrine (deep trench) commenced, new urinal completed.

Received DRO No. 1915-1920.

Scavenging from 10 day carts will be supplied as follows :- BRAQUEMONT - 4;
LES BREBIS - 4; PHILOSOPHE, MAZINGARBE, & PETIT SAINS - one each.

Army Form C. 2118.

WAR DIARY
or
INTELLIGENCE SUMMARY.
(Erase heading not required.)

Place	Date	Hour	Summary of Events and Information	Remarks and references to Appendices
BRAQUEMONT.	10 Dec.		Constructive work:- LES BREBIS:- Grease traps with pits, new urinal with screening latrine for 180/R.G.A fitted with box seats, at Siree 3A new urinal made + 6 box seats fixed over pails. PHILOSOPHE:- BRAQUEMONT:- new officers latrine (pail) complete erected this morning leaving of the whole area has progressed very favourably to-day + the next destructors have been burning all day. If a little more dry refuse can be obtained there will not be much difficulty in burning the greater part of the civilian refuse. Received D.R.O. N°: 1921-1924 + G.R.O. dated 4th Dec. 1916.	NSR
	to 11 Dec.		Constructive work:- LES BREBIS:- 24th W.T.M.B - new officers latrine complete erected; men's latrine repaired + rescreened, 14th/R.G. new box seat latrine erected. PHILOSOPHE:- new ablution bench erected under cover now a shelter. HAZINGARBE:- standard type incinerator supplied + fixed for 10/W. Yorks. WORKSHOP:- 12 box seats, 10 miscellaneous signs made + painted.	NSR

WAR DIARY
or
INTELLIGENCE SUMMARY.
(Erase heading not required.)

Army Form C. 2118.

Place	Date	Hour	Summary of Events and Information	Remarks and references to Appendices
BRAQUEMONT	Dec 11		BRAQUEMONT:- several minor repairs. In most artillery camps new latrines are being made by the units concerned. Received D.R.O. No. 1925-1927	WSL
	12 Dec		Constructive work:- HOUCHIN:- No.1 D.A.C. incinerator for burning excreta re-built on more convenient site. Cook house removed to new site. No.2 D.A.C. new pail latrine erected, new urinal constructed, ablution benches fixed, soakage pits & 2 urine pits made. Grease traps have now been made for all cook houses. H.Q. D.A.C. new pail latrine erected. Inoculation:- All men of the Section will be inoculated this week consequently constructive work will be a little disarranged. Billet inspection:- BRAQUEMONT - Corp. EDWARDS will take charge of billet inspection in this village from to-day. He will visit every billet & will report under following heads:- character, accommodation, overcrowding, cleanliness, conservancy arrangements &c. Received D.R.O. No. 1941-5.	WSL

Page 9

Army Form C. 2118.

WAR DIARY
or
INTELLIGENCE SUMMARY.
(Erase heading not required.)

Place	Date	Hour	Summary of Events and Information	Remarks and references to Appendices
BRAQUEMONT	13 Dec.	1	Constructive work:-	
			LES BREBIS:- cinema latrine re-canvased.	
			PHILOSOPHE:- drainage trenches dug.	
			WORKSHOP:- 10 small latrine boxes constructed.	
			sample waterproof box for bleaching powder to carry on water cart.	
			Scavenging. The work of incineration is now proceeding steadily & the majority of burnable refuse is now being burned. A new destructor will be necessary at the dump at FOSSE 2 BETHUNE.	
			Received:- A.D.M.S. R.O. No¹ 211-214	1052
	14 Dec.		Constructive work:-	
			BRAQUEMONT:- 2 latrines (Artillery Wagon lines) fitted with box seats, & re-canvased.	
			HAILLICOURT:- new deep trench latrine, box seats, completed	
			HOUCHIN:- No. 1 D.A.C.:- grease trap, new incinerator in course of erection.	
			No. 2 D.A.C.:- grease trap, new incinerator in course of erection.	
			No. 3 D.A.C. H.Q.:- grease trap, urinal. bucket system latrine now complete.	
			WORKSHOP:- 8 small box seats.	
			Received D.R.O. No¹ 1946-1951, & C.R.O. No¹ 218-224.	1052

Page 10

Army Form C. 2118.

WAR DIARY
or
INTELLIGENCE SUMMARY.

(Erase heading not required.)

Place	Date	Hour	Summary of Events and Information	Remarks and references to Appendices
BRAQUEMONT.	15th Dec	—	WORKSHOP :- 2 large latrine boxes for buckets.	
			MAZINGARBE :- 4 small ' trench, several latrine seats repaired, grease trap, soakage pits.	
			Public latrines: all these have now been cleaned & put in good condition.	
			FOSSE 2 BETHUNE :- new urinal, other urinal renewed.	
			BRAQUEMONT:- new box seat for latrine (M.M.P.); 3 latrines in artillery lines re-canvassed.	WSL
			Received W.O. 1952-1955. Constructive work :-	
	16th Dec		WORKSHOP :- 11 box lids for latrines, & 1 box seat made & painted.	
			MAZINGARBE :- scavenging :- it is found that one cart is insufficient to do the work efficiently :- a road is being made to the rubble destructor in the village where it is hoped to burn much of the vegetable refuse.	
			MARDC :- 6 latrines re-canvassed & put in good repair, the work of putting all latrines in good repair is now almost complete.	
			BRAQUEMONT :- 3 latrines fitted with box seats (artillery lines), 1 new latrine.	WSL
			Received D.R.O. No. 1956-1960 & G.R.O. dated 15%.	

WAR DIARY
or
INTELLIGENCE SUMMARY.
(Erase heading not required.)

Place	Date	Hour	Summary of Events and Information	Remarks and references to Appendices
BRAQUEMONT	Dec: 1st		Received D.R.O. No.s 1961-1965 & 1st L.Q.O. 2/16/12/16. Constructive work:—	

LES BREBIS:— 2 new deep trench bor seat latrines, 1 urinal, 1 latrine fitted with lids & re-screened.

PETIT SAINS:— 2 latrines roofed (public latrine), several minor repairs.

PHILOSOPHE:— new latrine (bor seats, deep trench for R.G.A. in gun position.

BRAQUEMONT:— 19th Company A.S.C. this unit is moving its camp & all new sanitary conveniences &c will be made under supervision of N.C.O. i/c this area.

HOUCHIN:— H.Qrs. D.A.C.:— new cookhouse erected.
  No. 1 D.A.C.:— incinerator still in process of construction, open trench latrine converted into closed with 2
  2. D.A.C.:— open trench latrine converted to new side bor seats, officers transferred to new side ablution bench roofed in & screened. [put down
  3. D.A.C.:— new ablution bench fixed simple soap scheme [scheme completed.

WAR DIARY or INTELLIGENCE SUMMARY

Army Form C. 2118.

Place	Date	Hour	Summary of Events and Information	Remarks and references to Appendices
BRAQUEMONT.	Dec 17		HOUGHIN cont:- 138th R.G.A.:- work of converting trench latrines to pail commenced, ablution bench fixed, base of shed cemented, structure roofed with corr: iron & covered with canvas. DROUVIN:- 36 M.V.S. :- officers' latrine roofed. Billet inspection:- all billets in BRAQUEMONT have now been inspected. New billets have beds fixed, but only four have been found unsatisfactory. These are to be replaced by one hut to accommodate 30-35 men. Received D.R.O. 1961-1965 - 1st C.R.O. dated 16th Dec.1916.	NSC
	18th Dec		Constructive work:- MAROC:- 5 latrines put in good repair. LES BREBIS:- new public latrine, trench type, 4 seats, unimil. roof & screen. MAZINGARBE:- ditto. BRAQUEMONT:- 1 latrine canvased, 1 new cook house, new latrine pit. WORKSHOP:- 6 latrine boxes (corrosion innovation) & 'hot' seats for buckets. Received D.R.O. 1966-1974 & 1st C.R.O. dated 14th Dec.1916.	NSC

WAR DIARY or INTELLIGENCE SUMMARY

Army Form C. 2113.

Place	Date	Hour	Summary of Events and Information	Remarks and references to Appendices
BRAQUEMONT	19th Dec		Constructive work:-	
			BRAQUEMONT:- 194 A.S.C. - new 4 bot seat latrine completed; new sergeants' latrine completed. Artillery wagon lines:- new cookhouse with grease trap &c, new latrine 1 bot seat, trench type. Various signs fixed.	NSL
			QUALITY ST:- new latrine complete. MAZINGARBE:- Bankers - 2 bot seats fixed (Men's latrine), 1 for Officers' latrine, cow iron incinerator. R.E.A. - 3 bot seats fixed, all necessary notice boards made, written fixed.	
			MAROC:- 2 latrines completed. Received D.R.O. Nos 1942 - 1945. G.R.O. No dated 14/12/16 & C.R.O. No 245-252. Constructive numb:-	1
	20th Dec		PHILOSOPHE:- Brick destructor completed, also shed for refuse. This shed is roofed with corr: iron & has concrete floor. BRAQUEMONT:- Burials, several minor repairs. latrine for Ordnance storemen put in repair & refuse cleared away	NSL

WAR DIARY
or
INTELLIGENCE SUMMARY.

Army Form C. 2118.

Page 14.

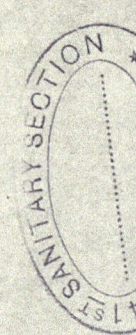

Place	Date	Hour	Summary of Events and Information	Remarks and references to Appendices
BRAQUEMONT.	20 Dec.		LES BREBIS:- WORKSHOP:- 16 latrine box seats, 5 urinals, 2 grease traps minor repairs to incinerator so served out. Received D.R.O. No. 1946-1981, + 1st b C.R.O. No. 253-261. Constructive work:-	WSL
	21st Dec.		WORKSHOP:- 6 urinals, 2 trough urinals, 9 box seats. LES BREBIS:- minor repairs to latrines + urinal Pt SAINS:- 1 latrine repaired, 1 demolished, + 1 received FOSSE 2. BETHUNE:- refuse shed received at the back, shed fitted with lock + key. MAZINGARBE:- 3 trough urinals fixed, 1 urinal demolished, 1 standard incinerator fixed for Sir Banter. Other small minor defects. Received D.R.O. No. 1982-1985 Received D.R.O. No. 1986-1990 + C.R.O. No. dated 21/12. Constructive work:-	WSL
	22 Dec.		WORKSHOP - 8 urinals, 2 grease traps, 6 box seats Owing to heavy weather little outdoor work was possible to-day. Men at HQ employed in whitewashing billet. Received D.R.O. No. 1991-2; 1st C.R.O. dated 22nd December 1916	WSL

Army Form C. 2118.

Page 15

WAR DIARY
or
INTELLIGENCE SUMMARY.
(Erase heading not required.)

Instructions regarding War Diaries and Intelligence Summaries are contained in F.S. Regs., Part II. and the Staff Manual respectively. Title pages will be prepared in manuscript.

Place	Date	Hour	Summary of Events and Information	Remarks and references to Appendices
BRAQUEMONT	23 Dec.		Constructive work:-  WORKSHOP:- 8 box seats, 1 grease trap, 1 urinal/ablution bench, commenced 1 food safe, 1 conversion deodorator. HOOCHIN:- Bucket latrine for 138 R.G.A. completed, soak-away, food safe, pit & abide of lime scheme completed in 1st Army Mining School camp. LES BREBIS area:- latrines to have suffered severely in the recent gale. Men have been engaged all day repairing same throughout the area.	WSL
	24 Dec.		Whitewashing of billet completed at 3/4/8. Constructive work:- PHILOSOPHE:- new latrine for Batt. area. Ft. SAINS:- public latrine re-sheeted & re-roofed, new bucket latrine for officers erected, conversion incinerator made & fixed for artillery lines. Other areas work of repairing after the gale continued. Received D.R.O. N°d 1993-8, G.R.O. N°d 2603-2015, + 6 G.O. N°d 270-282.	WSL

A5834 Wt W4973/M687 750,000 8/16 D.D. & L. Ltd. Forms/C.2118/13.

Army Form C. 2118.

WAR DIARY
or
INTELLIGENCE SUMMARY.
(Erase heading not required.)

Instructions regarding War Diaries and Intelligence Summaries are contained in F. S. Regs., Part II. and the Staff Manual respectively. Title pages will be prepared in manuscript.

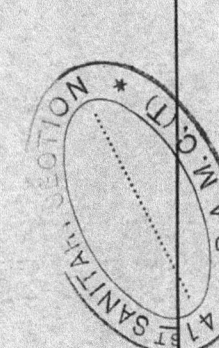

Place	Date	Hour	Summary of Events and Information	Remarks and references to Appendices
BRAQUEMONT	25th Dec.		Christmas Day :- all work suspended. Received D.R.O. No. 1999-2003.	NSC
	26th Dec.		Constructive work :- WORKSHOP :- 1 meat safe, 1 urin: non ineneraton, 5 box seats, several notice boards. LES BREBIS :- 8 latrines repaired, 3 re-screened. PT SAINS :- 4 " " 2 " BRAQUEMONT :- 4 " " 2 " new latrines for No.11 Examining Post commenced. Owing to scarcity of timber it is now impossible to roof in the new latrines erected. HOUCHIN :- all latrines here (except the public ones) are now of the bucket type & excreta is being burned. HALLICOURT :- this village is now being used as a rest area for battalions of the Canadian Corps. Improved sanitary arrangements are urgently needed. Received D.R.O. No. 2004-2007, D.R.O. No. 283-5. D.R.O. No. 2005 re correspondence with strangers will be included in the Orders of the Unit.	NSC

Page 17

Army Form C. 2118.

WAR DIARY
or
INTELLIGENCE SUMMARY.
(Erase heading not required.)

Place	Date	Hour	Summary of Events and Information	Remarks and references to Appendices
BRAQUEMONT	27 Dec.		Constructive work:—	
			WORKSHOP:— 1 cwt. iron destructor, 6 box seats, 3 separate lids, 10 signs	
			FOSSE 2:— 1 new public latrine, 1 for R.F. Transport lines erected & completed.	
			Billet inspection:— all billets in BRAQUEMONT area have now been inspected twice. (Only one case of overcrowding has been reported - no case of dirty billets have been noticed). The 5th inspection of all watercarts in the Division (excepting the Artillery carts) completed to-day. On the 29th the first inspection of all Artillery carts will be complete.	
			BRAQUEMONT:— 4 new latrines for No 11 Examining Post completed.	
			Received D.R.O. No^s 2008-2011, + C.R.O. No^s 286-288.	WSC
	28th Dec.		Constructive work:—	
			WORKSHOP:— 6 latrine boxes for buckets, 2 ditto for trench latrines cow: iron incinerator	
			LOOS:— new latine roofed (trench type – box seat), boxes supplied for 2 more latrines, usual minor repairs in other areas.	
			Received D.R.O. No^s 2012-2020, L.R.O. No^s 2016-2027, + C.R.O. No^s 289-298.	WSC

WAR DIARY
or
INTELLIGENCE SUMMARY.
(Erase heading not required.)

Army Form C. 2118.

Place	Date	Hour	Summary of Events and Information	Remarks and references to Appendices
BRAQUEMONT	29 Dec.		Constructive work:—	
			WORKSHOP:— 6 ordinary latrine box seats, 1 large box seat, 6 miscellaneous notice boards.	
			LES BREBIS:— 2 latrines roofed with corr: iron, 1 fitted with box seats.	
			MAROC:— 2 latrines re-erected, 1 fitted with box seats. All latrine urinals in this area have now been put in good order.	
			BRAQUEMONT:— new latrine, box seat, roof, screening, deep trench type erected for prisoners only in Elbe Camp.	
			New public latrine in Rue CANROBERT completed by us. Ablution benches (15 in all) are being supplied to camps requiring same. Arrangements are now satisfactory throughout the area. Received D.R.O. N° 2021-2028, G.R.O. N° 299-304.	WSL
	30th Dec.		Constructive work:—	
			WORKSHOP:— 9 box seats (standard type), 8 urinals.	
			LES BREBIS:— urinal in own camp, minor repairs to latrines, 2 ablution benches fixed.	
			BRAQUEMONT:— carting of bog for road to destructor, public latrines &c. Received D.R.O. N° 2029, 2030, 2032, Army R.O. N° 139, G.R.O. N° 305-308.	WSL

WAR DIARY or INTELLIGENCE SUMMARY.

Army Form C. 2118.

Place	Date	Hour	Summary of Events and Information	Remarks and references to Appendices
BRAQUEMONT	31st Dec.	—	Constructive work:- WORKSHOP:- 6 box seats for buckets nearly completed, 3 signs for LOOS. The billets at LES BREBIS are being limewashed. An exhibition ground is being prepared in the same village to illustrate how almost every sanitary appliance necessary in the field can be made out of boxes, drums or supplied with rations with a little timber, canvas, coir, iron. Full particulars will be noted in the January volume. Received DRO N°s 2033-2036.	NSC

41st SANITARY SECTION
WAR DIARY
(CONFIDENTIAL)
VOLUME 17
from Jan 1st to Jan 31st 1917

COMMITTEE FOR THE
MEDICAL HISTORY OF THE WAR
Date 13 MAR. 1917

T425
140/1942 Vol 17
24 Div
Jan 1917

Army Form C. 2118.

WAR DIARY
or
INTELLIGENCE SUMMARY.
(Erase heading not required.)

Page 1.

Instructions regarding War Diaries and Intelligence Summaries are contained in F.S. Regs., Part II. and the Staff Manual respectively. Title pages will be prepared in manuscript.

Place	Date	Hour	Summary of Events and Information	Remarks and references to Appendices
BRAQUEMONT	Jan. 1st 1917		Routine inspection work continued at Braquement. The following camps were visited:- 108A, 108B, 109A, 109C, 106A, 106B, 106C, 106D, 106B R.F.A., 194 C.A.S.C., 24th Divisional Signal Cy. Billet inspections were made as follows:- 106D, 109A, 108A, R.F.A. and all were in satisfactory condition. The following constructional work has been executed :- Ablution bench fixed at camp of 196 Coy A.S.C. and arrangements completed for copper made, two new into ablution drainage system. A deep throat latrine fixed with 8 box seats, made in our workshop has been completed at waggon lines 106B. R.F.A. at LES BREBIS the men of the out-section have visited the following camps — 2nd Leinsters, 139 Coy R.E. Dump, Divisional Employers, 3rd Siege Bty, Royal West Kents Transport, Queens Transport, Wells Derby Transport, R.F.A. Old Q.rs., 43rd Light T.M. Bty, Mining Coy R.E's, 107D R.F.A., 17th Bde Transport, 14th Bde Old Q.rs, 1st R.H's, 3rd Siege Bty R.G.A., 2nd Leinsters Transport, 13th Middlesex Transport, 108C Heavy Bty, 9th Queens, 106 M.G.Q.rs. R.F.A., 73rd M.G. Coy, The following constructive work has been executed :- Latrine completed at 108 R.F.A. Old Q.rs, new latrine (sqr) erected in Batt's Area Philosophe, 106 R.F.A. at Q.rs latrine re-screened, Middlesex Transport ablution bench fixed, D107 R.F.A. ablution bench fixed, Officers latrine Batt's Area Philosophe new box seat provided. In workshop 9 Mitre Boards, 3 large box seats & 3 standard box seats were constructed. Work for Sanitary Perbulation continued. Two Water carts belonging to 1st Royal Irish were inspected. Received D.R.O. 2034-3045 & R.O. 309 - 315	N.F.C

WAR DIARY
INTELLIGENCE SUMMARY

Army Form C. 2118.
41st SANITARY SECTION — R.A.M.C.(T)

Page 2.

Place: BRAQUEMONT
Date: Jan 2nd 1917

Routine Inspection work continues. From Braquemont the following camps were visited:— Batteries 3rd Coy Canadian Dt. Qrs, Model Bren Trench Billets — Junction 1st/S.A. D.A.C., 132 U.R.G.A., No 3 Sec D.A.C., A, B, C, D, 106 A+C/107, A+B/108 R.F.A., 194th Bny A.S.C., 245th Divisional Signal Co., Divisional Signal School, D/106, B/107, 195th, 196th, 197th Coy A.S.C., & Billets occupied by 9th Reserve Park A.S.C., B/107.

Constructional work:—
Steam Latrine at A/106, new incinerator at B/106, new urinal and Refuse Pit at A/108, extra canvas trench Latrines & apparatus attached to old line trench completed at 245th Divisional Signal Co., new screen for Public Latrine near DADOS office. Latrine screens completed at Model Billets.

Disinfection:—
At 132nd Sig Ambulance. An Annealing Oven sprayed with Crésol — opened four cars from the billets the following camps detailed have been inspected:—
160th Bty R.G.A., 3rd Section, 174th M.C.Coy, 2d Bty R.E., 53rd Siege Bty, 103 R.E.s, 6th Queens, 109/C Bty R.F.A., Steam Camp Dt. Qrs, Model Billets, Divisional Cavalry, 156 R.G.A., Intelligence Corps, 14th Bn Hants Transport, Snow Camp Dump, D/107 R.F.A., C/107 R.F.A., Horse Lines of 1st — 6th Queens, 184 RTs, 1st Hants Dump, 108th Coy R.G.A., Rajputana War, 29th Royal Sussex.

Constructional work:—
2 Billets Camps: new roof fixed to Latrine. New Latrine seats at 967 Reserve Park, new first circle latrine at 53 Field public latrine repaired at R.B. Transport, new whether system with Ann Philosophe converted from desp. wat. workshop 3 large buried boxes, trace & repaired & painted in workshop, now probably greased, completed, named & drawn for addition work.

Water Carts:—
3rd R.B. (two carts) 175 M.C.Coy, 139 Coy R.E. & 104 Coy R.E. inspected.

PHILOSOPHE:—
Standard Brick Drainhole completed.

[signature]
Capt R.A.M.C.
A.D.M.S. 2nd Army Standing Orders

WAR DIARY
or
INTELLIGENCE SUMMARY.

(Erase heading not required.)

Army Form C. 2118.

Page 3.

Place	Date	Hour	Summary of Events and Information	Remarks and references to Appendices
BRAQUEMONT	Jan 3rd 1917		A demonstration of Sanitary Appliances used in the field was given today in connection with the 1st Corps Course in Sanitation. Three Medical Officers and four Sanitary Officers attended. Three officers missed first the workshop & go to Bruáy to see sanitary appliances being made. They then went to an Infantry Brigade in a neighbouring place of ground, where they were actually in use, such as Italian herve biscuit tins, oil drums, & corrugated iron. Drawings were shown to the officers of the sanitary arrangements made to their billets. The class was also shown the sanitary arrangements made in the Colliers Camp, visits being paid to the 103rd & 104th Amb. and the 1783 Tunnelling Co. R.E. They also went to the Brigade Dump Town 27B or the latrines erected by the Sanitary Section.	
			Routine inspection work continues from Braquemont the following camps were visited — the 11 Examining Post, A.B. C.D./06. A.T.C./07., A+B/08. 19/12 & 15 F. Mtres, occupied by 11/108, 2nd Divisional Signal Co., 196 Co. A.S.C. Latrines for "Sepoys" commenced at 5. Latrine work:- Screening of latrine at No 11 Examining Post was made. Miscellaneous notice boards made.	
			From the Brehm the following camps, units & lorelanes were visited:- Hotchery transport, St. Quesin transport, 1st Staffs transport, 137 M.G. Coy transport, 1st R.F. Transport, 13 T.M.B 4th/4 TM.B trench St R.F., Cinnamon Canteen (Magnicourt), 3rd Sieg R.G.A, 21st Remain Billets (Manqo), Rennin transport, Nicholson transport, Lucan transport, D./107 R.F.A, 1st 8th Queens Billets (Philosophe).	
			Constructional work:- Features trough turned field, Phikeaph, Officers latrine convert from hired Structure erected, uned stores, Haymade, Soap trap constructed at 3rd Siege R.G.A. Petroleum Latrine repaired, Soap trap field in workshop – 1 corrugated iron incinerator, 2 standard latrine seats, 9 miscellaneous notice boards completed - 2 ambulance dustbins	

Received R.O. 562 — 566. C.R.O. 7 — 10. D.R.O. 2053 — 2055

WAR DIARY
or
INTELLIGENCE SUMMARY.

Army Form C. 2118.
41st SANITARY SECTION R.A.M.C. (T)

Page 1.

Place	Date	Hour	Summary of Events and Information	Remarks and references to Appendices
BRAQUEMONT	Jan 1st 1917		Routine Inspection Work continues. From Braquemont the following camps/billets were visited:— B/108 R.F.A., 2nd Divisional Signal Co., 196 Co. A.S.C., A.B.C.D/106, A.C/110, A.B/110, 194 Co. A.S.C. d'Divisional Signal School. Sanitational work:— New urinals arranged at A.S.C. reserve Latrine at Signal School. 5 standard latrine seats made from R. Buerie (?) the following camps, billets etc have been noted:— 2nd Lancs Fus., 73rd M.G. Coy transport, 75th T.M.B transport, 191st T.M.B transport, 106, 107, 108 R.F.A. HQ transport, 7th North Staffs, Divisional transport, Divisional transport, Rifle Bde transport. D/107, C/106 R.F.A., 12th N.F., 2 q.s. hospitals. Constructional work:— Duck board 153 re-constructed. Re-covered were urinals; divers urinal fixed, latrine 558 (Mane) re-covered. Borrowed fried in billets of Branches transport, latrine retried at Divisional transport. New urinal fixed in officers latrine, divisional magazine repaired. Received C.R.O. 11–13., D.R.O. 2056–2061. Water Carts have been inspected belonging to following units:— 13th Middlesex, 7th R Staffs (War Carts), D/107, B/108 R.F.A.	WSC
BRAQUEMONT	Jan 5th 1917		Routine Inspection work continues. From Braquemont the following camps/billets were visited:— 19 F.A., 195 Co., 196 Co. A.S.C., A.B.C.D/106, A.C/107, A.B/110, A.B/108, R.F.A., 3rd Bde R.C.A., Brit. Sec. 3rd Australian Tunnelling Co., divisional Signal School. Following camps/billets have been noted:— 73rd Bde dumps, Depots transport, 191st M.G. Co transport, 191st T.M.B., Y.T.M.B + 2 T.M.B. Balers, 73rd T.M.B. Shelters, 73rd M.G. Co. transport, 146th R.W. Kens + 4th Suffolks Infantry transport, N.F. 2nd R.F.A. H.Q, 7th North Staffs Divisional transport, Divisional transport, Div. Ammunition Transport. Constructional work:— I arranged new incinerators + standard latrine borne made, magazine repaired, latrine 315 R. Borne. Latrine screen repaired at Divisional transport, new incinerators erected + sanitation work at Middlesex transport. Water Carts belonging to following units have been inspected:— 103rd Cy R.E. 3rd Lancashire (War Carts), D.R.O. 2061–2066. Received 1st Army Special Order of the day. Two cases of diphtheria in different homes have been reported amongst civilians at HOUCHIN. An investigation showed that they went into premises where 2 prevision cases where (?) but the outbreak is ascribed (?) by a civilian practicing the charge of the consent.	WSC

WAR DIARY or INTELLIGENCE SUMMARY

Page 5.

Place	Date	Hour	Summary of Events and Information	Remarks and references to Appendices
BEAUMONT (continued)	Jan 5th 1917		No clinical evidence above; no antitoxin was used. The horses have been placed out of bounds to troops, and arrangements made to disinfect the termination of the diarrhoea. Two N.C.O's (Sergt Sanitary & Sgt Baylis) are being organised to replace him Jan 5th.	WSC
BEAUMONT	Jan 6th 1917		(at BEAUMONT) The Prime Automobile having intimated that they did not wish the ground which they had been using as a dump for refuse & manure, altho were obtained by the trench known as the Tranchée Quatre mille on an unlicensed piece of land west of the road 15 feet wide and pointed out to them. In heaps 4 feet high & feet wide and prolonged for any length, manure & refuse in dumps will be at a pinch by the side of the Avion - Oeleroy Rd, and may be formerly made of the Boisoo - Dévise Rd and the gleamy white hut immediately adjoining the Ravelway in the known dramplying its termanted by the Frigg Dept. of the Units. Routine Inspection Work continues — from Beaumont, the following camps billets &c: A+C/107, A+B/108, 3rd Siege By R.G.A. billet, — A.B.C.+D/106, 3rd Australian Trammeway Cos B/106, 3rd Siege Bty R.G.A. billet, Ammunition Signal School, A+C/107, A+B/108, 3rd Siege By R.G.A., 194 Co, A.S.C., 2nd Air Signal, Ammunition School Lead, No 2 DAC. D/106 + 12/107 Camps — 12th Canadian Riflemen House Billets, toad & Billets, 1st Army rineny school Leed School, No. 2 DAC. Convalescent Depot. Australian dug out all fitted, ground marked at 1st Canadian new horse lines, man Billets, advice re seepit of feature Billet — toe student latrine seats warted. Tren Ber Kutin, the following camps, billets, hospital, horse lines have been visited — 13th R Fr., 1st Sul Survey C R.E., Y.M.C.A., 190 B.T.T. R.G.A., 2nd Canadian Transport mobiles 9a Royal Irish Trans port Rifle Bon transport, D/107, C/106 R.F.A., 9th Royal House billet, 7/5 Hants, 73rd M.G. Coy, 91 Bn, 10B, G.R.E's Reeds, Inter Staff transport, 1st Ryrbs halimg transport, 73rd M.G. Cp transport, 94 Queens transport, 73rd Bde R.F.A. transport — "X" T.M. Bty, 'Y' & Z' T.M. Bty transport, 73rd M.C. Cp Billet Contructional work — latrine re-erected at Mauve, latrine + 2 urinals re-erected at Magnybo — Urinal erected at Y.M.C.A. (Magnygain), 6 miscellaneous masters bath, 6 standard latrine doors, and screen (to line) completed in workshop Material belonging following unit have been inspected — 195 Co, 196 Co, 197 Co ASC, 21st Divisional HQ Ops, 2nd Divisional Signal, C/107 R.F.A.	WSC

WAR DIARY
INTELLIGENCE SUMMARY. Page 6.

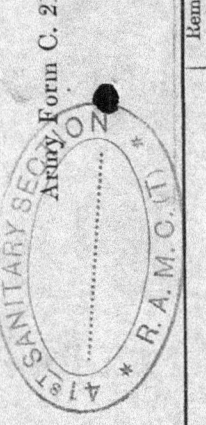

Army Form C. 2118.

Place	Date	Hour	Summary of Events and Information	Remarks and references to Appendices
BRAQUEMONT	Jan 7th 1917		The O/C visited HAILLICOURT and RUITZ with the acting Town Major, who is also O/C No 30 Supply Column. The O/C No 30 Supply Column, the Town Major LES BREBIS, going round the area with the acting Town Major. They visited a rest area for two Battalions of Canadian Infantry. Owing to lack of material the sanitary arrangements were made are faulty. Steps are being taken to remedy this state of affairs, and diagrams of sanitary appliances made from easily obtainable materials have been forwarded to the acting Town Major.

Routine Inspection work continued. From Braquemont the following billets, camps, etc have been visited:- 1950 ASC Sidings, D.A.D.O.S., 9th G Reserve Park, and road of slag being constructed at Refuse Dumps, whilst from F.S. Brohs the following billets, camps & transport lines have been visited:- R.W. Kents, 137th T.M. Bty, Queens, Hunts Derby Transport, Bays Transport, 73rd Bde M.Gun, Divisional Camp Attached Salvage Dump, Divisional Baths 3rd Suf Bty, 5rd Suf Bty, 75 Hortishani Buries, 9th P.Bunny host lines, 7505 M.G. Coy horse lines, 8th Queens horselines, 15 Bde Hd Qrs horse lines, 191st M.G. Coy and transport, 3rd R Bde Transport, Queens Circus (hayguards), 4th North Staffs, 14th Hants Batts Transport, Scotic Transport, 12th R. Irish Transport, D/107, C/108 R.F.A., Florida Scots.

Latrine work reported at 73rd Bde H Qrs, Divisional Officers Mess, latrine removal at Queens Transport, Latrine works at Quinins (Keroutri), Latrine 153 (horse) moved, 2 sample washing troves & 3 standard latrine tools were in evidence.

The public works (Vaughts) have been visited at four different points, and a good result obtained from each test. (LES BREBIS)

Water carts belonging to following units have been tested:- D/108 — C/108 R.F.A.

As does the water supply continues to be chlorinated each morning — and work of reconstructing sanitary arrangements commenced.

Received Routine Orders No 141, 567 - 572, C.R.O. 18 - 22, D.R.O. 5070 - 5072 | NSC |
| BRAQUEMONT | Jan 8th 1917 | | Routine Inspection Work continues. In Braquemont the following camps, billets, etc were visited:- A.B. C&D/106 A&C/107 A&B/106, 3rd Suf By R.Q.A, 315 Squad, 2th Division Signal School, HQ Sect D.A.C, No 3 Sect D.A.C., 21st Divisional Rest Camp, 138th By R.G.A, 10A C/W Ops | NSC |

WAR DIARY
INTELLIGENCE SUMMARY

Army Form C. 2118.

Instructions regarding War Diaries and Intelligence Summaries are contained in F.S. Regs., Part II. and the Staff Manual respectively. Title pages will be prepared in manuscript.

Page 1.

Place	Date	Hour	Summary of Events and Information	Remarks and references to Appendices
BRAQUEMONT (continued)	Jan 3rd 1/9/17		From Bas Bréhain the following camps, billets, transport lines were visited :— 181 L.G., R.E., 787 F.T.M.B9, 91st Queens GR without transport & Queens transport, 139th M.G. Co., transport, 191st G-R.E, 103 G.R.E., 101st Res H.Qrs, 91st Bn Surrey transport line, 91st Queens-Wilson, 9th R.W. Kent transport, 127th M.G. Co, howitzer Bty., 13th Bys, 191st M.G.C., Corps R.G.A. H.Qrs, 17th Bau transport, hitcher transport, 9th Horse Arbl transport, transport transport, D/107 R.F.A. Constructional work :— Batholic Sanitary Convenience erected near Church, Baskin, 3 standard latrine seats, 3 large latrine box seats 86 miscellaneous notices boards completed Wali Carts in progress. The following which have been inspected but C/106, A/108, B/107, D/106, C/107, B/106, +A/106 R.F.A. (on Inspection). Received C.R.O. 23 - 25, D.R.O. 2044 - 2045.	WDC
BRAQUEMONT	Aug 4th 1/9/17		Surgeon General Pike D.M.S., and D.D.M.S. 1st Corps, and A.D.M.S. 2nd Division visited the workshops LECREBIS this morning and after inspecting the constructional work being done, there went to the adjoining exhibition ground to see the sanitary appliances which had been erected for the 1st Corps Course in Sanitation. From Braquemont the following camps, billets, transport lines were visited :— A,B,C+D/106, A/107, A+B/108 R.F.A., 3rd Brig. Bty R.G.A., 2nd Squn G.D/107, B/107, R.F.A. Constructional work :— Public latrine in Rue Sebastopol reopened, and 2 standard latrine seats completed in workshops. From Bas Brehin the following camps, billets, transports lines were visited :— 17th M.G. Co, transport, 98 Bys, 8th Bys transport, 106 Bds, 107 Bd, 106 Bd, 108 Old G GR transport, 93rd M.G. Co, 75th T.M.B3, "X".T.M.B3," "Y" T.M.B3 2nd Female, 9 R.W. Kents, Royal Sussex Regt., 150 Bd R.G.A., South Since, Y.M.C.A, (Philosophe,) Kemall transport, Corporation transport, 13 R. Warwick transport, 3rd R. Berks transport, D/107, C/107, +C/108 R.F.A., 14th Hural Training, 9 Both, 191 M.G.C., 17 Bd, 36 Dfr @sc + Down Majors (Magrgarin). Constructional work :— 3 Urinals reopened at Hagnagne, near officer's latrine fixed. Gean trap emptied, wooden bench fixed at Hagnagne Public Latrine, received at Berthin officer's latrine reopened door repaired, pit dug at Philosophe, 10 miscellaneous notice boards, 2 urinals, 2 standard latrine seats arrangeled non inscriptive made in workshop.	WDC

WAR DIARY or INTELLIGENCE SUMMARY

Army Form C. 2118.

Page 8.

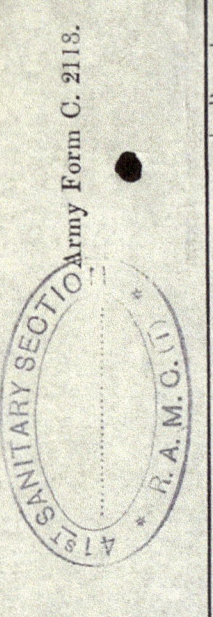

Place	Date	Hour	Summary of Events and Information	Remarks and references to Appendices
BRAQUEMONT (continued)	Jan 9th 1917		Water carts in possession of the following units were inspected:— No1. Sec DAC, No2 Sec DAC, No3 Sec DAC, 194 Co ASC, A/107 R.F.A. At LOOS Latrine at Right Batt. of Gun moustached and reasonable, and old latrine at Enemies Dump demolished. Examination of Village Water Supply continues, and all water supplies in working order. Received C.R.O. 26-32 and F.R.O. 2076-2078	WSC
BRAQUEMONT	Jan 10th 1917		A demonstration of Sanitary appliances in connection with 19 Corps bomb in Sanitation held this afternoon at the workshops and exhibition ground LES BREBIS. A full description of this Course is to be found in Jan 3rd. Six officers attended, three being Medical Officers of Units. Latrine inspection work continues. From Braquemont the following camps billets and horse-lines were visited: A/8106, C/107, D/106, B/107, R.F.A., 194th Co, 195 Co, 196 Co, 197 Co, A.S.C, 3rd Sup. Bty R.G.A, 31st Div. Sig. Co at Our. Signal School, 3rd Ambulance Dumbells Co. Water supplies moved by D/106 R.T.A were filled up. Domestic Tent (O.) 2 Stand pipe near billets in Rue Deroin & Remuignay, - 1 Stand pipe adjoining No 25 Rue Herman Remignay. Barth was showed a deep new main road as Rue Raphael Dump continues. The renovation of mine near Raphael Dump continues. From Petit-Sains the following camps billets & horse lines were visited - D/110, C/105 R.F.A, Siding transport, 5th Div's 6 Divisions 18th Sanitary Divisional Canteen (Magazins) 193 Bty R.G.A, 184 Bty R.G.A, 105 G.R.E, 139 G.R.E, 131 R.F.Rain Timeline, 9th C.Gunnery Rose line, 180 Bty R.G.A, 73rd M.G. Co, 73rd T.M.By, South Lanc Amb, 175 M.G.C, 85 Bty S. Transport, 72nd T.M.By, Z T.M.By, 1st Inuits Sig. Transport, 18th Royal Engineer Transport, and 137 M.G. Co transport. Latrines moustached and others in latrine re-erected at Magazin, 1 standard corrugated iron urinal erected at Magazins, 2 urinals & 2 standard latrines for units inspected in montcaliarp. Water carts in possession of the following units were inspected:— 8th R.W.Kents (Scarli), 6th Buffs (Scarli) & 8th Queens (Scarli). At Petit Sains the renovation of a large back distinctly for burning all refuse now being given to Public Distillers or horse-lines was commenced. Received Routine Order No.142, 573 - 583, + GR.0 2056 - 2065.	WSC

A5834 Wt. W4973/M687. 750,000 8/16 D.D. & L. Ltd. Forms/C.2118/13.

WAR DIARY
or
INTELLIGENCE SUMMARY. Page 9.
(Erase heading not required.)

Army Form C. 2118.

Place	Date	Hour	Summary of Events and Information	Remarks and references to Appendices
BRAQUEMONT	Jan 15th 1917		Routine Inspection Work continues. From Braquemont the following units have been visited:— A/B, C/D/106, A/B/C/107, A/B/108 R.F.A. 3rd Siege Bty R.G.A., 194 C.A.S.C., 1st & 2nd Schools at Div Signal School. Constructional work:— 9 notice boards "TO PUBLIC INCINERATOR" and directing arrows] made. 8 " " "TO LATRINE & URINAL " " From Fosse Bruhin the following units have been visited:— 8th Buffs transport, 6th R.W. Kent, 8th Buffs, 7rd T.M. (6th) Battery, Mining Co. R.E., C/106 R.F.A. 1st Corps Cyclists, 16 Divn Reserve, Y.M.C.A. (Maingarde), Divisional Canteen (Maingarde), 5th Pioneers, 4th Divisional Ammunition Sub park, Soma Transport, D/107 & C/108 R.F.A. Transport, 3rd Bus Transport. Constructional work:— 1 Officers latrine completed. 2 inside urinals completed at Fosse Bruhin. 1 Grease trap fixed at Y.M.C.A. (Maingarde). Urinals completed in workshop. Wall cards in pursuance of the following units were inspected:— 12/4 R?(2cents) Gt East Surreys (2cents), 108 North Devys (2cents.) 7th Machine Gun Co., +108/H2 R.F.A. Received C.R.O. 43–47, D.R.O. 2054–2056.	
BRAQUEMONT	Jan 16th 1917		Routine Inspection Work continues. From Braquemont the following units were visited:— 107/C R.F.A. (twenty hours), 3rd Siege Bty R.G.A. (eight hours) — all found to be clean & tidy, and no action of importance. Constructional work nil. From Fosse Bruhin Camp continues also road over Fosse Bruhin the following units were visited:— 8th R.W. Kents, 103 C.R.E., 4th Divn A.S.C. + 2 Gers, 5th Pioneers, A.C.P. Guards, Middlesex Transport, Guards Reserve Transport, Royal Irish Transport, D/107 + C/108 R.F.A. Mining Co. R.E., 2nd Div Artillery H.Q., Corps H.Q. R.G.A. 1st N Zealand, 3rd R. Bus Transport, Constructional work Futurna but re-search over new pit dug. MAROC Boveloin H.Q, new trough pit dug Corps H.Q. R.G.A. new officers latrine erected. Common cavalier roof created over urinal. MAZINGARBE 2nd R.F.A. H.Q. repair of latrine. FOSSE 2 BETHUNE. C/106 R.F.A. Latrine completed WORKSHOP. 4 large box seats made. Wall cards in pursuance of the following units were inspected:— HQ C.R.E., 12/R Rawlins (Dons), 3rd R. Bus (2cents.) 15 Lep. DENNIS and Cpt LOTT granted leave to England. A.S.C. order from Jan 1st to Jan 2nd inclusive. R.O 20ft–206, CRO 43–47, AS Order 66–67, 6R–79, Divisional Order 5/1917.	

WAR DIARY or INTELLIGENCE SUMMARY.

Army Form C. 2118.

Page 10.

Place	Date	Hour	Summary of Events and Information	Remarks and references to Appendices
BRAQUEMONT	Jan 13th 1917		Routine Inspection Work continues. From BRAQUEMONT the following Units were visited :— B/106 R.F.A. (14 killed), C/106 (60 killed), 9th Divnl Ammn Sqdn Co. (1st killed) From LES BREBIS the following Units were visited :— 5th Pioneers, 4th Divers, Middlesex Transport, Royal Sussex Transport, D/107, C/106 R.F.A., 11th Corps Cyclists, 103rd Bde Pioneers, 106 Bde A.Q. R.F.A., R.W. Kents, Y.M.C.A. (Mazingarbe), 1st Surrey G.R.E., Special Co R.E., 191st M.G. Co. Convalescent work :— LES BREBIS. (WORKSHOP) 6 standard latrine boxes completed 6 urinals 2 notice boards Frame work for Refuse Shed constructed General trays completed 1 Incinerator PETIT SAINS Malt carts in possession of the following Units were inspected :— 17th M.G.C., 104 Co R.E., 2nd Pioneers, 13th Middlesex (2 carts), 9th Royal Sussex (1 w.cart) from LOOS all water supplies were examined and found to be in good working order. Latrines at B West and A Keeps completed. Received C.R.O. 46—52. D.R.O. 3087—3090	WDSG
BRAQUEMONT	Jan 14th 1917		Routine inspection Work continues. From BRAQUEMONT the following Units were visited :— A/107 (25 killed), D/106 (17 killed), +A/108 R.F.A. (11 killed), Convalescent work :— 10 notice boards, Latrine Screens, Incinerators, "Refuse Dumps", 3 "Refuse Dumps", 1 Shed erected at Refuse Dump built for Refuse. From LES BREBIS the following Units were visited :— Stationary Hospital, 5th Buffs Transport, 137th M.G.Co. Transport, 13th Divisional Transport, 72nd Bn. H.Q. R.F.A., 72nd T.M. By, 73rd T.M.B., R.W.K. Transport, Y.M.C.A. (Mazingarbe), Special Co R.E., Middlesex Transport, Sussex Transport, 5th Pioneers, 4th Pioneers. Convalescent Work :— MAROC. Latrine boxes re-screened. PHILOSOPHE. Hutchinsons fired MAZINGARBE. Refuse pit dug. (15th Leinsters) new screens erected PETIT SAINS 3 grease traps, 2 soak pits constructed at Grange. 1 Urinal fixed. at LOOS a new urinal fixed at 104 G.R.E. and other conservational work proceeding. Received C.R.O. 53—56. D.R.O. 3091—3093. + two copies of "S.S. 535" "Gas Defence"	WDSG

WAR DIARY or INTELLIGENCE SUMMARY

Army Form C. 2118.
R.A.M.C.(T)
41st SANITARY SECT.

Place	Date	Hour	Summary of Events and Information	Remarks and references to Appendices
BRAQUEMONT	Jan 15th 1917		Routine Inspection Work continues. From BRAQUEMONT the following Units were visited:- No 1 Sec, No 2 Sec, No 3 Sec, HQ Off D.A.C., HQ Off Mobile Vet Sec, D/106 B/107 R.F.A., 138 Bty R.G.A., Divisional Bus School, 36th Mobile Vet Sec, D/106, 3rd. Sqdn., 39 Australian Tun. Coy., 195 Co, 196 Co, 197 C. A.S.C., 9th Reserve Park, No 11. Examining Post, D.A.D.O.S., Constructional work:- HOUCHIN. 5 notice boards fixed at Rest Camp. Trench latrines converted to bucket option at No 2 D.R.O. I latrine for high use (incinerator) completed " " " " Hd's. D.R.O. From LES BREBIS the following units were visited:- 5th Lancers, 4th Hussars, 16th Lancers (Dismtd. Trans), Artillery Baths, D/107, C/108 R.F.A., 18th Royal Train Transport, 8th R.W. Kents Inlists, 75th M.G.C., 3rd R. Bde. 1st North Staffs., 9th Survey Lit [?], Special Co R.E., 9th Norfolk, 191st M.G.C., 9th Batt, 13th Middlesex. Constructional work:- PHILOSOPHE. I latrine converted to bucket (6) system. I latrine re-erected over new trench. PETIT SAINS. I latrine erected (trench) for 5th Lancers. I latrine erected. I latrine erected. MAZINGARBE. I latrine erected (trench) for 915 Batt. WORKSHOP. 4 standard latrine seats & 2 urinal beams completed. Work continues in pursuance the following Units have been inspected:- D/107 R.F.A., B/106 R.F.A., 73rd M.G.Co., 103rd Co. R.E. Received C.R.O. 57-60, B/106 R.F.A. 2093-2094.	MO
BRAQUEMONT	Jan 16th 1917		Routine Inspection Work continues. From BRAQUEMONT the following Units were visited:- A.B.C. & D/106, A+B/107, A+B/106 RFA, 3rd Siege Bty R.GA, 21st Signals, 21st Sqn'c Section, 79th Co A.S.C. Constructional work:- RUTZ. 2 latrines (deep trenches system) completed. HALLICOURT. ashes path made, latrines, lighting at Reserve Baths. From LES BREBIS the following units were visited:- 8th Batts, 3rd R. Bde, 106 Bty R.G.A., 192nd Bty R.G.A., 107 Bde H.Q., 106 Bde H.Q., 106 Bde H.Q. R.T.A., 1st R. Irish, 73rd M.G.Co., 75th T.M. Bty, 5th Queens Transport, 8th R.W. Kents Transport, 9th R. Sussex Transport, 13th Middlesex, 5th Lancers, 4th Hussars, 2nd R. Irish Transport, 13th Middlesex Transport, 9th R. Sussex Transport, D/107 & C/108 R.F.A Transport, & 13th R. Fusiliers Transport. Constructional Work:- MAZINGARBE. I corrugated iron incinerator. I train latrine. I urinals. I mainseats (Annie) completed. LES BREBIS. I cover for man. hole. I latrine, bor. seat, trenches completed. PETIT SAINS. I incinerator (brick) completed. MAROC. Latrine refuse new pit. WORKSHOP. 4 standard latrine seats & 2 incinerators made with galvanised iron. Work sent in pursuance of the following Units were inspected:- 195 Co, 196 Co, 197 C A.S.C., 21st Divisional Sd Qtrs., 21st Divisional Sqn'c Co., Received: C.R.O. 2066-2083, C.R.O. 61 + bis. D.R.O. 2095-2097. Army Orders Jan to January 1917. Acting Corporal A returned for duty. 2 acting corporals legal returned for duty. 21 Jan 17.	MO

WAR DIARY or INTELLIGENCE SUMMARY

Army Form C. 2118.

Place	Date	Hour	Summary of Events and Information	Remarks and references to Appendices
BRAQUEMONT	Jan 17th 1917		Routine Inspection Work continues. From BRAQUEMONT the following units were visited :– A, B, C & D/106, A & C/107, A/108, B/106, D/106, B/107 RFA, 3rd Siege Bty R.G.A, 3rd Sqdn. 19th Co, 19th Co, 196 Co, 197 Co A.S.C, 9th Reserve Park, DADOS, 2nd Australian Tunnelling Co, Hosp. 11–13 Examining Post. Constructional work :– 6 standard latrine. 6 accidents completed – Shelter hatch points fixed, 1 new latrine completed behind CINEMA. From LES BREBIS the following units were visited :– 8th & R.W. Kents, 8th Queens. Transport, 73 M.G.Co Transport, 13th Batt. Daily Transport, 17th M.G.Co Transport, 15th N. Staff Billets, 7th T.M. Bty Wells, 7th T.M. Bty Wells, 1st Batt. T.M. Bty, "X" T.M. Bty, 9th Royal Sussex, 191st M.G.Co, 1st Surrey C, R.E, 5th Lancers, 4th Queens, 3rd Female Transport, 13th Middlesex Transport, 9th Suss.x Transport, 15th R.F.Williams Transport. A/106, C/107, C/106 R.F.A. Transport. Constructional work :– FOSSE 2. 1 Grease trap fixed. MAZINGARBE All purvée latrines cleaned & disinfected. WORKSHOP 6 Urinals, 1 standard latrine and 1 repair & completed. LOOS. 1 latrine for officer 173rd Co.R.E completed. Work carried on in possession of the following units inspected :– D/106, A/107, C/107, & C/108 R.F.A. Received C.R.O. 65–71, A.D.R.O. 2098–2099.	HAS
BRAQUEMONT	Jan 18th 1917		Routine Inspection Work continues. From BRAQUEMONT the following units were visited :– A, B, C & D/106, A & C/107, A & B/106 R.F.A., 3rd Siege Bty R.G.A., 19th Co, 195 Co, 196 Co, 197 Co A.S.C., 2nd Sqdn Co, 3rd Engine School, "D" DADOS, Siege "3rd Australian Tunnelling Co, 107 H.Q. R.F.A Transport, 193 Siege Bty Wells, 10th R.E's. L.H. From LES BREBIS' the following units were visited :– 73rd M.G.Co Wells, 9th E. Surrey Wells, 5th Lancers, M.G.Co Transport, 6th R.W. Kt. Transport, D/107, C/106 R.F.A Transport, C/106, A/106, B/107, D/106, A/106 R.F.A. 13th Middlesex Transport. 2nd Female Transport, similar areas 1st Female, Y.M.C.A (Mazingarbe) Constructional work :– LES BREBIS. Latrine 361 re-erected over new pit, unconv. fixed & new hole. Latrine 401 new pit, interior fixed, latrine re-erected over new pit. WORKSHOP. 1 Repair Wells, 1 soap latrine boxes sent, Invalid boards, 2 footscrap slip, 3 etc. for latrine units completed. Watercarts in possession of following units were inspected :– C/106, A/106, B/107, D/106, C/107, & A/106 R.F.A. at LOOS all water supplies in working order – new wash fixed at "D" Keep & reconstruction of latrine continues. Received :– Routine Orders. 584 – 586, C.R.O. 72 – 74, A.D.R.O. 2100–2101.	HAS

A 5834 Wt. W.45673/M687 750,000 8/16 D. D. & L. Ltd. Forms/C.2118/13.

WAR DIARY or INTELLIGENCE SUMMARY.

(Erase heading not required.)

Army Form C. 2118.

Place	Date	Hour	Summary of Events and Information	Remarks and references to Appendices
BRAQUEMONT	Jan 19th 1917		Routine Inspection Work continues. From BRAQUEMONT the following units were visited :- No 1 Sec, No 3 Sec. J.H.Q.D.A.C., 138 S/G Y TR. GTA, 2nd Divisional Baths School, 1st Army Musical School, 194 C. ASC, 3rd Siege By R.G.A., A.16 C+D/106, A/107, A+B/108 R.F.A., 2nd Divisional Signal Co, Surgical School, C/107 (4 Rifles) + B/106 (6 Rifles). From LES BREBIS the following units were visited :- 193rd M.G. Coy, 133rd Light T.M. Battery, "X" T.M. Bty, Rifle "Y" T.M. Bty Rifles, 69+13th Bn Transport, 1st R. Staffs Transport, Royal Irish Rifles "Transport," 1st Surreys Transport, 13th Middlesex Transport, 7th N. Hants Transport, 9th + 5 Gloucesters Transport, R.W. Kent Transport, 8th Queens Transport, 9th + 6 Surreys Transport, D/107, C/105, D/106 R.F.A, 3rd Bn Lanark, 13th Middlesex Transport, D/107, C/105 R.F.A. Transport, R.W. Kent Transport. Constructional work PHILOSOPHE 1 Latrine repaired + 1 latrine re-erected over a new pit. MAROC 1 latrine repaired. Latrine completed. PETIT SAINS Latrine commenced. WORKSHOP 1st refuse bins, 6 wash stands completed, 6 for seat party constructed. At LOOS all water supplies in working order. - New urinal fitted at 9th Bn to HQ. stretcher bearers tried in O to Keep and private latrines. Water carts in possession of the following units were inspected :- No 3 Section B.A.C. + 19th Co A.S.C. Received C.R.O. 48-61, 4 D.R.O. 2100-2109. 2 Q.M. LANNIGAN proceeds to UK on leave to England from Jan 19th to Jan 29th.	WAS?
BRAQUEMONT	Jan 20 1917.		Routine Inspection Work Continues. From BRAQUEMONT the following units were visited :- 1st Batt Canadian Model Rifles, 30 Supply Column, 1st Napoleons Park, 13th Canadian Bn, 195 G, 196 G, 197 G. A.S.C., 9th Reserve Park, Police Camp, B/107, D/108 R.F.A., 3rd Australian Tunnelling Co, D.A.D.O.S., 2nd Signal Co. Constructional work :- 197 Coy latrine re-erected. New urinals + seats. Repair to screens. Australian knock frees. From LES BREBIS the following units were visited :- It Artist Rifles, A.S.C workshops, 103 R.C.S. Transport, 8 Queens Transport, 2 R.W. Kent Transport, 9 +5 Surrey Transport, 7 Hants Transport, W. Ridings Rifles, 4 Bedsocks Surreys, 9 Royal Sussex Transport, D/107+C/105 R.F.A. Transport, 107 Bn. R.F.A. Transport, 192 Bde R.G.A., 10+ C.R.E., 17th M. G. Co Transport, 143rd T.M. Bty Rifles, 10th T.M. Bty Rifles, 18 + R. Fusiliers Transport, 106 Bde R.F.A. Transport, 108 Bde H.Q. Transport, 9 + 5 Surreys Billets. At LOOS all water recesses completed at B. Keep. Wear manholes completed at B Keep. 9th Queens (Rest Camp). Water carts in possession of following Units were inspected :- A/107 R.F.A., 9th Queens.	WAS?

WAR DIARY
or
INTELLIGENCE SUMMARY.
(Erase heading not required.)

Army Form C. 2118.

Nage Lt

Place	Date	Hour	Summary of Events and Information	Remarks and references to Appendices
BRAQUEMONT (Continued)	Jan 20th 1917		Constructional work :— MAROC. Repairs to latrine at Battalion H.Q. PETIT SAINS. Immersion proof FOSSE 2. Soap trap fixed. WORKSHOP. Lt. standard latrines completed to notice boards made and fixed. Received C.R.O 62–84, D.R.O D110–D114.	
BRAQUEMONT	Jan 21st 1917		Routine Inspection Work continues. From BRAQUEMONT the following units were visited :— 196 Co A.S.C (11 hours), 2nd Div. Salvage Co (1 hour), 197 Co A.S.C (14 hours). From LES BREBIS the following units were visited :— 5th Lancers, 13th Middlesex Transport, 9th Royal Sussex Transport, 164 Lancers, 104 Bde H.Q R.F.A, 3rd R Bde, Corps H.Q R.G.A, B.coy H.Q R.G.A, 9th & 6 Sussex Bns, 105th C.R.E, Transport, 9th R.W Transport, 8th Queens Transport, 553 Siege Transport, 73rd Light T.M Bty Billets, + Mining Co R.E. Constructional work :— MAZINGARBE. 4 metal man-holes and public urinal PETIT SAINS. 1 corrugated iron incinerator supplied + fixed. WORKSHOP. Several traps completed. Received Mother Army Orders 589–593. C.R.O 85–91. 8th Buffs (2oms), 8th R.W Bn (2ons) 1015 Water-cart in possession of the following units were inspected :— 8th Buffs (2oms), 8th R.W Bn (2ons) 1015 Notts a Derby (2cart) and 105th H.Q R.F.A	WSL
BRAQUEMONT	Jan 22nd 1917		Routine Inspection Work continues. From BRAQUEMONT the following units were visited :— C/107, A+B/106, R.F.A. 194th Co A.S.C, 3rd Siege Bty R.G.A + D/110 R.F.A (20 hours), B/110 R.F.A (13 hours), 8th R.W Kent Trans from LES BREBIS the following units were visited :— 103rd R.E Transport, 8th Queens Transport, 189 C.R.E, 107 H.Q R.F.A Transport, 19th Bty R.G.A billets, 8th Buffs Trans, 405 Bde Transport, 9th & 8 Sussex Transport, 3rd R Bde, 1st + 13th R. Fusiliers, 16th Lancers, 191 M.G.C Transport, 181 M.G.C Transport, 13 T.M Bty, 13th Middlesex Transport, 9th C.L Scout Transport, D/107+C/106 R.F.A Transport, 4 Sussex, 5th Lancers. WORKSHOP. 20 refuse bins made, 2 standard Latrine box seats Constructional work :— 1 Receiver Trap + 13 miscellaneous notice boards made + fixed MAZINGARBE. 2 Destructors repointed, 1 incinerator trap completed. PETIT SAINS. 4 night urinals fixed. Water-cart in possession of the following units were inspected :— 12th R Fusiliers, 9 E Surreys (2cart), 15th R Scots (2cart), 73rd M.G.Co.	WSL

WAR DIARY or INTELLIGENCE SUMMARY

Army Form C. 2118.

Page 15.

Place	Date	Hour	Summary of Events and Information	Remarks and references to Appendices
BRAQUEMONT	Jan 22 1917		Routine Inspection Work continues. From BRAQUEMONT the following units were visited:- A/B C+D/106 R.F.A., A/107, A/15/106 R.F.A., 241 Signal Co., 242 Divisional Signal Co., 16th Batt Canadian Light Model Railway, 2nd Canadian Divisional Train, 2nd Div Supply Column, 3rd Batt Canadian Infy, 10th Pontoon Park, & 20th & 21st Motor Pat Cos. From LES BREBIS the following units were visited:- 103rd G.R.E Transport, 8 R.W.Kent Transport, 9th & Surrey Transport, 121 Ball Transport, 751 M.G.C.Transport, 122 Queen's Transport, 121 Ball Transport, 8th Buffs Transport, 8th Queen's Rifles, 121 T.M.B.ty Rifles, Y.T.M.B.ty Rifles, 107 Ball H.Q. Transport, 8th Buffs Transport, 3rd R. Batt, 15th Shoeboxes, 193 B.ty R.G.A., 9th & Surrey Rifles, 4th Shoeboxes, 4 15th Middlesex Transport. Benefactional work:- LES BREBIS. 30 refuse bins fixed for combinatorial WORKSHOP. 15 drawers covered + latrine pan MAROC. Latrine hut small repair 2 Standard Urinals completed covered repaired 30 refuse bins notice boards completed B.D. " " " Reviewed one more pic 637 3 Notice boards fixed 2 latrines erected over machine 3 urinals PHILOSOPHE I was annoyed towards fried 1 great trap accommodated in MAZINGARBE. towards fried At LOOS another latrine completed at "B Keep East", also the latrines demolished at old A Keep completed. Waste carts in opposition at the following units were inspected- 195 Royal Ambulance, 195 Royal shoeboxes (Scouts) 177 Machine Guns & 3rd Rifle Bn (Scouts), 101st Co R.E. Received G.R.O. DP 4 - 2099. G.R.O. 88 - 93.	
BRAQUEMONT	Jan 24 1917		Routine Inspection Work continues. From BRAQUEMONT the following units were visited:- A/106 (B+ hitters) - A/106 (B+ hitters) - Div Signal Co., 24 Div Signal, B C +D/106 R.F.A., A/107, A/15/106 R.F.A., 3rd Siege Bty R.G.A., 24 Div Signal Co., 24 Div Signal School, 194 C 195 G 196 Q + 197 G.A.S.C., H.Q. Outham, + 2d Div M.M.P. From LES BREBIS the following units were visited - 8th Queen's Rifles, 103 G.R.E. Transport, 8 Queen's Transport, 8 R.W.Kent Transport, 9 G Surrey Transport, 121 M G.C. Transport, 107 Ball H.Q. Transport, 193 Bty R.G.A. Rifles, 8 Buffs Transport 4 Rifles, 10 L Co R.E. Transport, 121 M G.C. Transport assembly area, 151 T M.B.ty Rifles, 15t Sat T.M.B.ty Rifles, 9t R.W.Kent Rifles, 101 M G.C. assembly area, 173 Ball H.Q.Transport, 15t Notts Shoeboxes, 4 Shoeboxes. D/107 + C/106 R.F.A Transport. Combinatorial work:- LES BREBIS Latrines 511 small repair + new urinal fixed WORKSHOP. 1 washing trough + 30 refuse bins fixed for combination 561 3 manholes absorbers fixed engines bin refuse." ghat. 7088 H.Q. 1 notice board fixed 3 Tile shoeboxes " PHILOSOPHE. 2 brick drainholes repaired PETITSAINS' Soakage pit dug + R.F.A latrine The 1st Corps class on Sanitation was held at LES BREBIS during the afternoon. At LOOS air water supplies in working order - notice boards fixed 16 new latrines	

WAR DIARY
INTELLIGENCE SUMMARY

Army Form C. 2118.

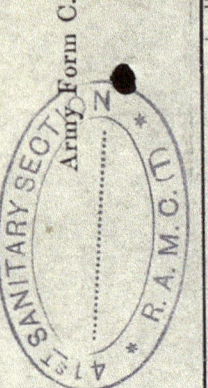

Page 16

Place	Date	Hour	Summary of Events and Information	Remarks and references to Appendices
BRAQUEMONT	Jan 24 1917 continued		Water carts in possession of the following units were inspected :— 139 C.R.E., 103rd G.R.E., 13th Middlesex, 19th Sussex. Received C.R.O. 93-103, D.R.O. 2119-2120.	MSL
BRAQUEMONT	Jan 25 1917		Routine Inspection Work continued from BRAQUEMONT. The following units were visited :— No 1 Sec. No 2 Sec. H.Q. D.A.C., 138th R.G.A, Divisional Gas School, Rest Camp, 194 Co. A.S.C, 3rd Siege Bde. R.G.A., 2nd Div. Signal Co., A.B. C+D/106, A+C/107, A+B/106 R.F.A. from LES BREBIS the following units were visited :— 8th Queens , 103rd G.R.E., 13th Middlesex, "C" Ant. among Section, D/107, 67th R.G.A. H.Q. 16th Lancers, 1st Army G.R.E., 1st Wheelers, 9th Sussex Transport, 13th R Sussex Transport, D/107 and C/106 R.F.A. pte R.W. Kirt Transport, 7th M.G.Co. Transport, 12th Queens Transport, 13th Middlesex Transport. 9th E. Surreys Transport, 13th T.M.Bn., 73rd M.G.Co. Transport, 19th Queens Transport, 13th Middlesex Transport, 1st M.G.Co. Bullets, 75th M.G.Co. Bullets. Constitutional work :— MAROC Latrine 93B two water shutes examined, framework dismantled renovated repainted. LES BREBIS, 20 R.G.A. Lines field for sunken urine. 12 Rd Latrine pits filled in. New 12th Staff Transport WORKSHOP 20 Refuse tins made Enclosed heads and Privies. 3 Latrine beds to floor made. Ventilation revived. PHILOSOPHE. Repairs Latrine (15th & 16th R.B. 9/10) Latrine floor re-made (Beck Ane) . 7th 3rd 45/50/65/ 13th Middlesex.	MSL
BRAQUEMONT	Jan 26 1917		Water carts in possession of the following units were inspected — 7th M.G.Co. in other proper duties. D/107 R.F.A., 73rd M.G.Co. Pte MILLS has intimated his name to write out at 17th M.G.Co. Received C.R.O 104-110 and A.R.O 2121-2121. LSjt DENNIS + LCpl LOTT reported for duty after leave to England. Routine Inspection Work continued from BRAQUEMONT the following units were visited :— 194 Co., 195 Co., 196 Co +197 Co. A.S.C., 9th Reserve Parks, 3rd Brigadeer Travelling Co. with 2nd Bde. 3rd 50th M.M.P., H.Q. R.F.A., A.B +D/106, A.B+D/107, D/107 R.F.A., 3rd Siege.Bde R.G.A., 2nd Air Signal School. from LES BREBIS the following units were visited :— 103rd R.E.Transport, 8th Queens Transport, 106 R.F.A. H.Q. Transport, 7th M.G.Co. Transport, 73rd M.G.Co., 13th Middlesex Bullet, 107 R.F.A. H.Q. Transport, 106 R.F.A. H.Q. Transport, 9th E.Surrey Transport, H.Q. T.M.Bn, 175th M.G.Co. Transport, 13th T.M. Bn., 73rd M.G.Co. Bullet, pte R.W. Kirt Bullet, 13th R Sussex N.R.A. R.G.A. Corps H.Q. 105 Coming H.Q., 19th M.G.Co., 9th Royal Sussex Transport, D/107, C/106 R.F.A. Transport. 13th Middlesex Transport, 125th Railway Transport, Bullets 65 / recommenced over new trench. Constructional work. :— MAROC. Latrine 65 / recommenced over new trench. LES BREBIS Latrines 53A and 93B repaired. Box seats and latine beater fixed at 8th Bn R LOOS. New latrines completed of new tolefield drain — old Latrine demolished pit filled in. WARFARE near (93/193,108 Z 875 m) &.L.R.A.M.C) (C.R.81873. 196 A.S.C. 73B C/106 R.F.A EDWARDS. Received R.O No 1145 — 594—601, C.R.O. III—115, SDRO 2125—2131. 15 FEB 53 Lcpl granted from Jan 26th	MSL

WAR DIARY or **INTELLIGENCE SUMMARY**

Army Form C. 2118.

Page 14.

Place	Date	Hour	Summary of Events and Information	Remarks and references to Appendices
BRAQUEMONT	Jan 27th 1917		Routine Inspection Work continues. From BRAQUEMONT the following units were visited :— A,B,C,+D/106, A/107, C/107, B/106 R.F.A., 3rd Bugl. Bg. R.G.A., 1st G.A.S.C., 2nd Div. Signal Co. & Signal School, A/106 (15 skiers), 9th Reserve Park (18 skiers), #C/106 (15 skiers), +A/107 (05 skiers). From LES BREBIS the following units were visited :— 3rd Bde Transport, Special Co. R.E., 9th Suffolks, 19th M.G.C. Transport, 16th Lancers, St Quesnoy, 13th M.G.C., 103rd G.R.E. Transport, 9th Co. Survey Transport, 8th R.W. Kent Transport, 13th M.G.C., 73rd T.M. Bty, X.T.M. Bty, 8th Queens Transport, 107th R.F.A. Transport, 13th Bde M. R.G.A., 13th Middlesex, 13th Shellwin Transport, C/108 +D/108 R.F.A. Transport. Constructional work :— LES BREBIS. Incinerator (brick) repaired in 2 areas, 2 loads of slag spread in Rue Bully. BRAQUEMONT, 2 disinfectors repaired. Inspected PHILOSOPHE Bath area. Latrine screens repaired. 150 R.G.A. 3 lids fixed. Latrine Boxes WORKSHOP 15 latrine box seats constructed, 3 lids for incinerators made and painted, 3 latrine boards constructed, 3 notice boards enamelled. 4 notice boards fixed. Latrine (for men & horses) completed at 3rd R.G.A. H.Q. LOOS Materials in possession of the following units were inspected :— 197 B, 195 B, A.S.C., 2nd Div. H.Q., 2nd Div. Signal Co., A/107, C/107, +D/106 R.F.A. Received C.R.O. 116 — 124.	WDC
BRAQUEMONT	Jan 28th		Routine Inspection Work continues. From BRAQUEMONT the following units were visited :— 18th Canadian Infty, 26th Mobile Ordnance Workshop, 4th Canadian Div. Transport, 10th Pontoon Park, A+D/106, A,B,+C/107, A+D/108, R.F.A., 194 G.A.S.C. & 2nd Div. M.M.P. From LES BREBIS the following units were inspected :— 195th Bde R.G.A., 16th Lancers, 1st M.G.Co., St Queens, Loos, Bas Loos, 103rd R.E., 1st R.W. Kent Transport, 8th Queens Transport, 9th E. Surrey Transport, 74th B.M & Co Transport, 9th Reserve Park, 14th Middlesex, 137th M. Bty Mules, 1st G. Trench Transport Working Area, 13th M.G. Co Transport, 18th Sherwin Transport, D/107 C/108 R.F.A. Transport, 9th Royal Sussex Transport, 13th R. Sussex Transport, A/108 R.F.A. Constructional work :— BRAQUEMONT, 194 G.A.S.C. Incinerator fixed, 26th Mobile Ordnance, 1 cesspit & 1 incinerator constructed. Rue de Plenville, Latrine screened. Windows of Billets covered with canvass. 2 notice boards made. 3 notice boards made and painted. MAZINGARBE, 16 latrine openings made. WORKSHOP 20 refuse tins made. LOOS, 1 urinalite box seat also stench completed on Queensway. LESBREBIS latrine 561. 1 seat fixed. 1 mule heads fixed cesspits & drainage. Materials in possession of the following units were inspected :— B/107, C/107, A/108, +D/106 R.F.A. Received C.R.O. 125 — 126. Circular 2nd Divn CCX. 908/5 re new Box Respirator in frosty weather.	WDC

WAR DIARY or INTELLIGENCE SUMMARY

Place	Date	Hour	Summary of Events and Information	Remarks and references to Appendices
BRAQUEMONT	Jan 29th 1917		Routine Inspection Work continued. from BRAQUEMONT the following units were visited :— A.B. C/D/106, A+C/107, A+B/106 R.F.A, 19th Co A.S.C, 24th Divisional Signal Co, Signal & Signal School, 3rd Australian Tunnelling Co, 196 Co A.S.C, D/106 R.F.A (16 mules) A/107 R.F.A (15 mules) Model Billet, 18 Army Training School, 1st Sea D.A.C, Divisional Gas School, 1st Rest Camp. From LES BREBIS the following were visited :— 9th hospital, 1st R.W. Division, 16th Lancers, 7th M.G.C, 8th Queens (mules), 12th Staff (mules), 13th M.G.C. Transport, 73rd Lgt. T.M. Bty (mules), 8th R.W.Kents (mules), 7th Hants (mules), 12th Staff Transport, 1st R. Fusiliers Transport, 13th Middlesex Transport, 12th Sherwood Foresters Transport, D/107 C/106 R.T.A. Transport. Sanitational Work :— HALLICOURT. Incinerator new incinerator made and fired, 2 refuse pits dug, urinal fired. Water carts in process of the following units were inspected :— No.1 Co, No.2 Co, No.3 Sec, No.3 Sec. D.A.C 194 A.S.C Recvd C.R.O. 129–132, D.R.O. 2132–2133, 1st Army Circular No.20 "Orders for the Prevention of Trench Fatalities". 1st Corp Circular Q.1/65 "Care of Motor Transport Vehicles".	NOSE
BRAQUEMONT	Jan 30th 1917		Routine Inspection Work continued. from BRAQUEMONT the following units were visited :— A.B. B+D/106, A+C/107, A+B/106, 19th Co A.S.C, 24th Divisional Signal Co, & Signal School, From LES BREBIS the following were visited :— 2nd Bde C.T.A, 8th R.W. Kents, 9th E. Surreys, 13th Devons (13th mules) Artil.Divy (1 mule), D/107 Transport (2 mules), 9th Co Supply Transport (1 mule), 13th hants Transport (3 mules), C/106 R.T.A Transport, 15th Middlesex Transport, 195 R.G.A (2 mules), 9th Arty Transport, 103 R.E. Transport, 8th Queens Transport, 8th R.W.Kent Transport, 73rd T.M. Bty, 8th R.W.K(1 mule 3 mules), 15th R. Fusiliers, 8th Bde Riding Party, 186 R.G.A, D/107 Bty R.F.A(11 mules), C/106 Bty R.F.A(12 mules). Sanitational Work :— BRAQUEMONT, New trench latrine completed at A/106 Bty R.F.A. LES BREBIS 4 mules cleaned, 1 latrine trench completed, 1 latrine trench completed in A area. Workshop. 2 standards urinals completed. MAZINGARBE. 2 tree exits for latrine supplied and fixed. FOSSE 2. Incinerator board fixed. Water carts inspection of the following units were inspected :— B/106, A/107, A/106, +C/106 R.F.A. A sample of water taken from well used by 7th Works Rl.E. (LES BREBIS) was tested and it destroyed Cue. and flue reaction reacted in Lt Gp. the well has been marked "Unfit for Drinking". Revcd:— G. R.O. 3160 – 3105 Gorder Memo B/5166 "General Orders" Memo D.G. 179/4/5 "measures to detection of Rats." War Office letter 105/gen. no./233/. (A. G. 3). Routine Order A/5543/3/3 "2nd Div, & Dub. Sec's 10 Q/S+59 C.R.O 183 – 186, D.R.O 2134 – 2138. Circular A/5543/3/3 "2nd Div, & Dub. Sec's 10 Q/S+59	NOSE

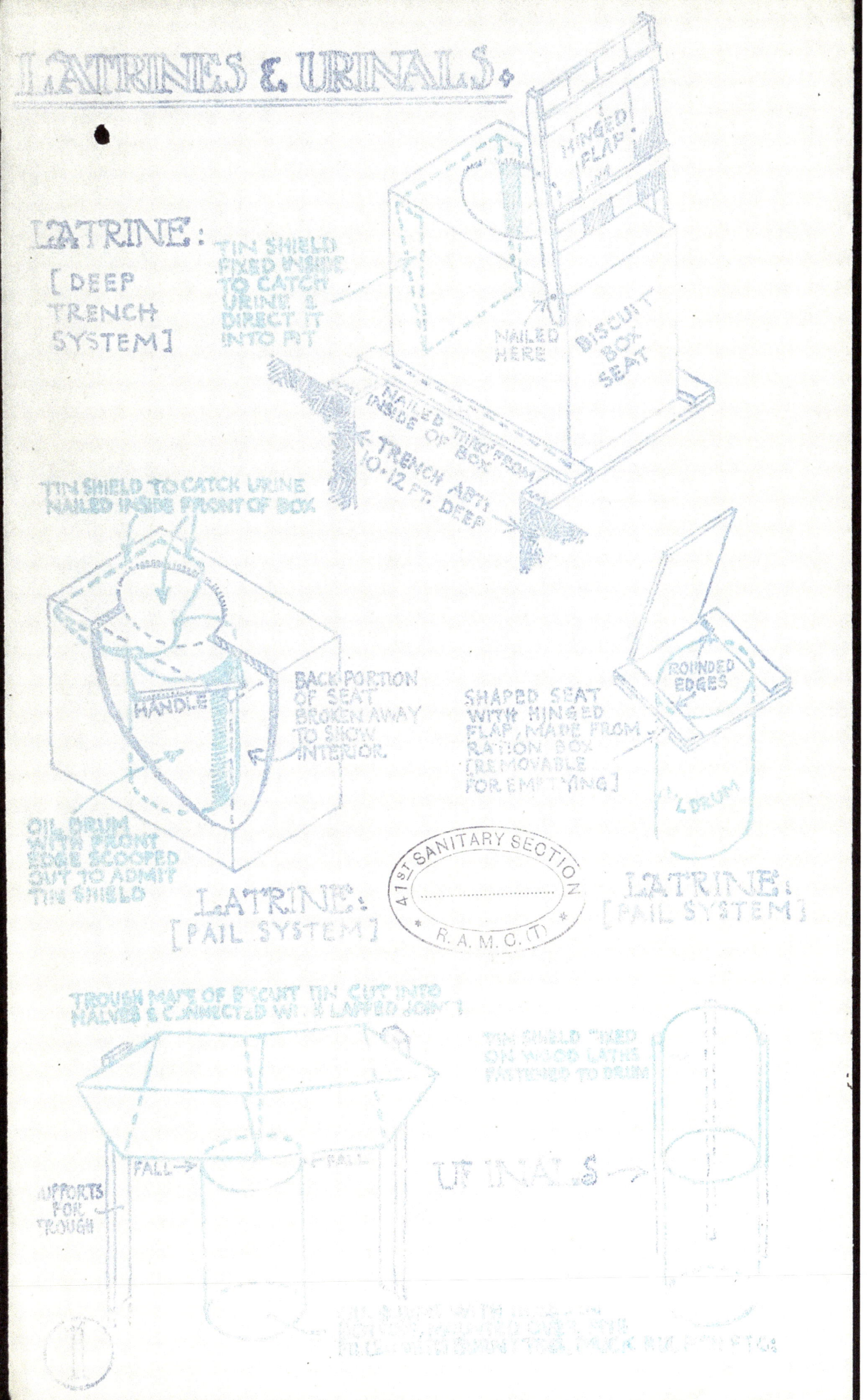

ABLUTION BENCH AND DISPOSAL OF SOAPY WASTE WATER

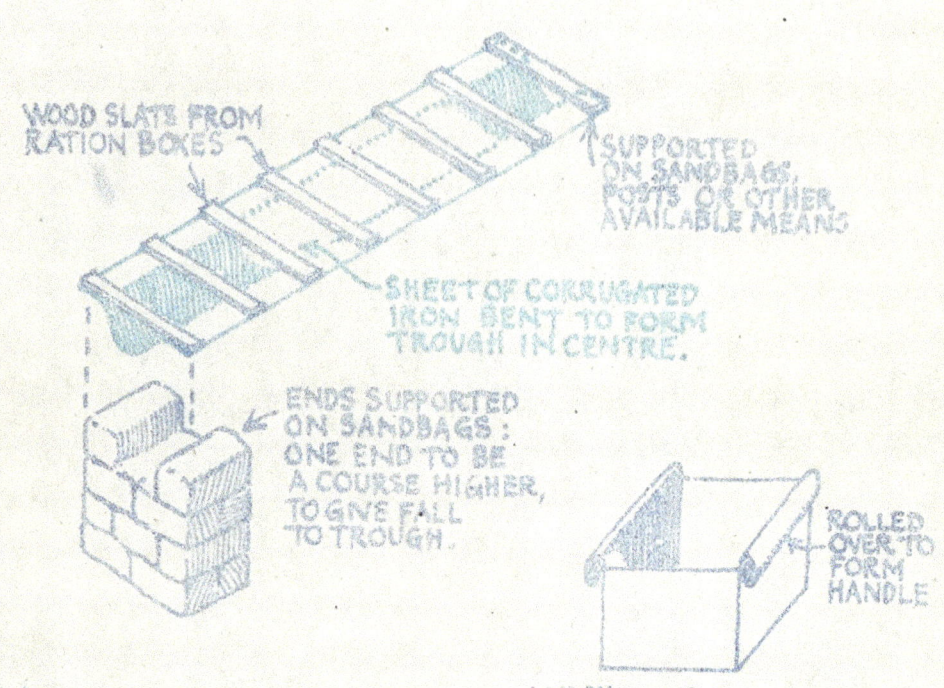

ABLUTION BENCH.

- WOOD SLATS FROM RATION BOXES
- SUPPORTED ON SANDBAGS, POSTS OR OTHER AVAILABLE MEANS
- SHEET OF CORRUGATED IRON BENT TO FORM TROUGH IN CENTRE.
- ENDS SUPPORTED ON SANDBAGS: ONE END TO BE A COURSE HIGHER, TO GIVE FALL TO TROUGH.
- ROLLED OVER TO FORM HANDLE
- WASHING BOWL MADE FROM BISCUIT TIN.

41st SANITARY SECTION R.A.M.C.(T)

NOTE:- CONTENTS OF DRUM TO BE CHANGED DAILY. PITS TO BE EMPTIED EVERY THIRD DAY.

2 PITS EACH 4FT. x 4FT. x 3FT. DEEP ARE SUFFICIENT FOR ONE COMPANY

- WOOD SCUM BOARDS EXTENDING 6" BELOW WATER LEVEL
- SCUM BOARD
- WATER LEVEL
- 2ND SETTLING PIT.
- 1ST SETTLING PIT.
- END OF ABLUTION BENCH
- 5 GALL. DRUM WITH HOLES IN BOTTOM
- 1" CHLORIDE OF LIME ON SURFACE OF COKE
- ½ FULL OF COKE
- TIN TRAY

TREATMENT OF SOAPY WATER FROM ABLUTION BENCH.

INCINERATORS & MANURE BURNING

SQUARE INCINERATOR
(For one Coy. 4'x 4'x 4')

BOTTOM FILLED UP TO TOP OF DRAUGHT HOLES WITH BURNT TINS

EMPTY BY MEANS OF SLOT AT SIDE OF GRATE FOR REMOVING ASH

HOLES IN STONE ON EACH SIDE OF GRATE FOR DRAUGHT

VALVE OPEN OR STRAIGHT FLUE

CORRUGATED IRON INCINERATOR

SIDE AND SIDE BAND OPPOSITE SIDE

COLLECTING HOLE IN OPPOSITE SIDE

WIRED TOGETHER
INTO GROUND

VIEW

MANURE BURNING DIAGRAM

THIN EVEN LAYER OF MANURE

DESCRIPTION: — WIRE SUCH AS THAT USED FOR BINDING BALES OF HAY IS COLLECTED AND MASSED TOGETHER IN A HEAP AS SHOWN IN DIAGRAM. THE MANURE IS SPREAD IN A THIN LAYER OVER THIS. WOOD SOAKED IN OIL IS PLACED AT THE LOWER EDGE OF THE PILE AND IGNITED. THE MANURE MERELY SMOULDERS AWAY: A FINE ASH RESULTING WHICH FALLS INTO THE CENTRE OF THE MASS OF WIRE.

FOOD SAFE & GREASE TRAP.

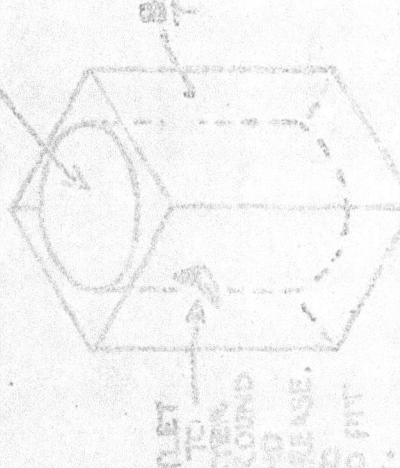

INNER DRUM [OR TIN] WITH HOLES IN BOTTOM, CONTAINING HAY OR SHAVINGS AND SUPPORTED ON STONES OF BROKEN BRICK.

BISCUIT TIN.

LIPPED OUTLET NEAR TOP TO FORM WATER JACKET ROUND DRUM AND SETTLE GREASE. OUTLET TO LEAD INTO PIT OR DITCH.

NOTE:- HAY TO BE RENEWED DAILY. REMAINDER OF TRAP TO BE CLEANED EVERY 3RD DAY.

GREASE TRAP.

*1ST SANITARY SECTION * R.A.M.C.(T)*

FRONT COVERED WITH FLAP OF SACKING NAILED AT TOP AND SECURED BY HOOKS AT BOTTOM.

TOP INSIDE TO BE PROVIDED WITH HANGING RAILS.

VENT HOLES IN SIDES.

REMOVABLE TIN TRAY TO BE PROVIDED TO CATCH DRIPPINGS FROM MEAT.

FRONT EDGE SLIGHTLY CURVED OR TURNED TO ACT AS SMALL FLAP TO MAKE FITTING CLOSELY.

FOOD SAFE MADE FROM 2 RATION BOXES.

140/99 L.

COMMITTEE FOR THE
MEDICAL HISTORY OF THE WAR
Date 4.— APR. 1917

Vol 18

41ST SANITARY SECTION
WAR DIARY
(CONFIDENTIAL)
VOLUME 18
from February 1st to February 28 1917.

WAR DIARY
or
INTELLIGENCE SUMMARY.
(Erase heading not required.)

Army Form C. 2118.

Instructions regarding War Diaries and Intelligence Summaries are contained in F.S. Regs., Part II. and the Staff Manual respectively. Title pages will be prepared in manuscript. **Page 1**

41st SANITARY SECTION * R.A.M.C. (T)

Place	Date	Hour	Summary of Events and Information	Remarks and references to Appendices
BRAQUEMONT.	Feb 1st 1917		Routine Inspection Work continues. - From BRAQUEMONT the following units were inspected:- A,B,C+D/106, A.B.+C/107, A,B+D/108 R.F.A., 194 Co., 195 G., 197 G., A.S.C., 21st Divisional Signal Co. & Signal School, 9th Reserve Park + 21st Divisional Train 31 Div. From LES BREBIS the following were inspected:- 1st N. Staffs, 2nd M.G.C., 135 Hotchkiss/Dvtp., 103rd G.R.E., 1st Scouts, 1st Corps Gas School, 1st Corps Sanitary Detachment, 1st Capt A.T. Q, R.E., 8th R.W. Kent, 73rd M.G.C., 73rd & 74th T.M. Bty, 1st Royal Fusiliers, 73rd Moving Co. R.E., 106 R.F.A., H.Q. Transport Train 104+107 R.F.A., H.Q. Transport Train 75th Howitzer, 9th R. Sussex 2nd Echelon, 2nd Rocket Transport, 13th Middlesex Transport, 75th Howitzer Transport, 9th R. Sussex Transport, D/107+C/108 R.F.A. Transport, 135 R. Fusiliers Transport, 129 Co. R.E., 2nd Bde E.F.A., 9th Bear Survey, 8th Queens Transport, 9th Norfolks, 1st Leicesters, 3rd Bde Transport, 1st Corps Advance Workshop A.S.C. Billets were inspected as follows:- LES BREBIS (37 billets) MAROC (21 billets) MAZINGARBE (5 billets) Wash-carts in possession of the following units were inspected:- 12th Hotchkiss/Dvtp (2 carts), 9th Bear Survey (2 carts), 8th R.W. Kent (2 carts), 12th Royal Fusiliers (2 carts), 72nd M.G.C. (1 cart). Constructional work:- WORKSHOP. 17 repair tins, 1 corrugated iron incinerator, 3 notices. Latrine complete. LES BREBIS: 1 latrine completed "A" area, 1 corrugated iron incinerator finished, refuse bins (large) finished. MAZINGARBE. 1 destructor repaired (Northumbria). MAROC. 1 refuse pit dug. BRAQUEMONT. Latrine at A/106 R.F.A. removed and fixed over new trench, old latrine filled in. LODS Main latrine at left Batt'y H.Q. recommenced. Received D.R.O. 2142 - 2146. C.R.O. 141 - 146.	R. not. m.
BRAQUEMONT.	Feb 2nd 1917		Routine Inspection Work continues. From BRAQUEMONT the following Units were inspected:- A,B, & C/107, A,B +D/108 R.F.A., 194 Co. & 197 Co. G.A.S.C., 21st Divisional Signal & Signal School, 3rd Australian Tunnelling Co., 21st Div. M.M.P. Corps., 21st Queens Band & 21st Ba DOS. From LES BREBIS the following units were inspected:- 104th Bde H.Q. R.F.A., 104th Co. R.E., 14th M.G.C., 9th E. Surrey., 1st Royal Fusiliers, 3rd Rifle Bde, 2nd Fusiliers, 8th Queens, 106th Bde H.Q. R.F.A., 105th Bde H.Q. R.F.A., 129 Area Co. R.E., 2nd Bde C.F.A., 9th R.W. Kent, 73rd M.G.C., 12th Hotchkiss Dvtp., 103rd G. R.E., 16 Lancers, 9th Norfolks, 13th Royal Fusiliers, 1st Corps Cy. Artillery 21 Div., 156 R.G.A., 17th Bde H.Q., 1st Survey G.R.E. and the following Transports:- 13th Middlesex, 9/5 Howitzers, 9th R. Sussex, D/107+C/107 R.F.A, 13th Royal Fusiliers, 73rd M.G.C., 8th R.W. Kent, 15th Hotchkiss Dvtp., 8th Queens. Billets were inspected as follows:- LES BREBIS (26 billets), MAZINGARBE (4 billets), PHILOSOPHE (21 billets), MAROC (21 billets), 3rd R. Bde (back), 17th G.Co.104 G.R.E. Water carts in possession of the following units were inspected:- 1st R. Fusiliers (2 carts),	

WAR DIARY or INTELLIGENCE SUMMARY

Army Form C. 2118.

Place	Date	Hour	Summary of Events and Information	Remarks and references to Appendices
BRAQUEMONT	Feb 2nd 1917 continued		Constructional work:- WORKSHOP 1 grease trap. LATRINES 1 notice board completed. MAZINGARBE, 1 Officers latrine renewed and refixed. 1 repair to dug. MAROC 1 notice board fixed. PHILOSOPHE 1 notice board fixed. LES BREBIS 1 latrine repaired. Received C.R.O. 149 - 151. D.R.O. Dury - 2151. S.P.I. ANGLN. Important from Sanitary Section on	R.W.M.
BRAQUEMONT	Feb 3rd 1917		Routine Inspection Work continues:- from BRAQUEMONT the following units were visited:- 194 G.A.S.C., 195 G, 196 G, 197 G A.S.C., 9th Reserve Park, 5th Australian Tunnelling Co, No 11 Browning Post, 21st Divisional Ordnance, 21st Divisional Signal Coy + Signal School, A.B.+D/106, A+B/107 A+D/108 R.F.A. from LES BREBIS the following units were visited:- D/96 R.E., II Bn C.F.A., 1st Huntsmen, 1st G.R.E., 1st R.W. Kent, 9th R. Sussex, A/110 R.F.A., 1st Corps Signal, 2nd female, 173 Manuq. R.E., 140th R.G.A., 150th R.G.A. "C" Anti-Aircraft Bty, 67th R.G.A. H.Q., 119th Bde. H.Q., 497 M.G.Co, 200th Siege Bty, and the following transport, Inn, 145 Bde, 101st R.F.A., 3rd Fem+Inn, 13th Middlesex, 75 honsaules, 9th Royal Sussex GRB+T.O., 75th Bde. 108 R.F.A. H.Q., 108th R.Sussex, 195 R.Irish. Billets were inspected also:- MAZINGARBE (4 billets). PETITSAINS (7 billets). LES BREBIS (51 billets). PHILOSOPHE (49 billets) + MAROC (26 billets). Constructional work :- LES BREBIS 1 ocean for urinal repaired 1 incinerator fired, 1 latrine complete. in "A" Area, 1 trench commenced for urinals. MAZINGARBE 1 latrine and urinal drainage trench filled in. MAROC 1 incinerator erected. BRAQUEMONT Invoices boards made and fixed. WORKSHOP, 3 cleaners hose carts made. 2 latrines, 13th Middlesex (Reads) + can't inspection of the following units were inspected - 2nd Remotes, 103rd Co R.E., 9th R. Sussex, D/107, R.F.A. Received E.R.O. 155 - 160 and See 30 "Personnel Hilden" D.R.O. 2152 - 2153	R.W.M.
BRAQUEMONT	Feb 4th 1917		Routine Inspection Work continues. from BRAQUEMONT the following Units were visited:- A/106 + B/106 R.F.A., 21st Divisional H.Q., 21st Divisional Ordnance, 21st Divisional Signal Co, "Sniper Billet" Cambayarea, 24th Divisional Artillery H.Q. from LES BREBIS the following were visited - 1st Leicesters, 9th R.W. Kent, 1st Hunts, 12nd Buffs, 1st Corps Cyclists, 2nd Remotes, 9th Royal Sussex Div. Sig. Co, B/108 R.F.A., 75th M.G.Co. 75 T.M. Bty, 9th R. Sussex, 9th R. Sussex, D/96 R.E., 75th Bde H.Q. Transport, 9th R.W.K. Transport + 5th Quartermaster. Billets were inspected as follows:- LES BREBIS (17 billets)	

WAR DIARY or INTELLIGENCE SUMMARY

Army Form C. 2118.

41st SANITARY SECTION R.A.M.C.(T)

Place	Date	Hour	Summary of Events and Information	Remarks and references to Appendices
BRAQUEMONT	April 4th 1917 continued		Water carts in possession of the following units were inspected :- 2nd Leinsters, 9th Royal Sussex, 173 M.G.Co. Constructional work :- MAROC. New stands dug for latrines and new grease trench. PHILOSOPHE. 1 notice board fixed at water supply. LES BREBIS 2 boxes fixed at latrine No. 510. WORKSHOP. 2 corrugated iron troughs urinals completed. Received G.R.O. 161-165, D.R.O. 2151 - 2157. The O.C. Capt CARRUTHERS W.D. R.A.M.C.(T) was evacuated to No.1. C.C.S. and Capt MACPHERSON R.W. R.A.M.C. has assumed command temporarily.	R.M.M.
BRAQUEMONT	April 5th 1917		Routine Inspection Work continues. From BRAQUEMONT the following were visited :- B/106, C/104 R.F.A., 195 Co, 196 Co, 194 Co A.S.C., 2nd Divisional Engineers and Pioneer Bathes. from LES BREBIS the following were visited :- 13th Middlesex, 103rd M.G.Co, 8th R.W.Kent, 103rd T.M.By, H.Q., C/107 D/107 R.F.A., 7th Northants, 2nd Leinster, 173 Mining Co R.E., 13th T.M.By., 13th Bde Wiring Party, C/108 D/107 R.F.A. 107 Bde R.F.A. H.Q., 1st Bde H.Q., 1st Royal Sussex, 173 M.G.Co, 173rd Light T.M.By, 1st Hants Dump, Loralis Bomb, 1st Corps Cyclists, 9th Queens, 13th Middlesex, and the following Transport Lines - 8th Buffs, 173 Bde H.Q., 8th R.W.Kent, 9th E Surrey, 9th Queens, 13th Middlesex, 173 Northants, 9th Royal Sussex, 108 R.F.A. Brebis were inspected as follows :- MAROC (10 trees) LES BREBIS (11 trees) BRAQUEMONT (4 trees) C/108 R.F.A. Water carts in possession of the following units were inspected :- 7th Northants (boards) D/107 (boards) 129 Co. R.E. Constructional work :- BRAQUEMONT. 1 grease trap fixed at "C" mess, 2 notice boards made and fixed. LES BREBIS. Latrine No.510 completed, New urinal fixed at Divisional Store, 1 pump repaired at Bowwow 665. 1 new urinal fixed at No. 103 C.R.E. WORKSHOP. 1 wash bowl, 1 large latrine box seat, and 3 standard latrine bowseats completed. Received :- Army Order Gen. No. 1352 "War Savings", G.R.O. 2109-2116, C: R.O. 166-193 D.R.O. 2156-2163.	R.M.M.
BRAQUEMONT	April 6th 1917		Routine Inspection Work continues. From BRAQUEMONT the following were visited :- A,B,C + D/106, A+C/104, A/105, 2nd Divisional Squad School + 2nd Divisional Squad (Motor Cyclists rider). From LES BREBIS the following were visited :- 12th Royal Sussex, 6th Buffs, 16th Lancers, Spoinet G.R.E. 7th Northants, C/108 R.F.A., 173rd Mining Co R.E., Divisional Scouts, D/107 R.F.A., 9th E Surreys, 13th T.M.By, 13th M.G.Co, 173rd M.G.Co, 8th R.W.Kent, 103rd Co R.E., 129 Field Co R.E., 2nd Bn C.F.A., Divisional Dump, 13th Middlesex, 1st Corps Schooling Co, 1st Corps Cyclists, and the following Transport Lines :-	

WAR DIARY or INTELLIGENCE SUMMARY

Army Form C. 2118.

Title: Page 4.

41st SANITARY SECTION R.A.M.C.(T)

Place	Date	Hour	Summary of Events and Information	Remarks and references to Appendices
BRAQUEMONT	Sep 6th 1917 continued		73rd Bde H.Q., 73rd M.G.Co., 8th R.W.Kent, 2nd Londons, C/107 R.F.A., 13th R. Fusiliers, 4th Northants, & 9th Royal Sussex. Billets were inspected as follows:- LES BREBIS 17th M.G.Co. (1 billet), 73rd M.By 4 billets), 13th Middlesex (3 billets), 4th Northants (3 billets), PETIT SAINS + FOSSE 2, 4th Northants Transport (6 billets) 9th R. Sussex Transport (6 billets), 13th Royal Fusiliers Transport (5 billets). MAZINGARBE 191st M.G.Co. (1 billet) 110th Bty R.G.A Transport (1 billet), Divisional Canteen (1 billet), 16th Lancers (1 billet), 1st Special R.E. (1 billet) Water carts in possession of the following units were inspected:- 195 Co, 196 Co, 197 Co A.S.C., 21st Divisional H.Q., 24th Divisional Signal Co, C/107 + D/106 R.F.A. Conditional works:- BRAQUEMONT. 1 trench dug for 2 weeks latrines at 21st Signal Co (motor cyclists) 1 latrine commenced at D/106. 1 greasetrap fixed at C/107. MAZINGARBE 13/5 R. Fusiliers. 1 latrine (blair cents + pails) completed PHILOSOPHE. Latrine at 15th Corps Cyclists rebuilt LES BREBIS. Billet 157. Urinal repaired. WORKSHOP 2 standard latrines were a notice boards completed. The D.G visited PHILOSOPHE to enquire about the defects reported to him by the inspection detailed for that district and the following units were warned that the defects should be remedied without delay:- 8th R.W.Kent, 13th Notts + Derbys, 15th Corps Cyclists + Y.M.C.A. Received: C.R.O. 194-160. D.R.O. 2164-2166. 15th Corps Cir. No. 9982.	
BRAQUEMONT	Sep 7th 1917		Routine inspection work continues. From BRAQUEMONT the following units were visited:- 21st Signal Co (Motor Cyclists), No 1 Sec., No 2 Sec., and H.Q.D.A.C., 131st Bty R.G.A., Divisional Rest Camp & baths, A/D/106, A+C/107 V.A/107. R.F.A. From LES BREBIS the following were visited:- 9th E. Surreys, 108th Bde H.Q., 73rd Bde H.Q., 9th Bde., 16th Lancers, 14th Hussars, 191st M.G.Co., 3rd Rifle Bde., Divisional Canteen (MAZINGARBE), 8th R.W.Kent, 73rd M.G.Co., 103rd Co. R.E., 12th Notts + Derbys, Tunnels Leonis, A/106 R.F.A., 3rd Somersets, 173rd Mining Co. R.E., 73rd L.T.M. Bty, 73rd Bde Wiring Party, D/106 R.F.A., 139 field Co R.E., Divisional Camp, and the following Transport lines:- D/107 R.F.A., 9th Royal Sussex, 4th Northants, 13th Middlesex, 3rd Somersets, 8th R.W.Kent, 9th Queens, 73rd Bde HQ. 4 9th Punjabi. Billets were inspected as follows:- LES BREBIS 13th Middlesex (17 billets), 3rd Somersets A Co. (4 billets) MAROC D/106 R.F.A. (4 billets), 73rd Bde. Wiring Party (7 billets), 9th Queens (2 billets) 3rd R. Bde (3 billets) 191st M.G.Co. (1 billet) MAZINGARBE 16th Lancers (2 billets), 14th Hussars (1 billet). Following units were inspected:- A/107, B/107, C/107, A/106, D/106 and A/106 R.F.A.	R.W.M.

WAR DIARY
or
INTELLIGENCE SUMMARY.

Army Form C. 2118.

Place	Date	Hour	Summary of Events and Information	Remarks and references to Appendices
BRAQUEMONT	Feb 1st 1917		Constructional work :- BRAQUEMONT. Latrine completed at 2nd R Signal Co (Motor Cyclist) LOOS. Latrines commenced at M.G.C. D/106 Latrine completed C/107. 2 Urinals dug for Latrine LES BREBIS. Urinal supplied and fixed at 3rd Bde C.F.A. WORKSHOP. 1 Standard Latrine housed PETIT SAINS. Urinal supplied and fixed at 9th R Sussex Transport. 1 pipe urinal & shelter trench made. The 1st Corps Class in Sanitation has been held at LES BREBIS. 5 officers attended. Received Major Routine Orders 620 - 629, C.R.O. 181 - 184, D.R.O. 2161 - 2193, J Circular No A/50/11/18/245.	R. to M.
BRAQUEMONT	Feb 2nd 1917		Routine Inspection Work continues From BRAQUEMONT the following units were visited :- 194 Co, 195 Co, 196 Co, 197 Co A.S.C., 2nd Divisional Band & M.M.P., 2nd Divisional Ordnance Salvage Squads, 3rd Australian Tunnelling Co, 9th Bourne Park, A. B & D/106, B & C/107, A & D/108 R.F.A. From LES BREBIS the following were visited :- 129 Field Co R.E., 2nd Bde C.F.A., Divisional Dump, 9 & E Sussex, 3rd Bde M.G.C., 135 Middlesex, Pts R.W. Kents, 13rd Bde H.Q., 106 Bn R.F.A. H.Q., 135 Notts & Derbys, 108 R.E., 1st Corps Cyclists, 1st Corps Lowering C, 73rd Bde H.Q., 16th Lancers, 13rd Dining Co R.E., 9th Yorkshires, 2nd Inniskillings, C/108 R.F.A., D/107 R.F.A, Divisional Escort & the following Transport Lines :- 2nd Inniskillings, 9th Yorkshires, 9th R Sussex, 13rd R Irish, 17th Bde, 8th Bugle, 3rd Rifle Bde, 1st N. Staffs, 73rd M.G.C, 8th R.W. Kent & 9th Queens. Briefs were inspected as follows :- MAZINGARBE (4 hutted) miscellaneous LES BREBIS 13th Middlesex (2 huts), miscellaneous (5 huts) MAROC 2nd Leicesters (16 shelves) Water carts in possession of the following units were inspected :- No 1 Sec No 2 Sec No 3 Sec D.A.C. 194 Co A.S.C. - B/106 R.F.A. Constructional work :- BRAQUEMONT. 2 Latrines completed at D/107. Urinal hand applied field at D/106 PETIT SAINS. Soap made screen reconstructed at 9th R Irish Transport. Iron seat field Latrine at 12 R.F. Transport 2 notice boards fixed at 9th Royal Sussex Transport. Officer latrine reconstructed as a urinal. Officer Latrine Field in reconstruction as a urinal trench at 13th Middlesex Transport. MAZINGARBE. Bone and Ash pit & new officers latrine erected at 7th Canadians. LES BREBIS. Latrine seat repaired at 75th M.G.Co. Urinal repaired and box seats repaired at Latrine near Cinema. Officers Urinal fixed at hostel, 3 box seats fixed to latrine approx 673, 1 grease trap fixed at R.F.A.T.M. Bay WORKSHOP. 1 Standard latrine box seats made, 1 notice boards made and furnished, 1 table made for disinfect of Forms. 15 Rogue Urinal made at Latrine in Biscuit Lane. Urinal fixed at D Keep. And a new latrine in course of construction at 17th Sherwood Foresters.	

WAR DIARY
or
INTELLIGENCE SUMMARY
(Erase heading not required.)

Army Form C. 2118.

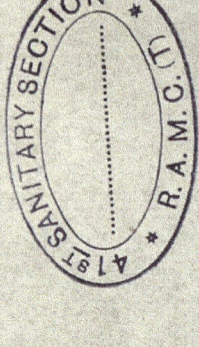

Place	Date	Hour	Summary of Events and Information	Remarks and references to Appendices
BRAQUEMONT	Aug 8th 1917 contd		No 685 Cpl EDWARDS reported for duty on return from leave in England. No 1214 Cpl KILBURN granted leave to England from Aug 9th to Aug 19th 1917. No 4750 L/Cpl LANIGAN. The above establishment of this unit on being transferred to this new Roads Construction Unit. No 4750 L/Cpl LANIGAN reverts to the rank of Sapper on being transferred to the new Roads Construction Unit. T.R.W.M. Received C.R.O. 165-169. D.R.O. 2173-2179.	
BRAQUEMONT	Aug 9th 1917		Routine Inspection Work continues. from BRAQUEMONT the following Units were visited: - 194 G, 195 G, 196 G, 197 G, A.S.C., 9th Reserve Park, 211th Divisional Reserve, 3rd Australian Tunnelling Co., Divisional Signal Co, Signal School, A, B, C & D/106, A & C/107, A & D/108 R.F.A. From LES BREBIS the following were visited: - 3rd Field Coy, 73rd Mining C.R.E., 133rd T.M. Bty, 173rd Mining Coy R.E., 176th Tunn Coy R.E. 9th R. Welsh Fus., 13th M.G.C., 12 Notts & Derby, 103rd G.R.E., Lewis Scouts, YMCA (Philosophe) 14th Hordouain Coy, 15th Coy Spahis, 15 Coy Spahis, 15 Coy Cyclists, 18 Sapeurs G.C., 2nd M.G.C., 19th Field G.R.E., Divisional Dump, 13th Minenwerfer, YMCA (MAROC), 15 Coy Cyclists (LES BREBIS) 9th G. Sumps, 1st Bde H.Q., 9th Jancers, 10th Bde R.F.A. H.Q., 8th Btty., School, Army Kitchen (LES BREBIS) 9th R. G.A. H.Q., "C" Anti-aircraft Bty, and the following Troops: 2nd Queens, 8th Queens, 1st Coy Artillery H.Q., 6th R.G.A. H.Q., 9th R. Sumps, 9th B/L12 Btty, 12 Field Bty, by Ferodin, 13th Huzzars, 4th Honvedeh, 9th R.W. Kent, 9th R. Sumps, & 12th R. Huzzars. Billets were inspected as follows: - BRAQUEMONT, 197 G, A.S.C., (17 billets), 195 G, A.S.C. (15 billets), B/106, (5 billets) and 9th Reserve Park, (5 billets). Water Carts in possession of the following units were inspected: - C/106 R.F.A., 108 Bde H.Q. R.F.A, 9th MAZINGARBE manoeuvre areas. The following units were inspected: - MAZINGARBE (6 billets) Queens (2 carts), 8th Bedis (2 carts). Water Carts in possession of the following units were inspected. Sanitational Work: - BRAQUEMONT, Latrine repaired at 2nd Div M.M.P. LES BREBIS New latrine holes supplied and fixed at 13th Midd'x. Also apertures filled in at "C" Anti-aircraft Bty. Newlatrine trench fixed at 8th Batt, 12 spare holes fixed at MAZINGARBE. Newchop on Aug 9th C Anti-aircraft Bty, Newlatrine trench fixed at 13th Coy Artillery H.Q. WORKSHOP. 4 urinal Tops made, & motor screens made and painted. LOOS. 1 new urinal field arB Keep seat, 1 notice board fixed at B Keep seat, 1 motice board & painted at B Keep-seat, 1 notice board fixed at B Keep seat. Billets not inspected by the Disinfection. 12th R. Irish Rifles. MEASLES 2nd/Lt PENROSE. Billet and household goods of his contacts disinfected necessary as they had already had measles — patients will be kept under observation by M.O. Regt. MAZINGARBE disinfector killed. Acts compiled & handed in by M.O. Regt. The O/C 37 Sanitary Section 37th Division came today preparatory to taking over, and was shown over the whole area by O/C. Received G.R.O. 2117-2121. C.R.O. 190-196. D.R.O. 2180-2183. Crown S.S. 377 Army Postal Services.	T.R.W.M.

A.5834 Wt. W.4973/M687 750,000 8/16 D.D. & L. Ltd. Forms/C.2118/13.

WAR DIARY or INTELLIGENCE SUMMARY

Army Form C. 2118.

41st SANITARY SECTION R.A.M.C. (T)

Place	Date	Hour	Summary of Events and Information	Remarks and references to Appendices
BRAQUEMONT.	Nov 10th 1917.		Routine inspections continue. From BRAQUEMONT the following units were visited :- 194 C. ASC. A/B/106, A/C/107 R.F.A. From LES BREBIS the following were visited :- 140th R.G.A. H.Q., 106th R.G.A., 3rd Rifle Bde, 14th M.G.Co., 101st Co. R.E., 73rd M.G.Co., 103rd & 9th Cr T.M.Bty, Pte Ambce, 1st Royal Marines, 106th R.F.A., H.Q., 1918 Siege. C.F.A., 2nd Bde C.F.A., 1st Middlesex, Pte R.W.Kent, 73rd M.G.Co. (LES BREBIS), 2nd Pioneers, 1st Hunts, and 175th Training Co. R.E., Church Army Hut, Run, 8th R.W.Kent., 13th Hunts & Devons, 1st R. Staff., 73rd Bde H.Q., 3rd Kensingtons, 13th Middlesex, 7½ hut (Conc) 9th Royal Sussex, 13th R. Sussex. Billets were inspected as follows :- LES BREBIS, Maustauxem (S hills), MAROC, St Germain (10 hills). BRAQUEMONT, D/103 R.F.A. (9 hills), B/107 R.F.A. (3 hills), 194 C. ASC. 10 hills and D/106 (2 hills). Water carts in possession of the following units were inspected :- A/107 R.F.A., 1st T.M.G.Co., 135 Ants + Ontrp (2 arts), 1st R.W. Kent (2 arts), 9th Cr R. Sussex (2 arts). Constructional work.- BRAQUEMONT. 1 incinerator, deep trench. 3 box seats completed. MAZINGARBE, Incinerator constructed at 140th R.G.A. H.Q., 1 new latrine constructed at Y.M.C.A. hut, latrines constructed at 106 R.F.A. H.Q., 1 new latrine constructed at E Keep (Hospicebrunt), 1 new urinal fixed at E Keep (Hospicebrunt), 1 new urinal fixed at A Keep, 1 incinerator and 1 latrine board fixed at the Fortified Farm, 1 incinerator board fixed at A Keep, 1 latrine board fixed at Owen Way. Received :- 104th Ambce. Order 628 - 638, D.R.O. 2164 - 2185, and Circular War H.Q. A/56.1/15/1.	R.W.Jn
BRAQUEMONT.	Dec 14th 1917		Preparations were made for moving into the next new area LABEUVRIERE, and an advance party of 1 N.C.O and 2 men were sent for purpose of taking over disinfection, laundries by French. MAROC, Aux douches, disposal of controls left in the hands of the M.O. of Units. Campaign. Earlier hour, 3rd Grenades MAROC, still disinfected, segregation of controls left in the hands of the M.O. of Unit. Received C.R.O. 199 - 203.	R.W.Jn
BRAQUEMONT.	Dec 12th 1917		Further preparations were made for moving into the new rest area LABEUVRIERE, and inspections made throughout the area to see that units were making necessary preparations for leaving their camps etc in a clean and satisfactory state. 2nd Lieut PENROSE who continued... ...disinfection of M.O.'s of Units. Received D.R.O. 2169 - 2185.	

WAR DIARY or INTELLIGENCE SUMMARY

Army Form C. 2118.

Page 8.

41st SANITARY SECTION — R.A.M.C. (T)

Place	Date	Hour	Summary of Events and Information	Remarks and references to Appendices
BRAQUEMONT	June 13th 1917		The headquarters and office of this unit were to-day moved to LABEUVRIERE. An inspection was made of the villages in the area in which are situated HESDIGNEUL, occupied as H.Q. of 9th Royal Sussex; no sanitary conveniences for troops, sanitary arrangements advised as being inadequate to the present number of troops, sanitary arrangements advised. LAPUGNOY, occupied by 13th Middlesex to contain a temporary manner the French latrines a temporary manner. FOUQUEREUIL occupied by 2nd Lincolns, enough sanitary conveniences for the company, two companies K.O. inspected the sanitary arrangements in the village of LABEUVRIERE with a view of making necessary improvements — a map of the village to be appended to this volume.	Appendix I R.W.M.
LABEUVRIERE	June 14th 1917		A party of 1 N.C.O and 4 men were sent to ALLOUAGNE (to be billeted and attached by 19th Field Ambulance) to work the following villages; LE HAMEL, BUSNETTES, BAS RIEUX, ECQUEDECQUES. A party of 1 N.C.O and 3 men were sent to FOUQUIERES (billeted and rationed by 19th G.A.S.C) to work the following districts — NOEUX-LES-MINES, ANNEZIN, FOUQUEREUIL. In both above out-stations men will inspect sanitary areas, camps, billets etc of the troops in occupation and report daily upon defects and improvements or lines to be dealt. Received GRO 203 – 207, 208 – 213 ; DRO 2193 – 2197.	R.W.M.
LABEUVRIERE	June 15th 1917		Routine Inspection work resumed. From LABEUVRIERE the village of LAPUGNOY and HESDIGNEUL were visited. LAPUGNOY was found to be occupied by the 7th Hertfords and 13th Middlesex and the work of emptying sanitary conveniences proceeding slowly owing to scarcity of materials. HESDIGNEUL was found to be occupied by the 9th Royal Sussex, and the work of emptying sanitary conveniences proceeding slowly owing to scarcity of materials. From ALLOUAGNE the villages of BAS RIEUX, CANTRAINNE, BUSNETTES and LE HAMEL were visited. BAS RIEUX was found to be occupied by the 9th Suffolks and Durhams and the sanitary conveniences sufficient for troops are billeted in barns and houses. The sanitary arrangements were simple and adequate. CANTRAINNE was found to be occupied by two companies of 9th Suffolks and the work of emptying sanitary conveniences in progress.	R.W.M.

WAR DIARY or INTELLIGENCE SUMMARY

Army Form C. 2118.

41ST SANITARY SECTION * R.A.M.C.(T)

Page 9

Place	Date	Hour	Summary of Events and Information	Remarks and references to Appendices
LABEUVRIERE	Sept 15th 1917 continued		BUSNETTES was found to be occupied by A.T.C. Coy. & R.W. Kent and Transport, and D Coy & Coys of 1st N. Staffs and Transport. The troops are billeted in barns and outhouses. No sanitary conveniences had been made but work of construction in progress. From FOUQUIERES the following villages have been visited:- ANNEZIN, and FOUQUEREUIL. The troops occupying FOUQUIERES are 1st Royal Irish Rifles, 189 Bde H.Q., an amount from H.Q., 19 Coy, 195 Coy + 197 Coy R.E., A.S.C. They are billeted in huts and houses. Sanitary conveniences improvement + construction in progress. Arrangements were made by the Town Major for collecting refuse for burning at incinerator. FOUQUEREUIL was found to be occupied by 189 Coy R.E. Transport. The troops are billeted in barns & houses. Since last visit new improvements have been made in the sanitary areas and work in progress to complete. The Town Major has made arrangements with the civilian occupation to permit the use of the Sanitary areas and collecting it to incinerator at Horse & Mule Stand for the purpose of collecting refuse and emptying it to incinerator. A P.B. man is in charge of same, two whole time men. ANNEZIN was found to be occupied by 3rd R.I.R Brigade and Transport C+D/107 R.F.A. + 107 Bde H.Q. R.F.A. Whole of completing sanitary conveniences is in progress and arrangements are being made by the Town Major for collection of refuse and this animal manure that has been erected by D/107 under their annual with area constructional work:- WORKSHOP, Standard arrangement. horse incinerator emptied. 1 corrugated Iron ablution bench emptied. 1 Kild oven + 1 grease trap emptied. LABEUVRIERE. 1 urinal erected and 1 notice board fixed at D.H.Q. 1 latrine commenced at 11.M.M.P. in traffic Police repairs & destruction and H.Q. Transport commenced.	
			A map of LAPUGNOY has been prepared and made, and a copy is appended to this volume. Received C.R.O. 346 - 347. D.R.O. 298 - 302. Lieut Col. ADMS. 1st Div Speaker of Units personnel being visiting by Watts Supplies throughout the area is being made, showing arrangement bricks + being fixed and where funds for transporting proper, as necessary. Notice boards are being fixed giving information as to the amount of BLEACHING POWDER to be used for water carts. Lately the supply of this supplies in LABEUVRIERE have been. Short.	Appendix II

R. W. 7-

WAR DIARY or INTELLIGENCE SUMMARY

Army Form C. 2118.

Place: LABEUVRIERE
Date: Feb 16th 1917

The O.C. accompanied by the D.A.D.M.S. 2nd Division, inspected Sanitary Arrangements of the 2nd Divisional Train and Bombing School about FOUQUIERES and found same in a very unsatisfactory condition. All present arrivals from Infantry Brigades in being supplied with a water supply. Cooks had rifles with drawn hafts — the unit producing an open entrenched hose, no latrines for officers or men, urine bays do not receive sufficient attention and are arranged quite in the open, some are broken down & soft, whilst not water etc. Dispersed at South side will receive attention and a recommendation made where these ice stain. The water supply from a pump in barn with filtrates. I have recommended that immediate steps should be taken to improve the various conditions and that the whole system of water disposal on account of water logged condition of ground are possibly be altered. A report has been forwarded to D.A.D.M.S. Divisions for information.

The R.O. made usual recommendation to the O.C. 131st F.A. Ambulance regarding measles, owing to a number of cases having occurred in the area.

A map has been prepared of HESDIGNEUL and is appended to this volume showing the remarks of the water supplies. Has been tested in LABEUVRIERE and in positions at the following units were inspected :— 1st Royal Dragoons (tents) 19 G. ASC, 1st G.A.S.C., 3rd Rifle Bde. (2 Coys.) D/107 R.F.A., and Remounts (tents), 7129 Co. R.E.

Routine inspection work continues, from MUDAGNE the following details were visited :— ECQUEDECQUES, DASRIEUX, CANTRAINNE, LE HAMEL & LE VALLEE, ECQUEDECQUES marching into be occupied by the 6th Middlesex Battn. 196 G. ASC. 106 Bn RFA Transport, 59th Motor Machine Gun R.E., 4th Qr. Engrs. 1st Army Corps and sanitary work in progress.

LE HAMEL marching into be occupied by 9th R.W. Fus. and Workshop, measures had been taken to provide sanitary conveniences.

LA VALLEE marching into be occupied by 1/9 & 1/5 N. Staffs and M.G. Section and temporary measures had been taken to provide sanitary conveniences.

From FOUQUIERES the following districts were visited :— ANNEZIN + NOEUX les MINES.
NOEUX les MINES was being occupied by 17th J. Bn. H.Q., 8 B.y F.C., 13th R. Fusiliers, 10 R.E., 17th M. G. Coy, 17 Light T.M. Bty, 8th Bn Transport + 13th R. Fus Transport, the sanitary arrangements of all these units were found to be in a satisfactory condition, commenced work. LAIBEUVRIERE 1 urinal pit and covered installation had pits at Christian Workshop. 2 refuse arranged.
FOUQUIERES. 2 latrine trenches dug, 1 refuse latrine constructed at 3rd R.L. urinal pits
ANNEZIN. Repairs to latrine urinal made.

Received Aug 150 Royston Cugder. 627 R M M
A534 Wt. W.4973/M.687 750,000 8/16 D.D. & L. Ltd. (Forms)/C.2118/13. GRO 2126-2139, CRO. 215-222. + DRO 2203-2285.

Remarks and references to Appendices: Appendix III

WAR DIARY or INTELLIGENCE SUMMARY

Army Form C. 2118.

Place	Date	Hour	Summary of Events and Information	Remarks and references to Appendices
LABEUVRIERE	July 4 1917		Routine Inspection Work continues:- From ALLOUAGNE the villages of LE HAMEL, LAVALLEE, BAS-RIEUX, CANTRAINNE and ECQUEDECQUES. Progress has been made in all areas of environmental sanitary measures but slowly owing to scarcity of materials. From FOUQUIERES the villages of FOUQUEREUIL + ANNEZIN were visited and work of installing sanitary appliances proceeding slowly owing to dearth of material. At LABEUVRIERE all sanitary areas were visited. A map of the village of ANNEZIN has been prepared and made, and a copy in appended to this volume. Water cart in possession of the following units were inspected :- 2nd Sqdn. C°, 13th Middx. (2 carts), 4th Hussars (2 carts), 73rd M.G.C, 21st Div H.Q., and 9th R.Sussex (2 carts). Water Supplies in FOUQUEREUIL (5) and FOUQUIERES (5) were tested by Horrocks Test. Disinfection 73rd Field Ambulance NOEUX LES MINES measles; controls 20; bullets (bags + worms) disinfected, kits disinfected, blankets to the fumigator; contacts under observation. Constructional work- LABEUVRIERE Latrines constructed at Div Ordnance repair Station and Div Gholera, latrines commenced to be made in the mule yard. 1 latrine seat and 1 grease trap fixed. WORKSHOP 1 aeroplane bench emptied, 5 closets pit latrines put out, made. FOUQUIERES 1 urinal pail at 1st R.F., 1 urinal pail at 3rd R.B., 1 latrine hole repaired. LE HAMEL 2 other latrines erected and covered (for ants + no disposal). 1 urinal pail made. 1 man latrine constructed temporarily (workshop later). BAS-RIEUX. refuse pit dug. 1 man 11548/5 latrine constructed (horsents over latrine). CANTRAINNE refuse pit dug. ECQUEDECQUES 4 temporary latrines constructed, 1 grease trap, 1 urinal + incinerator emptied. ALLOUAGNE 2 officers latrines erected + 5 mens latrines (temporary). Received No.157 Routine Orders 636 – 645. C.R.O 223 – 206. D.R.O 2206 – 2211, + Circular D.J.A.G. G.H.Q No.M/157152"	Appendix IV. R.W.M.

WAR DIARY or INTELLIGENCE SUMMARY

Army Form C. 2118.

Place	Date	Hour	Summary of Events and Information	Remarks and references to Appendices
LABEUVRIERE	July 11th 1917		The O.C. visited ALLOUAGNE re case CEREBRO SPINAL MENINGITIS the bacteriological examination of which proved positive and made the following recommendations:- (1) The contacts at present under observation of M.O. Bruxelin to be completely isolated. (2) The schools of the contacts be ordered and out bacteriological examination as soon as possible. (3) The room in which case was billeted not to be used by French civilian. (4) A report to be sent to office of A.D.M.S. 51st Division re present movements of the case amongst those contacts as (5) An estimate of the amount of clear content in barn with a view to its disinfection. Routine inspections were carried out. The following villages were visited :- TOUQUIERES, FOUQUEREUIL, ANNEZIN, ALLOUAGNE, ECQUEDECQUES, BUSNETTES, BASRIEUX, LAPUGNOY and LABEUVRIERE. The work of constructing artificial outerng convenience is still in progress. Billets were inspected and found in a satisfactory condition in FOUQUEREUIL & others at LAMOTTE, LABEUVR 139 Q R.E. 11 Artillery. Water carts in possession of the following units were inspected:- 6/107 R.F.A & 197 G.A.S.C. At HESDIGNEUL 6 water carriers used by troops were examined by homocock-Test and found satisfactory. DISINFECTION. Spray Form. Dr W H MACKAY. B Coy 2nd Genuine FOUQUEREUIL: movements for present broked:- MAROC in billets & evacuated 17-3-17; LABEUVRE N°597 & 417 ES BREBIS and was associated with LE HODGE whose men evacuated from MAROC suffering from Scarlet Fever 11-3-17; Contacts are $ offices of B. Coy and the latrines at LE MACKAY, they all were examined and are revealed no such an or burbis under observation of M.O. mess; Bedroom last occupied by 12 MACKAY has been disinfected, also his mess room by contacts; civilian occupants have painted with creosote mice which tender to seal bed cracks in order to make a solution to car dummy necessary. DISINFECTION. Murden Sundeman Ambulance belonging to H.C.S. 3rd Australian and 6 other units which had been used in evacuating a case dummy evening hundred. Emulsional work:- LABEUVRIERE. Incinerator (Orridart compression fresh) 1 notice servant field at Sn. Orphanage. 1 machine employed for 4th Coy. M.M.P. BAS RIEUX. 1 machine fresh WORKSHOP 1 advertisement compound 1 standard and complete new incinerator compleled. latrine box seats (with out lid) + 6 types to contain toilet paper " ECQUEDECQUES. 1 annual machine ALLOUAGNE. 2 other latine constructed. BUS 5 Arteries Co 1 moved fresh 1 query emptied + incinerators main. Received C.R. 0. 209-233; D.R. 0. 2012-2014. C.V. M.R. Staff Paymaster C.H. 1511	RWM

WAR DIARY or INTELLIGENCE SUMMARY

Army Form C. 2118.

Place: LABEUVRIERE
Date: July 15 1917

Routine Sanitation Work continued and latrines in the following villages have been inspected:— LABEUVRIERE, HESDIGNEUL, LAPUGNOY, GOSNAY, NOEUX LES MINES, ANNEZIN, FOUQUIERES, ECQUEDECQUES, BUSNETTES, BAS RIEUX, CANTRAINNE and ALLOUAGNE, and work of improving the sanitary arrangements in progress.

The following water supplies used by troops were tested by Divisional C.S.O:— BUSNETTES is approved. BAS RIEUX, 2 supplies, and CANTRAINNE 2 supplies. at BUSNETTES, are supply proved unsatisfactory and the M.O. of that unit having same has fixed a notice board saying "NOT TO BE USED". — 17th M.G.Co, 6th B.ytt. (Lower), & Water carts in provision of the following units were inspected:— 17th M.G.Co, 6th B.ytt. (Lower), 13th Royal Sussex (lower).

Billets have been inspected as follows:— C/107 R.F.A. FOUQUEREUIL, D/107 R.F.A. FOUQUEREUIL—Billet No127 occupied by 18 men of C/107 was found to be in an unsatisfactory condition. The civilian occupants being extremely dirty. The billet has been evacuated and reported to the Town Major. FOUQUIERES, A.S.C. attached men, 9 keeves J.B.109 & 110 R.F.A. in 17 keeves, 1st D.LH.Q. & 1st R.F. Battalion. Report rec'd 18-3-17. DISINFECTION: Nil. 2nd COLLINS W.T.: A134 Aust aerodrome 15th Army Troops. Report rec'd 18-3-17. GOSNAY, 6-3-17. Advised of trophies 18-3-17: location GOSNAY; Moreover, ANNEQUIN 20-7-17 & 8-3-17. GOSNAY, 6-3-17. Note 18-3-17: contacts members to any LETHIUNG L.I.R. and tradesmen who will be kept after some special appliances. Aircrew and billeting occupied that no work in canteens are at present employed but has been disinfected sheets and headrests accompanied been interviewed.

DISINFECTION: Ambulance bus sent the deinfectants by 73rd Field Ambulance. Servicing in the village of LABEUVRIERE has been sent to an outpatient town. The O.C. arranged with the Town Major that trails in completion should be made permanent, however, it may daily at 8 a.m. All the principle stables have been covered, and accumulations has been examined by Refuse Dumps.

The Refuse Dump selected in advance was (1st Corps Reg Stations) also not had been previously used by proceeding garrisons in occupation. This is already a smoke defected at the Dumps which when opened will cope with all the remainder of the accumulated refuse that is each list. Town has been decided for the purpose of sorting up refuse. A spring of all that possible Ambroses, dropping of all that produce Ambroses has been arranged man manure made and fed at Corps Refuse Workshop. 29 notice boards made and painted. A standard latrine bar seats made. WATER BOARD NOTICES fixed at supplies not previously marked in the villages of HESDIGNEUL, LAPUGNOY & LABEUVRIERE.

Received CRLO 234—238. Additions to 1st Corps Standing Orders, DRO 2015—226.

R.W.W.

Army Form C. 2118.

WAR DIARY
or
INTELLIGENCE SUMMARY.
(Erase heading not required.)

Page 1/4

41st SANITARY SECTION
R.A.M.C. (T.)

Place	Date	Hour	Summary of Events and Information	Remarks and references to Appendices
LABEUVRIERE	Jan 20th 1917		Routine Inspection work continues. Units in the following districts were visited :– LABEUVRIERE, ALLOUAGNE, BAS RIEUX, ECQUEDECQUES, BUSNETTES, LA VALLEE, NOEUX-LES-MINES, ANNEZIN, FOUQUIERES, FOUQUEREUIL and ANNEZIN and work of improving sanitary conveniences in progress. DISINFECTIONS. (1) Scarlet fever : 1st Royal Irish. NOEUX LES MINES : 2nd Lt COHEN. E : contacts 1 batman who reported: movements 17th, 18th, 19th, Loos, 10th, 11th, 12th, 15th, 16th (attracted), 13th, 14th MAZINGARBE, 14th, 17th, 18th NOEUX have separate sleeping place, huts disinfected. (2) Measles : 6th Brigade NOEUX LES MINES : Pt CLINCH H.J. 110 contacts who are segregated in huts are separated between LOOS camp, MAZINGARBE camp, NOEUX camp: movements between LOOS camp, MAZINGARBE camp, NOEUX camp 13th, 14th, 15th LOOS. (3) Suspected Cerebro spinal meningitis: 13th Glamorgan?: ALLOUAGNE. Pte DAMES. R : the village has been placed out of bounds to all troops: huts disinfected, straw burned and destroyed: movements 13th, 14th, 15th LOOS. 14th, 15th PHILOSOPHE, 14th, 15th, 17th PETITSANS, 15th, 17th, 18th ALLOUAGNE. (4) Measles : 1st Royal Irish : FOUQUIERES : Pte GREEN. E. : 1 platoon contacts who are segregated : movements 13th, 14th, 15th 7th Fusilier, 17th truth village line, 14th, 15th FOUQUIERES : killed a rough coal distribution 15th, 16th 4 brothers villagers who still have diarrhoea. (5) Measles : 1st Royal Irish : FOUQUIERES : Pte MOORE. G. : 2 platoons contacts are segregated : hulks a long hours who have been disinfected: movements 13th u 7th Fusilier, 15th truth village line, 14th, 15th. FOUQUIERES. This case probably contacted with Lt. COHEN. E or case (1). (6) Measles : 1st N. Staffs : BUSNETTES : Lt STAINER. W.D : contacts 5 officers who are segregated : hutmen occupied by Case are meet now used by the Case and contacts of officers : movements between 12th to 13th NOEUX 13th, 13th to 19th, BUSNETTES. (7) Measles : 1st N Staffs : BUSNETTES : Capt. ROBINSON. H. G : no contacts : sickroom and huts lines disinfected : adjoining rooms disinfected : movements between 12th, 17th NOEUX 13th, BUSNETTES 13th from LA HAMEL. Water supplies were tested by Norredis Coca as follows :– BUSNETTES. S supplies – 196 G A.S.C. A, B, C & D, 1106 R.F.A, BAS RIEUX, 5 supplies. CANTRAINNE, 2 supplies. LA VALLEE, 9 supplies. Half cards in procession of these following units went inspected :– 196 G A.S.C. A, B, C & D, 1106 R.F.A. Bills were imposed as follows :– FOUQUIERES : 1st Royal Irish : A.S.C. stores. Constructional work :– FOUQUIERES 1 grease trap constructed 3 lye pits added to existing latrines. BAS RIEUX. Two latrines (trench) filled in and also not latrines dug. ECQUEDECQUES. 2 urinal pits constructed 2 latrine trenches filled in, new latrines dug. WORKSHOP. 12 disposal latrine box seats made. 3 grease trays made. 16 metre trough made and punished stand and complete moving camps made. Scavenging in the village of ALLOUAGNE is now proceeding satisfactorily under the supervision of the N.C.O. of the station, whom criticisms etics. N.C.O.'s 10 men are being employed by Municipal Council. Received C.P.O 739 –215. P.R.O 3234 – 22.3.3 and accompanying sheet messages 22.1.	R. Ma [signature]

A 3534 Wt.W.4973 M687 750,000 8/16 D.D. & L. Ltd. Forms/C.2118/13.

Army Form C. 2118.

WAR DIARY or **INTELLIGENCE SUMMARY.**
(Erase heading not required.)

Instructions regarding War Diaries and Intelligence Summaries are contained in F.S. Regs., Part II. and the Staff Manual respectively. Title pages will be prepared in manuscript. **Page 15**

41st SANITARY SECTION — R.A.M.C. (T)

Place	Date	Hour	Summary of Events and Information	Remarks and references to Appendices
LABEUVRIERE	July 21st 1917		Routine Inspection Work continues. Units in the following districts were visited:— LABEUVRIERE, HESDIGNEUL, CROSNAY, LAPUGNOY, BUSNETTES, LE CORNET BOURDOIS, ALLOUAGNE, ECQUEDECQUES, FOUQUIERES, ANNEZIN & FOUQUEREUIL and the work of improving sanitary conveniences found to be in progress. Water carts in possession of the following units were inspected:— No 2 Coy. R.H.A.D.A.C. 9th B. Suffolk (scants), 8th R.W. Kent (scants), 13th N. Suffs. (scants). Water supplies were visited by Commandant. Test as follows:— ALLOUAGNE 18 Emplon. Emplacement made, 3 urinal pits dug, 3 latrine derricks & incinerator emplaced with new emplacement. ECQUEDECQUES 2 urinal pits, 3 latrines field & 3 ALLOUAGNE: 3 urinals field 3 latrine emplaced. BUSNETTES: 4 urinals field and new incinerator. 3 incinerator emplaced. 3 incinerators constructed. LE CORNET BOURDOIS: 1 incinerator constructed, FOUQUIERES: Latrine derrick emplaced. 2 pits renewed. PIERRE STRAY: 1 grease trap field, 1 soakpit field, 3 urinals field, 2 latrine derrick emplaced. ANNEZIN: Repair & construction of latrines. HESDIGNEUL. 13 horse field at Divisional, 1 urinal field. LAPUGNOY: 1 incinerator (large) made, 1 cumm. added, 1 movement bath at Battalion, 12 horse field, 15 latrine urinal field, 3 temporary latrines. 2 refuse pits dug. LABEUVRIERE. 8 latrine paper trees field. WORKSHOP. 4 horse travel latrine paper made, 15 tar anti-latrine made, 1 blanket covering for new movements made, 1 solution bench made. Maps of CANTRAINNE, BUSNETTES, and LE HAMEL were prepared to made today and a copy of each applied to the various. Received C.R.O. 216 – 250. D.R.O. 3344 – 3359.	APPENDICES V. VI. VII. R.W.M.
LABEUVRIERE	July 22nd 1917		Routine Inspection Work continues. Units in the following districts were visited:— LABEUVRIERE, FOUQUIERES, ANNEZIN, NOEUX-LES-MINES, ALLOUAGNE, LE HAMEL, CANTRAINNE, BAS RIEUX, & ECQUEDECQUES and the work of improving sanitary conveniences is in progress. To facilitate this, sanitary appliances made in the workshop of this Section have been issued today to the following units: 13th Machine Gun Coy. 1 grease trap; 9th B. Suffolk 1 latrine latrine complete, 9th Royal Sussex 18 loss ventilators main leads, scavenges. 13th Essex Knots 1314, 6 urinals and 6 seats; 7th Buffs 2 corrugated iron incinerators & latrine derrick, 6 night urinals in the seat, 12 fly screens; 1st West Kent 1 corrugated iron incinerators, latrine urinals emplaced & 5 notice boards. DISINFECTIONS: Measles 9th Buffs No 19655 Pte MERRITH. Diagnosed 21st: NOEUX-LES-MINES, Movements, blankets, 18th & 19th. MAZINGARBE 6th & 10th. NOEUX-LES-MINES 15th & 17th orderlies 60 who were isolated in a large hut, whose mess apparel, have been meals apparel, latrines, urinals apart from remainder of Battalion: its hut has been disinfected today by Machonich Spray and cresol solution & 9th: NOEUX-LES-MINES. No 18234 Pte BAINES. B: diagnosed 20th: movements same as previous one, as also cresols and remarks. Measles: 8th Buffs: NOEUX-LES-MINES: No 16234 Pte BAINES. B: diagnosed 20th: movements, blankets 37th & 5th, Comps. Rect. Station 6th & 15 19th, NOEUX 20th 17.29th remarks and cresols same as in two preceding cases. Water carts in possession of the following units were inspected:— 12th M. G. Co., 12th Hertz Derby (scants). 103rd R. E., 8th Queens (scants). Water applied to the villages of LABEUVRIERE and HESDIGNEUL were applied with notice boards.	

WAR DIARY or INTELLIGENCE SUMMARY

Army Form C. 2118.

Place	Date	Hour	Summary of Events and Information	Remarks and references to Appendices
LABEUVRIERE	Mar 30th Continued		Constructional work:- BAS RIEUX mortuaries dug, told in, filled in, cleaned and put into use. 6 company latrines demolished & 5 new ones erected. LE HAMEL 2 urinals erected, 1 new incinerator built, 6 company latrines demolished & 5 new ones erected. ECQUEDECQUES Incinerator improved. ALLOUAGNE Showers repaired, first incinerator & urinal, also pail latrine dug. WORKSHOP 36 latrine box seats made, 2 urinated rain incinerators emptied, CANTRAINNE Impost dug. WORKSHOP 36 latrine box seats made, 30 notice boards made and painted. Incinerators with rotating drum made. 6 grease traps made. Billets were inspected as follows- 3rd Rifle Bde. ANNEZIN A.C., 8 billets. B.C., 4 billets. C.Q., 6 billets. D.C., 3 billets. Transport towards 8 billets. A map of BAS RIEUX has been prepared and made, and a copy in appended to this volume.	R.10 m Appendix VIII
LABEUVRIERE	Mar 31st 1917		Routine inspection work continues. Units in the following divisions were visited:- LABEUVRIERE, ALLOUAGNE, CANTRAINNE, BAS RIEUX, ECQUEDECQUES, HESDIGNEUL, LA VALLEE, NOEUX-LES-MINES, FOUQUIERES, ANNEZIN, FOUQUEREUIL, and work of improving sanitary conveniences found to be in progress. DISINFECTIONS. (1). Measles: 104 C.R.E. NOEUX-LES-MINES; Spr: TAYLOR.H. contacts 6 in number who have been confined to billet & estaminets also placed out of bounds 15 days; billet occupied by case and soldiers sprayed with cresol solution. (2). Cerebro-spinal meningitis: 104th Bde. R.F.A; ANNEZIN: Bomb: JONES.W.; contacts 12 in number occupying two billets, child in inspected and isolated and medically observed; beds have been sprayed with cresol solution; civilian & French Authorities have been communicated with. (3). Measles: 12th Royal Scottish:NOEUX les MINES; Pte WEBBER.A.J: contacts 34 in number, all transport men, & they are kept apart from rest of Battalion, forbidden to visit estaminets etc; rooms occupied by soldiers sprayed with cresol solution. (4). Scabies: 12th Royal Fusiliers: NOEUX les MINES; Pte WHITE; this case examined in some billet as preceding one. (5). Measles: 3rd Lifeguards at R.F.C; HESDIGNEUIL; D/Lt SCARAMANGA G.J; contacts 34 in number, all living in 10 different new aggregated; sickroom occupied by officer sprayed with cresol; bedclothes to be washed. Water carts in possession of the following units were inspected:- A/107 (Depot) + B/110 R.F.A. Water supplies in ALLOUAGNE have been supplied with notice boards declaring it for drinking etc. Maps have been prepared of the following districts and a copy of each appended to this volume:- FOUQUIERES, FOUQUEREUIL + ECQUEDECQUES. Constructional work:- WORKSHOP. I arranged covers made for "A" mess, 30 ten-pin latrine box seats prepared, 30 notice boards made & painted. FOUQUIERES' new latrine supplied & old latrine demolished in all 15 R.F. 3 new latrine completed for the Police. ECQUEDECQUES grease trap fixed; 1 urinated fixed; 1 ventilator constructed. Billets were inspected as follows - ALLOUAGNE: Pa. MOCKETT.M: contacts 30 in number aggregated; sheets blankets & pillows examined. DISINFECTIONS (1) Measles: 10 M Field Ambulance: ALLOUAGNE; Sgt RUSSELL. J.W: 1 contact who is aggregated; sheet blankets & cart disinfect sanitized (2) Measles: R.E. 493rd S.B: ALLOUAGNE; Pte Queers; 13 RIEUX, LA HAMEL; 9 R.W. Kent 11 Hussars, ECQUEDECQUES. 10th Huss D5 Huss	Appendices IV, V + VI

A 3534 Wt. W.4973 M687 750,000 8/16 D.D. & L. Ltd. Forms/C.2118/13.

WAR DIARY or INTELLIGENCE SUMMARY.

Army Form C. 2118.

(Erase heading not required.)

Instructions regarding War Diaries and Intelligence Summaries are contained in F.S. Regs., Part II. and the Staff Manual respectively. Title pages will be prepared in manuscript.

41st SANITARY SECTION * R.A.M.C. (T)

Place	Date	Hour	Summary of Events and Information	Remarks and references to Appendices
LABEUVRIERE	Jan 24th 1917		Routine Inspection Work continues. Units in the following districts were inspected:— LABEUVRIERE, HESDIGNEUL, LAPUGNOY, LE HAMEL, FOUQUIERES, FOUQUEREUIL, ANNEZIN, NOEUX les MINES, ALLOUAGNE, ECQUEDECQUES, CANTRAINNE, BUSNETTES and work of improving sanitary conveniences in progress. 8 latrine box seats drawn and taken been issued to the 13th Middx. DISINFECTION. (1) Measles: 93rd Light T.M. By.; LABEUVRIERE: TP. EMENY, F.: contacts, 12 in number who have been isolated. List of contacts also handed Units. Water carts in possession of the following units were inspected:— 194 G, 195th A.S.C., 1st Royal Irish (2 carts), No 1 S.A.D.A.C., 3rd Rifle Bde (2 carts), C/107 D/107 R.F.A., 2nd Leinsters (2 carts). Water supplies in the district of LE HAMEL have been applied with water hand notices. Constitutional work:— WORKSHOP 16 repairing 8 grease traps. 1 draught screen. 12 lids of latrine seats made. Statues boxes made and painted. HESDIGNEUL, 9th Royal Sussex, 12 repaired ... 4 latrines, 2 urinals, 2 wash baths, ... 4 urinal, Field LAPUGNOY, 3rd Leinsters, 1 grease trap, 12 latrines, 1 urinal & incinerator. ... 22 horses hand fired 1 latrine fired for use at Hospital. Contacts ANNEZIN, 3rd Rifle Bde, 1 latrine (urinal) erected. CANTRAINNE, 5 urine latrine (trenches dug) 1 urinal fired, 2 grease traps fired, 1 incinerator built. LE CORNET BOURDOIS, 9 latrines completed. 8 latrines completed 2 grease traps fired ... MANQUEVILLE: Billets were inspected as follows:— CANTRAINNE 958 Survey IO Killed ECQUEDECQUES: 196 G.A.S.C 6 killed, 30 horses, 2 Shelter BUSNETTES, 9th R.W. Kents 11 billets 25 horses. 11th R.F.A has now been inspected ... She had required duty on hours, received the 18 men of C/107 R.F.A has now been inspected fit for habitation again MOY[?]: Cpl KILBURN, P. reported back from leave and resumed duties in change of WORKSHOP. The man in change of water cart at C/107 R.F.A was today vaccinated by R.A.M.C. Sam. S... in district. Received G.R.O. 2145-2151. G.R.O. 361-369. D.R.O. 2249-2250. 4th Army Runner Memos Nos 35 & 36. R.W.M.
LABEUVRIERE	Jan 25th 1917		Routine Inspection Work continues. Units in the following districts were inspected:— LABEUVRIERE, BAS RIEUX, CANTRAINNE, BUSNETTES, ALLOUAGNE, LE HAMEL, FOUQUIERES, ANNEZIN, LAPUGNOY, NOEUX les MINES and the work of improving sanitary conveniences found to be also in progress. 6 latrine box seats have been issued to 107th M.Q. R.F.A. DISINFECTIONS: (1) Measles: LAPUGNOY: Pt ROLLS, H.: contacts 16 in number are not isolated: billets, blankets &c (2) Measles: 93rd Light T.M.Br.: LABEUVRIERE: case evacuated to 4th Field Ambulance. Contacts sprayed and cresol solution. (3) Measles: 13 Middx, LAPUGNOY: 4/Cpl TUCKEY, W.H.: evacuated to 7th Field Ambulance: contacts nil: curtain billet scraped by cases & bidding sprayed with cresol solution. (4) Scarlatina Ambulance No 1 US.B.S used in conveying case No 1 & 2 to 7th Field Ambulance sprayed and cresol solution. (5) Measles: 107 Field Ambulance: ALLOUAGNE: Pt DENT, E.: case evacuated to No 7 General Hospital: contacts nil: billets sprayed and cresol solution. (8) Measles: 10th Royal Irish: NOEUX les MINES: 2/pl SIMS, C.E.: evacuated to 43 Field Ambulance: contacts 10 isolated in own hut. Huts sprayed and cresol solution. Water carts in possession of the following units were inspected:— 93rd M. G. Co., 129 C.R.E., 93 R.E. (2 carts). Water supplies in the village of BAS RIEUX, CANTRIANNE + BUSNETTES have been supplied with notice boards. Billets were inspected as follows:— ALLOUAGNE, 8th Queens, 31 billets. Constitutional work:— WORKSHOP. 16 notice boards made and painted. It has been explained to me that any workmen have heard that any latrines pit dug 1 from laid 15 ... new ... repaired. LABEUVRIERE: ... of latrines inspected & urinals erected. TECHNICAL SCHOOL, urine latrine. CANTRIANNE [?] ... Received A.F. No ... R.W.M.

Routine Orders No. 646 — 654

WAR DIARY or INTELLIGENCE SUMMARY

Army Form C. 2118

41st SANITARY SECTION R.A.M.C. (T)

Place	Date	Hour	Summary of Events and Information	Remarks and references to Appendices
LABEUVRIERE	31/12/26th 1917		Routine inspection work continues. Visits to the following districts were made:- ANNEZIN, FOUQUEREUIL, FOUQUIERES, NOEUX les MINES, ECQUEDECQUES, CANTRAINNE, BUSNETTES, LA VALLEE, ALLOUAGNE, LABEUVRIERE. Work of improving sanitary arrangements of the above areas is in progress. The following units were inspected:- 1914 A.S.C. Sub DP H.Q. 21st Div Supp. C. 135 Middlesex (Scot.) Imp. Fontaine (Scot.) Buses were inspected as follows:- 104 Field R.E. H.Q. 3 buses. Disinfectional work.— FOUQUIERES. Repairs at latrine cubicle ANNEZIN finish moveable hut. LABEUVRIERE. 2 new parts made to latrine. 1 officers latrine urinal replaced & [?] 30 metres hessian put round. 16 latrine seats (screens) made. 1 urinal (complete). WORKSHOP. Water supplies in the village of ECQUEDECQUES were today tested. Contacts isolated as begun:- DISINFECTIONS (1) Parotitis: 3rd R/R. Bn: ANNEZIN: Rifle Day: F returned to Coy: Duce Ambulance: contacts number 70 whom as usual. (2) Measles: B. WIDDOWSON, T: ANNEZIN: R/F/ Day: F returned to 93rd Field Ambulance: contacts number 31 [?] whom urinal opened with cresol solution. (3) Mumps: 5th Queens: ALLOUAGNE: Pte Peak C.W.: evacuated to No. 7 Gen Hospital: contacts: billet sprayed with cresol solution & men examined. Kits & billet hut disinfected. (4) Scarlet Fever (?): 13th Middx: LAPUGNOY: D/Cpl. KENDALL H.T.: evacuated to 1/2nd Lon Field Ambulance: contacts: No. 3294 Pte Storey H.G., 2nd London Sanitary Co. attached 41st Sanitary Section was this day evacuated to No. 23 C.C.S. suffering from N.Y.D.(?) Fever and was brought direct. The strength of the Section is now from this date 5. A map of ALLOUAGNE has been revised and a copy appended to this volume.	
LABEUVRIERE	27/12/1917		Routine inspection work continues. The following districts were visited:- LABEUVRIERE, LE HAMEL, BUSNETTES, ALLOUAGNE, ECQUEDECQUES, LAPUGNOY, ANNEZIN, FOUQUIERES, FOUQUEREUIL, NOEUX les MINES, and work of improving sanitary conveniences found to be in progress. The following units were inspected:- 104 Co R.E., 1st M.G.C., 8th Bn Rifle, 13th R Fusiliers (Scot.) Water points as printed on map of ANNEZIN are listed by specific sources. DISINFECTION (1) Measles: les Village of RADCLIFFE C.W.: 8th Bn R/F: evacuated to 135 Field Ambulance: contacts now in camp. Area. 1 billet disinfected by usual solution. (2) Diphtheria: 104 R.E. Co R.E.: NOEUX les MINES: Cpl ETHERIDGE: evacuated from no.4 Field Ambulance to 2nd W Riding C.C.S. contacts (3) Measles: 104 Field Co R.E. NOEUX les MINES: Cpl Schama M.H. evacuated from 1st F Amb to No. 7 General Hospital contact 1 Ambulance in barracks by usual solution billet sprayed with usual solution [?] (4) Measles: 8th Queens: ALLOUAGNE: Pte SHURLOCK M.J.: evacuated from 1st F Amb to No. 7 General Hospital. contacts number 31 and kept from active duties - form active solution. All billets disinfected as usual. (5) Measles: 135 Middlesex: LAPUGNOY: Cpl. SCHOOLING, Pte READING, Pte MITCHELL F.A., Pte MUNN, Pte BLACKBURN.A, Pte READ.C. evacuated from 1st F Amb Ambulance to the 7 General Hospital: contacts are A.G.C.C. who are isolated as usual. Disinfection. All billets sprayed with cresol solution. C. cress, Steam No.10 platoon, Barracks sprayed. Disinfectional work — [?] standard routine refused by C.P Renwick. ANNEZIN 1 moveable hut. 3 notice boards fixed. Received 6 R.P.	

Army Form C. 2118.

WAR DIARY
or
INTELLIGENCE SUMMARY.
(Erase heading not required.)

Page 19

Instructions regarding War Diaries and Intelligence Summaries are contained in F. S. Regs., Part II. and the Staff Manual respectively. Title pages will be prepared in manuscript.

Place	Date	Hour	Summary of Events and Information	Remarks and references to Appendices
LABEUVRIERE.	Feb 28th 1917		Routine Inspection Work continued. Units in the villages of LABEUVRIERE, HESDIGNEUL, ANNEZIN, ECQUEDECQUES, ALLOUAGNE, CANTRAINNE, BAS RIEUX, FOUQUIERES, FOUQUEREUIL and work of improving sanitary arrangements found to be in progress. DISINFECTION. Nissans: FOUQUEREUIL. 29 Jennulin. Lt CROW, F.H. measured furnitures Ambulance to 7 linear samples. I assisted am officer who was appointed and under instructions of M.O.I. will at tempted with creosote solution. With carts in possession of the following units were inspected 196.6. A.S.C, 103 & R.E. A.B. C+D1106. R.F.A. Water supplies in the village of ANNEZIN were inspected and notices issued. Constructional work. – WORKSHOP 16 notice boards made and painted. 6 long standard latrine screens 10 small standard latrine screens made and painted. 2 shelves latrine (new) constructed. 1 maintenance erected. LABEUVRIERE. 1 latrine repaired HESDIGNEUL. 1 notice board fixed. ECQUEDECQUES. 1 refuse pit dug, 1 grease trap repaired. ALLOUAGNE. 1 latrine erected over new pit, refuse pit dug. 3 ablution pits, 1 latrine CANTRAINNE. 1 refuse pit dug, 2 latrine seats. Into new trenches. FOUQUIERES 1 urinal fixed. Received. 6. R.O 265 – 288. D.R.O 3260 – 3265. Scavenging has proceeded satisfactorily throughout the area	R.M.M

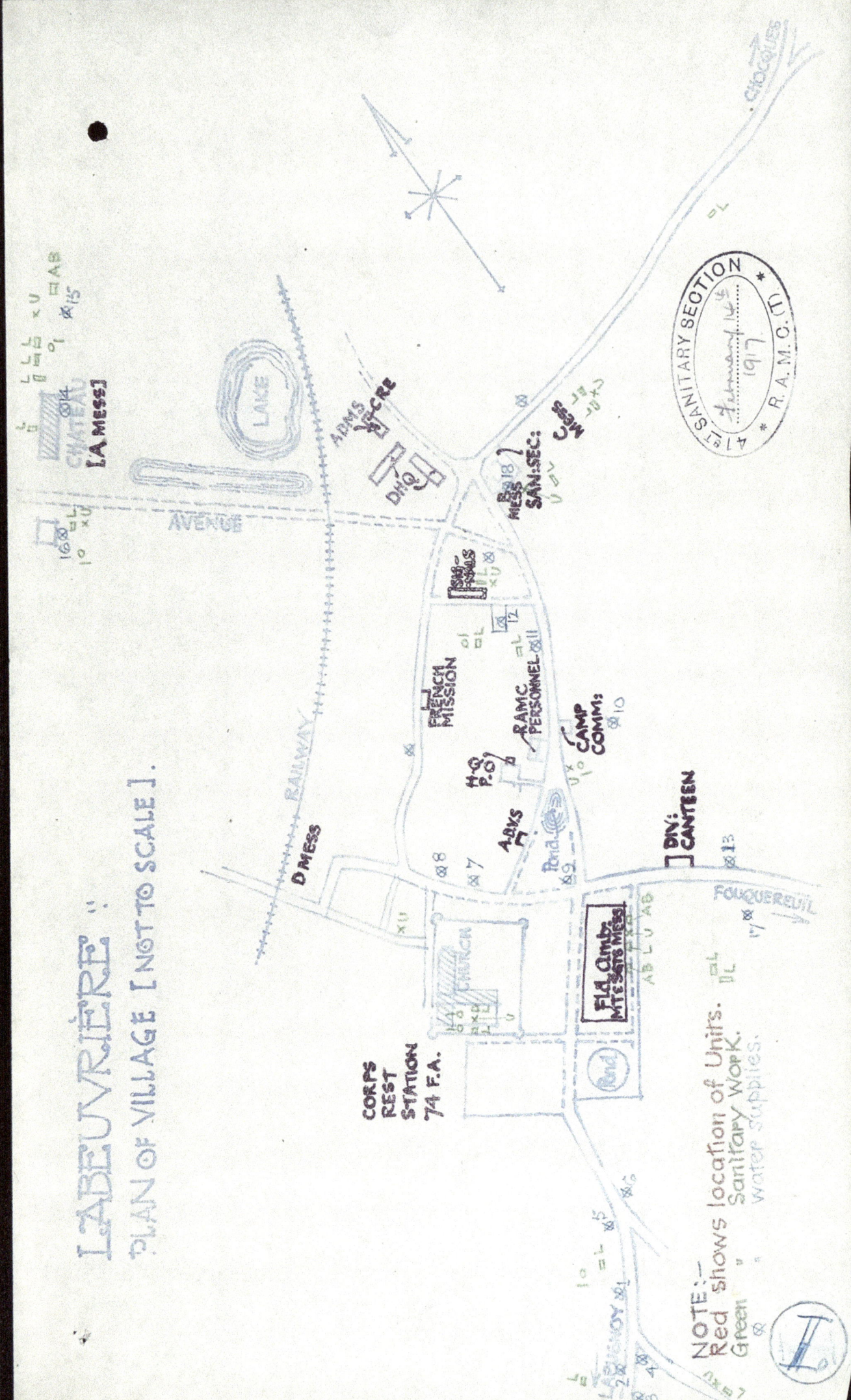

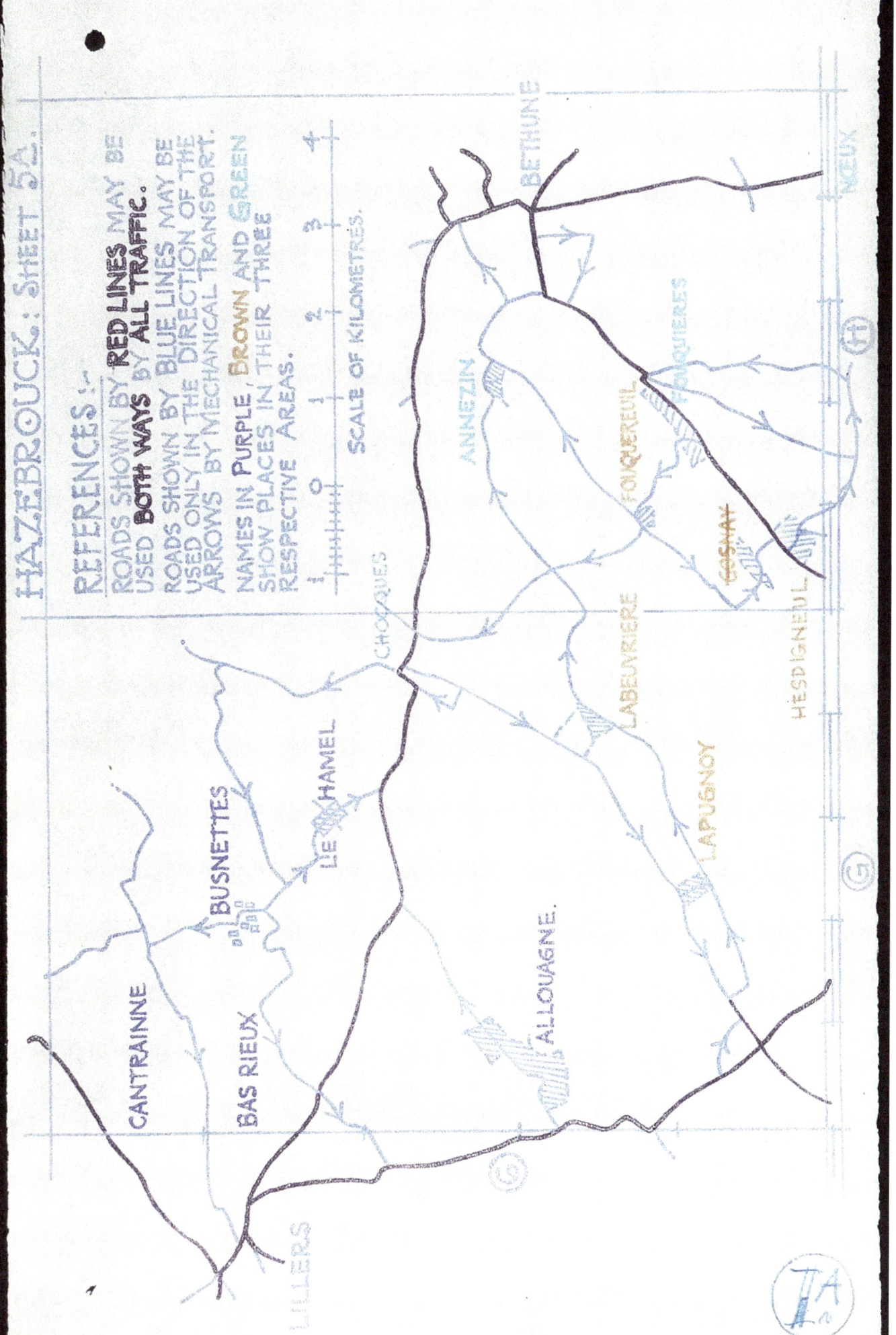

LAPUGNOY:
PLAN OF VILLAGE [NOT TO SCALE].

HESDIGNEUL:
PLAN OF VILLAGE: [NOT TO SCALE].

NOTE:—
1 Batt. [9th Sussex] and R.F.C. are billeted in this Area; but individual billets are not shown.

Green shows Sanitary Work.
× shows water supplies.

41st SANITARY SECTION
R.A.M.C. (T)

FOUQUIÈRES & BÉTHUNE

GOSNAY

Rue Nationale

Batt. H.Q

East St.

Baths
Model Billet

VAUDRICOURT

Church
HALLICOURT

Bath Rd.

GREEN

AERODROME

Woods

RUITZ & BRUAY

"ANNEZIN"
PLAN OF VILLAGE : [NOT TO SCALE].

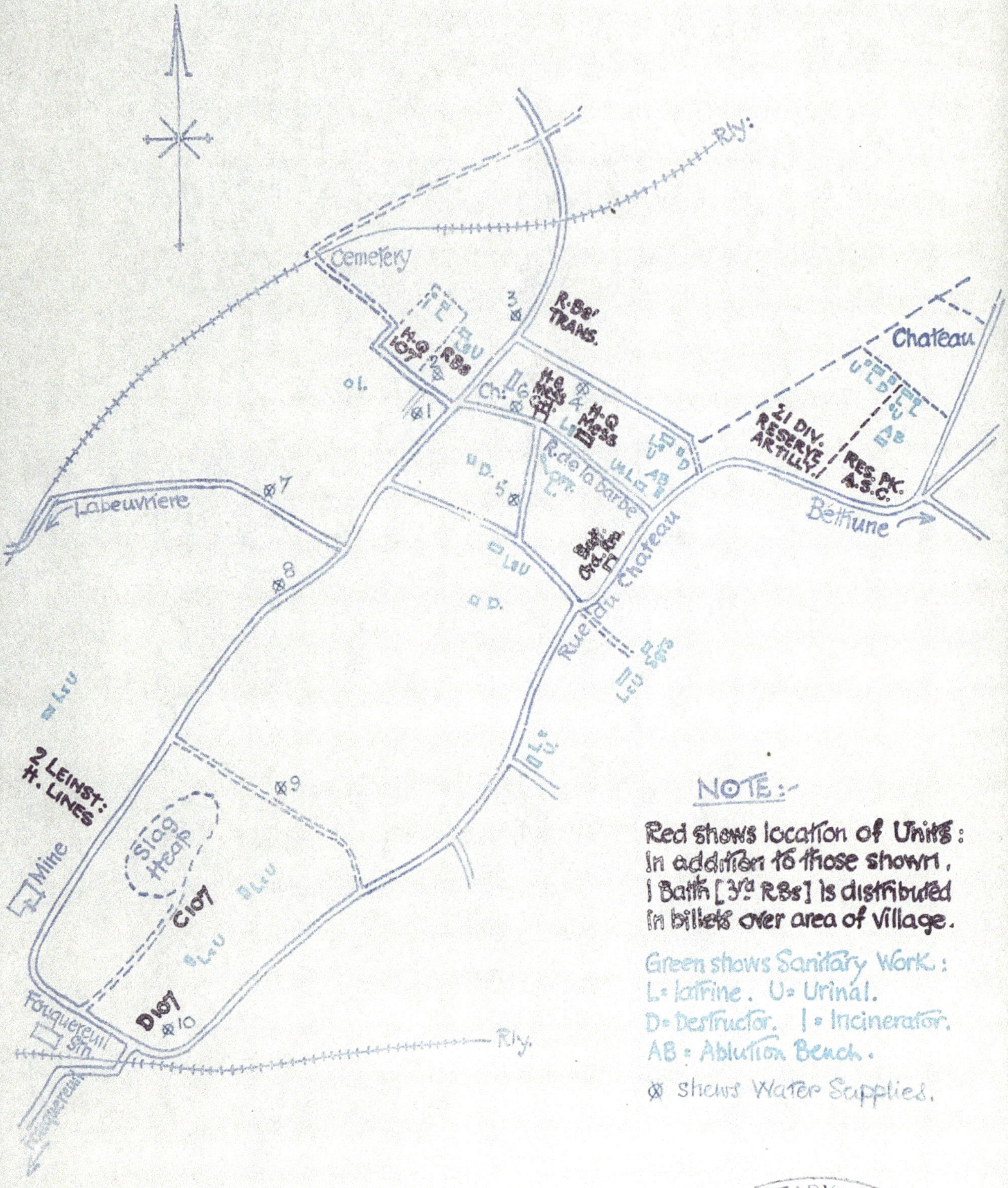

NOTE :—

Red shows location of Units:
In addition to those shown,
1 Battⁿ [3^d R.B^s] is distributed
in billets over area of village.

Green shows Sanitary Work :
L = Latrine.   U = Urinal.
D = Destructor.   I = Incinerator.
AB = Ablution Bench.
⊘ shows Water Supplies.

"CANTRAINNE"
PLAN OF VILLAGE [NOT TO SCALE].

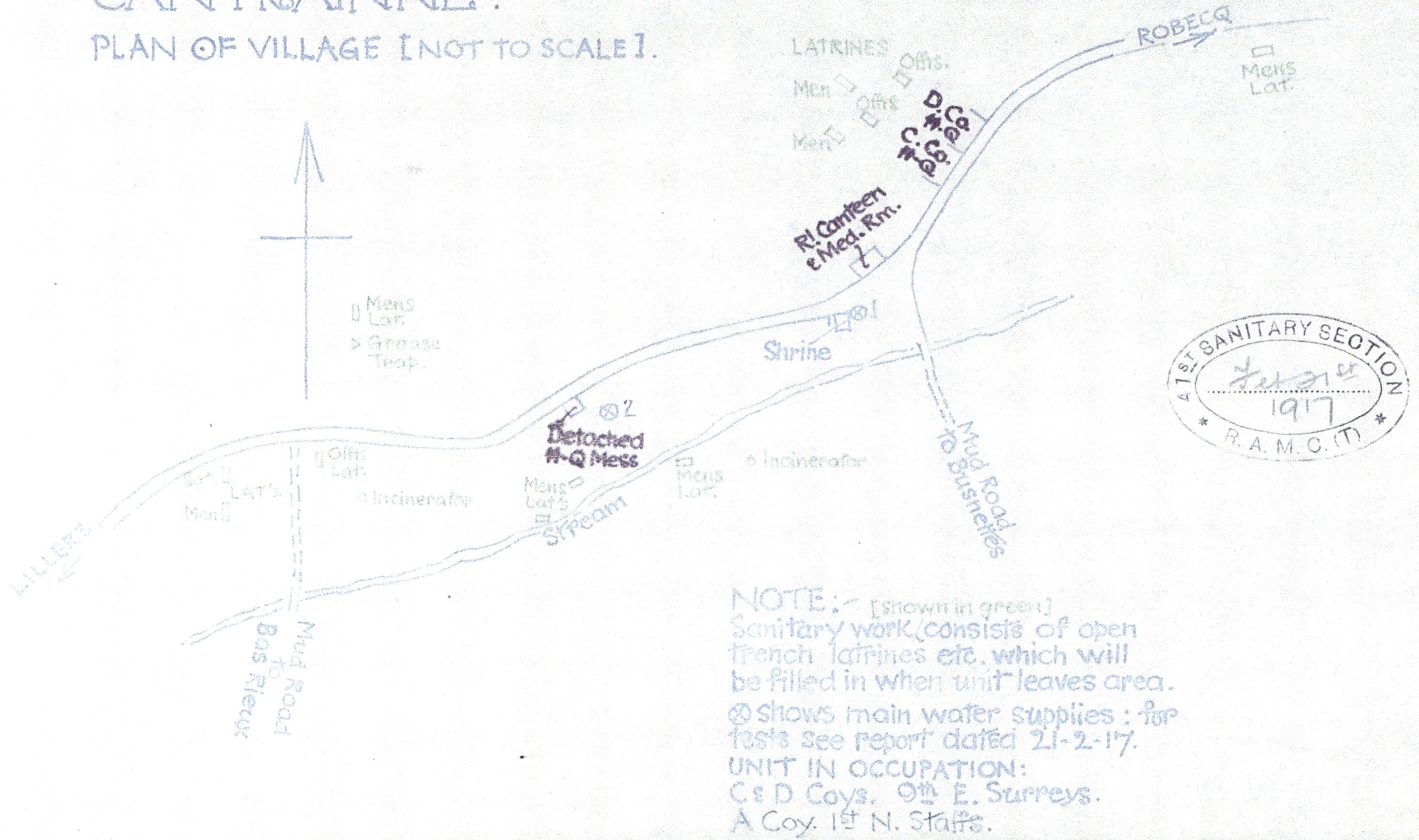

41ST SANITARY SECTION R.A.M.C. (T.)

ROBECQ

Men's Lat.

LATRINES Offrs.
Men Offrs
Men
D. Coy M.G.
C. M.G.
R. Orderly
E. Med. Rm.

Mud Road to Busnettes

Shrine

o Incinerator

Men's Lat.

⊗ 2

Detached H-Q Mess

Men's Lat's.

Stream

Men's Lat.
△ Grease Trap.

o Incinerator

Offrs Lat.
Men

Mud Road to Bas Rieux

LILLERS

NOTE:— [shown in green]
Sanitary work consists of open
trench latrines etc. which will
be filled in when unit leaves area.
⊗ shows main water supplies; for
tests see report dated 21-2-17.
UNIT IN OCCUPATION:
C & D Coys. 9th E. Surreys.
A Coy. 1st N. Staffs.

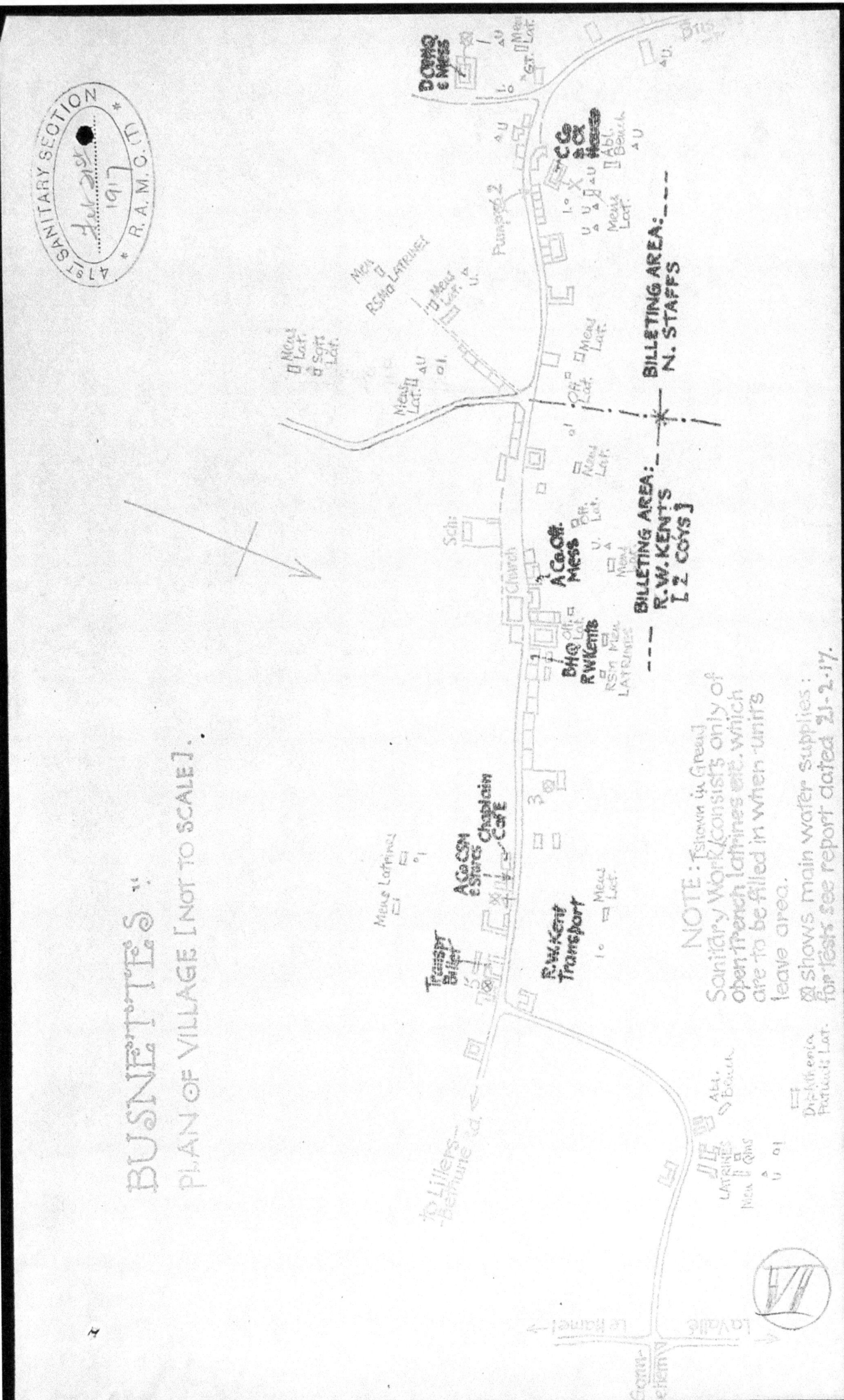

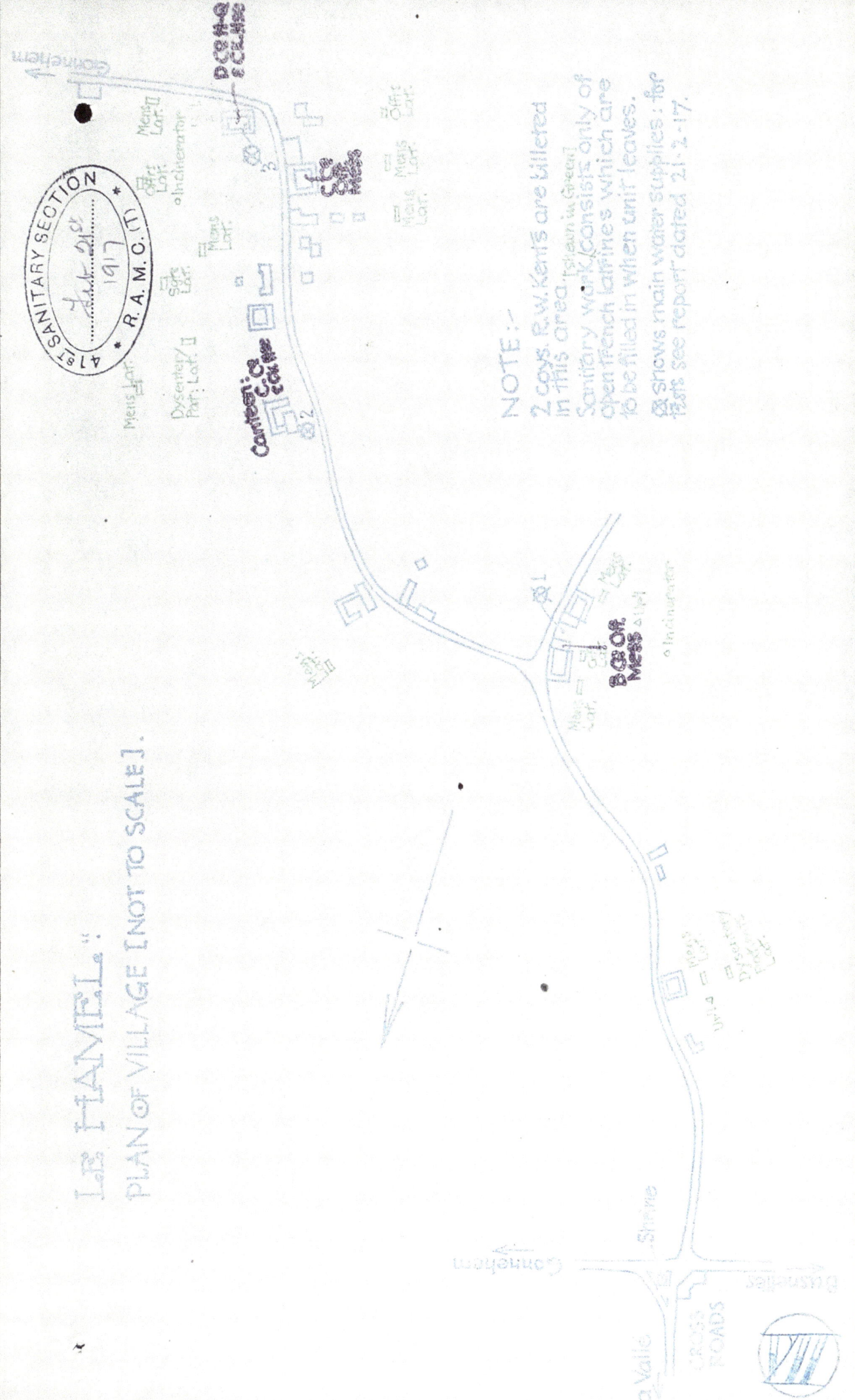

"BAS - RIEUX"
PLAN OF VILLAGE [NOT TO SCALE].

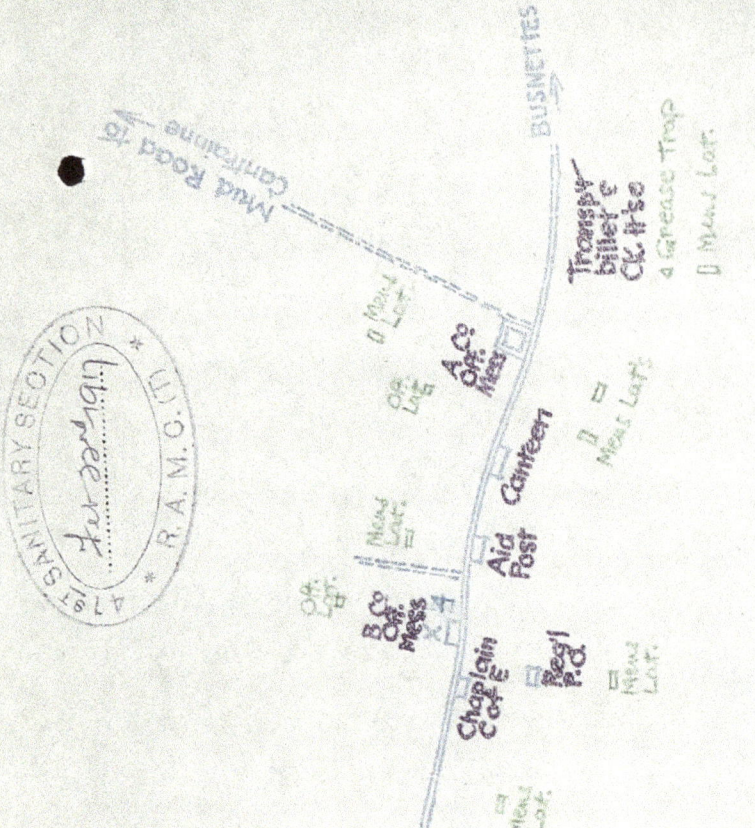

NOTE :- [shown in Green] Sanitary work consists of open trench latrines etc. which will be filled in when unit leaves area.

× shows main water supplies: for tests see report dated 21.2.17.

UNITS IN OCCUPATION :-
H.Q., A & B Cos. 9th E. Surreys.
Column Workshop.

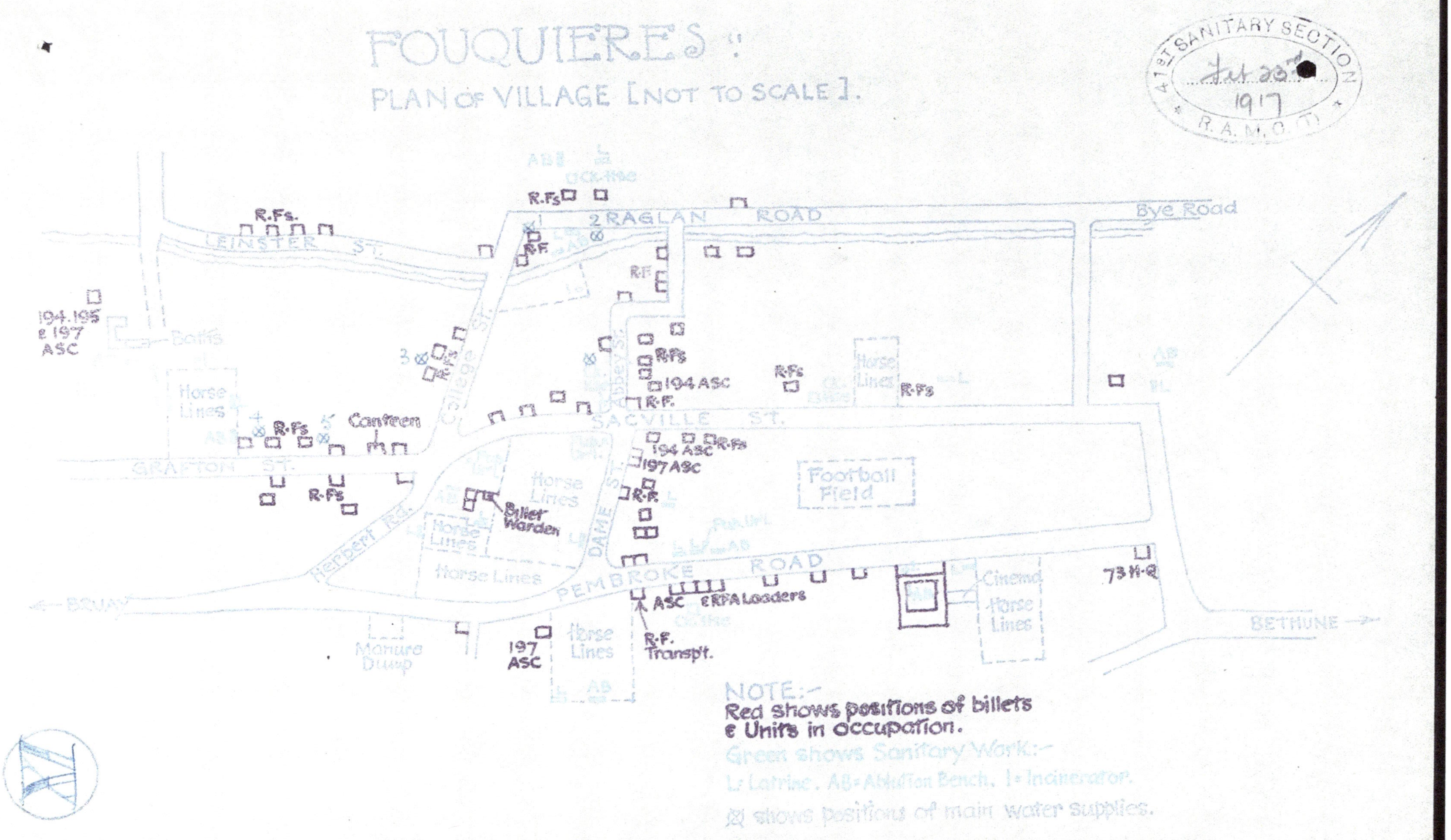

FOUQUIERES :
PLAN OF VILLAGE [NOT TO SCALE].
41ST SANITARY SECTION
Feb 23rd 1917
R.A.M.C. (T)
RAGLAN ROAD
Bye Road
LEINSTER ST.
College St.
Abbey St.
SACVILLE ST.
GRAFTON ST.
DAME ST.
Herbert Rd.
PEMBROKE ROAD
BRUAY
BETHUNE
Baths
Horse Lines
Canteen
Billet Warden
Football Field
Cinema
Manure Dump
R.Fs.
194.195 & 197 ASC
194 ASC
197 ASC
197 ASC
R.F.
ASC
ERPA Loaders
R.F. Transp't.
73 H.Q.
NOTE:-
Red shows positions of billets & Units in occupation.
Green shows Sanitary Work:-
L: Latrine. AB: Ablution Bench. I: Incinerator.
⊗ shows positions of main water supplies.

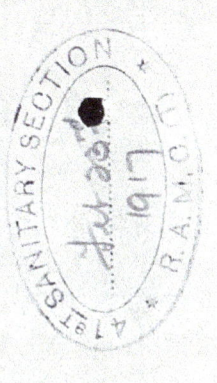

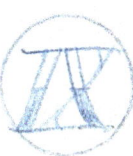

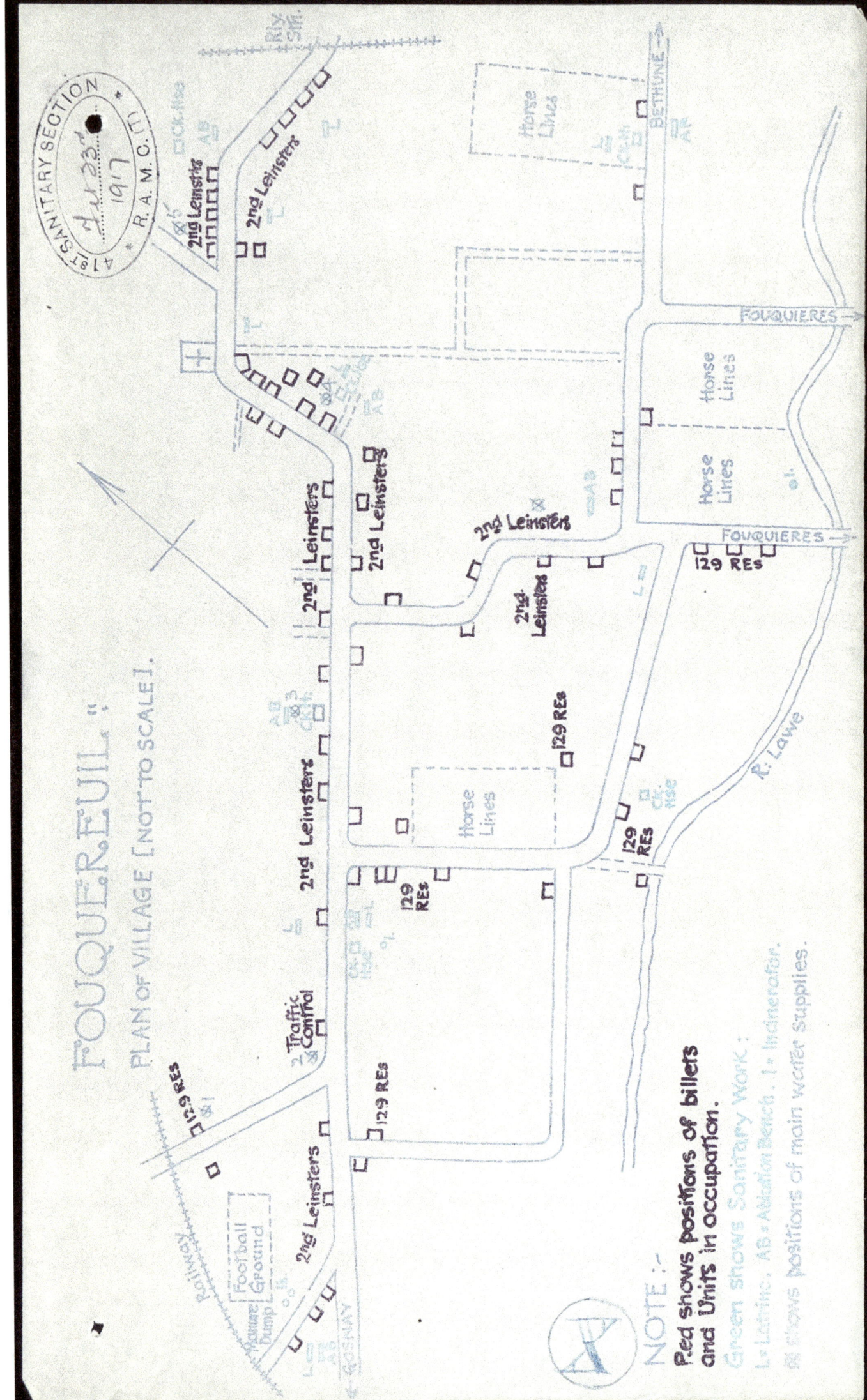

ECQUEDECQUES.
PLAN OF VILLAGE [NOT TO SCALE].

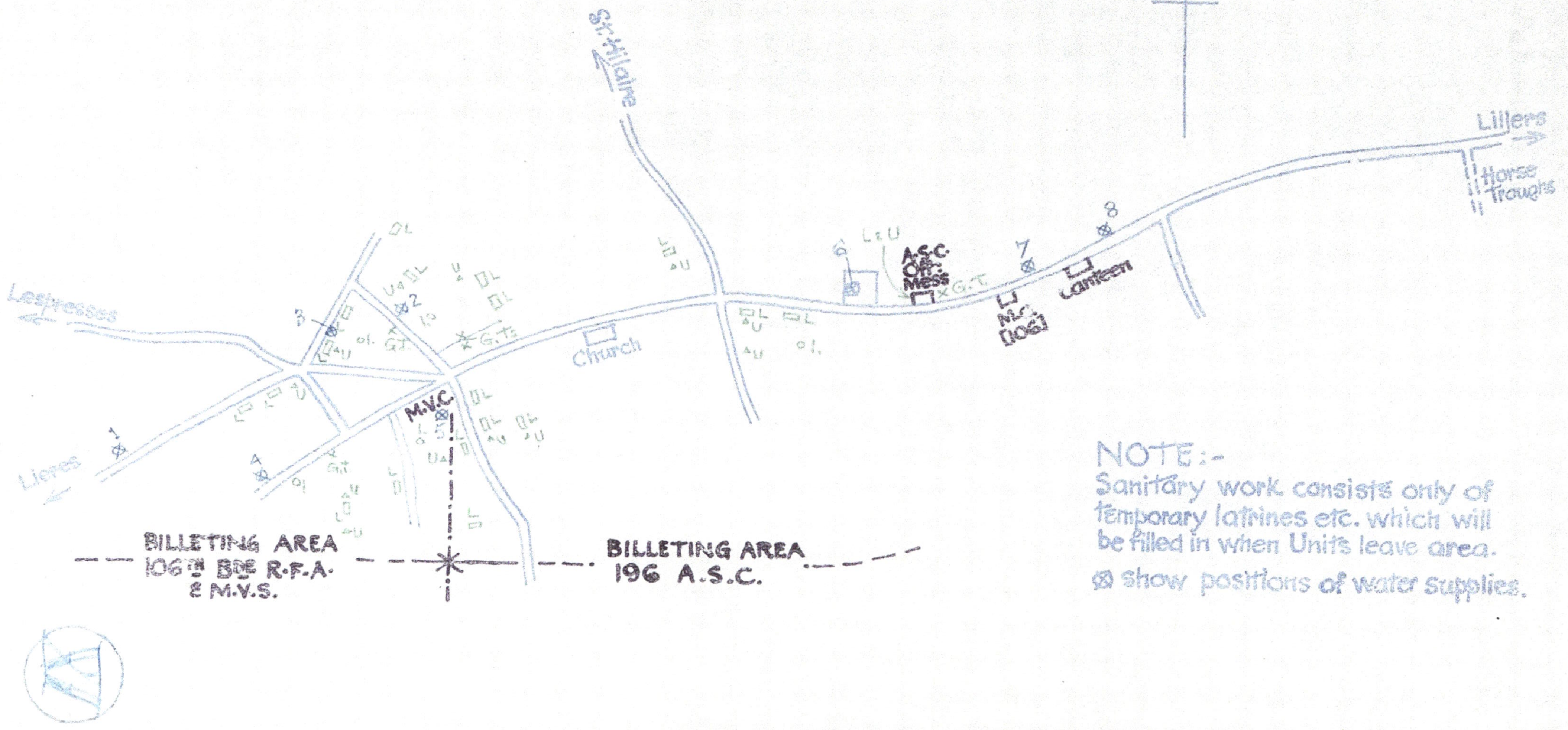

NOTE:—
Sanitary work consists only of temporary latrines etc. which will be filled in when Units leave area.
⊗ show positions of water supplies.

— — — BILLETING AREA — — — BILLETING AREA — — —
106th Bde R.F.A.   196 A.S.C.
& M.V.S.

ALLOUAGNE.

PLAN [NOT TO SCALE] SHOWING SANITARY WORK.
SURVEYED 2ND JANY. 1917.

NOTE:-

RED SHOWS BILLETS AS REGISTERED ON PLAN IN DIV. TRAINING BATT'S OFFICE.

GREEN SHOWS SANITARY WORK.

⊗ " " WATER SUPPLIES.

ALLOUAGNE.

DESCRIPTION OF LATRINES CORRESPONDING WITH NUMBERS IN GREEN ON ACCOMPANYING PLAN DATED 16TH FEB: 1917.

No	DESCRIPTION
1	Officers' latrine & urinal : 2 box seats.
2	" " " : 1 " "
3	" " " " : 4 " "
4	x [OLD] Covered Public Latrine & urinal [10 seats]
5	x " " " " "
6	Demolished.
7	Open trench latrine & urinal.
8	[Do Do Do Do also Offrs' Latrine : 1 box seat & urinal.
9	4 box seats over trench & urinal.
10	[Officers : 1 seat & urinal. [Men : 4 " "
11	4 box seats & urinal.
12	Disused: screening sufficient for 1 Offrs' seat.
13	x [OLD] New buckets & canvas provided.
14	[8 seats over pit & urinal. [5 " " " adjacent: no screening.
15	3 box seats & urinal.
16	10 " " "
17	3 cresol drums without seats.
18	4 box seats & urinal.
19	1 seat : disused.
20	6 " over pit & urinal.
21	4 " " "
22	1 box seat over tin, & urinal.
23	1 " " " } Emergency latrines behind
24	1 " " " } billets [for night use].
25	1 " " "
26	2 " " over pit & urinal.
27	1 " " " tin for Officers.
28	5 seats & urinal.
29	12 " "
30	1 " over cresol drum for Officers.

NOTE :-
X Existed prior to Sanitary Work executed by Corps.
Remainder constitute   "   "   "   "   "
Field Ambulance Latrines are not included.

Vol. 19

140/2043

CONFIDENTIAL
War Diary
of
41st Sanitary Section

from March 1st to March 30th 1917.

Volume No 19.

COMMITTEE FOR THE
MEDICAL HISTORY OF THE WAR

Date   11 MAY 1917

March 1917

Army Form C. 2118.

WAR DIARY
INTELLIGENCE SUMMARY.
(Erase heading not required.)

Instructions regarding War Diaries and Intelligence Summaries are contained in F. S. Regs., Part II. and the Staff Manual respectively. Title pages will be prepared in manuscript.

41st SANITARY SECTION R.A.M.C.(T)

Place	Date	Hour	Summary of Events and Information	Remarks and references to Appendices
LABEUVRIERE	Mar 1st 1917		Routine Inspection Work continued. Units in the following districts were visited :- LABEUVRIERE, NOEUX les MINES, ANNEZIN, FOUQUIERES, FOUQUEREUIL, MANQUEVILLE, LE CORNET BOURDOIS, ALLOUAGNE, LE HAMEL, + LAVALLEE, and work of improving sanitary arrangements found to be in progress. DISINFECTIONS (1) Measles : FOUQUIERES : 1st Royal Scots Ambulance : Pte RUTLAND M ; evacuated to 73rd Field Ambulance ; huts disinfected with cresol solution by Sanitary Section. (2) Scabies : LE CORNET BOURDOIS : 182nd Co. D.A.C. : evacuated : normal cresol solution by D.P.C. + disinfection by Sanitary Section. (3) German measles : NOEUX LES MINES : 12th Royal Scots : Cpl BAYLIS R.W, Pte BARKER G.H, Pte SMITH M.R, Pte TEAGUE A : evacuated to 73rd Field Ambulance ; 4 huts disinfected by San. Section ; contacts approximately 60 in number. Construction work :- 5 long standard latrine bases made ; all under cement construction, 2 standard urinals made ; 32 notice boards made and painted ; ALLOUAGNE 1 grease trap reconstructed, latrine pit dug, FOUQUIERES 1 urine urinal made, TECHNICAL SCHOOL 1 compl. wall screen reconstructed, 1 latrine remodelled, 9 subground notice boards fixed. Rifles were inspected in MANQUEVILLE system, D.A.C. 5 Units. Received C.R.O 289 - 293.	
LABEUVRIERE	Mar 2nd 1917		Routine Inspection Work continued. Units in the following districts were visited :- LABEUVRIERE, ALLOUAGNE, ECQUEDECQUES, BAS RIEUX, CANTRAINNE, LAPUGNOY, FOUQUIERES, ANNEZIN, NOEUX LES MINES, + FOUQUEREUIL. DISINFECTIONS (1) Measles : ALLOUAGNE : 103rd Co. R.E : Cpl STONE A.I.B ; Cpl REEVE H, Pte SEVERN : evacuated from 87th Field Ambulance to 7th General Hospital ; contacts number 21 and one patient ; disinfection + billet + equipment carried out. (2) Measles : NOEUX LES MINES : 12th Royal Scots : contacts latrine + hut disinfected by San. Sec. Construction work in progress in the following units were inspected. - Cpl R.W Tent (Canv.) 12th Saps (cav.) 18th Hos. Co.(sap.) lectures - WORKSHOP ; 1 large standard latrine hut made ; 20 standard urinals made ; notice boards completed ; LAPUGNOY 13th Maher 6 latrines completed enclosed 20 box seats ; 1 urinstone reserve dug, 1 grease trap construction fired ; 7th Wards 2 all water wells not after completed ; notice board fixed ; 3 grease traps made ; FOUQUIERES 1 trench latrine fixed on ALLOUAGNE 1 new latrine hut sent along and 1 trenches filled in latrine (including absorption pit also constructed (at trench) A.C. O. D. 21-300. D.R.O 2563 - 2566. and A.C.H.Q C.H.Q. Received CRO 294 - 300. D.R. O. 2563 - 2566.	
LABEUVRIERE	Mar 3rd 1917		The O.C. paid a further visit to the 2nd Divisional Technical + Bombing School, FOUQUIERES to see if the recommendations made by him on March 1st 16th had been carried out. The following improvements were noted :- latrines remodelled, improved arrangements, soap scheme fixed and working satisfactorily ; all fine ground washed + greasetrap tried, two tanks supplied, fixed + marked for drinking water. The drainage will be built as soon as materials are available. Preparations were made to the 1st move into the new line area, and a party of 2 N.C.O's + two men sent to BOYEFFLES to take over workshop from 1st Canadian Sanitary Sec.	

Forms/C.2118/13. A.F.34 Wt. W4973/M687 750,000 8/16 D.D. & L. Ltd.

WAR DIARY or INTELLIGENCE SUMMARY

Army Form C. 2118.

41st SANITARY SECTION R.A.M.C.(T.)

Page 2.

Place	Date	Hour	Summary of Events and Information	Remarks and references to Appendices
LABEUVRIERE	Mar 3rd 1917 continued		Routine Inspection Work continues. All distincts were visited to see that troops moving in & out their camps leave all clean. Camps were inspected as follows:— A/107 (details) B/107 R.F.A. DISINFECTIONS (1&2) Measles: LAPUGNOY: 1st Northants: Corpl BURNAPP T.M, Pte ROLLS T.: both evacuated to 1st Field Ambulance: contacts number 29: camp disinfected by San Sec. (3,4,5) Measles: 15th Royal Scots: NOEUX LES MINES: Pte SMITH H.R, Pte FORDER T, Pte SEAVEN F.S.: evacuated to 1st Field Ambulance: contacts are two platoons who are isolated. Received D.R.O. 2267—2270 C.R.O. 301—306.	Ruth
LABEUVRIERE	Mar 4th 1917		The men from AHLOUAGNE and FOUQUIERES were recalled to Head Quarters and further preparations made for moving into the area. DISINFECTIONS (1&2) Measles: AHLOUAGNE, A.S.C. M.T. att. 73rd Field Ambulance: Pte Griffith B, & Pte Gladden J.: evacuated to 1st General Hospital; billets & camp disinfected by San Sec. (3) Measles: BULLY GRENAY: 15th Royal Scots: Pte BENNETT J.W.: evacuated to 1st Field Ambulance: billet disinfected by San Sec: contacts left in charge of M.O. unit. (4) Paratide BULLY GRENAY: 75 Canadian Infantry Batt: evacuated to 73rd Field Ambulance: contacts number 4 and are segregated: billet disinfected by San Sec. Received G.R.O. & D.R.O. 2152—2159 D.R.O. 2292—2294.	Ruth
LABEUVRIERE	Mar 5th 1917		The men were today completed to the number and the head quarters to its establishment at BOYEFFLES.	Ruth
BOYEFFLES	Mar 6th 1917		An N.C.O. and two men were today sent to BULLY GRENAY to supervise the sanitary arrangements there in surrounding districts. An N.C.O. and one man were today sent to BARLIN to supervise the sanitary arrangements of the 24th Divisional troops in occupation there. A man was sent to make enquiry as to the following areas:— BOYEFFLES, AIX NOULETTE, NOEUX, CAUCHIES, PETIT SAINS, SAINS-EN-GOHELLE, FOSSE 10, BOUVIGNY WOODS, NOULETTE WOODS to locate & sanitary troops to enquire as to sanitary arrangements, wells, supplies, kinds etc. The O.C. visits BARLIN to arrange for inspection of sanitary arrangements in that part of BARLIN occupied by Divisional H.Qrs and also to meet the Town Mayors of BULLY GRENAY & AIX NOULETTE regarding the sanitation of these areas & improvements to be made in the sanitary circumstances there. DISINFECTIONS (1) SCARLET FEVER: FOSSE 10 4th Field Ambulance: evacuated to No 9 Casualty Clearing Station: contacts nil: dsinfected by San Sec. (2) Measles Trenches: 8th D.L.I. : L/C HEMSLEY P.: evacuated to No 9 General Hospital. (3) German Measles: BULLY GRENAY: Pte CHARWOOD H.W.: evacuated to 73rd Field Ambulance: contacts number 10 are isolated: billet disinfected by San Sec.	

Wt. W4973/M687 750,000 8/16 D.D. & L. Ltd. Forms/C.2118/13.

WAR DIARY or INTELLIGENCE SUMMARY

Army Form C. 2118.

Place	Date	Hour	Summary of Events and Information	Remarks and references to Appendices
BOYEFFLES	March 6 1917 continued		(4) Miners: BULLY GRENAY; 104 Field Co RE; 6th BOYES. O.R.F: evacuated 4/3rd Field Ambulance: civilians number who are isolated. Billet of cats and animals disinfected by San Sec. (5) Miners: NOUVETTE WOOD; 93rd Infantry Brigade Bde; Pte MARTIN W; evacuated 15 9th Field Ambulance: civilians number 35 who are installed in a large hut in day time, but attend working parties at night; hut disinfected by San Sec. (6) Miners: FOSSE 10; 9th Field Ambulance; Pte LAMB V.C. evacuated 15 to 7 Casualty Clearing Station; civilians number 41 who are isolated. Hut and relations were disinfected by San Sec. (7) Miners: at Sub-section LENS. 9/6 Surveys; Pte ROFFE W.E: evacuated 15 43rd Field Ambulance: civilians number 20 and are isolated and inspected daily. Huts disinfected by M.O. Received dose. R.O. 655 – 663. C.R. O 207 – 311, 315 – 316, 319 – 326. D.R. O 2245 – 2274.	signature
BOYEFFLES	March 7 1917		The O.C. visited doses 10 to make arrangements and saw two major regarding sanitation of that district, and improvements in existing sanitary conveniences. All cisterns with the water supply throughout the area are today examined. All supplies used by troops are to be tested by Horrocks tests, and notice boards will be provided with the packets of the effects required. Water supplies limited today as follows:- PETIT SAINS (1) SAINS-EN-GOHELLE (5) FOSSE 10 (4) BARLIN (1). Water carts in possession of the following units were inspected :- 12th Royal Irish (Sans), 1/9th London (Sans) from BOYEFFLES the following districts were visited:- AIX-NOULETTE, NOULETTE WOOD, NOEUX-LES-MINES, BRAQUEMONT, ABLAIN ST NAZAIRE, PETIT SAINS, SAINS-EN-GOHELLE, and FOSSE 10, DIVISIONAL Troops were inspected in each of these districts and sanitary requirements noted. Functional work:- Workshop. 2 Latrines (box seat, bucket) completed. 2 urinals with box seat and 12 pan of lattice work cats made. BARLIN 1 latrine, box seat, bucket 2/13 completed, 1 cookhouse dug. 1 urinal pail approved, 1 incinerator fixed, 1 damaged urn incinerator fixed. Received C.R. O 324 – 331. DR O.	signature
BOYEFFLES	Mar 8th 1917		Routine inspection work continues, from BOYEFFLES units in the following districts were visited :- AIX-NOULETTE, NOEUX-LES-MINES, BRAQUEMONT, BOUVIGNY FOSSE 10 PETIT SAINS, SAINS-EN-GOHELLE. The following points were noted in the majority of Royal Engineer and ammunition dumps and alternate latrine system was in use, 3 standard latrines. 1 general disposal pit of [OG] model sanitary ones and camps in BOYEFFLES and BULLY GRENAY. In BULLY GRENAY there are 13 Infantry dumps areas with a distinctive and refuse dumps in each. Over 10 incinerators and 3 latrines are properly used. The firm units in occupation of the property of existing refuse and resting seems to denote the ash-pits and dumps kept clear of refuse. A quantity of foreign wood was that refuse is entirely petitioned to [...] and in area on good condition. In other latrines regular minor repairs and in many cases many [repairs] were observed. The following much work was [noticed] :- 8th Rifle Brigade (Sans), 6th [...] (Sans), 757th M.G. Co. G & S. Surveys (2) 6th R. Welsh (Sans), 3 Rifle Bde (Sans). (13) Water supplies in the district of AIX-NOULETTE were tested by Horrocks Cases. A.8834 Wt.W.4973/M687 750,000 8/16 D.D.&L. Ltd. Forms/C.2118/13. DISINFECTION Practice: FOSSE 10: 3rd Rifle Bde: 10/1 HARDWICK. F: evacuated to 9th Field Ambulance civilians number 4 and are isolated in billets : billets disinfected by San. Sec.	signature

WAR DIARY or INTELLIGENCE SUMMARY

Army Form C. 2118.

Place	Date	Hour	Summary of Events and Information	Remarks and references to Appendices
BOYEFFLES	Mar 8th Continued		Sanitation work:- WORKSHOP. D. went after inspected BARLIN. 2 scotchmen whitewash 2 repair latrines. His assistant and one scotchman are busy with urine deflectors. Insecticide is not needed yet. Looks O.K. Received order AX/LBB/7. Skeleton maps to be supplied with details as to the districts are complete, have now been prepared today of the following:- BOYEFFLES, BULLY GRENAY + SAINSEN-GOHELLE and a copy of each will be appended to this volume when complete.	Appendices 1, 2, + 3. Rwh
BOYEFFLES	Mar 9th 1917		The D.O. visited the Town Major at Fosse 10 to complete arrangements regarding disinfector & latrines — and also inspected the horse lines camps & billets occupied by the 5th + 9th Bn. C.T.A. DISINFECTIONS. (1) Parrotin: BRAQUEMONT: 3rd Canadian Tunnelling Co. & BEWLEY; evacuated 675th Field Ambulance. no extras, new disinfector by San. Sec. (2151C). Parrotin: BRAQUEMONT: 3rd Canadian Tunnelling Co; Sapprs PUNCH T., PHILLIPS A., PHILLIPS B., HENRIKSON H., HARDIN C., CARRINGTON W., WILKINS G.B., WATSON., COOK, HOWE C., THOMAS A.D., RANDALL S.C., MARLOW, TASEAU W., MORRISON H., NICHOLSON C.W. + RODENOFF M.; evacuated from Field Ambulance to 1.R.7 General Hospital; contacts 35 who are noted & batches 15 were not wet; kits disinfected by San. Sec. Water carts in possession of the following units were inspected:— 194.C, 195.C, 196.C, 197.C, A.S.C, C/107. R.F.A., A.B.C + D/106. R.F.A. Routine Inspection work continues. Units in the following districts were visited:- BOYEFFLES, BOUVIGNY WOOD, FOSSE 10, BRAQUEMONT, SAINS-EN-GOHELLE, PETIT SAINS, BARLIN, BULLY GRENAY, LES BREBIS and the work of improving sanitary conveniences found to be progressing. In orderly rooms in the following units/billets were visited from San. Sec workshop:- 6 large abdominal bandages to 175 Bde H.Q. 2 unexample K/75th Div A. 21 notice boards to BULLY GRENAY. Sanitational work:- WORKSHOP. 1 corrugated iron water cart. 3 officers latrine / papier filtré / throughout cleaned. 12 standard lids for tar seats. 3 inscribed latrine buckets and 1 tea cleaner completed. / 4 Ferris Wheel sinks and re-seated Dr. Bar Ash H.Q. oil drained fires. 25 notice boards made and painted. BARLIN: 1 urinal pit, 2 notice boards / scotchman whitewashed, 2 urinal deflectors fixed, repairs to latrines + 3 tar sealed seats + seating repaired to latrines. DISINFECTIONS (continued)(19) Remembrance: BULLY GRENAY; 125 R Shoshone; Bn HOWES; evacuated 16 73rd F. Ambulance; contacts segregated; kits disinfected by San. Sec. (20). Measles: BULLY GRENAY; 18 N. Staffs; Pl.Opt LEATHER; evacuated 16 73rd F. Ambulance; contacts segregated; kits disinfected by San. Sec. (21). Measles: LES BREBIS; 1/7th M. & Co; RMQMARTIN T.W.; evacuated to 75th F. Ambulance; contacts segregated; kits disinfected by San. Sec. (22). Measles: BULLY GRENAY; 109 C.R.E.; Spr FOWLKES T.; evacuated to 75th F. Ambulance; contacts segregated; kits disinfected by San. Sec. Skeleton maps of BOIS DE NOULETTE, FOSSE 10, + AIX NOULETTE have been prepared and more today; these will be supplied with details of water supplies, sanitary conveniences as all they become available and when completed a copy of each will be appended to this volume.	Appendices 4, 5, 6 Rwh

Received No 154. R.O 164 - 67u, C.R.O 352 - 356, D.R.O 2260 - 2267.

A5834 Wt. W.4973/M687. 750,000 8/16 D.D. & L. Ltd. Forms/C.2118/13.

WAR DIARY or INTELLIGENCE SUMMARY

Army Form C. 2118.

41st SANITARY SECTION R.A.M.C.(T)

Place	Date	Hour	Summary of Events and Information	Remarks and references to Appendices
BOYEFFLES	Mar 10th 1917		The O.C. inspected the sanitary conveniences of the following units:— 9th R. Sussex, 10th W.R.E., 108th R.E., 148th R.E. Transport in SAINS-EN-GOHELLE, 9th Buffs Transport in PETIT SAINS and noted the defects in each case. Arrangements were made by the M.O concerned to remedy same. The O.C. also inspected the Divisional School at PRIEURE SY PRY made arrangements and fixed the erection of a shelter for disinfection. (i) Muller BRAQUEMONT O.C. ATKINSON A/107 R.F.A. evacuated to 70th F Ambulance. Contact number and segregated; Kit disinfected by San. Sec. Water carts in possession of the following units were inspected: — 103 Co, 104 Co, 139 Co R.E., 9th R. Sussex (3 carts) 9th Buffs (2 carts) & 13th Middlesex (3 carts), 13th Notts & Derbys, disinfected (2 carts), 13th Middlesex (3 carts). — BOYEFFLES, ABLAIN ST NAZAIRE, Routine inspection work continued. Units in the following districts were visited:— BOYEFFLES, ABLAIN ST NAZAIRE FOSSE 10, AIX NOULETTE, PETIT SAINS, BARLIN, MAROC, BULLY GRENAY and CALONNE and work of improving sanitary conveniences found to be in progress. Also in same district in some instances found and carried out new constructional work:— WORKSHOP 30 standard latrine seats made and fixed, 5 grease traps made and cemented, 15 tons of Bricks & constructional work:— WORKSHOP 30 standard latrine seats made and fixed, 17 notice boards made and fixed. BARLIN 1 grease trap repaired, 1 bathhouse refurnished, ABLAIN ST NAZAIRE 2 refuse pits, 1 soakage pit dug, 2 latrines completed, 3 urinals & 1 grease trap Received D.R.O. 2268 - 2293 2nd Div. H.Q. D.R.O. G H Q 1917. Lia polm emptied and details will be appended when volume is full. Sketch map of BOYEFFLES and FOSSE 2 CALONNE were seen.	Appendices 4 & 6
BOYEFFLES	Mar 11th 1917		The O.C. visited the trenches in the left sector and inspected the sanitary conveniences of the units occupying by battalions 9th R. Sussex and made recommendations to the M.O. regarding improvements. DISINFECTIONS (i) Scarlet Fever BOUVIGNY HUTS 9th R Sussex Lt BROOKS: evacuated to 137 F Ambulance: Contacts number (2) Enteric BRAQUEMONT 3rd Canadian Tunnelling Co Sr CHAMBERS: evacuated to 137 F Ambulance: contacts number 33 and are inoculated: kit disinfected by San Sec. Water carts in possession of the following units were inspected: — 2nd Canadian Siege Co 8th Div. H.Q. Constructional work — WORKSHOP: 15 lids for latrine tins made, 2 standard latrine boxes made, 3 standard urinals made with fine medicus, ? and fixed, PETIT SAINS repairs to 2 latrine I urinal fixed, I urinal renewed, 2 grease traps fixed. Mainsoil refuse bin workshop — 10 disinfected irrigation wires, 15 shovels I screen with 10 days latrines covered in (?) 10 benches dumb, 1 standard latrine vault in winter for ABLAIN ST NAZAIRE (13th Mid.). A map of the area occupied by 2nd Divisional troops has been prepared and a copy of same will be appended to this volume. The Town Major of BULLY GRENAY was visited today regarding dying on [illegible] ground as reported in this morning's Sm. Rep, and a fatigue party provided from the battalions in occupation reversed to remedy this defect. Constructional work:— BULLY GRENAY. 1 French latrine completed and 1 latrine completed with housing 2 tar vats fixed in existing latrine, 1 latrine completed for next improvement later.	Appendix 9.

Received G.R.O. March 7. 2160 - 2172. C.R.O. 334 - 349. D.R.O. 2393 - 2395.
Received G.R.O. March 14. D.D. & L. Ltd.

WAR DIARY or INTELLIGENCE SUMMARY

Army Form C. 2118.

41st SANITARY SECTION R.A.M.C. (T)

Place	Date	Hour	Summary of Events and Information	Remarks and references to Appendices
BOYEFFLES	Mar 12th 1917		The O.C. visited 195 G., 196 G., 197 G. A.S.C., and 107 Bde R.F.A. at BRAQUEMONT and made an inspection of the sanitary arrangements and noted the various defects requiring remedying, and made recommendations to have same carried out. DISINFECTIONS 4) BOUVIGNY VERQUIN; 6th Queens (Kitchen) Bar't: Pte BUTCHER W: evacuated from 74th & Ambulance to No 7 General Hospital contacts number to not and not isolated but disinfected by San. Sec. (MEASLES) (2) Huttes: AIX NOULETTE: 1/12 Siege Bty R.G.A. Gnr YOUNG F: evacuated from 74th F. Ambulance to No 7 General Hospital contacts number who in dug-out and are examined daily by M.O. at 115 H.Q. and disinfected (Scabies) by San. Sec. Notice sent in possession of the following units were inspected. — 137th By Co., 135 H.Q. huts and Dug-outs. 155 N Seige (beams), 17 M.G. Co., 135 huts and notices issued: — AIX NOULETTE, 6, Water supplies to the following districts were supplied with notices issued. — SAINS: 1. FOSSE 10. 51, SAINS-EN-GOHELLE 5. — BOYEFFLES, SAINS-EN-GOHELLE, FOSSE 10, BOUVIGNY WOODS in the following districts were inspected & sanitary arrangements examined. AIX NOULETTE, BULLY GRENAY, BARLIN and the work in progress. Sanitary appliances were issued from our workshop as follow. — BARLIN: 1 water cart stop, 6 latrine boxes, 6 latrine covers, 2 latrine seats, 3 refuse receptacles. BOYEFFLES: 1 grease trap, BULLY GRENAY: 14 latrine covers, 1 officers latrine complete, 2 grease traps, 10 fly nets, 18 notice boards, 1 19 wash boards. WORKSHOP 5 standard urinals, 6 large latrine boxes sent to 2 units within command, 10 water-tank pads for unit latrine complete, 15 tin officers latrine complete. BULLY GRENAY 1 officers latrine complete, 17 Bde H.Q. 3 latrines (Seats + covers). 17 Bde H.Q., new water carts issued but not complete at 17 Bde H.Q., 2 latrine seats complete & fixed at H. Stoffs (Sand), new Sewer 11 wheelbarrows. 17 Bde H.Q., BOUVIGNY WOODS 1 wheelbarrow & wheelbarrow. 1 notice board fixed. By R.G.A., 1 grease trap will be 11 Stoffs (Sand), BOUVIGNY WOODS 1 wheelbarrow, 1 notice board fixed. and now re-railing 4 hut seats complete. 1 Quartermaster stores completed. 11/3/17. Received C.R.O. 350 – 356, D.R.O. 2296 – 2301, 1st Army No 6053. A. No 6053. A.	Ruller
BOYEFFLES	Mar 13th 1917		Routine Inspection Work continues. Units in the following districts were visited: — BOYEFFLES, BRAQUEMONT, MAROC BULLY GRENAY, LES BREBIS, CALONNE, BARLIN, and the work of improving sanitary conditions found to be progressing. Sanitary appliances were issued from the workshop as follows. 12 box seats (latrine), 16 737 S.B. (dustbins) 1 officer latrine complete to B/107. DISINFECTIONS (1) Wounded: BULLY GRENAY: 5th Bn S. Stoffs: Sgt BRYANT J.W: evacuated 16 74th F. Ambulance: contacts number 5 and not segregated but disinfected by San. Sec. (2)(6) Parotitis: BRAQUEMONT: 3rd Canadian Tunnelling Co: Spr LEWIS H: Spr CALANCHINI G: evacuated to 73rd Field Ambulance 35 contacts who are not segregated but disinfected by San. Sec. Water supplies in districts of CALONNE (2), MAROC (5) and BULLY GRENAY (9) were being used for washing and were inspected. — A/107 (2 cans) D/107 R.F.A. No's 1, 2, 7 & 30 D.A.C. Construction work: — 11 urinals constructed, 10 small & large standard latrine seats constructed, 1 enamelled iron urinator and 16 officers latrine complete. BRAQUEMONT 1 officers latrine complete at B/107, MAROC 3 officers latrines (Sewer bar) completed. 2 new latrines erected with seats, 1 refrain head water-ball oil cans feed latrine complete, 1 notice board posted & fixed at 73rd M.G. Co., 2 latrines (new heads) completed BULLY GRENAY. WF Wt 4973. M687. 750,000 8/16. D.D. & L. Ltd. Forms/C2118/13 (Nov seats renewed), 1 officer latrine complete at 7th M.G.Co., 2 latrines BARLIN. 1 notice board fixed, 1 urinals fixed & drained, 2 officers latrine completed.	Ruller

Received DRO 2302-3.

Army Form C. 2118.

WAR DIARY or INTELLIGENCE SUMMARY.

(Erase heading not required.)

41st SANITARY SECTION
R.A.M.C.(T)

Place	Date	Hour	Summary of Events and Information	Remarks and references to Appendices
BOYEFFLES	March 14 1917		The O.C. visited BARLIN to inspect the arrangements made since his absence to arrange for technical school at PRIEURE ST PRY to inspect the new refuse destructor which had been completed there. Routine Inspection work continues. Units in the following districts were visited :- BOYEFFLES, AIX NOULETTE, BRAQUEMONT, BULLY GRENAY and BARLIN and work of improving sanitary conveniences are in progress. Sanitary appliances were issued from the workshop as follows :- 109th S.R.F.A. 2 urinals to 113th R.F.A., 1 grease trap and 3 refuse tins to 113th R.F.A. 1 workshop & 1 grease trap to BARLIN. 1 refuse tin to Queens Falours Batt. Constructional work :- Workshop 10 tins for latrine buckets made; 10 grease traps made; 3 refuse tin covers made; 1 urinal made; 1 grease tin cover made; BARLIN. Their latrine accessories & new apparatus fixed, 1 urinal seat & repair to latrine. Shoots will tanne completed; 1 notice board fixed. BULLY GRENAY 2 grease traps fixed, material being procured, excavation for new destructor completed; Water carts in possession of the following units :- 135th R.F.A. (2 carts), 12th R.W. Kent (2 carts), 6 dumps inspected at Calonne - R.R. Wiegent Rue Marles 3rd Rifle Bde (2 carts) 12th R. Buckhm & Queens (2 carts) 13th R. Durham, 15th Queen's Wocs etc. DISINFECTIONS (1) Measles: CALONNE. 8. R.W. KENT, Rue Marles 3rd Rifle Bde 1 (2) Measles: BULLY GRENAY 9. 6th Surreys: 20 contacts of Pte Roffe W.E. reported are well known in Half 5th scrying billets to 9th during their period of segregation billet vacated then disinfected by San Sec. Water supplies have been today tested by Horrocks Case as follows :- BOYEFFLES (3) BOUVIGNY (4) BARLIN and PETIT SAINS 5. Maps have been today prepared and issued of BARLIN and PETIT SAINS and a copy of each will be appended to this volume. Received Nos 155 Routine Orders 675 – 686 C.R.O. 357 – 359 D.R.O. 3304 – 3305	Rough appendices 10 & 11
BOYEFFLES	Mar 15th 1917		The O.C. visited the 9th D.R. Siege Transport and inspected the sanitary area, also the water carts in possession of B/107 and D/107 which had been deposited as being in a dirty condition and the recommendations as to their being kept clean in the future. Routine Inspection work continues. Units in the following districts were visited :- BOYEFFLES, BULLY GRENAY, LES BREBIS, FOSSE 10, BARLIN & SAINS-EN-GOHELLE, and the work of improving sanitary conveniences found R.E. progressing. Sanitary appliances were issued as follows :- 2 standard latrine seats & 1 No 9 A.R.E. 3 standard latrine seats & 1 urinal to 75th Sqn R.F. 10 notice boards to BARLIN. DISINFECTIONS (1) Measles: SAINS-EN-GOHELLE. "B" Special Co. R.E. Pioneer SIMPSON A.: evacuated to the 7 General Hospital contacts 20 and are segregated; billet sprayed by San Sec. (2) Measles: FOSSE 10: 153rd Coy Transport. Pte OAKLEY C. evacuated to the 41st Field Ambulance; contacts number 11 but are not isolated, billet disinfected by San Sec. Billets were inspected as follows :- BULLY GRENAY. 43rd M.G.C. (6.) 3rd T.M.B. (4). One H.Q. Sig Sqe 7. Miscellaneous (8) 103rd Co R.E. (20). 109 Co. R.E. (7). - one billet was found to be dirty and the matter has been today prepared and issued of BRAQUEMONT and a copy has been appended to this volume. Received W.W. Forms C.2118 Forms / C.2118/13. 20 standard latrine trough (under private attention details made / 13. 1 to be sent made. BULLY GRENAY, 2 urinals fixed, 1 work repaired 1 grease trap field, 1 grease trap re-escallated. 1 refuse failure completed BARLIN 2 urinals, 1 field waypipe & 2 latrines. Received A.F.O. 183, A.R.O. 13th D.R.O. 15th	appendix 12

WAR DIARY or INTELLIGENCE SUMMARY

Army Form C. 2118.

Page 8

Place	Date	Hour	Summary of Events and Information	Remarks and references to Appendices
BOYEFFLES	March 16th 1917		Routine Inspection Work continued. Units in the following districts were visited – BOYEFFLES, FOSSE 10, BOUVIGNY, BARLIN, BULLY GRENAY, MAROC, AIX-NOULETTE and work of improving sanitary conveniences found to be progressing. Sanitary appliances were issued from the workshop as follows: – 6 urinal troughs w/ 1 inlet each to BARLIN, 4 latrine box seats 3 miners', 1 fabric bucket, 1 corrugated iron movement to 13th Divisional, 6 latrine boxes and 6 urinals to 190 Co R.E. Water seats on the following units were inspected – 194, 195, 196, 197 Co A.S.C, 9/107 R.F.A, 8 Buffs (Details) w 9/107 R.F.A (Brds), 9/R Surreys (Details) 8Buffs were inspected as follows: BULLY GRENAY, (1) miscellaneous anti latrines, boxes etc and painted. WORKSHOP 3 upper latrine enclosed. 12 large standard latrines were removed. MAROC 17 small standard latrines have been erected and remain (standard) anti-fly treated with 1 shelter large anti-fly spread shelter used being made with 2 shelters for walling. MAROC seats also erected in dug out. WORKSHOP 10 latrines completed & repaired BOYEFFLES 10 R.E.'s & dining seats put up in the E/N Buffs dug out. BARLIN 5 urinal seats installed at the R.W.G.R. 10 officers' latrines completed at D/108, BARLIN 6 notice boards erected in line, 2 urinals & 1 set in the Cycles' Base Depot. No 912 No MELLER H. V/London Sanitary Co R.A.M.C (T) reported from the Cyclists' Base Depot and has been taken on the strength of this unit from this date. No 3340 PHE CLARK T.W. of London Sanitary Co R.A.M.C (T) reported from the Cyclists Base Depot and has been taken on the strength of this unit from this date. Received C.R.O 365 – 577, D.R.O D517 – D518.	Rwfu
BOYEFFLES	March 17th 1917		The Co visited ADLAIN & NAZAIRE to inspect the sanitary arrangements of the 46th BH? in occupation of 9th R. Gds. Routine Inspection Work continued. Units in the following districts were visited. – BOYEFFLES, BARLIN, BRAQUEMONT, AIX NOULETTE, NOEUX LES MINES, SAINS & FOSSE 10 and scheme of improving sanitary arrangements found to be progressing. Sanitary appliances were issued as follows: – 30 urinals to BULLY GRENAY. 36 latrine box seats (small), 10 latrine box seats (large), 10 latrine pails 20 urinals 7 fabric buckets 5 grease traps, 3 latrine erected; 3 notice boards. BARLIN 3 notice boards. 7th R. Warks 1 corrugated iron movement 1 urinal & 3 latrines box seats, 146 Siege Bty, 1 corrugated iron movement. 73rd M.G.C, 3 tin rails, 8 Buffs 2 notice boards 1st R. Sussex 1 notice board. Water carts in possession of the following units were inspected. – A.B.C+D/106 R.F.A, 9/R. Sussex (?) Constructional work. – WORKSHOP 2 large latrines boxes for 16 arrivals, 1 arsenic rails & 1 house for tar seats made. BOYEFFLES Repairs to public latrine. SAINS GOHELLE Separate latrine 10 R.F.E for seats completed. AIX NOULETTE 1 urinal bench (trench) Complete. BARLIN 2 notice boards fixed LES BREBIS 1 iron bog fixed in some latrine. BULLY GRENAY 1 man's latrine announced at fixed CALONNE 3 new urinals fixed. 3 lids to latrine seat fixed; 1 hose seat fixed and latrines completed. 5 Marti-Italy (6 box seats) completed. Waste outflow in "CALONNE UP" "HURDLE ALLEY" have been masked with notice boards. Received C.R.O 156 Routine Orders 658 – 706 D.R.O 5516 – 5518.	Rwfu

WAR DIARY or INTELLIGENCE SUMMARY

Army Form C. 2118.

Place	Date	Hour	Summary of Events and Information	Remarks and references to Appendices
BOYEFFLES	Mar 18th 1917		Routine Inspection Work continues. Units in the following districts were visited:- BOYEFFLES, BARLIN, BULLY GRENAY, BOUVIGNY WOODS, MARQUEFFLES FARM, SAINS-EN-GOHELLE, and work of improving sanitary arrangements found to be in progress. Sanitary Appliances have been issued from the workshop as follows:- 15 Urinal H.M.P., 2 Tar seats, 2 Dixies to 107 R.F.A. H.Q., 1 officers latrine complete, 1 latrine seat, 1 urinal pail, 1 Lid for incinerator D/106 R.F.A. Water carts in possession of the following units have been inspected :- 13th M.G.C, 134th M.G.C. (Infantry) 14th Howitzers (2) Sanitational work:- WORKSHOP. 13 Standard latrine top seats + 9 Standard and finished. BOUVIGNY 2 latrines (each with 3 box seats) completed. 1 latrine (12 seats) completed, 1 latrine (6 seats) completed. 1 urinals head & 2 grease traps completed. MAROC. Stoves with 2 Pts Maréchal E.H. in progress. AUBEET. Regimental Aid Post and Ambulance dressing completed by San Sec. Posts were inspected in LES BREBIS as follows:- 9 G.B. Sausage Trench (10). 13rd M.G.C. 14. 17th M.G.C. (5). Ich Sgt. Honorez (4) Ich Sgt. Honorez DISINFECTION WORKS SHOP No 1. C.C.S.	S.C.H.
BOYEFFLES	Mar 19th 1917		Received D.R.O. 2319 - 2330. Also 459 Rd CANNON WIT today inspected and was given authority to work in BARLIN today and also withdrawn from BARLIN and given authority to work in BOYEFFLES. BARLIN, FOSSE 10. Routine Inspection Work continues. Units in the following districts were visited:- BOYEFFLES, BARLIN, FOSSE 10, SAINS-EN-GOHELLE, BRAQUEMONT and BULLY GRENAY and the work of improving sanitary arrangements found to be in progress. Sanitation work completed to 2nd A.D.D.S. Water carts in possession of the following units were inspected:- 123rd Heavy Bdy, 13th M.G.C, 17 M.G.C. (5th Divy.) A/07 R.F.A. (Sec. 7) 12 M.G.C. (Sec. 3) 2 standard latrine top seats, 2 standard animal bomb made. Construction work:- WORKSHOP. 12 Standard latrine top seats with 2 standard animal troughs made. BOYEFFLES 1 cesspit + seats scheme completed. 1 brick disinfector drying chamber (Standard) established. 1 frame work behind latrine, 1 trench field and gravel for FOSSE 10. 1 deep trench latrine completed. 1 grease trap fixed cookup pt ring. SAINS-EN-GOHELLE 3 grease traps and 1 latrine bench refixed + soak-away made. 1 Impresspit dug. BULLY GRENAY. 6 anderson trenches fixed, 3 cesspit for washing water dug. Our N.C.O and 1 man were today sent to BRAQUEMONT to be billeted and to attend to the 4 A.S.C. Companies transport lines and also the Artillery lines in BRAQUEMONT. They will inspect the 4 A.S.C. Companies transport lines and also the Artillery lines in BRAQUEMONT and district. DISINFECTIONS (1) Measles. BRAQUEMONT. 3rd Australian Tunnelling Co. Capt. KIDD. L.S. evacuated to 43rd Field Ambul. There are no contacts but disinfected by Sn Sec. (2) Paratyphoid. BRAQUEMONT. 3rd Australian Tunnelling Co. Spr. MAYNE.E : evacuated to 43rd Field Ambulance : 36 contacts are isolated : hut disinfected by San Sec. Three at ASLAIN ST NAZAIRE and NURSE have today been detailed to report to the Officers	S.C.H.

WAR DIARY or INTELLIGENCE SUMMARY

Army Form C. 2118.

Place	Date	Hour	Summary of Events and Information	Remarks and references to Appendices
BOYEFFLES	Mar 20th 1917		Routine Inspection. Work continued. Units in the following districts were visited:— AIX NOULETTE, BOYEFFLES, BOUVIGNY WOODS, FOSSE 10, SAINS BARLIN, BULLY GRENAY & LES BREBIS and the work of improving sanitary arrangements found to be in progress. Sanitary appliances were today issued to:— 2 large standard latrine boxes and 1 latrine boxes for the workshop as follows:— 2 large standard latrine boxes and 16 latrine troughs to 107 Bde R.F.A. H.Q. 8 notice boards to Traffic Police. 1 abandoned latrine board battened round. 1 corrugated iron incinerator to 136 Siege Bty R.G.A.; 12 matchet board to BULLY GRENAY. DISINFECTIONS. (1) mealies FOSSE 10 1 2 N.C.Os. & Orderlies. Pte JAMES W. Pte LAWRISH. F.W. Pte YOUNG H.N. contacts number 25 and are aggregated. 2 huts disinfected by Sec See. cases evacuated to 7u/s of Ambulance. (4) mealies: CALONNE; 12 N.Stoke: PARADE J. Evacuated to 1/3rd Fd Ambulance. Contacts number 8 and are under observation. M.O. only cellar depot till 6 S/KIELPIR. evacuated to No 7 General Hospital. contacts number 30 (5) Scabies: BRAQUEMONT Stanhope Tunnelling Co. Contacts and are isolated by day but go to working parties at night. Work carried out today:—Water carts inspected:— 13th Hussars Cav. Pool D/110, R.F.A. 1st Sqn. 9th Cav. HQ. have today been prepared and made of LES BREBIS and a copy of same appended to this summary. A map has been prepared and made of LES BREBIS and a copy of same appended to this summary. Construction work:— WORKSHOP 9 standard latrine boxes, 6 grease trap and 1 corrugated iron incinerator made. AIX NOULETTE. 5 latrines built, 5 urinals (tins) latrines fixed (standard) 1 grease trap. BULLY GRENAY 1 grease trap. FOSSE 10. 5 new urinals fixed (standard) 1 trough urinal repaired. Two public latrines in BULLY GRENAY have today been repaired and are now fit for use. A new drain was built for the purpose of draining a well at the two public urinals in BULLY GRENAY. Received:— G.R.O. 2159-2200, Routine Orders 404-415, C.R.O. 373-379, 380-381, D.R.O. 330-2386.	APPENDIX 13
BOYEFFLES	Mar 29 1917		The O.C. Capt R.W. MACPHERSON preceded on leave to the United Kingdom and Capt. C.D. FAULKNER, 7 D.A. Field Ambulance temporarily assumed command. Routine Inspection work continued. Units in the following districts were visited:— BOYEFFLES, BARLIN, BULLY GRENAY, MAROC, FOSSE 10, SAINS-EN-GOHELLE, BOUVIGNY, MARQUEFFLES FARM, and BRAQUEMONT, and the whole of improving of the sanitary convenience found to be progressing. The Town Major of BOYEFFLES was asked in regard to occupying of the village, and arrangements were made to provide a wagon and team to commence same. All ambulances refuse to be dumped at a site at the field latrine area selected and approved, and after inspection from Sen. San. Officer workshops as follows:— 5 horse stalls. 1 incinerator. 2 grease traps to the kitchen. One in FOSSE 10. 1 meat safe. 1 horse trough. 1 public brand at AIX NOULETTE. 1 latrine complete. 1 meuse latrine (wash) 10 urinals. 3 bar seats. 10 latrine troughs for mince to BULLY GRENAY. construction work:— WORKSHOP. 16 coverts, 16 hinges, standard latrine, hood. SAINS-EN-GOHELLE. 1 standard brick defecator and manure chamber commenced. 1 horse trough manure completed. FOSSEIO. 2 horse seats first of urinals. 1 corrugated iron manure fence built. 1 grease trap and 1 mud hand funnels fixed. BULLY GRENAY. 1 mud hand urinal and 2 tubs, 1 incinerator staff and shows seats. Water carts inspected. Patients are constantly met on their BRAQUEMONT 1 grease trap fixed. Received D.R.O. 2524 – 2532. Water carts were inspected as follows:— No. 1 Sec. No 3 Sec. D.A.C. BHQ R.F.A.	

Received D.R.O. 2524 – 2532.

(A 583) W.L. W4283/M687 750,000 8/16 D,D. & L. Ltd. Forms/C2118/13

WAR DIARY or INTELLIGENCE SUMMARY

Army Form C. 2118.

41st SANITARY SECTION R.A.M.C.(T)

Title Page 11.

Place	Date	Hour	Summary of Events and Information	Remarks and references to Appendices
BOYEFFLES	Mar 22nd 1917		Routine Inspection Work continued. Units in the following districts were visited:- BARLIN, BOYEFFLES, AIX NOULETTE, CALONNE, BRAQUEMONT and the work of improving sanitary appliances was carried out at BRAQUEMONT. (approx.) Improvements completed is as under:- (1) Latrine benches for N/91 M.G.C. Instructional work:- WORKSHOP. A standard latrine screen, 4 urine deflectors, 6 latine seats transparent completed. AIX NOULETTE. Public Latrine cradicated and the men did their work under fearful conditions. Water cart in permanence of the following units were made:- A/106 R.F.A., 3rd R.W (Decoy) 3rd R.F transferred. 3rd R.F.S., 2nd R (Secondly) (2nd R (Decoy)) This work was today commenced by the men. Instructions were received from A.D.M.S. to provide latrine accommodation for the Lewis motor vehicle of 1000 men (approx.) at the new 139 Field Ambulance BRAQUEMONT for referring wounded at the premises of 139 Fld. Amb. Latrine, 3 standard urinals dug. Received MISS R.O. 716-797 CRO 365-391 D.R.O 2333-2535 2nd Army No AS 48/51/9/1.	SCH
BOYEFFLES	Mar 23rd 1917		Routine Inspection Work continued. Units in the following districts were visited:- BOYEFFLES, BARLIN, FOSSE 10, BRAQUEMONT, SAINS-EN-GOHELLE, AIX NOULETTE, BULLY GRENAY and LES BREBIS and the work of improving sanitary appliances commenced continued. Sanitary Appliances erected as follows:- (1) R Charles: 1 refuse latrine complete, 6 latrine seats continued. 3 standard urinals & improved traps (water 10). Water carts in permanence of the following units were inspected:- 19th Co, 19 S.C., 195 Co, 197 Co, A.S.C., 1st Royal Scottish (Decoy), 1st Berks (Decoy). Charlaine (Decoy), 2/Lt BURKE T.T. concerned to the 7 General hospital. DISINFECTIONS(1) Paratyphi. BRAQUEMONT. 3rd Australian Tunnelling Co: 2/Lt BAXTER T: evacuated to No. 7 General hospital. Decoration. (2) Paratyphi: BRAQUEMONT. 3rd Australian Tunnelling Co: two dispatched by Sa. Sc. BAXTER T. The work of providing latine accommodation to proposed hospital being considered, 3 urinals made, so mobile hand sanitation made and carried. BRAQUEMONT. The work of providing latrine accommodation to proposed hospital camp continued. A distinct report of the conditional will be given in connection. Impartially latrine continued. 1 grease trap made. LES BREBIS: 1 latrine re-sited, 4 urinals dug. Incorporated for burying manure; receive pit dug. BULLY GRENAY: 2 diffusion latrine completed. Received DRO 2334-2540. 2nd Army AS 485/9/1.	SCH
BOYEFFLES	Mar 24th 1917		Routine Inspection Work continued. Units in the following districts were visited and the work of improving sanitary appliances found to be in progress:- MARQUEFFLES FARM, FOSSE 10, BOYEFFLES, BULLY GRENAY, CALONNE, BRAQUEMONT, SAINS-EN-GOHELLE, PETIT SAINS. Sanitary Appliances erected in S.Co Workshop:- 6 wash bowls. 16 1/3rd field Ambulance, 1 grease trap, 1 rubbish check to 13th Middlesex. DISINFECTIONS (1+2) Measles: CALONNE. 8th Queen Pte METCALFE Pte GARDNER. Both evacuated to 1/3rd field Ambulance: huts disinfected by S.S M.O as in (1) MSS WOODS T.H. evacuated to 1/3rd field Ambulance: 1 coat (3) (b) A5354 W.C.W By H687, 798.655 8/75 P.D. D.& L. Royal Forms C.2118/13. by Sans Sc. (4) Measles: FOSSE 10. 316th Road Construction Unit: Pte McGEE: evacuated V/K & Rus Stretchers released: Kittie disinfected by S.S.	SCH

Army Form C. 2118.

WAR DIARY
or
INTELLIGENCE SUMMARY.
(Erase heading not required.)

Instructions regarding War Diaries and Intelligence Summaries are contained in F. S. Regs., Part II. and the Staff Manual respectively. Title pages will be prepared in manuscript.

Place	Date	Hour	Summary of Events and Information	Remarks and references to Appendices
BOYEFFLES	Mar 24th 1917 Continued		Latrine seats in possession of the following units were inspected:- B.C.& D/106, C/107, R.F.A, 9th & Scame (Beauts), 9th R.E., 2 secs (Beauts), 129 C.B., R.E. 9th R. Invic siding BEAUMONT. Construction Work: The sanitary arrangements for the proposed hospital train siding BEAUMONT have been completed as follows:- 2 hand latrines, pail system, 6 seats, roofed & screened. 1 Officers latrine " " 2 " (partition) " " " 1 N.C.Os latrine " " 2 " " " " 1 N.C.Os urinal. pail system 1 pail " " " 1 Mens " " 6 " " " " 1 Officers " " 1 " " " " In addition 8 canvas screens with high windscreens, 6 latrine paper boxes with lids and 12 notice boards have been made and fixed. It is proposed to dispose of the excreta when latrines are used by incineration in 73rd field Ambulance. WORKSHOP. 6 large and 6 small latrine seats completed. AIX NOULETTE. Latrines making 11 box seats and 6 have been completed. 1 grease trap MARQUEFFLES FARM. 3 latrines completed making 5 box seats. 1 Latrine, 4 new seats, 1 grease trap SAINS-EN-GOHELLE. 3 box seats, 1 urinal, 1 pail 1 grease trap fixed BULLY GRENAY. 4 latrines completed, 12 new seats. SAINS 1 trial derrick completed Received - D.R.O D5III	S.Eliff
	March 25. 1917.		Routine inspection work continued. Work on the following stations were carried on:- BOYEFFLES, BARLIN, CABONNE, BULLY GRENAY, BRAQUEMONT and work on improving sanitary conveniences found to be in progress. Several appliances issued from workshop. 10 large latrine seats, 7 old (new?) latrines, 3 field Ambulance seats sent in possession of the following units were inspected:- 73rd M.G.C. 103 G.R.E., 3 hand carts. 13th M.G.C., 10th G.R.E., 134 M. Rom Co., Ambulance man. DISINFECTION. (1) Measles ?: CALONNE: 8th Queens Pte Garry R. evacuated to 73rd Ambulance. 19 and valise, 3 pillow dampened Sac, Se. Environmental work - WORKSHOP. 5 hange of horseshoe latrines, box seat brushes dampened up made. Notice boards made and fixed. BULLY GRENAY. Latrine (other side area block) washed & new parts for new Environmental "latrines to obtain & have new models, connected with SAINS-EN-GOHELLE. 1 man latrine, 1 box seat, 2 pail fittings completed and new material supplied, washed and roofed at Gen. Solvent. 1 latrine, 2 box seat brackets, installed and roofed at Gen Solvent. 2 brackets made from a pump attached to his water wells wwte to O.C. 17.26 M.V.S. re: went out, and the pump removed this used was sent to him. A large meeting was held of NCO for the trials. NoQuin PACHISNALL L. was today admitted to 74th Field Ambulance diagnosed scabies. Received E.R.O. 390 - 391. D.R.O. D313 - D315.	S.Eliff

WAR DIARY or INTELLIGENCE SUMMARY

Army Form C. 2118.

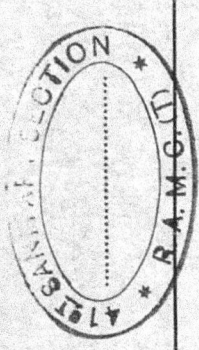

Place	Date	Hour	Summary of Events and Information	Remarks and references to Appendices
BOYEFFLES	Mar 26 1917		Routine Inspection Work continues. Units were visited in the following districts :- BARLIN. BOYEFFLES. BULLY GRENAY, LES BREBIS. PETIT SAINS. SAINS-EN-GOHELLE, FOSSE 10 and CALONNE and the work of improving sanitary convenience found to be in progress. Sanitary appliances were received from the workshop as follows :- 1007 C.R.E. 5 latrine box seats, 1 urinal, 1 grease trap. 10 meat safes. Hauls BARLIN, 1 urinal. A.P.M. No notice boards at BULLY GRENAY. Water carts in possession of the following units were inspected :- 45" M.G. Co. 1st N Staffs (joins), 17. M.G. Co. [illegible] 2nd [illegible] 1st [illegible] 4/35 Middlesex. 25" drills inspected by 199" G. A.S.C. were inspected at BRAQUEMONT and no instances of [illegible]. SAINS-EN-GOHELLE: Hygiène (1) Huguet. SAINS-EN-GOHELLE; 129 Co. R.E.: Ptr KENNY.M. evacuated to 7th Fld Ambulance: some no cases who are entered to village were met in a dirty state. Should still be See. (2) Mercadiè CALONNE (Ranchol); 8th Queens: Pte CLARK A.W. evacuated to 138 Fld Ambulance. Contacts number 9 and we related two others in the field. By See. [illegible] work – WORKSHOP 9 range and 20 small standard latrine box seats – 10 standard urinals made. BULLY GRENAY, 10 standard urinals fixed, 1 Officers latrine box seat + toilet roofed inspected. Sanitary latrine holding of the seals new inspection + connect installed over new trenches, 1 new latrine trench dug. 5 new L.B. box seals fixed, latrine repaired, 20 notice boards fixed, 1 new grease trap fixed, lately roads sprinkled with continued. BRAQUEMONT. 1 latrine trench dug. SAINS-EN-GOHELLE. 1 latrine trench dug. 1 latrine sprinkled with crelin carbol. Received no 159. R.O. 736 – 739, C.R.O. 295 – 299. D.R.O. 2344 – 2365 Lt G.C. HARTLEY R.A.M.C. assumed temporary command vice Capt. C.B. FAULKNER R.A.M.C.	S.C.H
BOYEFFLES	Mar 27 1917		Routine Inspection Work continues. Units were visited in the following districts :- BARLIN, BOYEFFLES, BULLY GRENAY, BRAQUEMONT, SAINS EN GOHELLE, FOSSE 10, AIX-NOULETTE, and the work of improving sanitary convenience is in progress. 2 large latrine box seats were received from H.Q. Sing Coy R.G.A. DISINFECTIONS (1) Mercadiè: NOEUX-les-MINES; C1/104 R.F.A. QM Sgt SMITH S. evacuated to 138 Fld Ambulance, 3 contacts are not contacts – contacts disinfected by See. (2) Hughette: AIX NOULETTE, HQ2 Sub. Bde R.G.A.: Gnr HACKETT D. evacuated to 43rd Field Ambulance – contacts number 4 and are isolated. Billet disinfected by See. Sanitary work in possession of the following units were inspected :- 13th [illegible], A1 D/107 R.F.A. and Barnington H.Q. Sub. Div. Supply Co. Small carts in possession of the following units were inspected :- 13th [illegible], A1 D/107 R.F.A. and Barnington H.Q. Sub. Div. Supply Co. Constructional work – change and so small standard and barrack huts seats, 6 standard urinals completed. 31 notice boards were made and painted. AIX NOULETTE 2 latrines reconnicated over new trenches. 1 box seat fixed, meat safe fixed. BULLY GRENAY 2 latrine trenches dug, 1 grease trap fixed, 2 latrines (box seats and top not completed) completed. FOSSE 10, 3 box seats fixed, urinal fixed, 1 box seat fixed, 1 boiler set for dug. The O.C. visited the town major, SAINS-EN-GOHELLE in reference to the sanitary arrangements for new D.H.Q. at the Chateau. Lulin were fired by military labour for officers common latrine for french etc and the work of emanation commenced. BARLIN. 10 notice boards fixed & male supplied. Received: C1/R. Ω. 2201 – 2209 C.R.O. 400 – 401 D.R.O. 2346 – 2348	S.C.H

WAR DIARY or INTELLIGENCE SUMMARY

Army Form C. 2118.

Page 14

Place	Date	Hour	Summary of Events and Information	Remarks and references to Appendices
BOYEFFLES	Mar 28th 1917		Routine Inspection work continued. Units were visited in the following districts – BARLIN, BOYEFFLES, BULLY GRENAY, BRAQUEMONT, CALONNE, MAROC, SAINS-EN-GOHELLE, HOUCHIN, + FOSSE 10 and work of improving sanitary arrangements found to be in progress. Sanitary Appliances were viewed from the workshop – 12 small standard latrines were sent to BARLIN complete and 5 notice boards K 9 & 5 incin. to be sent (small). 5 urine seats (large). 8 trough urinals, 12 standard urinals, 9 standard lavatories complete to units in BULLY GRENAY. Wall seat in position of the following units were inspected – No 1, 2nd Sec D.A.C., B/107 R.F.A. Constructional work – WORKSHOP. 5 trough urinals + 10 standard latrines on seats made. HOUCHIN latrines complete. The sawmill. The paper is better than before C.R.O.E. completed, 16 notice boards made and painted. MAROC. 1 low seat urinal trench latrine. CALONNE. Latrine pits dug, 2 wooden trench DISINFECTION. (1) urinals. FOSSE 10: No 310 Road Construction Co. Pnr THOMPSON C. evacuated to 7th Amb... contacts named & and are isolated. No 625 Sqn GOODING W E granted special short leave from March 28th to March 31st to ST POL. Received C.R.O. 405-407. D.R.O. 3349-3351.	G.E.H
BOYEFFLES	Mar 29th 1917		Instructions were received from the Town Major BOYEFFLES to vacate billets but occupied by 16 men of this section, as the billet was to be occupied by officer of an Artillery group. These were examined and kit billets shown were Lt Col's Battalion Quarters. 9 small large latrine tent out 4 pail 473rd Infantry Labour Appliances were issued as follows – 1 Standard latrine, 1 small standard urinal from BULLY GRENAY + 3 latrines ST NAZAIRE. Latrines complete urinals, 1 urinal on large latrine tent on seat, 6 grease traps ABLAIN ST NAZAIRE. DISINFECTION. Parade: 3rd Australian Tunnelling Co. Spr LANGFORD L.: 30 contacts are isolated who are not on duty, but thoroughly disinfected by San Sec. Constructional work – WORKSHOP. 108 notice boards were painted, signature to be held at D.H.Q. begun. BULLY GRENAY. 1 grease trap put Received D.R.O. 3917, No 2353-2355. 1 urinal... between the wall and 4 latrines were inspected in A/107 R.F.A were inspected.	G.E.H
BOYEFFLES	Mar 30th 1917		At BOYEFFLES sanitary appliances were made for new billets occupied by men of this section yesterday, a latrine was also constructed. Type and over field, dry pack made, and drain repair to from wall + trap of killed cavalry. CONSTRUCTIONAL WORK: WORKSHOP. 15 small and 6 large standard latrines were sent to D.H.Q. enclosed Bhy. 3 Sectn Sanitary Appliances were issued from workshop to units at following: AIX NOULETTE. 1 trough urinal + 5 grease traps at D.R.O. 3917 & D.R.O. 3037. 1 urinal. 1 urinal was moved to ... Received No 160 Routine Orders 24th.	G.E.H

SA/NS 1/4 ... A 8347 A.W.T. W4973/M687 750,000 8/16 D.D.& L. Ltd. Forms/C2118/13.

Army Form C. 2118.

WAR DIARY
or
INTELLIGENCE SUMMARY.
(Erase heading not required.)

Ragulta

Place	Date	Hour	Summary of Events and Information	Remarks and references to Appendices
BOYEFFLES	March 1917 cont'd		The appointment of Captain R.W. MACPHERSON, R.A.M.C., T.C., as Specialist Sanitary Officer, Commanding No 41st Sanitary Section, is approved from the 25th February 1917 inclusive, under the terms of War Office letter No 48/A.M.C/3915 (A.M.D.1) dated 6/12/14. (Ref: D.G.M.S. No 1516/25 dated 16.3.17)	

WAR DIARY or INTELLIGENCE SUMMARY

Army Form C. 2118.

41st SANITARY SECTION
R.A.M.C. (T)

Place	Date	Hour	Summary of Events and Information	Remarks and references to Appendices
BOYEFFLES	Mar 31. 1917		Routine Inspection Work continued. Units in the following districts were visited:- BOYEFFLES, BARLIN, BULLY GRENAY, AIX NOULETTE, BOUVIGNY, BRAQUEMONT, FOSSE 10, SAINS-EN-GOHELLE and the work of improving sanitary arrangements progressing. Walls erected in persuance of the following:- 9th Quin – A/106 R.F.A, 3rd Rifle Bde (scouts), 12th Royal Fusiliers (Scouts), 9th R.W.Kent (60) (deaths), 13th Royal Fusiliers (Scouts), 9th Suff (60) (death). isolated: Whilst Branquot by Sen. Sec. A/Branch W.T. evacuated to 14th Fd Ambulance: Canada. DISINFECTIONS: (1) Measles. FOSSE 10: 1 D/- females, RE BRANCH W.T. evacuated to 14th Fd Amb: Canada (2) Parotitis. BRAQUEMONT: 3 D/- Australians, including C: S.M. HOWE C. evacuated from 75th Field Ambulance K.M.F. Service Hospital. 120 contacts who are employed whilst NOT on duty, this arranged by Sen. Sec. Anti-malarial work. – WORKSHOP. Latrine trench, urinals men made, grease stand made. 30 metres trench made at BARLIN. 5 horse stands fed re trench latrines. 2 horse stands over trench pits covered. At SAINS-EN-GOHELLE I latrine improved pit dug, 1 latrine recovered over new latrine. FOSSE 10 1 latrine/urinal 3 horse stands over pit & hay sacks. AIX NOULETTE 3 new urinals pits & 1 urinal per Generals dug. I have Surface Water SAINS-EN-GOHELLE the following sanitary arrangements have been completed for D.H.Q. W Chateau 1 latrine box seat pit. newly scavenged for O.O. C. 1 urinal pit & defects. for Officers 1 ditto 2 box seat 2 pit for A+Q Staff 1 latrine 3 " 3 " " Other men 1 latrine 3 " 3 " a sawdust fire bucket, & soap provided for each latrine, 6 paper holders provided, 10 aluminium notice boards fixed. Scavenging manure proceeding satisfactorily throughout the area. Incinerators of BRAQUEMONT, BULLY GRENAY, FOSSE 10, BOYEFFLES tip carts have been allotted and are now under supervision of Town Major concerned. Assisted by own N.C.O. or men from the sanitary remainder of area scavenging is carried on by the units in occupation.	G.G.

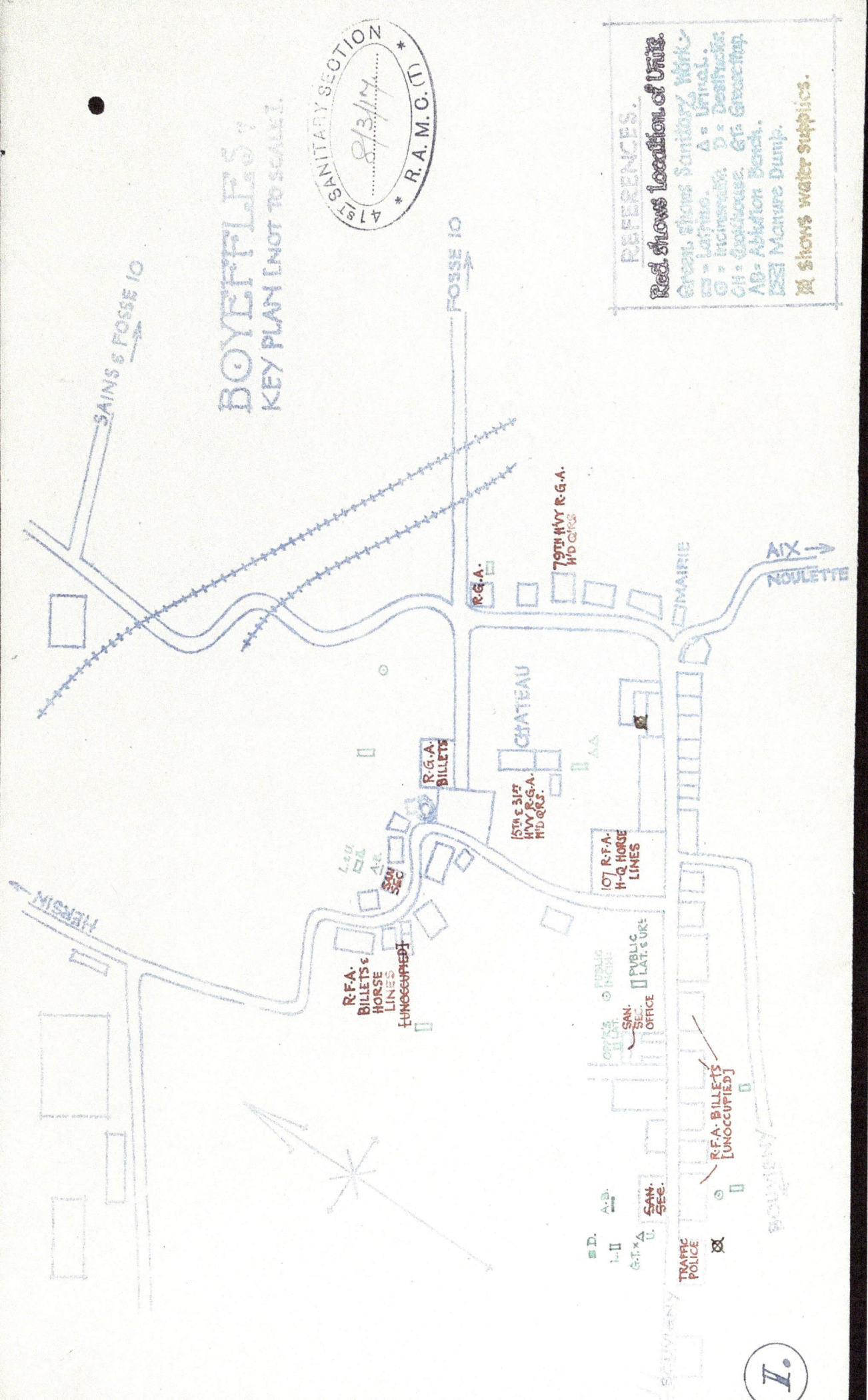

BULLY-GRENAY
KEY PLAN [NOT TO SCALE]

41st SANITARY SECTION — R.A.M.C. (T) — 8/3/17

REFERENCES:
Red shows Location of Units.
Green shows Sanitary Units.
□ = Urinal.
▽ = Latrine.
⊙ = Incinerator. △ = Receptacle.
C.H. = Cookhouse. G.T. = Greasetrap.
A.B. = Ablution Bench.
▦ = Manure Dump.
▨ = Sacks holding Supplies.

Units marked on map (red):
- 19TH R.G.A.
- 186TH R.G.A.
- R.E. DUMP
- 106TH R.F.A.
- BATT. H.Q. 2 & 3
- 172ND B'DE H.Q.
- 172ND M.G. Co.
- BDE GRENADE SCHOOL
- 72ND T.M.B. H.Q.
- CANTEEN
- 109RD R.E. H.Q.
- 252ND R.G.A. H.Q.
- BATHS
- 172ND B'DE H.Q.
- 104TH RES H-Q
- 1ST WELSH R.G.A.
- LOVAT'S SCOUTS
- SALVAGE
- 17TH M.G.C. H-Q.
- D.N. T.M.B.
- B'DE A.D.S.
- BATT. H.Q.
- 1ST CORPS CYCLISTS

Features / streets:
- Ligne de Béthune à Arras
- Rue de la Fosse
- FOSSE No 1
- GRANGE PLACE
- GRANDE RUE
- Rue des Chiens
- Rue Bailly
- Rue de la Chapelle
- Chemin de Bully-Lievin
- Rue Bully-Lievin
- CITÉ ALLOUETTE
- CITÉ D'AIX
- CITÉ ARENDIA
- Gendarmerie
- Cinema
- Ecole
- CEMETERY
- REFUSE DUMP
- 4-8 HYDRANTS ON MAIN SUPPLY

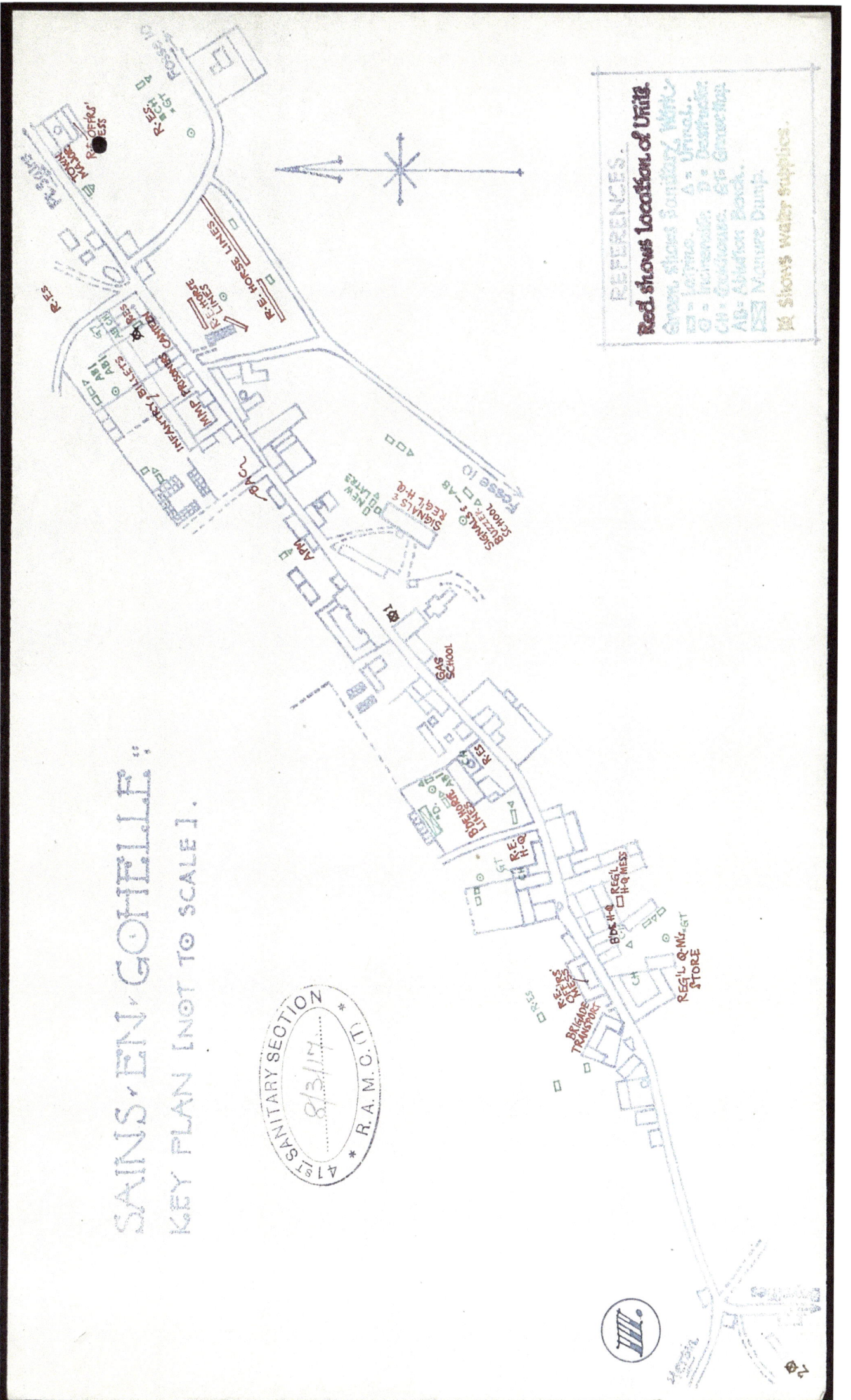

BOIS DE NOULETTE
PLAN OF CAMP [NOT TO SCALE]

REFERENCES.

Red shows Location of Units.
Green shows Sanitary Work:-
⊠ = Latrine.   △ = Urinal.
⊙ = Incinerator.   D = Destructor.
C.H. = Cookhouse.   G.T. = Grease Trap.
A.B. = Ablution Bench.
▨ = Manure Dump.

⊠ Shows water supplies.

41ST SANITARY SECTION 9/3/17 R.A.M.C.(T)

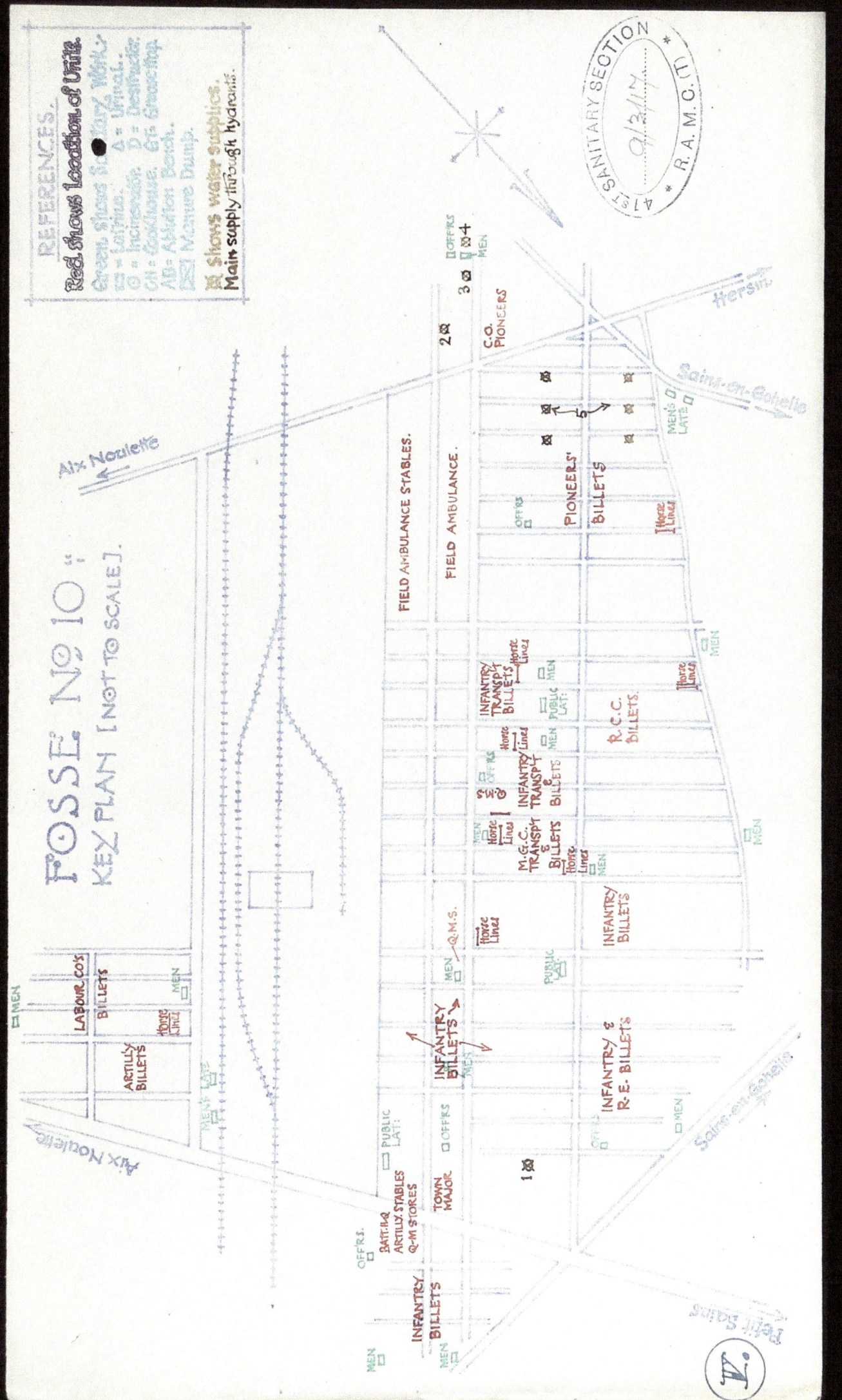

"AIX-NOULETTE"
KEY PLAN [NOT TO SCALE].

REFERENCES.
Green shows location of Utils.
L = Latrine.   U = Urinal.
O = Incinerator.   D = Destructor.
CH = Cookhouse.   G = Greasetrap.
AB = Ablution Bench.
▨ Manure Dump.
Red shows location of Utils.
⌧ Shows water supplies.

41st SANITARY SECTION — R.A.M.C.(T)

"BOUVIGNY"
KEY PLAN [NOT TO SCALE]

REFERENCES.

Red shows Location of Units.
Green shows Sanitary Works.
- L = Latrine.
- U = Urinal.
- I = Incinerator.
- D = Destructor.
- C.H = Cookhouse.
- G.D = Grease Trap.
- A.B = Ablution Bench.
- M.D = Manure Dump.

⊠ shows water supplies.

NOTE:- Remainder of Village is not occupied by Divl Troops.

Aix Noulette
Maisnonville Farm
Bouvigny Wood
Standpipe
M.G. Co.
A.E.
Church
Chateau
Sains
Bouvigny

[Stamp: A 1st SANITARY SECTION R.A.M.C.(T) 10/3/17]

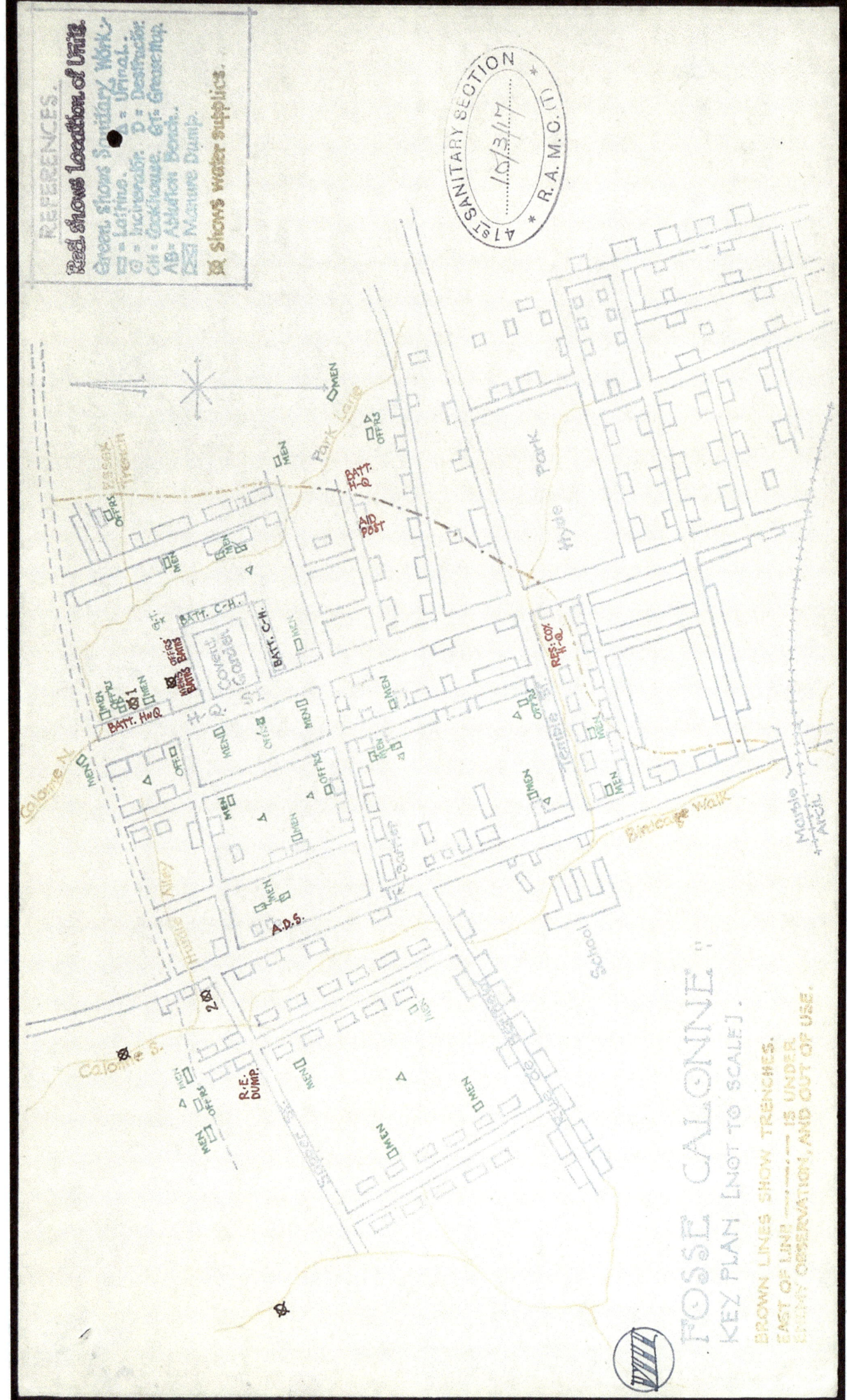

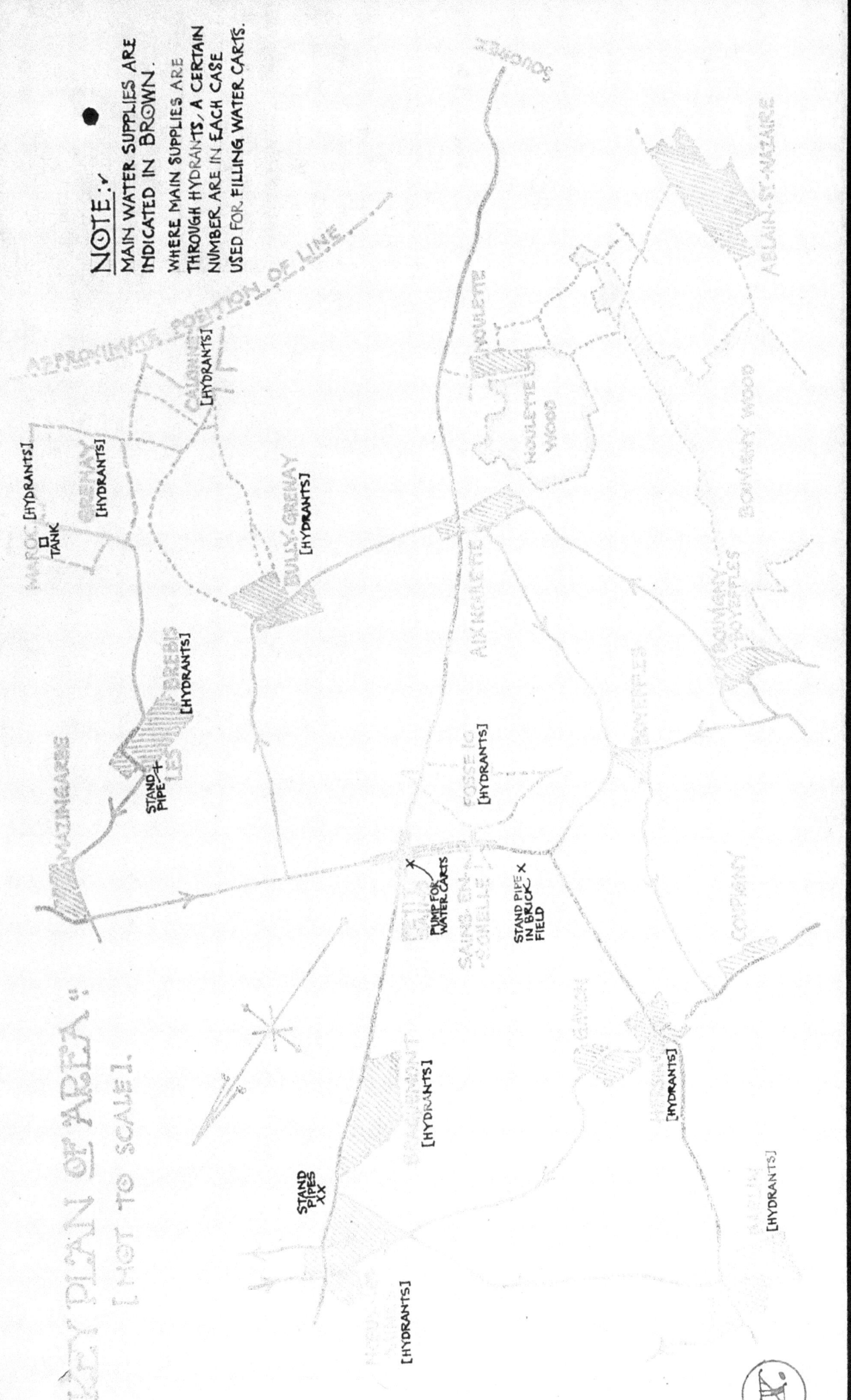

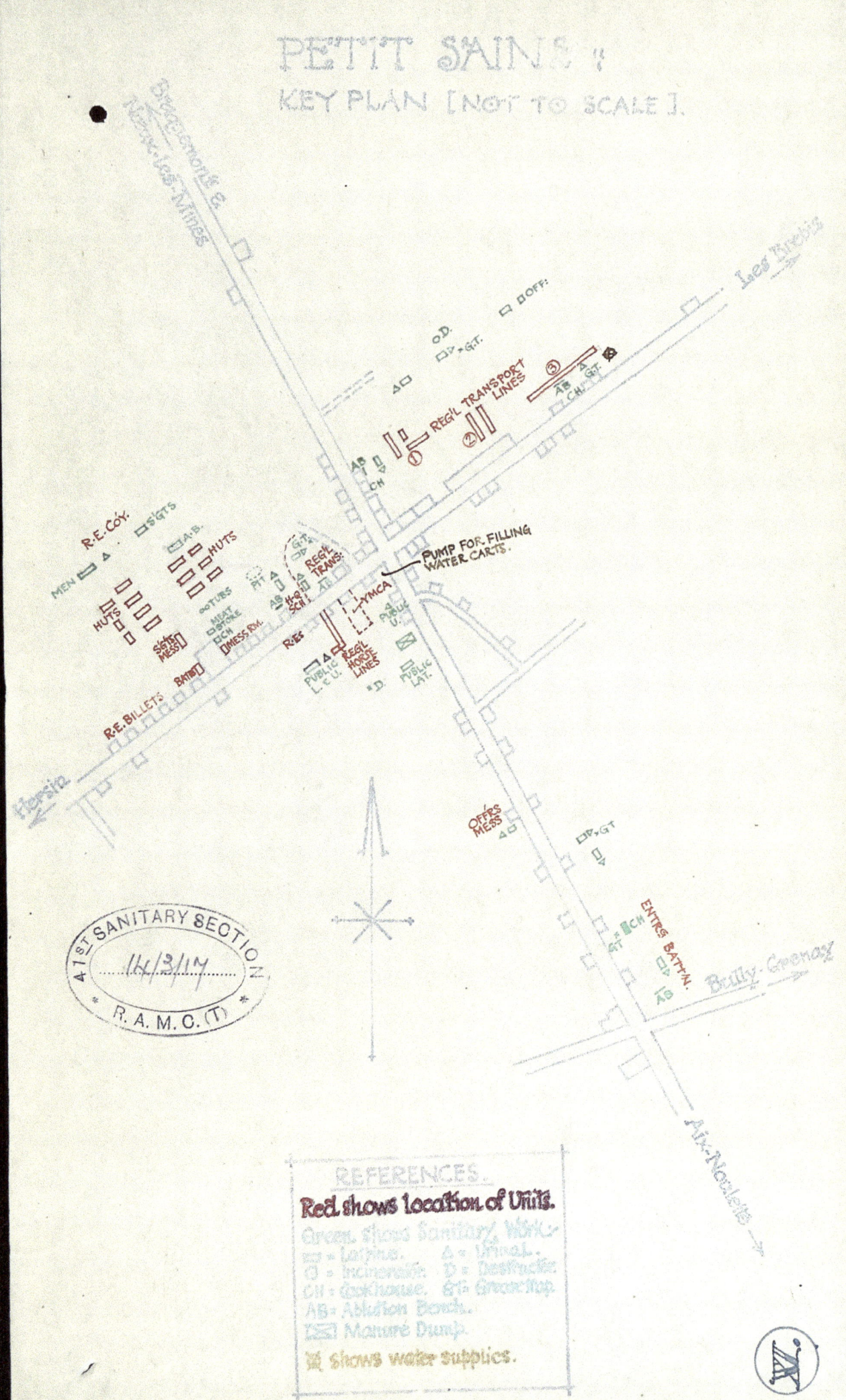

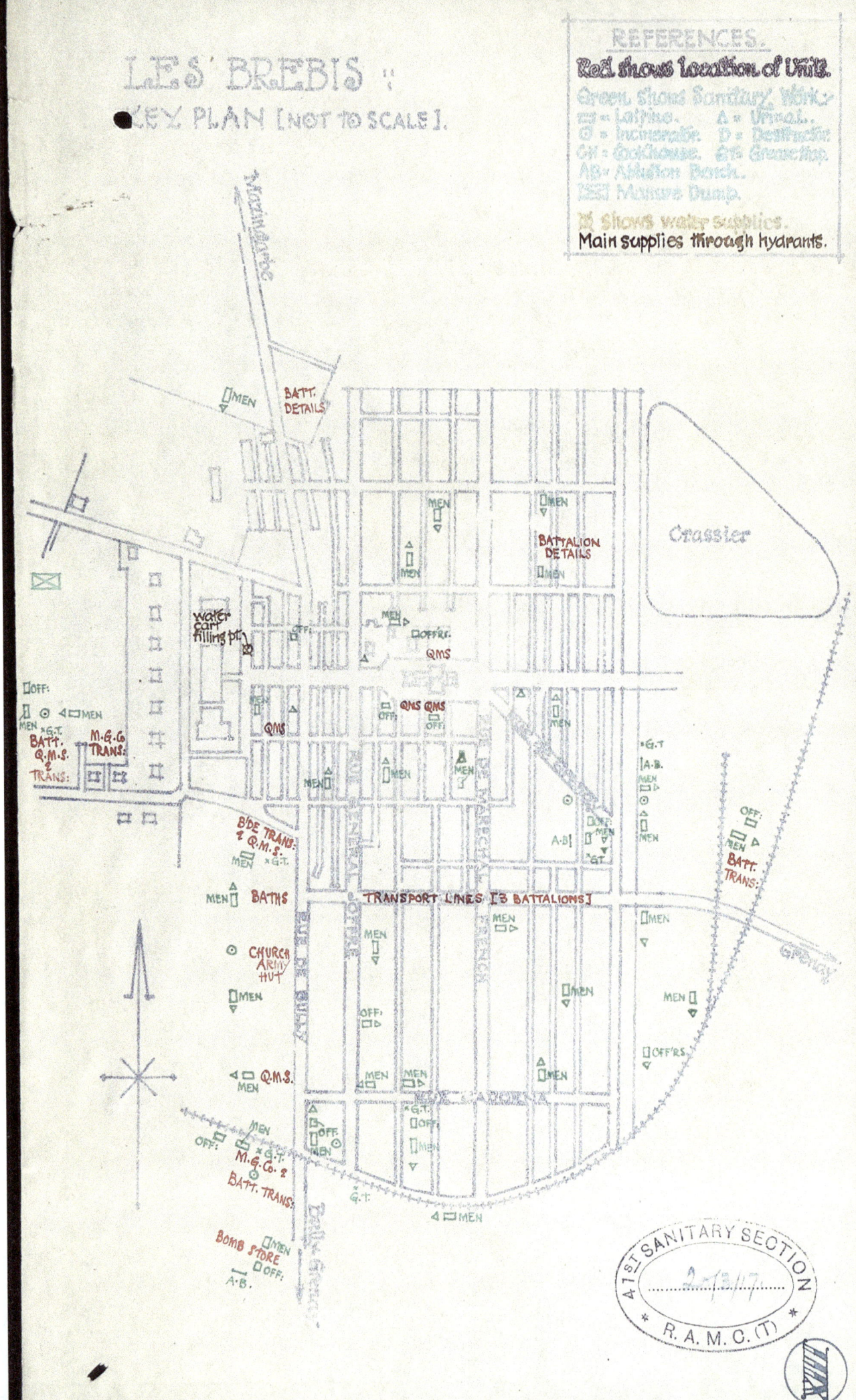

www.ingramcontent.com/pod-product-compliance
Lightning Source LLC
Chambersburg PA
CBHW081428300426
44108CB00016BA/2328